Hands-On Design F
Best Practices with Julia

Proven solutions to common problems in software design for Julia 1.x

Tom Kwong, CFA

BIRMINGHAM - MUMBAI

Hands-On Design Patterns and Best Practices with Julia

Commissioning Editor: Richa Tripathi
Acquisition Editor: Karan Gupta
Content Development Editor: Tiksha Sarang
Senior Editor: Afshaan Khan
Technical Editor: Ketan Kamble
Copy Editor: Safis Editing
Project Coordinator: Francy Puthiry
Proofreader: Safis Editing
Indexer: Rekha Nair
Production Designer: Nilesh Mohite

First published: January 2020

Production reference: 1170120

Published by Packt Publishing Ltd.
Livery Place
35 Livery Street
Birmingham
B3 2PB, UK.

ISBN 978-1-83864-881-7

www.packt.com

To my lovely family, Mei, Keith, and Karen.

Packt.com

Subscribe to our online digital library for full access to over 7,000 books and videos, as well as industry leading tools to help you plan your personal development and advance your career. For more information, please visit our website.

Why subscribe?

- Spend less time learning and more time coding with practical eBooks and Videos from over 4,000 industry professionals

- Improve your learning with Skill Plans built especially for you

- Get a free eBook or video every month

- Fully searchable for easy access to vital information

- Copy and paste, print, and bookmark content

Did you know that Packt offers eBook versions of every book published, with PDF and ePub files available? You can upgrade to the eBook version at www.packt.com and as a print book customer, you are entitled to a discount on the eBook copy. Get in touch with us at customercare@packtpub.com for more details.

At www.packt.com, you can also read a collection of free technical articles, sign up for a range of free newsletters, and receive exclusive discounts and offers on Packt books and eBooks.

Foreword

Design patterns are the negative space of a programming language. They are the techniques that programmers come up with to effectively leverage a language's strengths and compensate for its weaknesses. We all use them whether we mean to or not. The classic Gang of Four *Design Patterns* book took existing patterns that were already being used *in the wild* and catalogued and classified them. Perhaps even more importantly, it gave them names so that programmers could refer to common patterns easily and immediately understand each other. It gave programmers a lingua franca for the tools of their trade.

Whereas classic design pattern books have focused almost exclusively on patterns themselves, assuming language proficiency as a given, *Hands-on Design Patterns and Best Practices with Julia* weaves together both the positive and negative space images of Julia. It introduces the language features that patterns depend on as they are used, making the book accessible even for readers who are not already fluent Julia programmers. This approach provides a comprehensive introduction of the language, while also covering advanced subjects as the book progresses. The later chapters delve into the kinds of sophisticated design patterns used by *Julia wizards*, so by the time you get to the end, you will truly have mastered the language. Be forewarned, however, as with most of the best programming books, it may require more than one read through before you've fully digested the content.

One of the more interesting aspects of creating a widely used programming language is seeing the remarkable and surprising things that people do with it. This includes incredible and sometimes world-changing applications that people have built in Julia—from specifying the FAA's next generation air collision avoidance system, to mapping all the visible universe's celestial bodies, to modeling climate change with unprecedented accuracy and resolution. But it also includes the clever programming tricks that people come up with to make it do their bidding. One of my favorites is the *(Tim) Holy Trait Trick*, discussed in `Chapter 5`, *Reusability Patterns*, which leverages the fact that Julia can efficiently dispatch on as many arguments as we want, to work around the language's lack of multiple inheritance. Not only does this technique *get the job done*, it goes well beyond: traits can depend on computed properties of types, allowing them to express relationships that multiple inheritance cannot. It turns out that the language already had the expressive power that was needed, it just took a clever design pattern to unlock it.

Tom's background gives him an expertly nuanced and balanced perspective on programming languages and their design patterns. He started programming in BASIC. But since those early days, he's used a broad variety of languages in professional settings, including: C++, Java, Python, TypeScript, Scheme and—of course—Julia. The set of technological sectors he's applied these languages in are equally diverse: finance, search engine, e-commerce, content management, and currently asset management. Perhaps not coincidentally, Julia is gaining significant traction in many of these sectors, especially those which are computationally demanding. Our backgrounds shape how we see the world and sometimes you find a new tool that feels like it was made for you. Sometimes you encounter a new programming language and think *This is how I've always wanted to write programs!* Julia has been that language for Tom and for many others. Hopefully it will be for you as well. Whether you are just trying Julia for the first time, or have used it for years and want to *level up* with more advanced techniques, you will find what you're looking for in this book. Enjoy and happy coding!

Stefan Karpinski

Co-creator of the Julia programming language

Co-founder of Julia Computing, Inc.

Contributors

About the author

Tom Kwong, CFA, is an experienced software engineer with over 25 years of industry programming experience. He has spent the majority of his career in the financial services industry. His expertise includes software architecture, design, and the development of trading/risk systems. Since 2017, he has uncovered the Julia language and has worked on several open source packages, including `SASLib.jl`. He currently works at Western Asset Management Company, a prestige asset management company that specializes in fixed income investment services. He holds an MS degree in computer science from the University of California, Santa Barbara (from 1993), and he holds the Chartered Financial Analyst® designation since 2009.

I would like to thank my colleagues at Western Asset, especially Team Nebula, the DevOps Team, and some of the risk managers, for their encouragement and support in my enthusiasm for the Julia language. This includes Sal Kadam, Chandra Subramani, Rony Chen, Kevin Yen, Khairil Iqbal, Michael Li, Anila Kothapally, Porntawee Nantamanasikarn, Ramesh Pandey, Louie Liu, Patrick Colony, John Quan, and many others. I also want to thank Jacqueline Farrington for teaching me valuable life lessons, such as having a growth mindset and keeping myself challenged.

I would like to thank the community members from the JuliaLang Slack and Discourse forum for being so kind in teaching me and enlightening me about various programming techniques in Julia. There are too many to mention here, but the first ones who come to mind are Tamas Papp, David Anthoff, Scott P. Jones, David P. Sanders, Mohamed Terek, Chris Elrod, Lyndon White (oxinabox), Cédric St. Jean, Twan Koolen, Milan Bouchet-Valat, Chris Rackauckas, Stefan Karpinski, Kristoffer Carlsson, Fredrik Ekre, and Yichao Yu.

About the reviewer

Zhuo Qingliang (also known as KDR 2 online) is presently working at paodingai.com, which is a start up FinTech company in China that is dedicated to improving the financial industry by using artificial intelligence technologies. He has over 10 years of experience in Linux, C, C++, Python, Perl, and Java development. He is interested in programming, doing consulting work, and participating in, and contributing to, the open source community (including the Julia community, of course).

Packt is searching for authors like you

If you're interested in becoming an author for Packt, please visit authors.packtpub.com and apply today. We have worked with thousands of developers and tech professionals, just like you, to help them share their insight with the global tech community. You can make a general application, apply for a specific hot topic that we are recruiting an author for, or submit your own idea.

Table of Contents

Section 3: Implementing Design Patterns

Preface

Julia is a powerful programming language that is designed to enable high-performance applications with developer productivity in mind. Its dynamic nature allows you to quickly perform small-scale experiments and then migrate to larger applications. Its introspection tools allow us to optimize performance by analyzing how high-level code is translated into lower-level instructions and machine code. Its metaprogramming facility helps more advanced programmers to build custom syntax for their specific domain usage. Its multiple dispatch and generic function features make it easy to build new capabilities by extending existing functions. For these and many more reasons, Julia is an excellent tool for developing applications across a wide spectrum of industries.

This book fulfills several demands from Julia developers. *A desire to write better code. A desire to improve system performance. A desire to design software that is easy to maintain.* From the time that the Julia language was born to its magnificent milestone of version 1.0 in August 2018, many design patterns have already emerged from the brightest minds, ranging from the core developers of the language to heavy users of the language. At times, these patterns were presented in blog posts and conferences. Sometimes, they showed up in random discussion threads on the Julia Discourse forum. At other times, they come up in casual talks between community members on various Julia Slack channels. This book is a collection of patterns, documenting the best approaches to designing high-quality Julia applications.

The primary objective of this book is to organize these well-proven patterns into a format that is easily consumable by the Julia developer community. There are several benefits to organizing and naming these patterns:

- It allows developers to communicate with each other more easily.
- It allows developers to better understand code that uses these patterns.
- It allows developers to articulate when a pattern should be applied.

The goal of this book is simple but powerful – after reading this book, you should be more knowledgeable about how to design and develop software in Julia. In addition, the material presented in this book can serve as a reference for any future discussions regarding design patterns in Julia. As we know from history, new design patterns will continue to emerge alongside the continuous evolution of the Julia language.

I hope you enjoy this book. *Happy reading!*

Who this book is for

This book is for beginner-to-intermediate Julia developers who want to get better at writing *idiomatic* Julia code for larger applications. It is not an introductory book, so you are expected to have some basic programming knowledge. If you are familiar with the object-oriented programming paradigm, then you may find this book helpful where it shows how the same problem can be solved differently, and often in a better way, in Julia.

Many of the patterns described in this book are applicable to any industry domain and use cases. Whether you are a data scientist, researcher, system programmer, or enterprise application developer, you should be able to benefit from using these patterns in your projects.

What this book covers

`Chapter 1`, *Design Patterns and Related Principles*, introduces the history of design patterns and how they are useful for developing applications. It covers several industry-standard software design principles that are applicable across any programming language and paradigm.

`Chapter 2`, *Modules, Packages, and Data Type Concepts*, discusses how larger programs can be organized and how dependencies can be managed. Then, it explains how to develop new data types and express their relationship in a custom type hierarchy.

`Chapter 3`, *Designing Functions and Interfaces*, explains how functions are defined and how multiple dispatch come into play. It also discusses parametric method and interfaces, for which different functions can work with each other properly based on a pre-determined contract.

`Chapter 4`, *Macros and Metaprogramming Techniques*, introduces macro programming facility and how it can be used to transform source code into a different form. It describes several techniques for developing and debugging macros more effectively.

`Chapter 5`, *Reusability Patterns*, covers design patterns that relate to code reuse. This includes the Delegation pattern for reusing code via composition, the Holy Traits pattern for a more formal interface contract, and the Parametric Type pattern for creating new types from a parameterized data structure.

Chapter 6, *Performance Patterns*, covers design patterns that relate to improving system performance. This includes the Global Constant pattern for better type stability, the Memoization pattern for caching prior computation results, the Struct of Arrays pattern for rearranging data for a more optimal layout, the Shared Array pattern for optimizing memory usage with parallel computing, and the Barrier Function pattern for improving performance via function specialization.

Chapter 7, *Maintainability Patterns*, covers design patterns about code maintainability. This includes the Sub Module pattern for better organization of larger code bases, the Keyword Definition pattern for creating data types that can be constructed more easily, the Code Generation pattern for defining many similar functions with less code, and the Domain-Specific Language pattern for creating a new syntax for a specific domain.

Chapter 8, *Robustness Patterns*, covers design patterns that help you write safer code. This include the Accessor pattern for providing standard access to fields, the Property pattern for controlling access to fields, the Let-Block pattern for limiting the variable scope, and the Exception Handling pattern for handling errors.

Chapter 9, *Miscellaneous Patterns*, covers several design patterns that do not fit into the preceding categories. It includes the Singleton Type pattern for use with dynamic dispatch, the Mocking pattern for building isolated tests, and the Functional Pipe pattern for building linear data processing pipelines.

Chapter 10, *Anti-Patterns*, covers patterns that should be avoided. The main anti-pattern is Piracy, which involves defining or extending functions for data types that you do not own. Then, it covers the Narrow Arguments and Non-Concrete Type Fields patterns, which hinder system performance.

Chapter 11, *Traditional Object-Oriented Patterns*, covers the traditional object-oriented patterns described in the *Design Patterns* book by Gang-of-Four. It discusses how those patterns can be simplified or implemented differently in Julia.

Chapter 12, *Inheritance and Variance*, discusses how Julia supports inheritance and why it is designed as such since its approach is quite different from mainstream object-oriented programming languages. Then, it covers the topic of type variance, an important concept in terms of subtyping relationships between data types used by multiple dispatch.

To get the most out of this book

You should download the latest version of Julia from the Julia Language website (https://julialang.org/).

The code samples are available on GitHub, as described in the *Technical requirements* section of each chapter. At the time of writing, the code has been tested with Julia version 1.3.0. To download the code samples, clone the project from GitHub as follows:

```
$ git clone https://github.com/PacktPublishing/Hands-on-Design-Patterns-and-
Best-Practices-with-Julia.git
Cloning into 'Hands-on-Design-Patterns-and-Best-Practices-with-Julia' ...
remote: Enumerating objects: 31, done.
remote: Counting objects: 100% (31/31), done.
remote: Compressing objects: 100% (24/24), done.
remote: Total 862 (delta 10), reused 18 (delta 7), pack-reused 831
Receiving objects: 100% (862/862), 3.44 MiB | 377.00 KiB/s, done.
Resolving deltas: 100% (377/377), done.
```

You are encouraged to run and experiment with the code samples accompanying this book. The code samples are typically stored in one of the following formats:

- Code snippets in a Julia source file. These snippets can be copied and pasted into the REPL.
- Code residing in a package directory. The package can be instantiated as follows:

For example, in Chapter 5, *Reusability Patterns*, the content is listed as follows:

```
$ cd Hands-on-Design-Patterns-and-Best-Practices-with-Julia
$ cd Chapter05
$ cd DelegationPattern
$ ls -l
total 16
-rw-r--r--  1 tomkwong  wheel  3581 Jan 16 20:04 Manifest.toml
-rw-r--r--  1 tomkwong  wheel   318 Jan 16 20:04 Project.toml
drwxr-xr-x  3 tomkwong  wheel    96 Jan 16 20:04 misc
drwxr-xr-x  6 tomkwong  wheel   192 Jan 16 20:04 src
drwxr-xr-x  4 tomkwong  wheel   128 Jan 16 20:04 test
```

To use the code for `DelegationPattern`, just start a Julia REPL in that folder with the `--project=.` command-line argument:

```
[$ julia --project=.
               _
   _       _ _(_)_      |  Documentation: https://docs.julialang.org
  (_)     | (_) (_)     |
   _ _   _| |_  __ _     |  Type "?" for help, "]?" for Pkg help.
  | | | | | | |/ _` |    |
  | | |_| | | | (_| |    |  Version 1.3.0 (2019-11-26)
 _/ |\__'_|_|_|\__'_|   |  Official https://julialang.org/ release
|__/                     |

julia> 
```

Then, go to the package mode and instantiate the package by entering the `]  instantiate` command:

```
(DelegationPattern) pkg> instantiate
```

After that, you can use the package as usual:

```
julia> using DelegationPattern
[ Info: Precompiling DelegationPattern [03117b61-9e61-518c-8c62-ec09d203ee1c]
```

If there is a test directory, then you can read and run the test scripts provided.

Download the example code files

You can download the example code files for this book from your account at www.packt.com. If you purchased this book elsewhere, you can visit www.packtpub.com/support and register to have the files emailed directly to you.

You can download the code files by following these steps:

1. Log in or register at www.packt.com.
2. Select the **Support** tab.
3. Click on **Code Downloads**.
4. Enter the name of the book in the **Search** box and follow the onscreen instructions.

Once the file is downloaded, please make sure that you unzip or extract the folder using the latest version of:

- WinRAR/7-Zip for Windows
- Zipeg/iZip/UnRarX for Mac
- 7-Zip/PeaZip for Linux

The code bundle for the book is also hosted on GitHub at `https://github.com/PacktPublishing/Hands-on-Design-Patterns-and-Best-Practices-with-Julia`. In case there's an update to the code, it will be updated on the existing GitHub repository.

We also have other code bundles from our rich catalog of books and videos available at `https://github.com/PacktPublishing/`. Check them out!

Code in Action

Visit the following link for the Code in Action videos:

`http://bit.ly/36Z4oXs`

Conventions used

There are a number of text conventions used throughout this book.

`CodeInText`: Indicates code words in text such as variable names, function names, data types, etc. For example, "The `format` function takes a `formatter` and a numeric value, `x`, and returns a formatted string."

A block of code is set as follows:

```
abstract type Formatter end
struct IntegerFormatter <: Formatter end
struct FloatFormatter <: Formatter end
```

Any experiment or output from the REPL is presented as screenshots:

```
julia> using HTTP

julia> url = "https://hacker-news.firebaseio.com/v0/topstories.json";

julia> response = HTTP.request("GET", url);

julia> typeof(response)
HTTP.Messages.Response
```

Bold: Indicates an important word or concept. For example, "The **Bridge pattern** is used to decouple an abstraction from its implementation so that it can evolve independently."

Italics: Emphasizes a new concept that will be explained later in the text. For example, "The cases presented in previous chapters include various situations that we can solve by writing *idiomatic* Julia code."

 Important notes appear like this.

 Tips and tricks appear like this.

Get in touch

Feedback from our readers is always welcome.

General feedback: If you have questions about any aspect of this book, mention the book title in the subject of your message and email us at `customercare@packtpub.com`.

Errata: Although we have taken every care to ensure the accuracy of our content, mistakes do happen. If you have found a mistake in this book, we would be grateful if you would report this to us. Please visit `www.packtpub.com/support/errata`, selecting your book, clicking on the Errata Submission Form link, and entering the details.

Piracy: If you come across any illegal copies of our works in any form on the Internet, we would be grateful if you would provide us with the location address or website name. Please contact us at `copyright@packt.com` with a link to the material.

If you are interested in becoming an author: If there is a topic that you have expertise in and you are interested in either writing or contributing to a book, please visit `authors.packtpub.com`.

Reviews

Please leave a review. Once you have read and used this book, why not leave a review on the site that you purchased it from? Potential readers can then see and use your unbiased opinion to make purchase decisions, we at Packt can understand what you think about our products, and our authors can see your feedback on their book. Thank you!

For more information about Packt, please visit `packt.com`.

Section 1: Getting Started with Design Patterns

The aim of this section is to introduce you to how design patterns are used in general and how Julia is different from the object-oriented programming paradigm.

This section contains the following chapter:

- Chapter 1, *Design Patterns and Related Principles*

Design Patterns and Related Principles

Nowadays, learning and applying design patterns is an important aspect of software engineering. Design patterns are like water – you can't live without them. Don't believe me? Just ask hiring managers, and you will find that many of them have design patterns in their job postings as well as related questions in job interviews. It is a common belief that design patterns are important ingredients for software development and everyone should know them.

In this chapter, we will provide some context about why design patterns are useful and how they have served us well in the past few decades. By understanding the motivation behind design patterns, we will be able to set forth a set of guiding principles for developing software. The following topics will be discussed in this chapter:

- The history of design patterns
- Software design principles
- Software quality objectives

Let's get started!

The history of design patterns

Design patterns is not a new concept to computer programmers. Since personal computers became more affordable and popular in the 1980s, the programming profession flourished and a lot of code was written for a variety of applications.

I remember that, when I was 14 years old, learning the GOTO statement for a BASIC program was one of the coolest things. It literally allowed me to take a control flow to a different part of the code at any time. Perhaps not too surprisingly, when I learned about structured programming and the Pascal language in college, I started to realize how GOTO statements produce messy spaghetti code. Using GOTO for branching purposes is a pattern. It's just a bad one because it makes code difficult to understand, follow, and debug. In today's *lingua franca,* we call them anti-patterns. When it comes to structured programming techniques, organizing code in small functions is a pattern as well, one that has been taught as a mainstream subject in programming courses.

When I graduated from college, I started my programming career and spent plenty of time *hacking away.* I had the opportunity to do various kinds of research and find out how systems are designed. For example, I realized that the Unix operating system has a beautiful design. That is because it consists of many small programs, which individually do not have a ton of functionality, but you can compose them in any number of ways to solve more complex problems. I was also fond of the Scheme programming language, which came out of MIT's AI Lab. The simplicity and versatility of the language still amazes me today. Scheme's heritage can be traced to Lisp, which had some influence on how the Julia language was designed.

The rise of design patterns

In 1994, while I was diving deep into C++ and distributed computing for a financial application, four software professionals, also known as the Gang of Four or GoF, came together and published a book about design patterns, and it took the object-oriented programming community by storm. The group collected and classified 23 design patterns that were commonly utilized when developing large-scale systems. They also chose to explain the concepts using **Unified Modeling Language** (UML) and C++ and Smalltalk.

For the first time, a set of design patterns had been collected, organized, explained, and widely distributed to software developers. Perhaps one of the most significant decisions by the group was to organize these patterns in a highly structured and easily consumable format. Since then, programmers have been able to communicate with each other easily about how they design their software. In addition, they can visually present software design with a universal notation. When one person talks about the Singleton pattern, another person can immediately understand and even visualize in his/her mind how that component works. Isn't that convenient?

Even more surprisingly, design patterns suddenly became the gospel when it come to building good software. In some ways, using them was even perceived as the only way to write good software. GoF patterns were so widely preached across the development community that many people abused them and used them everywhere without good reason. The problem is – *When all you have is a hammer, everything looks like a nail!* Not everything can be solved or should be solved by the same patterns. When design patterns are overused or misused, the code becomes more abstract, more complicated, and more difficult to manage.

So, what have we learned from the past? We recognize that every abstraction comes with a cost. Every design pattern comes with its own pros and cons. One of the main objectives of this book is to discuss not just the how but also the why and why not, and under what circumstances a pattern should be used or not used. We, as software professionals, will then be equipped with the information we need to make good judgment calls about when to apply these patterns.

More thoughts about GoF patterns

GoF design patterns are classified into three main categories:

- **Creational patterns**: These cover how to construct objects in various ways. Since object-oriented programming brings together data and behavior, and a class may inherit the structure and behavior of an ancestor class, there are some complexities involved when building a large application. Creational patterns help standardize object creation methods in various situations.
- **Structural patterns**: These cover how objects can be extended or composed to make bigger thing. The purpose of these patterns is to allow software components to be reused or replaced more easily.
- **Behavioral patterns**: This cover how objects can be designed to perform separate tasks and communicate with each other. A large application can be decomposed into independent components and the code becomes easier to maintain. The object-oriented programming paradigm requires solid interaction between objects. The purpose of these patterns is to make software components more flexible and more convenient for collaboration with each other.

One school of thought is that design patterns are created to address limitations in their respective programming language. Two years after the GoF book was published, Peter Norvig published research showing that 16 of the 23 design patterns are either unnecessary or can be simplified in a dynamic programming language such as Lisp.

This is not an unimportant observation. In the context of object-oriented programming, additional abstraction from a class hierarchy requires the software designer to think about how objects are instantiated and interact with each other. In a strong, statically typed language such as Java, it is even more necessary to reason about the behavior and interaction of objects. In Chapter 11, *Traditional Object-Oriented Patterns*, we will circle back to this topic and discuss how Julia works differently compared to object-oriented programming.

For now, we will start with the basics and review some software design principles. These principles are like the North star, guiding us as we build applications.

How do we describe patterns in this book?

If you are new to Julia programming, this book will help you understand how to write more idiomatic Julia code. We will also focus on describing some of the most useful patterns that are already used in the existing open source Julia ecosystem. That includes Julia's own Base and stdlib packages as the Julia runtime is largely written in Julia itself. We will also reference other packages that are used for numerical computing and web programming.

For ease of reference, we will organize our patterns by name. For example, the Holy Traits pattern refers to a specific method for implementing traits. The Domain-Specific Language pattern talks about how to build new syntax to represent specific domain concepts. The sole purpose of having a name is just ease of reference.

When we discuss these design patterns in this book, we will try to understand the motivation behind them. What specific problem are we trying to solve? What would be a real-world situation where such a pattern would be useful? Then, we will get into the details of how to solve these problems. Sometimes, there may be several ways to solve the same problem, in which case we will look into each possible solution and discuss the pros and cons.

Having said that, it is important for us to understand the ultimate goal of using design patterns. Why do we want to use design patterns in the first place? To answer this question, it would be useful for us to first understand some key software design principles.

Software design principles

While this book does not cover object-oriented programming, some object-oriented design principles are universal and could be applied to any programming language and paradigm. Here, we will take a look at some of the most well-known design principles. In particular, we will cover the following:

- **SOLID**: Single Responsibility, Open/Closed, Liskov Substitution, Interface Segregation, Dependency Inversion
- **DRY**: Don't Repeat Yourself
- **KISS**: Keep It Simple, Stupid!
- **POLA**: Principle of Least Astonishment
- **YAGNI**: You Aren't Gonna Need It
- **POLP**: Principle of Least Privilege

Let's start with SOLID.

SOLID

The SOLID principle consists of the following:

- **S**: Single Responsibility Principle
- **O**: Open/Closed Principle
- **L**: Liskov Substitution Principle
- **I**: Interface Segregation Principle
- **D**: Dependency Inversion Principle

Let's understand each concept in detail.

Single Responsibility Principle

The Single Responsibility Principle states that every module, class, and function should be responsible for a single functional objective. There should be only one reason to make any changes.

The benefits of this principle are listed here:

- The programmer can focus on a single context during development.
- The size of each component is smaller.

- The code is easier to understand.
- The code can be tested more easily.

Open/Closed Principle

The Open/Closed Principle states that every module should be open for extension but closed for modification. It is necessary to distinguish between enhancement and extension—enhancement refers to a core improvement of the existing module, while an extension is considered an add-on that provides additional functionality.

The following are the benefits of this principle:

- Existing components can be easily reused to derive new functionalities.
- Components are loosely coupled so it is easier to replace them without affecting the existing functionality.

Liskov Substitution Principle

The Liskov Substitution Principle states that a program that accepts type T can also accept type S (which is a subtype of T), without any change in behavior or intended outcome.

The following are the benefits of this principle:

- A function can be reused for any subtype passed in the arguments.

Interface Segregation Principle

The Interface Segregation Principle states that a client should not be forced to implement interfaces that it does not need to use.

The following are the benefits of this principle:

- Software components are more modular and reusable.
- New implementations can be created more easily.

Dependency Inversion Principle

The Dependency Inversion Principle states that high-level classes should not depend on low-level classes; instead, high-level classes should depend on an abstraction that low-level classes implement.

The following are the benefits of this principle:

- Components are more decoupled.
- The system becomes more flexible and can adapt to changes more easily. Low-level components can be replaced without affecting high-level components.

DRY

We'll now cover the DRY principle:

- **D**: Don't
- **R**: Repeat
- **Y**: Yourself

This acronym is a good way of reminding programmers that duplicate code is bad. It is obvious that duplicate code can be difficult to maintain—whenever logic is changed, multiple places in the code are affected.

What do we do when duplicate code is found? Eliminate it and create a common function that is reusable from multiple source files.

In addition, sometimes code is not 100% duplicated but instead is 90% similar. That is not an uncommon scenario. In that case, consider redesigning the relevant components, possibly refactoring code to a common interface.

KISS

Let's talk about the KISS principle:

- **K**: Keep
- **I**: It
- **S**: Simple
- **S**: Stupid!

Often, when we design software, we like to think ahead and try to deal with all kinds of future scenarios. The trouble with building such *future-proof* software is that it takes exponentially more effort to design and code properly. Practically speaking, it's a conundrum—there is no 100% future-proof solution because technology changes, business changes, and people change. Also, over-engineering could lead to excessive abstraction and indirection, making a system more difficult to test and maintain.

In addition, when using Agile software development methods, we value faster and high-quality delivery over perfection or excess engineering. Keeping the design and code simple is a virtue that every programmer should keep in mind.

POLA

Let's look at the POLA principle:

- **P**: Principle
- **O**: Of
- **L**: Least
- **A**: Astonishment

POLA states that a software component should be easy to understand and its behavior should never be a surprise (or, more accurately, *astonishing*) to the client. How do we do that?

The following are some things to keep in mind:

- Make sure that the names of the module, function, or function arguments are clear and unambiguous.
- Ensure that modules are right-sized and well maintained.
- Ensure that interfaces are small and easy to understand.
- Ensure that functions have few positional arguments.

YAGNI

Let's move on to the YAGNI principle:

- **Y**: You
- **A**: Aren't
- **G**: Gonna
- **N**: Need
- **I**: It

YAGNI says you should only develop software that is needed today. This principle came from **Extreme Programming** (**XP**). See what Ron Jeffries, co-founder of XP, wrote in his blog:

> *"Always implement things when you actually need them, never when you just foresee that you need them."*

Software engineers are sometimes tempted to develop functionality that they feel the customer will need in the future. It's been proven time and time again that this is not the most effective way to develop software. Consider the following scenarios:

- The functionality is never needed by the customer and so the code is never used.
- The business environment changes and the system has to be redesigned or replaced.
- The technology changes and the system has to be upgraded to use a new library, a new framework, or a new language.

The cheapest software is the one that you didn't write. *You aren't gonna need it!*

POLP

Now, for POLP:

- **P**: Principle
- **O**: Of
- **L**: Least
- **P**: Privilege

POLP states that a client must be given access only to the information or functions that they need. POLP is one of the most important pillars for building secure applications, and it is widely adopted by cloud infrastructure vendors such as Amazon, Microsoft, and Google.

There are quite a few benefits when POLP is applied:

- Sensitive data is protected and not exposed to non-privileged users.
- The system can be tested more easily since the number of use cases is limited.
- The system becomes less prone to misuse because only limited access is given and the interface is simpler.

The software design principles that we have learned about so far are great tools. Although SOLID, DRY, KISS, POLA, YAGNI, and POLP seem to be just a bunch of acronyms, they are useful in designing better software. While SOLID principles came from the object-oriented programming paradigm, SOLID's concepts can still be applied to other languages and environments. As we work through the rest of the chapters in this book, I would encourage you to keep them in mind.

In the next section, we will go over several software quality objectives when designing software.

Software quality objectives

Everyone likes beautiful design. I do, too. But, the use of design patterns is not just to make something look good. Everything we do should have a purpose.

The GoF classified object-oriented design patterns as creational, structural, and behavioral. For Julia, let's take a different perspective and classify our patterns by their respective software quality objectives as follows:

- Reusability
- Performance
- Maintenance
- Safety

Let's understand each of these in the following sections.

Reusability

People often talk about top-down and bottom-up approaches when designing software.

The **top-down approach** starts with a large problem and breaks it down into a set of smaller problems. Then, if the problems are not small enough, as discussed when we looked at the Single Responsibility Principle, we further break down the problem into even smaller ones. The process repeats and eventually the problem is small enough to design and code.

The **bottom-up approach** works in the opposite direction. Given domain knowledge, you can start creating building blocks, and then create more complex ones by composing from these building blocks.

Regardless of how it is done, eventually there will be a set of components that work with each other, thereby forming the basis of the application.

I like the metaphor. Even a 5-year old child can build a variety of structures using just several kinds of Lego block. Imagination is the limit. Do you ever wonder why it is so powerful? Well, if you recall, every Lego block has a standard set of connectors: one, two, four, six, eight, or more. Using these connectors, each block can plug into another block easily. When you create a new structure, you can combine it with other structures to create even larger, more complex structures.

When building applications, the key design principle is to create pluggable interfaces so every component can be reused easily.

Characteristics of reusable components

The following are important characteristics of reusable components:

- Each component serves a single purpose (the S in SOLID).
- Each component is well defined and ready for reuse (the O in SOLID).
- An abstract type hierarchy is designed for parent-child relationships (the L in SOLID).
- Interfaces are defined as a small set of functions (the I in SOLID).
- Interfaces are used to bridge between components (the D in SOLID).
- Modules and functions are designed with simplicity in mind (KISS).

Reusability is important because it means we can avoid duplicated code and wasted effort. The less code we write, the less work we need to do to maintain software. That includes not just the development effort but also the time testing, packaging, and upgrading. Reusability is also one of the reasons why open source software is so successful. In particular, the Julia ecosystem contains many open source packages and they tend to borrow functionalities from each other.

Next, we will discuss another software quality objective—performance.

Performance

The Julia language is designed for high-performance computing. It does not come for free, however. When it comes to performance, it takes practice to write code that is more compiler-friendly, thus making it more likely to translate the program into optimized machine code.

For the past few decades, computers have seemed to become faster and faster every year. What used to be performance bottlenecks are more easily solved using today's hardware. At the same time, we are also facing more challenges due to the explosion of data. A good example is the field of big data and data science. As the amount of data grows, we need even more computing power to handle these new use cases.

Unfortunately, the speed of computers has not grown as rapidly as it did in the past. Moore's Law states that the number of transistors on a microchip doubles roughly every 18 months, and since 1960 it has been correlated with the growth in CPU speed. However, it is well known that Moore's Law will no longer be applicable soon due to a physical limitation: the number of transistors that can be fitted to a chip and the precision of the fabrication process.

In order to address today's computational needs, especially in the world of artificial intelligence, machine learning, and data science, practitioners have been gearing toward a *scale-out* strategy that utilizes multiple CPU cores across many servers, and looking at exploiting the efficiency of GPUs and TPUs.

Characteristics of high-performance code

The following are characteristics of high-performance code:

- Functions are small and can be optimized easily (S in SOLID).
- Functions contains simple logic rather than complex logic (KISS).
- Numeric data is laid out in contiguous memory space so the compiler can fully utilize CPU hardware.
- Memory allocation should be kept to a minimum to avoid excessive garbage collection.

Performance is an important aspect of any software project. It is particularly important for data science, machine learning, and scientific computing use cases. A small design change can make a big difference—depending on the situation, it could possibly turn a 24-hour process into a 30-minute process. It could also give users real-time experience when using a web application rather than a **please wait...** dialog.

Next, we will discuss software maintainability as another software quality objective.

Maintainability

Software can be maintained more easily when it is designed properly. Generally speaking, if you are able to effectively use the design principles listed previously (SOLID, KISS, DRY, POLA, YAGNI, and POLP), then your application is more likely to be well architected and designed for long-term maintenance.

Maintainability is an important ingredient for large-scale applications. A research project from graduate school may not last long. On the contrary, an enterprise application may last for decades. Recently, I heard from a colleague that COBOL is still in use and COBOL programmers are still making a good living.

We often hear about technical debt. Similar to monetary debt in real life, technical debt is something that you must pay for whenever code is changed. And the longer the technical debt stays in place, the more effort you have to spend.

To understand why, consider a module that is bloated with duplicate code or unnecessary dependencies. Whenever a new functionality is added, you have to update multiple parts of the source code, and you have to perform regression testing for a larger area of the system. So, you end up paying (in terms of programming time and effort) for the debt every time the code is changed until the debt is fully repaid (that is, until the code is fully refactored).

Characteristics of maintainable code

The following are characteristics of maintainable code:

- No unused code (YAGNI).
- No duplicate code (DRY).
- Code is concise and short (KISS).
- Code is clear and easy to understand (KISS).
- Every function has a single purpose (the S in SOLID).
- Every module contains functions that relate to and work with each other (the S in SOLID).

Maintainability is an important aspect of any application. When designed properly, even large applications can be changed frequently and easily without fear. Applications can also last a long time, reducing the cost of the software.

Next, we will discuss software safety as another quality objective.

Safety

"Safety—the condition of being safe from undergoing or causing hurt, injury, or loss."

– Merriam-Webster Dictionary

Applications are expected to function correctly. When an application malfunctions, there could be undesired consequences and some of those could be fatal. Consider a mission-critical rocket-launch subsystem used by NASA. A single defect could cause the launch to be delayed; or, in the worst-case scenario, it could cause the rocket to explode in mid-air.

Programming languages are designed to allow flexibility but at the same time provide safety features so software engineers can make fewer mistakes. For example, the compiler's static type checking ensures that the correct types are passed to functions that expect those types. In addition, most computer programs operate on data, and as we know, data is not always clean or available. Hence, the ability to handle bad or missing data is an important software quality.

Characteristics of safe applications

Some characteristics of safe applications follow:

- Each module exposes a minimum set of types, functions, and variables.
- Each function is called with arguments such that the respective types implement the expected behavior of the function (the L in SOLID; POLA).
- The return value of a function is clear and documented (POLA).
- Missing data is handled properly (POLA).
- Variables are limited to the smallest scope.
- Exceptions are caught and handled accordingly.

Safety is one of the most important objectives here. An erroneous application can cause major disasters. It can even cost a company millions of dollars. In 2010, Toyota recalled over 400,000 of its Prius hybrid cars due to a software defect with the **Anti-lock Braking System (ABS)**. In 1996, the Ariane 5 rocket launched by the European Space Agency exploded just 40 seconds after launch. Of course, these are only a few more extreme examples. By utilizing best practices, we can avoid getting into these kinds of embarrassing and costly incidents.

Now, we understand the importance of software design principles and software quality objectives.

Summary

In this chapter, we started by going back in time and reviewing the history of design patterns. We discussed why design patterns can be useful for software professionals and how we would like to organize design patterns in this book given what we have learned in the past.

We went over several key software design principles that can be applied universally in any programming language, as it is important that we keep them in mind when developing code and applying design patterns in Julia. We covered SOLID, DRY, KISS, POLA, YAGNI, and POLP. These design principles are well known and well received by the object-oriented programming community.

Finally, we discussed some software quality objectives that we want to achieve by using design patterns. In this book, we have decided to focus on reusability, maintainability, performance, and safety objectives. We also appreciated the benefits of these objectives and reviewed some general guidelines for achieving these objectives.

The next chapter is going to be exciting! We will get our hands dirty and look into how Julia programs are organized and how to use Julia's type system, along with some basics about Julia.

Questions

Review the following questions to reinforce your understanding of the subjects in this chapter. Answers are provided at the back of the book:

1. What are the benefits of using design patterns?
2. Name some key design principles.
3. What problem does the Open/Closed Principle solve?
4. Why is interface segregation important for software reusability?
5. What are the simplest ways to keep an application maintainable?
6. What is a good practice for avoiding over-engineered and bloated software?
7. How does memory usage affect system performance?

Section 2: Julia Fundamentals

2

The aim of this section is to quickly bring you up to speed regarding the fundamental concepts and features of the Julia programming language. A clear understanding of Julia Fundamentals is essential for you to be able to fully appreciate the beauty of the design patterns that we will look at in upcoming chapters.

This section contains the following chapters:

Modules, Packages, and Data Type Concepts

2

This chapter discusses several organizational techniques for developing large-scale applications. Believe it or not, this is often something that is easily overlooked. When developing applications, we typically focus on building data types, functions, control flows, and so on. It is equally important, however, to organize the code properly so that it is clean and maintainable.

In the later part of this chapter, we will introduce Julia's type system. Data types are the most fundamental building blocks of any application. Julia's type system is one of its strongest features when compared to other programming languages. A solid understanding of the type system will enable us to achieve better designs.

The following topics will be covered in this chapter:

- The growing pains of developing applications
- Working with namespaces, modules, and packages
- Managing package dependencies
- Designing abstract types and concrete types
- Understanding parametric types
- Converting between data types

By the end of the chapter, you should know how to create your own packages, divide code into separate modules, and start creating new data types for your application.

Let's go!

Technical requirements

The sample source code from this chapter is located at `https://github.com/PacktPublishing/Hands-on-Design-Patterns-and-Best-Practices-with-Julia/tree/master/Chapter02`.

The code is tested in a Julia 1.3.0 environment.

The growing pains of developing applications

"Start where you are. Use what you have. Do what you can. "

- Arthur Ashe

Everyone's journey is different. Julia is a versatile, dynamic programming language that can be used in many interesting use cases. More specifically, you can use it to easily code and solve a problem without thinking too much about system architecture and design. This is often sufficient for small research projects; however, when a project becomes more critical to the business, or when you have to harden a proof of concept into a production environment, it requires better organization, architecture, and design so that the project or application can live longer and be more maintainable.

What kinds of project do we typically deal with? Let's explore some examples.

Data science projects

A typical data science project starts with the idea of learning from a set of data and making a prediction. A lot of the upfront work goes into data collection, data cleaning, data analysis, and visualization. Then, data is further digested into features as inputs a machine learning model. The process up until this point is called *data engineering*. The data scientist then chooses one or more machine learning models and keeps on refining and tuning the model to arrive at a good level of accuracy for the predictive model. This process is called *model development*. When the model is ready for production, it is deployed and sometimes a frontend is created for the end user. The final process is referred to as *model deployment*.

The data engineering and model development processes can be interactive at the beginning, but they usually end up getting automated. That's because the process needs to be repeatable and the results have to be consistent. Data scientists may use a variety of tools during development, ranging from a number of Jupyter notebooks to a suite of related libraries and programs.

When a predictive model becomes production-ready, it can be deployed as a web service so that it can be used to make real-time predictions. At this point, the model needs to have a life cycle and be maintained, just like any other production software.

Enterprise applications

People developing enterprise applications have a different mindset. Unlike data science projects, software engineers typically know upfront what they need to build the system. They also know whether they have to live with certain assumptions and policies. For example, the technology stack may already be known when the project starts. Other factors that may already be familiar include the system architecture that will be used, which cloud vendor will be utilized, what database the application must integrate with, and so on.

Enterprise applications typically require a rich business domain object model. Data objects are created, manipulated, and transferred to different layers of the application. The system architecture may include a user interface, a middle tier, and a database backend.

Enterprise applications also tend to require a high level of integration with other systems. For example, a trading system used by an investment firm is typically hooked up to an accounting system, a trade-settlement system, a reporting system, and so on. As such, these applications are often designed to handle both *data at rest* (for example, data stored in a database) or *data in motion* (for example, data being streamed to another system). Furthermore, data movement may happen in real-time or as an overnight batch process.

Adapting to growth

No matter what kind of application you develop, it should not be hard to recognize growing pains.

For a data science project, the following signs typically indicate a growth-related problem:

- *"My notebook is getting too long. I often have to scroll up and down to understand what I have done before and what I'm doing now. There are too many variables created in between and I'm losing track of what they mean and how they are used."*
- *"The data structure is too complex. I was working on a data frame and have transformed it in ten different ways. I have now lost track of which transformed version represents what, and why they were needed in the first place."*
- *"I have saved a bunch of machine learning models on disk, and I'm losing track of how each one was trained and what assumptions were made for each of those models."*
- *"I have too much code scattered across many notebooks. Some code is duplicated or tweaked for a slightly different purpose. I am unable to achieve consistent results."*

As for an enterprise application, similar symptoms may surface:

- *"The application logic is too complicated, and there is a huge component performing too many functions."*
- *"It's becoming difficult to add new features without breaking existing functions."*
- *"It takes a lot of time for a new person to comprehend the code in this module and it seems that the same person has to relearn it again every now and then."*

It's not fun to handle unorganized code and data. If you find yourself uttering some of the preceding phrases, it may be a good time to rethink your strategy and start organizing your program properly.

Now, let's start our learning journey by organizing code better with Julia. As we are working at a high level, we will introduce the concept of namespaces, and we will go over how to create modules and packages.

Working with namespaces, modules, and packages

The Julia ecosystem lives on a namespace; in fact, this is the only way we can keep things in order. Why do I say that? The reason is that namespaces are used to logically separate fragments of source code so that they can be developed independently without affecting each other. If I define a function in one namespace, I will still be able to define another function in a different namespace even though both functions have the same name.

In Julia, namespaces are created using modules and submodules. In order to manage distribution and dependencies, modules are generally organized as packages. There is a standard directory structure for Julia packages. Although the top level directory structure is well defined, the programmer still has a lot of freedom in organizing source files.

In this section, we will explore the following topics:

- Understanding and using namespaces
- How to create modules and packages
- How to create submodules
- How to organize files in a module

Let's learn about each in detail in the following sections.

Understanding namespaces

What is a namespace? Let's try a real-life example.

Every language has its own set of words as defined in its dictionary. When people from different cultures talk to each other, they often end up in amusing situations. Consider these examples:

Conversation 1:

- American: *Your pants look dirty. You should change them.*
- British: *Do you mean my trousers? My underpants are... quite clean and well!*

Conversation 2:

- American: *These biscuits are yummy!*
- British: *Where? Where are the cookies...?*

Conversation 3:

- American: *I want to get back in shape and have tried many trainers but none of them are good.*
- British: *Have you tried the new running ones from Nike? I found them comfortable enough for my daily jogging routines.*

In fact, you don't even need to be from a different culture to experience this problem. Sometimes the same word already has different meanings depending on the context. For example:

- Pool - swimming pool or a group of things?
- Squash - the vegetable or the sport?
- Current - electrical current or a flow of water?

There is no way that we can enforce a single vocabulary across all domains because of ambiguities such as these. Fortunately, computer scientists are smart and long ago solved the problem as it pertains to their field: to distinguish two different meanings for a single word, we can just prefix the word with the respective context. Using the examples from the preceding list, we can qualify each word as follows:

- `Facility.Pool` and `Grouping.Pool`
- `Vegetable.Squash` and `Sport.Squash`
- `Electricity.Current` and `Liquid.Current`

The prefix is known as a **namespace**. Now that the words are qualified with their respective namespaces, they are no longer ambiguous and have a clear meaning.

In Julia, namespaces are created using modules, which we will learn about in the following section.

Creating modules and packages

Modules are used to create new namespaces. In Julia, creating a module is as simple as wrapping your code around a module block, like so:

```
module X
  # your code
end
```

In general, modules are created for the purpose of sharing and reuse, and the best way to achieve this is to organize code in Julia packages. A Julia package is a directory and file structure for maintaining module definitions, test scripts, documentation, and related data.

There is a standard directory structure and convention for Julia packages; however, it would be a hassle to manually configure a new program in the same structure every single time. Fortunately, there are some open source tools that automatically create the structure for a new package. Without officially endorsing any specific tool, I have chosen the PkgTemplates package for demonstration, as follows.

If you have not installed the PkgTemplates package before, it can be installed as follows:

```julia
julia> using Pkg

julia> Pkg.add("PkgTemplates")
```

Once it is installed, we can use it to create our sample module. The first step is to create a Template object, as follows:

```julia
julia> using PkgTemplates
[ Info: Precompiling PkgTemplates [14b8a8f1-9102-5b29-a752-f990bacb7fe1]

julia> template = Template(; license = "MIT", user = "tk3369")
Template:
  → User: tk3369
  → Host: github.com
  → License: MIT (Tom Kwong <tk3369@gmail.com> 2019)
  → Package directory: ~/.julia/dev
  → Minimum Julia version: v1.0
  → SSH remote: No
  → Add packages to main environment: Yes
  → Commit Manifest.toml: No
  → Plugins: None
```

Basically, the `template` object contains some default values that will be used to create new packages. Then, creating a new package is easy as calling the `generate` function.

```
julia> generate(template, "Calculator")
Generating project Calculator:
    ~/.julia/dev/Calculator/Project.toml
    ~/.julia/dev/Calculator/src/Calculator.jl
[ Info: Initialized Git repo at /Users/tomkwong/.julia/dev/Calculator
[ Info: Set remote origin to https://github.com/tk3369/Calculator.jl
Activating environment at `~/.julia/dev/Calculator/Project.toml`
 Resolving package versions...
  Updating `~/.julia/dev/Calculator/Project.toml`
  [8dfed614] + Test
  Updating `~/.julia/dev/Calculator/Manifest.toml`
  [2a0f44e3] + Base64
  [8ba89e20] + Distributed
  [b77e0a4c] + InteractiveUtils
  [56ddb016] + Logging
  [d6f4376e] + Markdown
  [9a3f8284] + Random
  [9e88b42a] + Serialization
  [6462fe0b] + Sockets
  [8dfed614] + Test
  Updating registry at `~/.julia/registries/General`
  Updating git-repo `https://github.com/JuliaRegistries/General.git`
 Resolving package versions...
  Updating `~/.julia/dev/Calculator/Project.toml`
[no changes]
  Updating `~/.julia/dev/Calculator/Manifest.toml`
  [2a0f44e3] - Base64
  [8ba89e20] - Distributed
  [b77e0a4c] - InteractiveUtils
  [56ddb016] - Logging
  [d6f4376e] - Markdown
  [9a3f8284] - Random
  [9e88b42a] - Serialization
  [6462fe0b] - Sockets
  [8dfed614] - Test
Activating environment at `~/.julia/environments/v1.3/Project.toml`
[ Info: Committed 6 files/directories: src/, Project.toml, test/, README.md, LICENSE, .gi
tignore
 Resolving package versions...
  Updating `~/.julia/environments/v1.3/Project.toml`
  [e1d37511] + Calculator v0.1.0 [`~/.julia/dev/Calculator`]
  Updating `~/.julia/environments/v1.3/Manifest.toml`
  [e1d37511] + Calculator v0.1.0 [`~/.julia/dev/Calculator`]
[ Info: New package is at /Users/tomkwong/.julia/dev/Calculator
```

By default, the package generator creates the new directory in the `~/.julia/dev` folder, but it is customizable with the `dir` keyword argument of the `Template` object.

The `generate` command is used to create a new package called `Calculator`. It automatically creates a directory with the following package structure:

```
$ ls -1R ~/.julia/dev/Calculator
LICENSE
Manifest.toml
Project.toml
README.md
src
test

/Users/tomkwong/.julia/dev/Calculator/src:
Calculator.jl

/Users/tomkwong/.julia/dev/Calculator/test:
runtests.jl
```

At this time, you can start editing the `Calculator.jl` file and replace the file contents with your own source code.

 If you are new to Julia, make sure that you check out the `Revise` package, which allows you to edit source code and have your working environment updated automatically. Your productivity using Julia will be increased by a factor of 10, guaranteed.

Let's work on the `Calculator` module by implementing some financial calculations. Over the course of this example, we will learn how to manage the accessibility of variables and functions from external clients. Our initial code is set up as follows:

```julia
# Calculator.jl
module Calculator

export interest, rate

"""
  interest(amount, rate)

Calculate interest from an `amount` and interest rate of `rate`.
"""
function interest(amount, rate)
  return amount * (1 + rate)
end

"""
  rate(amount, interest)
```

```
Calculate interest rate based on an `amount` and `interest`.
"""
function rate(amount, interest)
 return interest / amount
end

end # module
```

This code should be saved to the `Calculator.jl` file.

Defining functional behavior

Our `Calculator` module defines two functions:

- The `interest` function is used to calculate the interest for a deposit amount, `amount`, with the specified interest rate, `rate`, for a full investment period.
- The `rate` function is used to calculate the interest rate for which you can invest the deposit amount, `amount`, and receive the interest amount, `interest`.

Remember that *interest* and *rate* may mean completely different things outside the context of Calculator.

Exporting functions

Functions defined inside a module are not exposed to the outside world. To expose them, the `interest` and `rate` functions can be exported using the `export` statement, so that users of this module can easily bring them into their own namespace:

```
export interest, rate
```

Once the functions are exported, they will be available in the client's scope where the module is loaded with the `using` keyword. Let's try to reference these functions from the Julia REPL before loading the module:

```
julia> interest
ERROR: UndefVarError: interest not defined

julia> rate
ERROR: UndefVarError: rate not defined
```

Because we have not loaded the `Calculator` package yet, neither `interest` nor `rate` is defined. Let's bring them in now:

```
julia> using Calculator

julia> interest
interest (generic function with 1 method)

julia> rate
rate (generic function with 1 method)
```

When the `using` statement is executed, all symbols exported from the module are brought into the current namespace. From the Julia REPL, the current module is called `Main`, as shown in the following diagram:

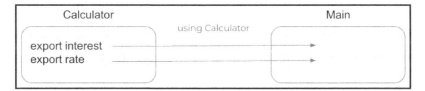

It is possible for us to bring in a subset of the names by qualifying the `using` statement with specific names. Let's restart the Julia REPL and try again:

```
julia> using Calculator: interest

julia> interest
interest (generic function with 1 method)

julia> rate
ERROR: UndefVarError: rate not defined
```

In this case, only the `interest` function was brought into the `Main` module:

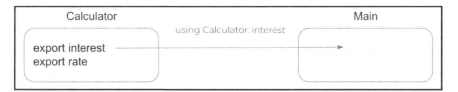

There are actually several ways to import names from another module into the current namespace. For the sake of simplicity, we can summarize them as follows:

Ref	Statement	What is brought into the scope

1	`using Calculator`	`interest`
		`rate`
		`Calculator.interest`
		`Calculator.rate`

2	`using Calculator: interest`	`interest`
3	`import Calculator`	`Calculator.interest` `Calculator.rate`
4	`import Calculator: interest`	`interest`
5	`import Calculator.interest`	`interest`

As you can see, there are four ways (namely, 1, 2, 4, and 5 in the preceding table) to bring the `interest` function into the current namespace. There are some subtleties in choosing between `using` and `import` statements. A good rule of thumb is to use the `using` statement when you are using the functionality, but choose the `import` statement when you need to extend the functionality from the module. Extending functions from another package is a key language feature of Julia, and you will learn more about that from various examples in this book.

Resolving conflicts

The picture, however, is not always rosy. Let's imagine that the main program needs to use another module called `Rater`, which provides rating services for online books. In this scenario, the main program may try to take functions from both modules, as shown in the following:

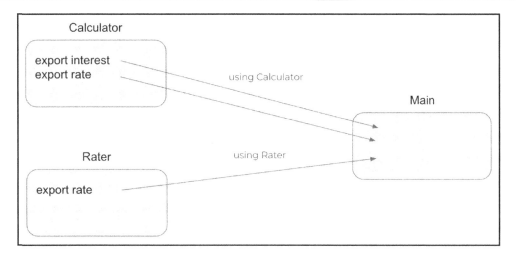

But, *Houston, we have a problem!* The `rate` function was brought in from the `Calculator` module, but it happens to be in conflict with the other one from the `Rater` module. Julia automatically detects this conflict on first use, prints a warning, and, from then on, requires the programmer to use their fully qualified names to access either function:

```
julia> using Calculator

julia> using Rater

julia> rate
WARNING: both Rater and Calculator export "rate"; uses of it in module Main
must be qualified
ERROR: UndefVarError: rate not defined
```

If you are not happy with this, especially the ugly-looking warning, then there is an alternative. First, you can ask yourself whether both `rate` functions are actually needed in the main program. If only one `rate` function is needed, then just bring one into scope so that there is no more conflict:

```
using Calculator: interest
using Rater: rate

# Here, the rate function refers to the one defined in Rater module.
```

From my experience, bringing specific names into the current namespace is indeed the best choice for most use cases. The reason for this is that it will be immediately obvious which functions you depend on. Such dependency is also self-documented in the code.

Occasionally, you may need to use both `rate` functions. In such cases, you can solve the problem by using the regular `import` statement:

```
import Calculator
import Rater

interest_rate = Calculator.rate(100.00, 3.5)
rating = Rater.rate("Hands-On Design Patterns with Julia")
```

This way, it only loads the packages and does not bring any name into the current namespace. You can now refer to both `rate` functions with their fully qualified names—that is, `Calculator.rate` and `Rater.rate`. After creating these modules, let's move on to see how to create submodules.

Creating submodules

When a module becomes too large, it may make sense to split it into smaller parts so that it's easier to develop and maintain. One way to solve this problem is to create submodules.

Creating submodules is convenient as they are just defined within the scope of the parent module. Let's say we organize the `Calculator` module with two submodules—`Mortgage` and `Banking`. These submodules can be defined in separate files and can be included directly into the parent module. Consider the following code:

```
# Calculator.jl
module Calculator

include("Mortgage.jl")
include("Banking.jl")

end # module
```

Submodules, just like regular modules, are also defined using module blocks. The source code for `Mortgage` looks just like a regular module definition:

```
# Mortgage.jl
module Mortgage

# mortgage related source code

end # module
```

Because the source code from `Mortgage` is included inside the `Calculator` module block, it forms a nested structure. The usage of submodules is the same as that of any regular module, except that you have to reference them via the parent module. In this case, you'd use `Calculator.Mortgage` or `Calculator.Banking`.

Using submodules is an effective way to separate code for larger codebases. Next, we will go over how to organize source code in a module.

Organizing files in a module

The source code for modules is typically organized as multiple source files. Although there is no hard and fast rule about how source files are organized, the following are useful guidelines:

- **Coupling**: Highly coupled functions should be placed in the same file. Doing so allows less context switching when editing source files. For example, when you change the signature of a function, all callers of that function may need to be updated. Ideally, you would want to minimize the *blast radius* and not have to change many files.
- **File size**: Having more than a few hundred lines of code in a single file could be a warning sign. If the code inside the file is all tightly coupled, then it may be better to redesign the system to reduce coupling.
- **Ordering**: Julia loads the source files in the order in which you include them. As data types and utility functions are usually shared, it is better to save them in a `types.jl` and `utils.jl` file respectively and include them at the beginning of the module.

Similarly, the same considerations apply when organizing test scripts.

By now, we have learned how to create new namespaces using modules and submodules. More conveniently, a module is organized in a package so that it can be reused from an application. Once we have created multiple packages, it is unavoidable that they may have to depend on each other. It is important that we know how to handle these dependencies properly; this will be our primary topic in the next section.

Managing package dependencies

The Julia ecosystem has a rich set of open source packages. When packages are designed with a single objective, they can be reused more easily; however, working with a large codebase is not an easy task because it is more likely to depend on third-party packages. It takes a considerable amount of time and effort for a developer to maintain and manage these dependencies in order to avoid *dependency hell*.

It is important to understand that dependencies exist not just between packages, but also between specific versions of packages. Luckily, the Julia language has strong support for semantic versioning, which can help solve a lot of problems.

In this section, we will cover the following topics:

- Understanding the semantic versioning scheme
- Specifying dependencies for Julia packages
- Avoiding circular dependencies

Now, let's take a quick look at the semantic versioning scheme.

Understanding the semantic versioning scheme

Semantic versioning (https://semver.org/) is a scheme developed by Tom Preston-Werner, most famously known as the co-founder and CTO of GitHub. Semantic versioning serves a very specific purpose, which is to provide the meaning—that is, the semantics—of version number changes.

When we use a third-party package and it is upgraded, how do we know whether our application needs to be updated? What kind of risk are we taking if we just upgrade the dependent package without doing any testing with our own application?

Before semantic versioning, it was almost always a guess. A more diligent and risk-averse developer, however, would at least examine the release notes of the dependent package, try to figure out whether there are any breaking changes, then take proper actions.

Here, we will quickly summarize how semantic versioning works. First of all, a version number is constructed using the following components:

```
<major>.<minor>.<patch>
```

If we wish, the version number can be followed by a release tag and a build number at the end:

```
<major>.<minor>.<patch>-<pre-release>+<build>
```

Every part of the version number reveals a meaning:

- The `major` release number, when changed, means that a major change has been introduced in this release that is incompatible with the previous release. It is highly risky for applications to incorporate the new release as existing functions will likely break.
- The `minor` release number, when changed, means that there are nonbreaking enhancements in this release. It is moderately risky for applications to incorporate the new release because previous functions should, at least in theory, continue to work as they are.
- The `patch` release number, when changed, means that there are nonbreaking bug fixes in this release. The risk is low for applications to incorporate the new release.
- The `pre-release` tag, when present, indicates a pre-release candidate, such as alpha, beta, or **release candidates** (**RCs**). The release is considered unstable and applications should never use it in a production environment.
- The `build` tag is considered to be meta information and can be ignored.

Note that semantic versioning is only useful when all packages use it properly. Semantic versioning is like a common language that package developers can use to easily indicate the impact of their changes when making new releases.

The Julia package ecosystem encourages semantic versioning. Next, we will take a look at how the Julia package manager, `Pkg`, handles dependencies using semantic versioning.

While Julia encourages semantic versioning, many open source packages still have a pre-1.0 version number, even though they can be quite stable for production use. A major version number of zero is special—it basically means that every new release is breaking.

As the Julia language matures, more package authors will mark their packages as 1.0, and the situation regarding package compatibility will get better over time.

Specifying dependencies for Julia packages

We can tell when a package depends on another by examining the `using` or `import` keywords in the source files; however, the Julia runtime environment is designed to be more explicit by tracking the dependencies. Such information is stored in the `Project.toml` file in the package directory. In addition, a `Manifest.toml` file in the same directory contains more information about the complete dependency tree. These files are written in the TOML file format. Although it is easy enough to edit these files by hand, the `Pkg` package manager's **command-line interface (CLI)** could be used to manage dependencies more easily.

To add a new dependent package, you just need to carry out the following steps:

1. Start the Julia REPL.
2. Enter `Pkg` mode by pressing the `]` key.
3. Activate the project environment using the `activate` command.
4. Add the dependent package using the `add` command.

For example, let's add the `SaferIntegers` package to our `Calculator` package as follows:

```
(Calculator) pkg> status
Project Calculator v0.1.0
    Status `~/.julia/dev/Calculator/Project.toml`
    (no changes since last commit)

(Calculator) pkg> add SaferIntegers
 Resolving package versions...
 Installed SaferIntegers — v2.5.0
  Updating `~/.julia/dev/Calculator/Project.toml`
  [88634af6] + SaferIntegers v2.5.0
  Updating `~/.julia/dev/Calculator/Manifest.toml`
  [864edb3b] + DataStructures v0.17.6
  [1914dd2f] + MacroTools v0.5.3
  [bac558e1] + OrderedCollections v1.1.0
  [88634af6] + SaferIntegers v2.5.0
  [2a0f44e3] + Base64
  [8ba89e20] + Distributed
  [b77e0a4c] + InteractiveUtils
  [56ddb016] + Logging
  [d6f4376e] + Markdown
  [9a3f8284] + Random
  [9e88b42a] + Serialization
  [6462fe0b] + Sockets
  [8dfed614] + Test
```

Let's first examine the contents of the `Project.toml` file, as shown in the following screenshot. The funny-looking hash code `88634af6-177f-5301-88b8-7819386cfa38` represents the **universal unique identifier** (UUID) of the `SaferIntegers` package. Note that there is no version number specified for the `SaferIntegers` package, even though we know version 2.5.0 was installed from the preceding output:

```
Users > tomkwong > .julia > dev > Calculator > ⚙ Project.toml
  1    name = "Calculator"
  2    uuid = "ed85bbf7-223e-44d4-8ae7-39755d48a39c"
  3    authors = ["Tom Kwong <tk3369@gmail.com>"]
  4    version = "0.1.0"
  5
  6    [deps]
  7    SaferIntegers = "88634af6-177f-5301-88b8-7819386cfa38"
  8
  9    [compat]
 10    julia = "1"
 11
 12    [extras]
 13    Test = "8dfed614-e22c-5e08-85e1-65c5234f0b40"
 14
 15    [targets]
 16    test = ["Test"]
 17
```

The `Manifest.toml` file contains the complete dependency tree of the package. First, we find the following section regarding our `SaferIntegers` dependency:

```
 43    [[SaferIntegers]]
 44    deps = ["MacroTools", "Random"]
 45    git-tree-sha1 = "6296e51150b2b5907eb14fd304e51e994d7e7c72"
 46    uuid = "88634af6-177f-5301-88b8-7819386cfa38"
 47    version = "2.5.0"
```

Note that the `SaferIntegers` package now has a specific version. `2.5.0`, in the manifest file. Why? It's because the manifest is designed to capture the exact version information for all directly dependent *and* indirectly dependent packages. A second observation is that officially bundled packages, such as `Serialization`, `Sockets`, and `Test`, do not carry version numbers:

```
49    [[Serialization]]
50    uuid = "9e88b42a-f829-5b0c-bbe9-9e923198166b"
51
52    [[Sockets]]
53    uuid = "6462fe0b-24de-5631-8697-dd941f90decc"
54
55    [[Test]]
56    deps = ["Distributed", "InteractiveUtils", "Logging", "Random"]
57    uuid = "8dfed614-e22c-5e08-85e1-65c5234f0b40"
```

These packages do not have version numbers because they are always released with the Julia binary. Their actual versions are pretty much determined by the specific Julia version.

It is important to realize that neither `Project.toml` and `Manifest.toml` contains any versioning compatibility information, even though we know version 2.5.0 of `SaferInteger` was installed. To specify compatibility constraints, we can manually edit the `Project.toml` file using the semantic versioning scheme. For example, if we know that `Calculator` is compatible with `SaferIntegers` version 1.1.1 and later, then we can add this requirement to the `[compat]` section of the `Project.toml` file, as follows:

```
[compat]
SaferIntegers = "1.1.1"
```

This compatibility setting provides the necessary information for the Julia package manager to ensure that at least `SaferIntegers` version 1.1.1 is installed in order to use the `Calculator` package. Since the package manager is sensitive to semantic versioning, the preceding setting means that `Calculator` can work with all versions of `SaferIntegers` from 1.1.1 to the latest 1.*x.y* version, right up to 2.0. In mathematical notation, the range of compatible versions is [1.1.1, 2.0.0), where 2.0.0 is excluded.

Now, what if `SaferIntegers` is improved and the package owner decides to release 2.0.0? Well, because the major version number has advanced from 1 to 2, we have to expect breaking changes. If we don't do anything, the latest version, 2.0.0, will never be installed in the `Calculator` environment because we specifically implemented an exclusive upper bound of 2.0.0.

Let's say that, after thorough examination and testing, we conclude that `Calculator` is not affected by any breaking changes from `SaferIntegers` 2.0.0. In that case, we can just make a small change to our `Project.toml` file, as follows:

```
[compat]
SaferIntegers = "1.1.1, 2"
```

This line specifies the *union* of these two compatible version ranges:

- The `1.1.1` specification indicates that the package is compatible with `SaferIntegers` versions [1.1.1, 2.0.0]
- The `2.0` specification indicates that the package is compatible with `SaferIntegers` versions [2.0.0, 3.0.0]

Such information is important. If the `Calculator` package is used by someone who has an environment pinned to `SaferIntegers` version 1.1.1, then we know that `Calculator` is still compatible in that environment and can be loaded in it.

The package manager is actually very flexible, and it implements a few more version-specifier formats. You can refer to of `Pkg` reference manual for more information (https://julialang.github.io/Pkg.jl/v1/compatibility/#Version-specifier-format-1).

It is important to specify compatibility between packages. By using the `Pkg` interface and editing the `Project.toml` file manually, we can manage dependencies properly, and the package manager will help us maintain the working environment in working order.

However, sometimes, we may run into tricky dependency issues—for example, circular dependencies. We will look at how to handle such situations next.

Avoiding circular dependencies

Circular dependencies are problematic. To understand why, consider the following example.

Let's say we have five packages (A, B, C, D, and E) with the following dependencies:

- A depends on B and C
- C depends on D and E
- E depends on A

To illustrate these graphically, we can create a diagram where we can use an arrow notation to indicate dependencies between components. The direction of the arrow indicates the direction of the dependency.

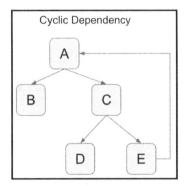

What's the problem?

Clearly there is a cycle, as A depends on C, C depends on E, and E depends on A. What is the problem with a cycle like this? Say that you have to make a change in package C that is supposed to be backward-compatible. To properly test the system with this change, we must make sure that C continues to have proper functionality given its dependencies. Now, if we trace this down the dependency chain, we must test C with D and E, and as E depends on A, we must include A as well. Now that A is included, we must include B and C. Because of the cycle, we now have to test all of the packages!

How do we fix this?

The *acyclic dependency principle* states that dependencies between packages must be a **directed acyclic graph (DAG)**—that is, the dependency graph must have no cycle. If we do see a cycle in the graph, then it is a sign of a design problem.

When we encounter such a problem, we must refactor the code so that the specific dependent function is moved to a separate package. In this example, suppose that there's some code in package A that is used by the package internally and also used by package E. This dependency is basically E -> A.

We can then take this code and move it to a new package F. After this change, packages A and E would both depend on package F, effectively removing the cyclic dependency:

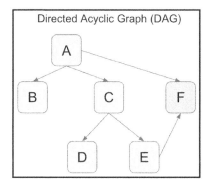

After this refactoring, when we make changes to C, we can just test the package with its dependencies, which would be D, E, and F only. Packages A and B can both be excluded.

In this section, we learned how to leverage semantic versioning to clearly communicate the impact of new versions of a package. We can use the `Project.toml` file to specify the compatibility of the current package with its dependent packages. We also reviewed a technique for resolving circular dependencies.

Now we know this, we will look into how to design and develop data types in Julia.

Designing abstract and concrete types

Julia's type system is the foundation of many of its language features, such as multiple dispatches. In this section, we will learn about both abstract types and concrete types, how to design and use them, and how they are different from other mainstream object-oriented programming languages.

In this section, we will cover the following topics:

- Designing abstract types
- Designing concrete types
- Understanding `isa` and `<:` operators
- Understanding the difference between abstract and concrete types

Let's first take a look at abstract types.

Designing abstract types

Similar to many other objected-oriented programming languages, Julia supports a hierarchy of abstract types. Abstract types are typically used to model real-world data concepts; for example, an `Animal` could be an abstract type for a cat or dog, and a `Vehicle` can be an abstract type for a car, truck, or bus. Being able to group types together and give the group a single name allows Julia programmers to apply generic code that is common to those types.

Abstract types are often conveniently defined in a type hierarchy for a specific domain. We can describe the relationship between abstract types as *parent–child*, or more technically, an *is-a-subtype-of* relationship. The terminology for the parent type and child type is *supertype* and *subtype* respectively.

A unique feature of Julia's design, unlike the majority of other languages, is that abstract types are defined without any fields. For this reason, abstract types do not specify how data is actually stored in the memory. It may seem somewhat restrictive at first glance, but as we learn more about Julia, it will seem more natural when used in this design. As a result, abstract types are used solely to model behaviors for a set of objects rather than to specify how data is stored.

The Rectangle and Square object model is a classic example of how things can break down when an abstract type is allowed to define data fields. Suppose that we were able to define a Rectangle with `width` and `height` fields. A Square is a kind of Rectangle, so intuitively, we should be able to model Square as a subtype of Rectangle. But we soon get into trouble because a square does not need two fields to store the length of its sides; we should rather use a single `side length` field instead. Therefore, inheriting fields from supertypes makes no sense in this case. We will discuss this case with more details in `Chapter 12`, *Inheritance and Variance*.

In the following sections, we will work through an example of building an abstract type hierarchy.

A personal asset type hierarchy example

Let's say we are building a financial application that keeps track of a user's wealth, which may include various types of asset. The following diagram shows a hierarchy of abstract types and their parent–child relationship. In this design, an Asset may be a Property, an Investment, or just Cash types. A Property can be a House or an Apartment. An Investment could be FixedIncome or Equity. As a convention, in order to indicate that they are abstract types rather than concrete types, we have chosen to italicize their names in the boxes:

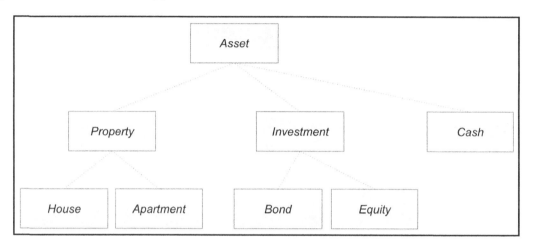

To create an abstract type hierarchy, we can use the following code:

```
abstract type Asset end

abstract type Property <: Asset end
abstract type Investment <: Asset end
abstract type Cash <: Asset end

abstract type House <: Property end
abstract type Apartment <: Property end

abstract type FixedIncome <: Investment end
abstract type Equity <: Investment end
```

The <: symbol represents an *is-a-subtype-of* relationship. So, the Property type is a subtype of Asset, the Equity type is a subtype of Investment, and so on.

While the Asset abstract type seems to be at the top level of the hierarchy in reality, it also has a supertype called Any, which is implicit when no supertype is specified and an abstract type is defined. The Any code phrase is the top-level supertype in Julia.

Navigating the type hierarchy

Julia provides some convenient functions to navigate the type hierarchy. To find the subtypes of an existing type, we can use the subtypes function:

```
julia> subtypes(Asset)
3-element Array{Any,1}:
 Cash
 Investment
 Property
```

Similarly, to find the supertype of an existing type, we can use the supertype function.

```
julia> supertype(Equity)
Investment
```

Sometimes, it's convenient to see the complete hierarchy in a tree format. Julia comes with no standard function that we can use to achieve this, but we can easily create one ourselves using a recursion technique, as follows:

```
# Display the entire type hierarchy starting from the specified `roottype`
function subtypetree(roottype, level = 1, indent = 4)
    level == 1 && println(roottype)
    for s in subtypes(roottype)
        println(join(fill(" ", level * indent)) * string(s))
        subtypetree(s, level + 1, indent)
    end
end
```

This function can be quite convenient for new Julia users. In fact, I have the code saved in my startup.jl file so that it is loaded into the REPL automatically.

> The startup.jl file is a user-customized script that is located in the $HOME/.julia/config directory. It can be used to store any code or functions that the user wants to run every time the REPL is started.

We can now display the personal asset type hierarchy easily, as follows:

```
julia> subtypetree(Asset)
Asset
        Cash
        Investment
                Equity
                FixedIncome
        Property
                Apartment
                House
```

Note that this function can only display a hierarchy of types that have already been loaded into memory. Now that we have defined abstract types, we should be able to associate functions with them. Let's do that next.

Defining functions for abstract types

So far, all we have done is create a hierarchy of related concepts. With that limited knowledge, we can still define some functions to model behaviors. But how is this useful when we have no concrete data elements? When dealing with abstract types, we could just focus on specific behavior and the possible interaction between them. Let's continue with the example and see what kinds of function we can add.

Descriptive functions

Although it does not sound very interesting, we can define functions that are solely based on the type itself:

```
# simple functions on abstract types
describe(a::Asset) = "Something valuable"
describe(e::Investment) = "Financial investment"
describe(e::Property) = "Physical property"
```

Now, if we ever call describe with a data element that has a supertype of Property, then the description method for Property will be invoked accordingly. As we did not define any description function with the Cash type, when describe is called with a Cash data element it will return the description from the higher-level type, Asset.

Because we have not defined any concrete types yet, we cannot prove the claim here that the describe function for a Cash object will resort to the describe(a::Asset) method. As it is a simple thing to do, I encourage the reader to do this as an exercise after reading this chapter.

Functional behavior

The reason to have a hierarchy is to create an abstraction about common behaviors for types. For example, the `Apartment` and `House` types have the same supertype, `Property`. This is intentional because they both represent some kind of physical dwelling at a certain location. So, we can define a function for any `Property` as follows:

```
"""
    location(p::Property)

Returns the location of the property as a tuple of (latitude, longitude).
"""
location(p::Property) = error("Location is not defined in the concrete
type")
```

You may ask, *What have we done?* We have just implemented a function that does nothing but return an error! Well, believe it or not, defining this function actually serves several purposes:

- It makes it clear that any concrete subtype of `Property` must implement the `location` function.
- At runtime, if the `location` function is not defined for the respective concrete type, then this particular function will be called and a reasonable error will be thrown so that the programmer can correct the bug.
- The document string right above the function definition contains a useful description that concrete subtypes of `Property` should implement.

Alternatively, we can define an empty function instead:

```
"""
    location(p::Property)

Returns the location of the property as a tuple of (latitude, longitude).
"""
function location(p::Property) end
```

What is the difference between an empty function and one that throws an error? For this empty function, there will be no runtime error if the concrete type does not implement this function.

Interaction between objects

It is also useful to define interactions between abstract types. Now that we know that every `Property` should have a location, we can define a function that calculates the walking distance between any two properties, as follows:

```
function walking_disance(p1::Property, p2::Property)
    loc1 = location(p1)
    loc2 = location(p2)
    return abs(loc1.x - loc2.x) + abs(loc1.y - loc2.y)
end
```

The logic completely lives in the abstract types! We have not even defined any concrete types, and yet we are able to develop generic code that works for any concrete subtypes of `Property` going forward.

The power of the Julia language allows us to define these behaviors at this level of abstraction. For a moment, let's imagine what we would have to do if we were not allowed to define functions at this level and could only implement logic with specific concrete types. In this case, we would have to define a separate `walking_distance` function for every combination of different types of properties. It would be too mundane and boring for programmers!

Now that we understand how abstract types work, let's continue our journey and take a look at how to create concrete types in Julia.

Designing concrete types

A concrete type is used to define how data is organized. In Julia, there are two kinds of concrete type:

- Primitive type
- Composite type

Primitive types carry pure bits. Julia's `Base` package comes with a variety of primitive types—signed/unsigned integers that are 8-, 16-, 32-, 64-, or 128-bits wide. Currently, Julia only supports primitive types with numbers of bits that are multiples of 8. For example, it is possible to define a 256-bit integer type (32 bytes) if we have a use case that requires very large integers. How to do this is outside the scope of this book. If you feel that this is an interesting project, you can consult Julia's source code on GitHub and see how existing primitive types are implemented. The Julia language is indeed largely written in Julia itself!

Composite types are defined by a set of named fields. Grouping fields into a single type allows easier reasoning, sharing, and manipulation. Composite types may be designated a specific supertype or defaulted to `Any`. Fields can also be annotated with their own types, if you wish, and types can be either abstract or concrete. When type information is absent for fields, they default to `Any`, which means that the field can hold objects of any type.

We will focus on composite types in this section.

Designing composite types

Composite types are defined with the `struct` keyword. Let's carry on the example from the preceding abstract type section and continue building our personal asset type hierarchy. We will now create a concrete type called `Stock` as a subtype of `Equity`. To keep things simple, we will just represent a stock as a trading symbol and the name of the company:

```
struct Stock <: Equity
    symbol::String
    name::String
end
```

We can instantiate a composite type using the standard constructor, which just takes all the fields as an argument:

```
julia> stock = Stock("AAPL", "Apple, Inc.")
Stock("AAPL", "Apple, Inc.")
```

Now, since `Stock` is a subtype of `Equity`, which is a subtype of `Investment`, which in turn is a subtype of `Asset`, we should obey the *contract* that we set forth earlier by defining the `describe` function:

```
function describe(s::Stock)
    return s.symbol * "(" * s.name * ")"
end
```

The `describe` function just returns a string representation of the stock with both the trading symbol and company name.

Immutability

Composite types are by default immutable. This means that their fields are not changeable after the object is created. Immutability is a good thing as it eliminates surprises when system behavior changes unexpectedly because of data modification. We can easily prove that the concrete `Stock` type that we created in the last section is immutable:

```
julia> stock.name = "Apple LLC"
ERROR: setfield! immutable struct of type Stock cannot be changed
```

That's great! Now, the immutability guarantee actually stops at the field level. If the type contains a field and the field's own type is mutable, then changing the underlying data is allowed. Let's try a different example by creating a new composite type called `BasketOfStocks`, which is used to hold a vector (that is, a one-dimensional array) of stocks and the reason that we are holding them:

```
struct BasketOfStocks
    stocks::Vector{Stock}
    reason::String
end
```

Let's just create an object for testing:

```
julia> many_stocks = [
          Stock("AAPL", "Apple, Inc."),
          Stock("IBM", "IBM")
       ];

julia> basket = BasketOfStocks(many_stocks, "Anniversary gift for my wife")
BasketOfStocks(Stock[Stock("AAPL", "Apple, Inc."), Stock("IBM", "IBM")], "An
niversary gift for my wife")
```

As we already know, `BasketOfStocks` is an immutable type, so we cannot change any of the fields in it; however, let's see if we can take away one of the stocks from the `stocks` field:

```
julia> pop!(basket.stocks)
Stock("IBM", "IBM")

julia> basket
BasketOfStocks(Stock[Stock("AAPL", "Apple, Inc.")], "Anniversary gift for my
 wife")
```

Here, we just call the `pop!` function directly on the `stocks` object, and it will happily take away half of the presents for my wife! Let me repeat—the immutability guarantee does not have any effect on the underlying fields.

This behavior is by design. The programmer should be cautious about making any assumptions about immutability.

Mutability

In some situations, we may actually want an object to be mutable. The immutability constraint can be removed easily by just adding the `mutable` keyword in front of the type definition. To make the `Stock` type mutable, we do the following:

```
mutable struct Stock <: Equity
    symbol::String
    name::String
end
```

Now let's try to update the `name` field in a hypothetical case where Apple changes its company name:

```
julia> stock = Stock("AAPL", "Apple, Inc.")
Stock("AAPL", "Apple, Inc.")

julia> stock.name = "Apple LLC"
"Apple LLC"

julia> stock
Stock("AAPL", "Apple LLC")
```

The `name` field has been updated as we wish. Note that, when a type is declared mutable, all of its fields become mutable. So, in this case, we would be allowed to change the symbol as well. Depending on the situation, such behavior may or may not be desirable. In Chapter 8, *Robustness Patterns*, we will go over some design patterns that we can use to build a more robust solution.

Mutable or immutable?

As you can see, mutable objects seem more flexible and give us good performance. But if that's the case, then why wouldn't we want everything to be mutable by default? There are a couple of reasons:

- Immutable objects are easier to handle. Because the data in the object is fixed and never changes, a function that operates on these objects will always return consistent results. That is a very nice property to have because there are no surprises. And if we build a function that caches calculation results from such objects, the cache will always be good and return consistent results.
- Mutable objects are more difficult to work with in a multi-threaded application. Let's say that a function is reading from a mutable object, but the content of the object is modified by another function from a different thread. Then the current function may produce incorrect results. In order to ensure consistency, the programmer must use a locking technique to synchronize the read/write operations to the object. Having to handle such a concurrent situation makes the code more complex and difficult to test.

On the other hand, mutability could be useful for high-performance use cases because memory allocation is a relatively expensive operation. We can reduce the system overhead by reusing allocated memory over and over again.

All things considered, immutable objects are usually the better choice.

Supporting multiple types using Union types

Sometimes, we need to support multiple types in a field. This can be done using a Union type, which is defined as a type that can accept any specified types. To define a Union type, we can just enclose the types within curly braces after the Union keyword. For example, the Union type of Int64 and BigInt can be defined as follows:

```
Union{Int64,BigInt}
```

These `Union` types are quite useful when you need to incorporate data types that come from different data type hierarchies. Let's extend our personal asset example further. For instance, say that we need to incorporate some exotic items into our data model, which may include things such as art pieces, antiques, paintings, and so on. These new concepts may have already been modeled with a different type hierarchy, as follows:

```
abstract type Art end

struct Painting <: Art
    artist::String
    title::String
end
```

As it turns out, my wife likes to collect paintings, and so I can just generalize the `BasketOfStock` type as `BasketOfThings`, as follows:

```
struct BasketOfThings
  things::Vector{Union{Painting,Stock}}
  reason::String
end
```

The things inside the vector can be `Stock` or `Painting`. Remember that Julia is a strongly typed language, and it is important that the compiler knows what kinds of data type can fit into an existing field. Let's see how it works:

```
julia> stock = Stock("AAPL", "Apple, Inc.",)
Stock("AAPL", "Apple, Inc.")

julia> monalisa = Painting("Leonardo da Vinci", "Monalisa")
Painting("Leonardo da Vinci", "Monalisa")

julia> things = Union{Painting,Stock}[stock, monalisa]
2-element Array{Union{Painting, Stock},1}:
  Stock("AAPL", "Apple, Inc.")
  Painting("Leonardo da Vinci", "Monalisa")

julia> present = BasketOfThings(things, "Anniversary gift for my wife")
BasketOfThings(Union{Painting, Stock}[Stock("AAPL", "Apple, Inc."), Painting
("Leonardo da Vinci", "Monalisa")], "Anniversary gift for my wife")
```

To create a vector that contains either `Painting` or `Stock`, we just specify the element type of the array in front of the square brackets, as in `Union{Painting, Stock}[stock, monalisa]`.

The syntax for Union types can be very verbose, especially when there are more than two types, so it is quite common for a constant to be defined with a meaningful name that represents the Union type:

```
const Thing = Union{Painting,Stock}

struct BasketOfThings
    thing::Vector{Thing}
    reason::String
end
```

As you can see, Thing is much easier to read than Union{Painting,Stock}. Another benefit is that the Union type may be referenced in many parts of the source code. When we need to add more types later—for instance, an Antique type—then we only need to change it in one place, which is the definition of Thing. This means that the code can be maintained more easily.

In this section, although we have chosen to use concrete types such as Stock and Painting for our example, there is no reason why we cannot use abstract types such as Asset and Art for the Union type.

 Another common usage of the Union type is to incorporate Nothing as a valid value for a field. This can be achieved by declaring a field with the Union{T,Nothing} type, where T is the real data type that we want to use. In that case, the field can be assigned with a real value or just Nothing.

Next, we will continue to learn how to work with type operators.

Working with type operators

Julia's data types are first-class citizens themselves. This means that you can assign them to variables, pass them to functions, and manipulate them in various ways. We will take a look at two commonly used operators in the following sections.

The isa operator

The isa operator can be used to determine whether a value is a subtype of a type. For example, look at the following code:

```
julia> 1 isa Int
true

julia> 1 isa Float64
false

julia> 1 isa Real
true
```

Let me explain each of these results:

- The number 1 is an instance of the Int type, so it returns true.
- Because Float64 is a different concrete type, it returns false.
- Because Int is a subtype of Signed, which is a subtype of Integer, which is a subtype of Real, it returns true.

The isa operator could be useful for checking types in a function that accepts generic type arguments. For example, if the function can only work with Real numbers, then it may throw an error when a Complex value is passed by accident.

The <: operator

The *is-a-subtype-of* operator, <:, is used to determine whether a type is a subtype of another type. Taking the third example from the preceding section, we can check whether Int is indeed a subtype of Real as follows:

```
julia> Int <: Real
true
```

Sometimes the developer may be confused about the usage of the `isa` and `<:` operators because they are very similar. We can keep in mind that `isa` checks a *value* against a type, and `<:` checks a *type* against another type. The document string for these operators is actually quite helpful. From the Julia REPL, type a ? character and enter the operator to find the documentation:

```
help?> isa
search: isa isascii isapprox isabspath isassigned

  isa(x, type) -> Bool

  Determine whether x is of the given type. Can
  also be used as an infix operator, e.g. x isa
  type.

  Examples
  ≡≡≡≡≡≡≡≡≡≡

  julia> isa(1, Int)
  true

  julia> isa(1, Matrix)
  false

  julia> isa(1, Char)
  false

  julia> isa(1, Number)
  true

  julia> 1 isa Number
  true
```

```
help?> <:
search: <:

  <:(T1, T2)

  Subtype operator: returns true if and only if
  all values of type T1 are also of type T2.

  Examples
  ≡≡≡≡≡≡≡≡≡≡

  julia> Float64 <: AbstractFloat
  true

  julia> Vector{Int} <: AbstractArray
  true

  julia> Matrix{Float64} <: Matrix{AbstractFloat}
  false
```

As it turns out, both `isa` and `<:` are just functions, but they can also be used as infix operators.

These operators are quite useful for type-checking purposes; for example, we can throw an exception from a constructor function if the arguments being passed do not have the right types. They can also be used to execute different logic dynamically based upon the types being passed to a function.

Abstract types and concrete types are the fundamental building blocks for data types in Julia. It may be worth looking at a quick summary of the differences between them. Next, we will look at specific details.

Differences between abstract and concrete types

Having discussed abstract types and concrete types, you may be wondering how they differ from each other. We can summarize their differences in the following table:

Property	Abstract Type	Concrete Type
Has a supertype?	Yes	Yes
Allows subtypes?	Yes	No
Contains data fields?	No	Yes
First class?	Yes	Yes
Can be part of a `Union` type?	Yes	Yes

For abstract types, we can build a hierarchy of types. The top-level type is just `Any`. Abstract types cannot contain any data fields as they are used to represent concepts rather than data storage. Abstract types are first-class, meaning that they can be stored and passed around, and there are functions that work with them—for example, the `isa` and `<:` operators.

A concrete type is associated with an abstract type as a supertype. If the supertype is not specified, then it is assumed to be `Any`. A concrete type does not allow subtypes. This means that every concrete type must be final, and would be a leaf node in a type hierarchy. Concrete types are also first class, just like abstract types.

Both abstract types and concrete types can be referred to in a `Union` type.

What we just mentioned may be surprising to people who come from an object-oriented programming background. First, you may wonder why concrete types do not allow subtypes. Second, you may wonder why abstract types can't be defined with fields. This design is actually intentional and was debated heavily by the core Julia development team. The debate is related to behavioral inheritance versus structural inheritance, which will be discussed in `Chapter 12`, *Inheritance and Variance*.

Now, let's switch gear and go over the parametric type feature of the Julia language.

Working with parametric types

One of the most powerful features of the Julia language is the ability to parameterize types. It is actually quite difficult to find any Julia package that does not use this feature. Parametric types allow the software designer to generalize types, and let the Julia runtime automatically compile to the concrete version based on the specified parameters.

Let's take a look at how this works with composite and abstract types.

Working with parametric composite types

When designing composite types, we should assign each field a type. Oftentimes, we don't really care exactly what those types are, as long as the type provides the functionality that we want.

A classic example would be numeric types. The concept of numbers is simple: basically the same as we were taught in elementary school. In practice, many numeric types are implemented in computer systems because of the different physical storage and representations of data.

By default, Julia ships with the following numeric types; concrete types are darker:

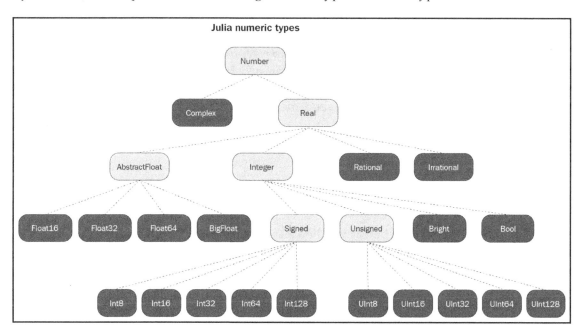

Do you remember when we designed a composite type to represent a stock in an investment portfolio earlier in this chapter? Let's revisit that example here:

```
struct Stock <: Equity
    symbol::String
    name::String
end
```

If I have to hold some stocks in my brokerage account, then I should also keep track of the number of shares that I own. To do this, I can define a new type called `StockHolding`, as follows:

```
struct StockHolding
    stock::Stock
    quantity::Int
end
```

The `Int` data type is by default aliased to either `Int64` or `Int32`, depending on whether you are using the 64-bit or 32-bit version of Julia. This seems reasonable just to get started, but what if we need to support fractional shares for a different use case? In that case, we can just change the type of `quantity` to `Float64`:

```
struct StockHolding
    stock::Stock
    quantity::Float64
end
```

We basically widen the type of `quantity` field to a type that supports both integer and floating-point values. It may be a reasonable approach, but if we need to support both `Int` and `Float64` types, then we would have to maintain two slightly different types. Sadly, if we do create two different types, then it becomes a maintenance nightmare.

To make it more flexible, we can redesign the `StockHolding` type with a parameter:

```
struct StockHolding{T}
    stock::Stock
    quantity::T
end
```

The symbol `T` inside the curly braces is called a *type parameter*. It serves as a placeholder that can be used as a type in any of the fields.

Now, we have the best of both worlds. The `StockHolding{Int}` type refers to the type that contains a `quantity` field of the `Int` type. Likewise, the `StockHolding{Float64}` refers to the type that contains a `quantity` field of the `Float64` type.

In practice, the `T` type parameter can only be a numeric type, so we could further qualify `T` as any subtype of `Real`:

```
struct StockHolding{T <: Real}
    stock::Stock
    quantity::T
end
```

Here's how we read this—*the* StockHolding *type contains a stock and a quantity of the* T *type that is a subtype of* Real. The second part of the sentence is important; it means that we can create a new StockHolding with the type of quantity as Float16, Float32, Float64, Int8, Int16, Int32, and so on.

Let's try instantiating the StockHolding object with different kinds of type parameter, such as Int, Float64, and Rational:

```
julia> stock = Stock("AAPL", "Apple, Inc.");

julia> holding = StockHolding(stock, 100)
StockHolding{Int64}(Stock("AAPL", "Apple, Inc."), 100)

julia> holding = StockHolding(stock, 100.00)
StockHolding{Float64}(Stock("AAPL", "Apple, Inc."), 100.0)

julia> holding = StockHolding(stock, 100 // 3)
StockHolding{Rational{Int64}}(Stock("AAPL", "Apple, Inc."), 100//3)
```

We can see that different StockHolding{T} types are created automatically according to the argument that was passed to the constructor.

Another use of parametric types is to enforce the consistency of field types. Suppose that we want to design another kind of stock-holding object to track the price and market value of the holding. Let's call it StockHolding2 to avoid confusion with the preceding one. The following is what it looks like:

```
struct StockHolding2{T <: Real, P <: AbstractFloat}
    stock::Stock
    quantity::T
    price::P
    marketvalue::P
end
```

Knowing that the type for quantity may not be the same as the type for price and marketvalue, we have added a new type parameter, P. Now, we can instantiate a StockHolding2 object that contains an integer quantity while having floating-point values for price and market value fields:

```
julia> holding = StockHolding2(stock, 100, 180.00, 18000.00)
StockHolding2{Int64,Float64}(Stock("AAPL", "Apple, Inc."), 100, 180.0, 18000.0)
```

Note that the type is `StockHolding2{Int64, Float64}`, as shown in the preceding screenshot. In this case, the type parameter `T` is `Int64` and the parameter `P` is `Float64`.

As we declared that both the `price` and `marketvalue` fields must be of the same type, `P`, does Julia enforce this rule for us? Let's give it a try:

```
julia> holding = StockHolding2(stock, 100, 180.00, 18000)
ERROR: MethodError: no method matching StockHolding2(::Stock, ::Int64, ::
Float64, ::Int64)
Closest candidates are:
  StockHolding2(::Stock, ::T, ::P, ::P) where {T<:Real, P<:AbstractFloat}
  at REPL[51]:2
Stacktrace:
 [1] top-level scope at REPL[53]:1
```

Yes, it does! We correctly received an error because we passed a `Float64` value for `price`, but an `Int64` for `marketvalue`. Let's take a closer look at the error message, which revealed what the system expects. The closest candidate function for `StockHolding2` takes a `P` type for the third and fourth arguments, where `P` is any subtype of `AbstractFloat`. Because `In64` is not a subtype of `AbstractFloat`, there is no match and so an error was thrown.

Parametric types can be abstract as well. We will go over this next.

Working with parametric abstract types

Abstract types can be enhanced in the same way that composite types can be parameterized. Let's continue with the preceding example. Suppose that we want to build an abstract type called `Holding` that keeps track of a `P` type that is used by its subtypes. We can code it as follows:

```
abstract type Holding{P} end
```

Then, every subtype of `Holding{P}` must also take a `P` type parameter. As an example, we can create two new types —`StockHolding3{T,P}` and `CashHolding{P}`:

```
struct StockHolding3{T, P} <: Holding{P}

  stock::Stock
  quantity::T
  price::P
  marketvalue::P
end
```

```
struct CashHolding{P} <: Holding{P}
  currency::String
  amount::P
  marketvalue::P
end
```

We can examine how these types are related as follows:

```
julia> StockHolding3{Int64,Float64} <: Holding{Float64}
true
```

Let's create a new `StockHolding3` object:

```
julia> certificate_in_the_safe = StockHolding3(stock, 100, 180.00, 18000.00)
StockHolding3{Int64,Float64}(Stock("AAPL", "Apple, Inc."), 100, 180.0, 18000.0)

julia> certificate_in_the_safe isa Holding{Float64}
true
```

As expected, the `certificate_in_the_safe` object is a subtype of `Holding{Float64}`.

Note that, when a type is parameterized, each variation is considered as a separate type that is unrelated to the others, except that they have a common supertype. As an example, `Holding{Int}` is a different type from `Holding{Float64}`, but they are both subtypes of `Holding`. Let's quickly prove this to ourselves:

```
julia> Holding{Float64} <: Holding
true

julia> Holding{Int} <: Holding
true
```

In summary, Julia comes with a very rich type system that a programmer can use to reason how each type relates to other types. Abstract types allow us to define behaviors in a hierarchy of relationships, and concrete types are used to define how data is stored. Parametric types are used to extend existing types to variations of field types. All of these language constructs allow the programmer to model data and behavior effectively.

Next, we will look into data type conversions and how they apply to functions.

Conversion between data types

We often need to convert data from one type to another in order to leverage existing library functions. A great working example would be the standard numerical data types. It is a common use case to convert a piece of date from an integer to a floating-point number in most mathematical functions.

In this section, we will learn about how data type conversion is performed in Julia. As it turns out, data type conversions are expected to be implemented explicitly; however, a set of rules has been implemented so that some conversions are automatically invoked.

Performing simple data type conversion

There are two ways to convert a value from one data type to another. The obvious choice is to construct a new object from an existing value. For example, we can construct a `Float64` object from a rational number as follows:

```
julia> Float64(1//3)
0.3333333333333333
```

Another way is to use the `convert` function:

```
julia> convert(Float64, 1//3)
0.3333333333333333
```

Either way works fine. There is an advantage from using the `convert` function when considering performance optimization, as we will explain later in this section.

Beware of lossy conversions

When it comes to conversion, it is important to consider whether the conversion is lossless or lossy. In general, it is expected that data type conversion is lossless, which means that, when you convert from one type to another and back, you get the same value.

Because of the numerical representation of floating-point numbers, such perfect conversion is not always possible. For example, let's try to convert `1//3` to `Float64` and then convert it back to `Rational`:

```
julia> convert(Float64, 1//3)
0.3333333333333333

julia> convert(Rational, convert(Float64, 1//3))
6004799503160661//18014398509481984
```

Because of a rounding error, it is not possible to reconstruct `1//3` after it was converted to a `Float64` type. The problem is not restricted to the `Rational` type. We can easily break this again by converting the value from an `Int64` to a `Float64` and back, as follows:

```
julia> 2^53+1
9007199254740993

julia> convert(Int64, convert(Float64, 2^53+1))
9007199254740992
```

We can see that there is a loss of precision here. While we may not be very satisfied with these results, there is really not much that we can do here as long as we use the `Float64` type. The `Float64` type is implemented according to the IEEE 754 floating-point specification, and it is expected to carry precision errors. If you need more precision, you can use `BigFloat` instead, which solves this particular problem:

```
julia> convert(Int64, convert(BigFloat, 2^53+1))
9007199254740993
```

When handling floating-point values, we should be cautious about precision issues.

Understanding numeric type conversions

Julia does not automatically perform conversion on data types for safety reasons. Every conversion must be explicitly defined by the programmer.

To make it easier for everyone, Julia already contains conversion functions for numeric types by default. For instance, you can find this interesting piece of code from the `Base` package:

```
convert(::Type{T}, x::T) where {T<:Number} = x
convert(::Type{T}, x::Number) where {T<:Number} = T(x)
```

Both functions take the first argument of the `Type{T}` type, where `T` is a subtype of `Number`. Valid values include all standard numeric types, such as `Int64`, `Int32`, `Float64`, `Float32`, and so on.

Let's try to understand these two functions further:

- The first function says that it's as easy as returning the argument `x` itself when we want to convert `x` from the `T` type and to the `T` type (the same type) as long as `T` is a subtype of `Number`. This can be considered a performance optimization because there is really no need to do any conversion when the target type is the same as the input.
- The second function is a little more interesting. In order to convert `x`, which is a subtype of `Number`, to type `T`, which is also a subtype of `Number`, it just calls the constructor of the `T` type with `x`. In other words, this function can handle the conversion of any `Number` type to another type that is a subtype of `Number`.

You may wonder why we don't just use the constructor in the first place. This is because the `convert` function is designed to be invoked automatically for various common use cases. As you can see from what we looked at previously, this extra indirection also allows us to bypass the constructor when conversion is unnecessary.

When does `convert` get called? The answer is that Julia does not automatically do that, except for a few scenarios. We will explore these scenarios in the next section.

Reviewing the rules for automatic conversion

As data type conversion is a fairly standard operation, Julia is designed to automatically call the `convert` function in the following scenarios:

1. Assigning a value to an array converts the value to the array's element type.
2. Assigning a value to a field of an object converts the value to the declared type of the field.
3. Constructing an object with `new` converts the value to the object's declared field type.
4. Assigning a value to a variable with a declared type converts the value to that type
5. A function with a declared return type converts its return value to that type.
6. Passing a value to `ccall` converts the value to the corresponding argument type.

Let's confirm that these are indeed working as advertised.

Case 1: Assigning a value to an array

In the following example, assigning the 1 value to a Float64 array would convert the former into a floating-point value, 1.0:

```
julia> x = rand(3)
3-element Array{Float64,1}:
 0.7382481817919213
 0.9383605464352593
 0.600077313229175

julia> x[1] = 1
1

julia> x
3-element Array{Float64,1}:
 1.0
 0.9383605464352593
 0.600077313229175
```

Case 2: Assigning a value to a field of an object

In the following example, the Foo struct accepts a Float64 field. When the field is assigned a value of 2, it is converted to 2.0:

```
julia> mutable struct Foo
           x::Float64
       end

julia> foo = Foo(1.0)
Foo(1.0)

julia> foo.x = 2
2

julia> foo
Foo(2.0)
```

Case 3: Constructing an object with the new function

In the following example, the `Foo` constructor automatically converts 1 to 1.0 when creating the `Foo` object:

```julia
julia> struct Foo
           x::Float64
           Foo(v) = new(v)
       end

julia> Foo(1)
Foo(1.0)
```

Case 4: Assigning to a variable that has a declared type

In the following example, the local variable x is declared as a `Float64` type. When it is assigned the 1 value, it is converted to 1.0:

```julia
julia> function foo()
           local x::Float64
           x = 1
           println(x, " has type of ", typeof(x))
       end
foo (generic function with 1 method)

julia> foo()
1.0 has type of Float64
```

Case 5: Function has a declared return type

In the following example, the `foo` function is declared to return a `Float64` value. Even though the `return` statement says 1, it is converted to 1.0 before it is returned:

```julia
julia> function foo()::Float64
           return 1
       end
foo (generic function with 1 method)

julia> foo()
1.0
```

Case 6: Passing a value to ccall

In the following example, the exp function from the C library is used to calculate the exponent of a number. It expects a Float64 value as an argument, so when the value of 2 is passed to ccall, it is converted to 2.0 before being passed to the C function:

```
julia> ccall((:exp, "libc"), Float64, (Float64,), 2)
7.38905609893065
```

All that is good, but something seems to be missing. What about the most common use case: passing an argument to a function? Wouldn't it be called if Julia auto-converts the arguments as well? The answer may be a little surprising. Let's look at this in more detail in the following sections.

Understanding the rules for function dispatches

Julia is a strongly typed language, which means that the programmer has to be very clear about the types being passed around. A function can only be called (also known as dispatched) when the types of its arguments are matched properly. A proper match can be defined as one that matches exactly (same type) or when the argument being passed is a subtype of what is expected in the function's signature.

To illustrate this, let's create a function that doubles the value of its argument of the AbstractFloat type. We will use our subtypetree utility function to quickly find out its subtypes:

```
julia> subtypetree(AbstractFloat)
AbstractFloat
    BigFloat
    Float16
    Float32
    Float64

julia> twice(x::AbstractFloat) = 2x;

julia> twice(1.0)
2.0

julia> BigFloat("1.5e1234")
1.500000000000000000000000000000000000000000000000000000000000000000000000000
000007e+1234
```

What happens if we pass an integer to the function? Well, it doesn't work too well:

```
julia> twice(2)
ERROR: MethodError: no method matching twice(::Int64)
```

Naively, we may think that the system should auto-convert the argument to `Float64` and then double the value. Well, it does not. It is not a conversion issue. To get that effect, we could obviously write another function that takes an `Int` argument, then converts it to `Float64`, and calls the original function. But the code would look exactly the same, and it's a duplication of effort. This problem can be solved by just writing the function more generically:

```
julia> twice(x) = 2x
twice (generic function with 2 methods)

julia> twice(1.0)
2.0

julia> twice(1)
2
```

If we feel that the argument has to be a `Number`, then we can restrict it again as such:

```
julia> twice(x::Number) = 2x
twice (generic function with 3 methods)

julia> twice(2.0)
4.0

julia> twice(2)
4

julia> twice(2//3)
4//3
```

What we choose to do here depends on how flexible we want the function to be. The benefit of specifying an abstract type, such as `Number`, is that we feel sure the function will work well for any type that implements the behavior set down by `Number`. On the other hand, if we leave it as untyped in the function definition, then we open up the possibility for other objects to be passed to the function as long as the `*` operator is defined.

In this section, we have learned about how data type conversion can be performed in Julia. In certain scenarios, Julia can also automatically convert numeric types.

Summary

In this chapter, we started discussing the importance of organizing source code for larger applications. We explored in detail how to establish namespaces and how to implement them using modules and submodules. To manage package dependencies, we introduced the concept of semantic versioning and learned how to use it properly with Julia's package manager.

Then, we went over the details of how to design an abstract type hierarchy and define functions for abstract types. We also discussed concrete types and the concepts of immutability and mutability. We demonstrated how to use union types when working with data types from different abstract type hierarchies. We looked at two common operators (`isa` and *is-a-subtype-of*) for data types. To further reuse data types, we introduced parametric types and looked at how they apply to both concrete types and abstract types.

Finally, we looked at the `convert` function in Julia and how it is invoked automatically under certain circumstances. We learned how Julia's function dispatch works and how to make a function more flexible by accepting broader abstract types in its arguments.

At this point, you should have a good understanding about how to organize code and designing your own data types.

In the next chapter, we will look at how to define application behavior using functions and Julia's multiple-dispatch facility.

Questions

Go through the following questions to test your understanding of the subjects in this chapter. The answers are provided at the back of the book:

1. How do we create a new namespace?
2. How do we expose the functions of a module to the outside world?
3. How do we reference the proper function when the same function name is exported from different packages?
4. When do we separate code into multiple modules?
5. Why is semantic versioning important in managing package dependencies?
6. How is defining functional behavior for abstract types useful?
7. When should we make a type mutable?
8. How are parametric types useful?

3
Designing Functions and Interfaces

This chapter will continue looking at the fundamental concepts of Julia. The topics that we have chosen here will provide a solid foundation of the key concepts of Julia programming. In particular, we will discuss the core Julia programming techniques that are related to functions and interfaces. Functions are the fundamental building blocks of software. Interfaces are contractual relationships between different components of the software. Effective use of functions and interfaces is a must for building robust applications.

The following topics will be covered in this chapter:

- Functions
- Multiple dispatch
- Parametric methods
- Interfaces

As part of the learning process, we will go over a use case of game design. More specifically, we will pretend that we are building a space war game that contains a game board with spaceships and asteroid pieces. We will build functions that move the game pieces around and equip the spaceships with weapons to blow things up.

By the end of this chapter, you will have the necessary knowledge to design and develop functions effectively. Through the use of multiple dispatch and parametric methods, your application will become more extendable. Once you have learned these techniques, you should also be able to design a system that contains pluggable components based on interfaces.

I can't wait any longer. Let's get started!

Technical requirements

The sample source code is located at `https://github.com/PacktPublishing/Hands-on-Design-Patterns-and-Best-Practices-with-Julia/tree/master/Chapter03`.

The code is tested in a Julia 1.3.0 environment.

Designing functions

Function is a core construct in Julia for defining the behaviors of an application. In fact, Julia works more like a procedural/functional programming language as opposed to an object-oriented programming language. In object-oriented programming, you focus on building classes and defining functions for those classes. In Julia, you focus on building functions that operate on data types or data structures.

In this section, we will demonstrate how functions are defined and the powerful features that come with functions.

Our use case – a space war game

Throughout this chapter, we will illustrate programming concepts by building parts of a space war game. The design of the game is very simple and straightforward. It consists of game pieces such as spaceships and asteroids that are scattered around a two-dimensional grid. These game pieces are called widgets in our program.

Let's first define our data types as follows:

```
# Space war game!

mutable struct Position
    x::Int
    y::Int
end

struct Size
    width::Int
    height::Int
end

struct Widget
    name::String
    position::Position
```

```
    size::Size
end
```

As data types are central to our design, this warrants a little more explanation:

- The `Position` type is used to store the coordinates of a game piece. It is represented by two integers: `x` and `y`.
- The `Size` type is used to store the size of a game piece. It is represented by two integers: `width` and `height`.
- The `Widget` type is used to hold a single game piece. It is represented by a `name`, `position`, and `size`.

Note that the `Position` type is mutable because we expect our game pieces to move around by just updating their coordinates.

Next, we will go over a number of topics related to how functions are defined.

Defining functions

There are actually two different syntaxes that we can use to define a function:

- The first way is a simple one-liner that contains both the signature and body of the function.
- The second way uses the `function` keyword with the signature, followed by the code block and the `end` keyword.

If the function is simple enough—for example, if it just has a single instruction—then it is usually more preferable to write the function in a single line. This style of function definition is very common for scientific computing projects, as many functions simply mimic the corresponding mathematical formulae.

For our game, we can just write four functions for moving the game pieces around the board by modifying the coordinates of the widget:

```
# single-line functions
move_up!(widget, v)    = widget.position.y -= v
move_down!(widget, v)  = widget.position.y += v
move_left!(widget, v)  = widget.position.x -= v
move_right!(widget, v) = widget.position.x += v
```

It is indeed quite idiomatic in Julia to write single-line functions. People coming from a different background may find it more intuitive to write the following, more verbose, form. There is nothing wrong with this; both forms work just fine:

```
# long version
function move_up!(widget, v)
    widget.position.y -= v
end
```

There are a few things to bear in mind about how these functions are written:

- **Use of underscore**: The preceding function names use an underscore to separate the words. According to the official Julia manual, the convention is to just smash the words together without any separators unless it becomes too confusing or hard to read. My personal opinion is that underscore should always be used for multi-word function names because it enhances the readability and makes the code more consistent.
- **Use of exclamation mark**: The preceding function names contain exclamation mark to indicate that the function mutates the state of the object that is being passed into the function. This is a good practice because it reminds the developer that there will be side effects when calling the function.
- **Duck typing**: You may wonder why the function arguments are not annotated with any type information. In the `move_up!` function, although we do not have any type annotation, we expect the `widget` argument to have the `Widget` type and `v` to have the `Int` type when the function is used. This is an interesting topic, and we will discuss it further in the next section.

As you can see, defining functions is a fairly straightforward task, and the way Julia handles function arguments is quite interesting. We will go over this next.

Annotating function arguments

In a statically typed language without any polymorphism, such as C or Fortran, every argument must be specified with the exact type. Julia, however, is dynamically typed and supports duck typing—*if it walks like a duck and quacks like a duck, then it is a duck*. Type information is not required in the source code at all. Instead, the compiler looks at runtime types that you pass into the function and compiles the appropriate method specialized for those types. The process of deducing types throughout a method body based on the argument types is called **type inference**.

Therefore, there is no need to annotate function arguments with type information at all. People sometimes get the impression that putting type annotations all over their Julia code will improve performance. That is not usually the case. For method signatures, types have no effect on performance: they are only useful to control dispatch.

So, what would you choose? Annotate arguments with types or not?

Untyped arguments

When function arguments are not annotated with type information, the function is actually more flexible. Why? That's because it can work with any type that you pass into the function. Let's say that, in the future, the coordinate system is changed from Int to Float64. When this happens, the function will not need to be changed: it just works!

In contrast, keeping everything untyped may not be the best idea either because the function cannot really work with every possible data type that is defined in the world. In addition, it could often lead to obscure exception messages and make the program more difficult to debug. For instance, if we were to pass an Int value as the Widget argument to the move_up! function by mistake, then it will complain about the type not having a position field:

```
julia> move_up!(1, 2)
ERROR: type Int64 has no field position
```

The error message is quite obscure. Is there anything that we can do to make debugging a little easier? The answer is that we could provide the type of function arguments. Let's see how this can be done.

Typed arguments

We know that our implementation of the move functions comes with some implicit design assumptions:

- The value of v should be a numerical value, as implied by the + or – operator.
- The widget has to be a Widget object, or at least something that contains a Position object, as implied by the access of the position field.

For these reasons, it's generally safer to define functions with some type information. Having said that, the `move_up!` function can be redefined as follows:

```
move_up!(widget::Widget, v::Int) = widget.position.y -= v
```

If we just define all `move` functions the same way, then debugging becomes easier. Suppose that we make the same mistake as we did in the preceding code by passing an integer as the first argument: we will now receive a more sensible error message:

```
julia> move_up!(1, 2)
ERROR: MethodError: no method matching move_up!(::Int64, ::Int64)
Closest candidates are:
  move_up!(::Widget, ::Int64) at REPL[4]:1
```

So instead of trying to run the function and failing miserably with an unknown effect, the Julia compiler will now tell us that the method does not exist for the argument types that we pass into the function.

Before we move on to the next topic, let's at least play a little bit of the game. In order to display these objects more nicely in the Julia REPL, we can define some `show` functions, as follows:

```
# Define pretty print functions
Base.show(io::IO, p::Position) = print(io, "(", p.x, ",", p.y, ")")
Base.show(io::IO, s::Size) = print(io, s.width, " x ", s.height)
Base.show(io::IO, w::Widget) = print(io, w.name, " at ", w.position, " size
", w.size)
```

These `Base.show` functions provide the implementation that is used when `Position`, `Size`, or `Widget` objects need to be shown at the specific I/O device, such as the REPL. By defining these functions, we get a much nicer output.

Note that the `show` function for the `Widget` type prints the name, position, and size of the widget. The respective `show` functions for the `Position` and `Size` types are going to be called from the `print` function.

The `show` function comes with another form, `show(io, mime, x)`, so that the value `x` can be displayed in different formats for different MIME types.

MIME stands for Multipurpose Internet Mail Extensions. It is also called Media Type. It is a standard that is used to specify the type of a data stream. For example, `text/plain` represents a plain text stream and `text/html` represents a text stream that has HTML content.

The default MIME type for a `show` function is `text/plain`, which is essentially the type we use in a Julia REPL environment. If we use Julia in a notebook environment, such as Jupyter, then we can provide a `show` function that provides additional formatting in HTML using the MIME type of `text/html`.

Finally, let's give it a test drive. We can move around an asteroid game piece by calling various `move` functions, as follows:

```
# let's test these functions
w = Widget("asteroid", Position(0, 0), Size(10, 20))
move_up!(w, 10)
move_down!(w, 10)
move_left!(w, 20)
move_right!(w, 20)

# should be back to position (0,0)
print(w)
```

The result is as follows. Note that the output of the asteroid widget is formatted exactly as how we coded it:

```
julia> w = Widget("asteroid", Position(0, 0), Size(10, 20))
asteroid at (0,0) size 10 x 20

julia> move_up!(w, 10)
-10

julia> move_down!(w, 10)
0

julia> move_left!(w, 20)
-20

julia> move_right!(w, 20)
0

julia> print(w)
asteroid at (0,0) size 10 x 20
```

Defining functions with typed arguments is generally considered a good practice because the function can only work with the specific data types of the arguments. Also, from a client usage perspective, you can clearly see what is required by the function just by looking at the function definition.

Sometimes it is more beneficial to define a function with untyped arguments. The standard `print` function, for instance, has a function signature that looks like `print(io::IO, x)`. The intention is that the `print` function is guaranteed to work with all possible data types.

Generally speaking, this should be an exception rather than the norm. In most situations, it makes more sense to use typed arguments.

Next, we will discuss how to provide default values for the arguments.

Working with optional arguments

Sometimes, we do not want to hardcode any values in a function. The general solution is to extract the hardcoded values and work them into function arguments. In Julia, we can also provide default values for the arguments. When we have default values, then the arguments become optional.

To illustrate this concept, let's write a function that makes a bunch of asteroids:

```
# Make a bunch of asteroids
function make_asteroids(N::Int, pos_range = 0:200, size_range = 10:30)
    pos_rand() = rand(pos_range)
    sz_rand() = rand(size_range)
    return [Widget("Asteroid #$i",
                Position(pos_rand(), pos_rand()),
                Size(sz_rand(), sz_rand()))
        for i in 1:N]
end
```

The function takes an argument of N for the number of asteroids. It also accepts a position range, `pos_range`, and `size_range`, for creating randomly sized asteroids that are placed randomly on our game map. You may notice that we have also defined two single-line functions, `pos_rand` and `sz_rand`, directly inside the body of the `make_asteroid` function. These functions only exist within the scope of the function.

Let's try this out without specifying any value for `pos_range` or `size_range`:

```
julia> asteroids = make_asteroids(5)
5-element Array{Widget,1}:
 Asteroid #1 at (86,130) size 15 x 29
 Asteroid #2 at (110,138) size 10 x 20
 Asteroid #3 at (188,69) size 29 x 15
 Asteroid #4 at (187,194) size 15 x 13
 Asteroid #5 at (33,124) size 29 x 20
```

But the fact that they are optional also allows us to provide custom values. For instance, we can place the asteroids closer to each other by specifying a much narrower range:

```
julia> asteroids = make_asteroids(5, 1:10)
5-element Array{Widget,1}:
 Asteroid #1 at (9,3) size 12 x 28
 Asteroid #2 at (6,8) size 19 x 17
 Asteroid #3 at (8,10) size 19 x 22
 Asteroid #4 at (5,5) size 12 x 11
 Asteroid #5 at (4,1) size 14 x 13
```

Where does the magic come from? If you hit the *Tab* key while entering the `make_asteroid` function from the REPL, you may notice that the single function definition ends up with three methods.

What are functions and methods?

Functions are *generic* in Julia. This means that we can extend the purpose of a function by defining various methods that have the same name, but take different types of argument.

Hence, every function in Julia may be associated to one or more associated methods.

Internally, Julia automatically creates these three methods, one for each signature:

```
julia> make_asteroids
make_asteroids (generic function with 3 methods)

julia> make_asteroids(          ⟵——— press Tab key twice
make_asteroids(N::Int64) in Main at REPL[18]:3
make_asteroids(N::Int64, pos_range) in Main at REPL[18]:3
make_asteroids(N::Int64, pos_range, size_range) in Main at REPL[18]:3
```

Another way to find the methods of a function is to just use the `methods` function that comes from the Julia `Base` package:

```
julia> methods(make_asteroids)
# 3 methods for generic function "make_asteroids":
[1] make_asteroids(N::Int64) in Main at REPL[18]:3
[2] make_asteroids(N::Int64, pos_range) in Main at REPL[18]:3
[3] make_asteroids(N::Int64, pos_range, size_range) in Main at REPL[18]:3
```

Of course, we can fully specify all arguments as such:

```
julia> asteroids = make_asteroids(5, 100:5:200, 200:10:500)
5-element Array{Widget,1}:
 Asteroid #1 at (140,180) size 360 x 470
 Asteroid #2 at (150,155) size 210 x 420
 Asteroid #3 at (150,130) size 250 x 430
 Asteroid #4 at (140,170) size 340 x 450
 Asteroid #5 at (135,190) size 500 x 250
```

As you can see, it is quite convenient to provide default values for positional arguments. In the case that the default values are generally accepted, the calling function becomes simpler because it does not have to specify all arguments.

Something feels a little weird here, though—the code is becoming more difficult to read: `make_asteroids(5, 100:5:200, 200:10:500)`. What does 5, `100:5:200`, and `200:10:500` mean? These arguments look quite opaque, and the programmer may not remember what they mean without looking up the source code or the manual. There has to be a better way! Next, we will check how to solve this problem using keyword arguments.

Utilizing keyword arguments

A drawback of optional arguments is that they must be in the same order in which they are defined. When there are more arguments, it is not easily readable which values are bound to which arguments from the call site. In that case, we may use keyword arguments to improve readability.

Let's redefine the `make_asteroid` function as follows:

```
function make_asteroids2(N::Int; pos_range = 0:200, size_range = 10:30)
    pos_rand() = rand(pos_range)
    sz_rand() = rand(size_range)
    return [Widget("Asteroid #$i",
```

```
                    Position(pos_rand(), pos_rand()),
                    Size(sz_rand(), sz_rand()))
            for i in 1:N]
    end
```

The only difference between this function and the one from the previous section is just a single character. The positional arguments (in this case, `N`) and keyword arguments (`pos_range` and `size_range`) just need to be separated by a `;` character.

From the caller's perspective, keyword arguments must be passed with the names of the arguments:

```
julia> asteroids = make_asteroids2(5, pos_range = 0:100:500)
5-element Array{Widget,1}:
 Asteroid #1 at (500,500) size 23 x 14
 Asteroid #2 at (0,0) size 16 x 16
 Asteroid #3 at (500,100) size 15 x 20
 Asteroid #4 at (0,100) size 24 x 11
 Asteroid #5 at (400,400) size 19 x 11
```

Using keyword arguments has made the code a lot more readable! In fact, the keyword arguments do not even need to be passed in the same order as they were defined in the function:

```
julia> asteroids = make_asteroids2(5, size_range = 1:5, pos_range = 0:10:100)
5-element Array{Widget,1}:
 Asteroid #1 at (20,40) size 2 x 1
 Asteroid #2 at (40,90) size 4 x 2
 Asteroid #3 at (70,80) size 3 x 5        specified in different order
 Asteroid #4 at (30,70) size 5 x 2
 Asteroid #5 at (80,20) size 3 x 3
```

Another cool feature is that keyword arguments do not have to carry any default values. For example, we could define the same function where the first argument `N` becomes a mandatory keyword argument:

```
function make_asteroids3(; N::Int, pos_range = 0:200, size_range = 10:30)
    pos_rand() = rand(pos_range)
    sz_rand() = rand(size_range)
    return [Widget("Asteroid #$i",
                Position(pos_rand(), pos_rand()),
                Size(sz_rand(), sz_rand()))
            for i in 1:N]
end
```

At this point, we could just call the function with N specified:

```
julia> make_asteroids3(N = 3)
3-element Array{Widget,1}:
 Asteroid #1 at (166,195) size 13 x 27
 Asteroid #2 at (100,105) size 21 x 13
 Asteroid #3 at (2,196) size 27 x 25
```

Using keyword arguments is a good way to write self-documenting code. Some open source packages, such as Plots, make extensive use of keyword arguments. It works very well when a function needs many arguments.

 While we specify default values for keyword arguments in this example, they are not really required. In the case that there is no default value, the keyword argument becomes mandatory when the function is called.

Another cool feature is that we can pass a variable number of arguments to a function. We will look into this next.

Accepting variable numbers of arguments

Sometimes, it is more convenient if the function can just accept any number of arguments. In this case, we can add three dots . . . to a function argument and Julia will automatically roll up all passed arguments into a single variable. This feature is known as **slurping**.

Here is an example:

```
# Shoot any number of targets
function shoot(from::Widget, targets::Widget...)
    println("Type of targets: ", typeof(targets))
    for target in targets
        println(from.name, " --> ", target.name)
    end
end
```

In the shoot function, we first print the type of the targets variable and then print every shot that was fired. Let's set up the game pieces first:

```
spaceship = Widget("Spaceship", Position(0, 0), Size(30,30))
target1 = asteroids[1]
target2 = asteroids[2]
target3 = asteroids[3]
```

Now we can start shooting! Let's first call the `shoot` function by passing a single target and then do that again by passing three targets:

```
julia> shoot(spaceship, target1)
Type of targets: Tuple{Widget}
Spaceship --> Asteroid #1

julia> shoot(spaceship, target1, target2, target3)
Type of targets: Tuple{Widget,Widget,Widget}
Spaceship --> Asteroid #1
Spaceship --> Asteroid #2
Spaceship --> Asteroid #3
```

It turns out that the arguments are just combined as a tuple and bound to a single `targets` variable. In this case, we just iterate the tuple and perform an action on each of them.

Slurping is a fantastic way to combine function arguments and handle them all together. This makes it possible to call the function with any number of arguments.

Next, we will learn about a similar feature called splatting, which essentially performs the opposite function of slurping.

Splatting arguments

Slurping is very useful in its own right, but the triple-dot notation actually has a second usage. At the call site, when a variable is followed by three periods, the variable will be automatically assigned as multiple function arguments. This feature is known as **splatting**. In fact, this mechanism is very similar to slurping, except that it is doing the opposite action. We will take a look at an example.

Let's say that we have written a function to arrange a couple of spaceships in a specific formation:

```
# Special arrangement before attacks
function triangular_formation!(s1::Widget, s2::Widget, s3::Widget)
    x_offset = 30
    y_offset = 50
    s2.position.x = s1.position.x - x_offset
    s3.position.x = s1.position.x + x_offset
    s2.position.y = s3.position.y = s1.position.y - y_offset
    (s1, s2, s3)
end
```

We have also constructed a couple of spaceships ahead of a space war:

```
julia> spaceships = [
           Widget("Spaceship $i", Position(0,0), Size(20, 50))
               for i in 1:3
        ]
3-element Array{Widget,1}:
 Spaceship 1 at (0,0) size 20 x 50
 Spaceship 2 at (0,0) size 20 x 50
 Spaceship 3 at (0,0) size 20 x 50
```

We can now call the triangular_formation! function using the splatting technique, which involves appending three periods after the function argument:

```
julia> triangular_formation!(spaceships...);

julia> spaceships
3-element Array{Widget,1}:
 Spaceship 1 at (0,0) size 20 x 50
 Spaceship 2 at (-30,-50) size 20 x 50
 Spaceship 3 at (30,-50) size 20 x 50
```

In this case, the three elements inside the spaceships vector are distributed to the three arguments as the triangular_formation! function expects.

Splatting can technically work with any collection type—vector and tuple. It should work as long as the variable being splatted supports the general iteration interface.

In addition, you may wonder what happens when the number of elements in the variable does not equal the number of arguments as defined in the function.

You are encouraged to check this behavior out as an exercise.

Splatting is a good way to build up function arguments and then pass them into the function directly without having to split them up into separate arguments. It is therefore quite convenient.

Next, we will discuss how functions can be passed around to provide higher-order programming facilities.

Understanding first-class functions

Functions are said to be **first-class** when they can be assigned to variables or struct fields, passed into functions, returned from a function, and so on. They are treated as first-class citizens just like regular data types. We will now take a look at how functions can be passed around like regular data values.

Let's design a new function that can propel a spaceship to leap in a random direction for a random distance. You may recall from the beginning of this chapter that we have already defined four move functions—move_up!, move_down!, move_left!, and move_right!. Here's our strategy:

1. Create a random_move function that returns one of the possible move functions. This provides the basis for choosing a direction.
2. Create a random_leap! function that moves the spaceship using the specified move function and leap distance.

The code is as follows:

```
function random_move()
    return rand([move_up!, move_down!, move_left!, move_right!])
end

function random_leap!(w::Widget, move_func::Function, distance::Int)
    move_func(w, distance)
    return w
end
```

As you can see, the random_move function returns a function that is randomly chosen from the array of move functions. The random_leap! function accepts a move function, move_func, as an argument and then it just makes the call with the widget and distance. Let's test the random_leap! function now:

```
julia> spaceship = Widget("Spaceship", Position(0,0), Size(20,50))
Spaceship at (0,0) size 20 x 50

julia> random_leap!(spaceship, random_move(), rand(50:100))
Spaceship at (0,-85) size 20 x 50

julia> random_leap!(spaceship, random_move(), rand(50:100))
Spaceship at (0,-35) size 20 x 50

julia> random_leap!(spaceship, random_move(), rand(50:100))
Spaceship at (0,56) size 20 x 50
```

We have successfully called a randomly chosen move function. All of this can be done easily because we can store functions as if they are regular variables. The first-class nature makes it very convenient.

Next, we will learn about anonymous functions. Anonymous functions are commonly used in Julia programs because they are a quick way to make a function and pass it around to other functions.

Developing anonymous functions

Sometimes, we just want to create a simple function and pass it around without assigning it a name. This style of programming is actually fairly common in functional programming languages. We can illustrate its use with an example.

Suppose that we want to explode all of the asteroids. One way to do this is to define an explode function and pass it into the foreach function as follows:

```
function explode(x)
    println(x, " exploded!")
end

function clean_up_galaxy(asteroids)
    foreach(explode, asteroids)
end
```

The results look good:

```
julia> clean_up_galaxy(asteroids)
Asteroid #1 at (20,40) size 2 x 1 exploded!
Asteroid #2 at (40,90) size 4 x 2 exploded!
Asteroid #3 at (70,80) size 3 x 5 exploded!
Asteroid #4 at (30,70) size 5 x 2 exploded!
Asteroid #5 at (80,20) size 3 x 3 exploded!
```

We can achieve the same effect if we just pass an anonymous function into foreach:

```
function clean_up_galaxy(asteroids)
    foreach(x -> println(x, " exploded!"), asteroids)
end
```

The syntax of the anonymous function contains the argument variables, followed by the thin arrow -> and the function body. In this case, we only have a single argument. If we have more arguments, then we can write them as a tuple that is enclosed in parentheses. An anonymous function can also be assigned to a variable and passed around. Let's say we want to explode the spaceships as well:

```
function clean_up_galaxy(asteroids, spaceships)
    ep = x -> println(x, " exploded!")
    foreach(ep, asteroids)
    foreach(ep, spaceships)
end
```

We can see that there are some advantages for using anonymous functions:

- There is no need to come up with a function name and pollute the namespace of the module.
- The anonymous function logic is available at the call site, so the code is easier to read.
- The code is slightly more compact.

By now, we have gone over most of the pertinent details regarding how to define and use functions. The next topic, do-syntax, is closely related to anonymous functions. It is a great way to enhance code readability.

Using do-syntax

When working with anonymous functions, we may end up having a code block that is in the middle of a function call, making the code more difficult to read. The do-syntax is a great way to address this problem and produce clear, easy-to-read code.

To illustrate the concept, let's build up a new use case for our battle fleet. In particular, we will enhance our spaceships with the ability to launch missiles. We also want to support the requirement that launching a weapon requires that the spaceship is in a healthy state.

We can define a `fire` function that takes a `launch` function and a spaceship. The `launch` function is executed only when the spaceship is healthy. Why do we want to take a function as an argument? Because we want to make it flexible so that, later on, we can use the same `fire` function to launch laser beams and other possible weapons:

```
# Random healthiness function for testing
healthy(spaceship) = rand(Bool)

# make sure that the spaceship is healthy before any operation
```

```
function fire(f::Function, spaceship::Widget)
    if healthy(spaceship)
        f(spaceship)
    else
        println("Operation aborted as spaceship is not healthy")
    end
    return nothing
end
```

Let's try this out using an anonymous function to fire the missile:

```
julia> fire(s -> println(s, " launched missile!"), spaceship)
Spaceship at (0,56) size 20 x 50 launched missile!

julia> fire(s -> println(s, " launched missile!"), spaceship)
Operation aborted as spaceship is not healthy
```

So far so good. But what happens if we need a more complex procedure to fire missiles? For example, say that we would like to move the spaceship up before firing and move it back down afterward:

```
fire(s -> begin
        move_up!(s, 100)
        println(s, " launched missile!")
        move_down!(s, 100)
    end, spaceship)
```

The syntax now looks quite ugly. Fortunately, we can rewrite the code using the do-syntax and make it more readable:

```
fire(spaceship) do s
    move_up!(s, 100)
    println(s, " launched missile!")
    move_down!(s, 100)
end
```

How does it work? Well, the syntax is translated so that the do-block is turned into an anonymous function and it is then just inserted as the first argument of the function.

An interesting usage of the do-syntax can be found in Julia's open function. Because reading a file involves opening and closing a file handler, the open function is designed to accept an anonymous function that takes an IOStream and do something with it, while the opening/closing housekeeping tasks are handled by the open function itself.

The idea is quite simple, so let's just replicate it here with our own `process_file` function:

```
function process_file(func::Function, filename::AbstractString)
    ios = nothing
    try
        ios = open(filename)
        func(ios)
    finally
        close(ios)
    end
end
```

Using the do-syntax, we can focus on developing the logic of file processing without having to worry about the housekeeping chores, such as opening and closing files. Consider the following code:

```
julia> process_file("/etc/hosts") do ios
           lines = readlines(ios)
           println(length(lines))
       end
```

As you can see, the do-syntax can be useful in two ways:

- It makes the code more readable by rearranging the anonymous function argument in a block format.
- It allows the anonymous functions to be wrapped in a context for which additional logic can be executed before or after the function.

Next, we will take a look at multiple dispatch, which is a unique feature that is not commonly found in object-oriented languages.

Understanding Multiple Dispatch

Multiple dispatch is one of the most unique features in the Julia programming language. They are used extensively in the Julia Base library, `stdlib`, as well as many open source packages. In this section, we will explore how multiple dispatch work and how one can utilize them effectively.

What is a dispatch?

A dispatch is the process by which a function is selected for execution. You may wonder why there is any controversy in selecting which function to execute. When we develop a function, we give it a name, some arguments, and a block of code that it should execute. If we come up with unique names for all functions in a system, then there will be no ambiguity. However, there are often times when we want to reuse the same function name and apply it to different data types for similar types of operation.

Examples are abundant in Julia's Base library. For example, the `isascii` function has three methods, and each one takes a different argument type:

```
isascii(c::Char)
isascii(s::AbstractString)
isascii(c::AbstractChar)
```

Depending on the type of the argument, the proper method is dispatched and executed. When we call the `isascii` function with a `Char` object, the first method is dispatched. Likewise, when we call it with a `String` object, which is a subtype of `AbstractString`, then the second method is dispatched. Sometimes, the type of the argument being passed to the method is not known until runtime, and in that case, the proper method is dispatched right at that moment, depending on the specific value being passed. This behavior is called **dynamic dispatch**.

Dispatch is a key concept that will come up over and over again. It is important that we understand the rules as related to how a function being dispatched. We will go over these next.

Matching to the narrowest types

As discussed in Chapter 2, *Modules, Packages, and Data Type Concepts*, we can define functions that take abstract types as arguments. When it comes to dispatch, Julia will find the method that matches the narrowest type in the arguments.

To illustrate this concept, let's return to our favorite example in this chapter regarding spaceships and asteroids! In fact, we will improve our data types as follows:

```
# A thing is anything that exist in the universe.
# Concrete type of Thing should always have the following fields:
#     1. position
#     2. size
abstract type Thing end

# Functions that are applied for all Thing's
position(t::Thing) = t.position
size(t::Thing) = t.size
shape(t::Thing) = :unknown
```

Here, we have defined an abstract type, `Thing`, which can be anything that exists in the universe. When we design this type, we expect its concrete subtypes will have the standard `position` and `size` fields. Therefore, we just happily define `position` and `size` functions for `Thing`. By default, we do not want to assume any shape of anything, so the `shape` function for `Thing` only returns an `:unknown` symbol.

To make things more interesting, we will equip our spaceships with two types of weapon—laser and missiles. In Julia, we can conveniently define them as **enums**:

```
# Type of weapons
@enum Weapon Laser Missile
```

Here, the `@enum` macro defines a new type called `Weapon`. The only values of the `Weapon` type are `Laser` and `Missile`. Enums are a good way to define typed constants. Internally, they define numeric values for each constant, and so it should be quite performant.

Now, we can define the `Spaceship` and `Asteroid` concrete types as follows:

```
# Spaceship
struct Spaceship <: Thing
    position::Position
    size::Size
    weapon::Weapon
end
shape(s::Spaceship) = :saucer

# Asteroid
struct Asteroid <: Thing
    position::Position
    size::Size
end
```

Note that both `Spaceship` and `Asteroid` include `position` and `size` fields as part of our design contract. In addition, we have a `weapon` field added for the `Spaceship` type. Because we have designed our state-of-the-art spaceships like saucers, we have defined the `shape` function for the `Spaceship` type as well. Let's test it out:

```julia
julia> s1 = Spaceship(Position(0,0), Size(30,5), Missile);

julia> s2 = Spaceship(Position(10,0), Size(30,5), Laser);

julia> a1 = Asteroid(Position(20,0), Size(20,20));

julia> a2 = Asteroid(Position(0,20), Size(20,20));

julia> position(s1), size(s1), shape(s1)
(Position(0, 0), Size(30, 5), :saucer)

julia> position(a1), size(a1), shape(a1)
(Position(20, 0), Size(20, 20), :unknown)
```

We have now created two spaceships and two asteroids. Let's turn our focus to the results of the preceding `shape` function calls for a moment. When it was called with a spaceship object s1, it was dispatched to `shape(s::Spaceship)` and returned `:saucer`. When it was called with an asteroid object, it was dispatched to `shape(t::Thing)` because there are no other matches for the `Asteroid` object.

To recap, Julia's dispatch mechanism always looks for the function with the narrowest type in the arguments. Judging between `shape(s::Spaceship)` and `shape(t:Thing)`, it will choose to execute `shape(s::Spaceship)` for a `Spaceship` argument.

Are you familiar with multiple dispatch? If not, don't worry. In the next section, we will dive deep into how multiple dispatch works in Julia.

Dispatching with multiple arguments

So far, we have only seen dispatch examples for methods that take a single argument. We can extend the same concept for multiple arguments, and that's simply called multiple dispatch.

So how does it work when multiple arguments are involved? Let's say we continue developing our space war game with the ability to detect collisions between different objects. To look at this in detail, we'll go through a sample implementation.

First, define functions that can check whether two rectangles overlap each other:

```
struct Rectangle
    top::Int
    left::Int
    bottom::Int
    right::Int
    # return two upper-left and lower-right points of the rectangle
    Rectangle(p::Position, s::Size) =
        new(p.y+s.height, p.x, p.y, p.x+s.width)
end

# check if the two rectangles (A & B) overlap
function overlap(A::Rectangle, B::Rectangle)
    return A.left < B.right && A.right > B.left &&
        A.top > B.bottom && A.bottom < B.top
end
```

Then, we can define a function that returns `true` when two `Thing` objects collide. This function can be called for any combination of `Spaceship` and `Asteroid` objects:

```
function collide(A::Thing, B::Thing)
    println("Checking collision of thing vs. thing")
    rectA = Rectangle(position(A), size(A))
    rectB = Rectangle(position(B), size(B))
    return overlap(rectA, rectB)
end
```

Of course, this is a really naive idea because we know that spaceships and asteroids have different shapes, possibly nonrectangular ones. Nonetheless, this is not a bad default implementation.

Let's run a quick test before we go further. Note that I have intentionally suppressed the output of the return values only because they're unimportant for our discussion here:

```
julia> collide(s1, s2);
Checking collision of thing vs. thing

julia> collide(a1, a2);
Checking collision of thing vs. thing

julia> collide(s1, a1);
Checking collision of thing vs. thing

julia> collide(a1, s1);
Checking collision of thing vs. thing
```

Knowing that the collision-detection logic may be different depending on the type of objects, we can further define these methods:

```
function collide(A::Spaceship, B::Spaceship)
    println("Checking collision of spaceship vs. spaceship")
    return true    # just a test
end
```

With this new method, based upon the narrowest-type selection process, we can safely handle spaceship-spaceship collision detection. Let's prove my claim with the same test as the preceding code:

```
julia> collide(s1, s2);
Checking collision of spaceship vs. spaceship

julia> collide(a1, a2);
Checking collision of thing vs. thing

julia> collide(s1, a1);
Checking collision of thing vs. thing

julia> collide(a1, s1);
Checking collision of thing vs. thing
```

It looks good. If we just continue defining the rest of the functions, then everything will be covered and perfect!

Multiple dispatch is indeed a simple concept. Essentially, all function arguments are considered when Julia tries to determine which function needs to be dispatched. The same rule applies—the narrowest type always wins!

Unfortunately, sometimes it is unclear which function needs to be dispatched. Next, we will look into how this can happen and how the problem can be resolved.

Possible ambiguities during dispatch

Of course, we can always define all possible methods with concrete type arguments; however, that may not be the most desirable option when designing software. Why? It's because the number of combinations in argument types could be overwhelming, and it is often unnecessary to enumerate them all. In our game example here, we only need to detect collisions between two types—spaceship and asteroid. So we just need to define 2 x 2 = 4 methods; however, imagine what we would do when we have 10 types of object. We would then have to define 100 methods!

The idea of abstract types can save us. Let's just imagine that we do have to support 10 concrete data types. If the other eight data types have similar shapes, then we could cut down the number of methods tremendously by accepting an abstract type as one of the arguments. How? Let's take a look:

```
function collide(A::Asteroid, B::Thing)
    println("Checking collision of asteroid vs. thing")
    return true
end

function collide(A::Thing, B::Asteroid)
    println("Checking collision of thing vs. asteroid")
    return false
end
```

These two functions provide the default implementation for detecting collisions between an Asteroid and any Thing. The first method can handle the first argument being Asteroid and the second argument being any subtype of Thing. If we were to have 10 concrete types in total, this single method can handle 10 scenarios. Likewise, the second method can handle the other 10 scenarios. Let's just have a quick check:

```
julia> collide(a1, s1);
Checking collision of asteroid vs. thing

julia> collide(s1, a1);
Checking collision of thing vs. asteroid
```

Great! these two calls are working fine. Let's finish our test:

```
julia> collide(a1, a2);
ERROR: MethodError: collide(::Asteroid, ::Asteroid) is ambiguous. Candi
dates:
  collide(A::Asteroid, B::Thing) in Main at REPL[29]:2
  collide(A::Thing, B::Asteroid) in Main at REPL[30]:2
Possible fix, define
  collide(::Asteroid, ::Asteroid)
```

But wait, what happened when we tried to check the collision between two asteroids? Well, the Julia runtime has detected an ambiguity here. When we pass two `Asteroid` arguments, it is unclear whether we want to execute `collide(A::Thing, B::Asteroid)` or `collide(A::Asteroid, B::Thing)`. Both methods seem to be able to take the task, but neither of their signatures is narrower than the other, and so it just gave up and throws an error.

Fortunately, it actually suggested a fix as part of the error message. A possible fix is to define a new method, `collide(::Asteroid, ::Asteroid)`, as follows:

```
function collide(A::Asteroid, B::Asteroid)
    println("Checking collision of asteroid vs. asteroid")
    return true # just a test
end
```

Because it has the narrowest signature, Julia can properly dispatch to this new method when two asteroids are passed to the `collide` function. Once this method is defined, there will be no more ambiguity. Let's try again. The result is as follows:

```
julia> collide(a1, a2);
Checking collision of asteroid vs. asteroid
```

As you can see, when you encounter ambiguity for multiple dispatch, it can be resolved easily by creating a function with more specific types in its arguments. The Julia runtime will not try to guess what you want to do. As a developer, we need to provide clear instructions to the computer.

However, ambiguities may not be obvious from just looking at the code. In order to reduce the risk of hitting the problem at runtime, we can proactively detect which part of the code may introduce such ambiguities. Fortunately, Julia already provides a convenient tool to identify ambiguities. We will take a look at that in the next section.

Detecting ambiguities

It is often difficult to find ambiguous methods until you happen to hit a specific use case at runtime. That's not good. I don't know about you, but software engineers like me don't like surprises in production!

Fortunately, Julia provides a function in the `Test` package for detecting ambiguities. We can try this out using a similar test. Consider the following code:

```julia
julia> using Test

julia> module Foo
           foo(x, y) = 1
           foo(x::Integer, y) = 2
           foo(x, y::Integer) = 3
       end
Main.Foo
```

We have created a small module in the REPL that defines three `foo` methods. It's a classic example of ambiguous methods—if we pass two integer arguments, then it is unclear whether the second or the third `foo` method should be executed. Now, let's use the `detect_ambiguities` function and see if it can detect the problem:

```julia
julia> detect_ambiguities(Main.Foo)
1-element Array{Tuple{Method,Method},1}:
 (foo(x::Integer, y) in Main.Foo at REPL[37]:3, foo(x, y::Integer) in
Main.Foo at REPL[37]:4)
```

The result is telling us that the `foo(x::Integer, y)` and `foo(x, y::Integer)` functions are ambiguous. As we've already learned how to fix that problem, we can do that and test again:

```julia
julia> module Foo
           foo(x, y) = 1
           foo(x::Integer, y) = 2
           foo(x, y::Integer) = 3
           foo(x::Integer, y::Integer) = 4
       end
WARNING: replacing module Foo.
Main.Foo

julia> detect_ambiguities(Main.Foo)
0-element Array{Tuple{Method,Method},1}
```

In fact, the `detect_ambiguities` function is even more useful when you have functions that extend functions from other modules. In this case, you can just call the `detect_ambiguities` function with the modules that you want to check all together. Here's how it works when you pass two modules:

```julia
julia> module Foo2
           foo(x, y) = 1
           foo(x::Integer, y) = 2
           foo(x, y::Integer) = 3
       end
Main.Foo2

julia> module Foo4
           import Main.Foo2
           Foo2.foo(x::Integer, y::Integer) = 4
       end
Main.Foo4

julia> detect_ambiguities(Main.Foo2, Main.Foo4)
0-element Array{Tuple{Method,Method},1}
```

In this hypothetical example, the `Foo4` module imports the `Foo2.foo` function and extends it by adding a new method. The `Foo2` module by itself would be ambiguous, but combining both modules resolves the ambiguity.

So when should we make use of this great detective function? A good way to do this is to add the `detect_ambiguities` test in the module's automated test suite so that it is executed in the continuous integration pipeline for every build.

Now that we know how to use this ambiguity detection tool, we can use multiple dispatch without fear! In the next section, we will go over another aspect of dispatch called dynamic dispatch.

Understanding dynamic dispatch

Julia's dispatch mechanism is unique not only because of its multiple dispatch features, but also the way that it treats function arguments dynamically when deciding where to dispatch.

Let's say we want to randomly pick two objects and check whether they collide. We can define the function as follows:

```
# randomly pick two things and check
function check_randomly(things)
    for i in 1:5
        two = rand(things, 2)
        collide(two...)
    end
end
```

Let's run it and see what happens:

```
julia> check_randomly([s1, s2, a1, a2])
Checking collision of thing vs. asteroid
Checking collision of asteroid vs. asteroid
Checking collision of asteroid vs. thing
Checking collision of asteroid vs. thing
Checking collision of spaceship vs. spaceship
```

We can see that different `collide` methods are called depending on the types of the arguments that are passed in the `two` variable.

This kind of dynamic behavior can be found as polymorphism in object-oriented programming languages. The main difference is that Julia supports multiple dispatch, utilizing all arguments for dispatch at runtime. By contrast, in Java, only the object being invoked is used for dynamic dispatch. Once the proper class is identified for dispatch, the method arguments are then used for static dispatch when there are several overloaded methods with the same name.

Multiple dispatch is a powerful feature. When combined with custom data types, it allows the developer to control which methods are called for different scenarios. If you are more interested in multiple dispatch, you can watch a video on YouTube with the title *The Unreasonable Effectiveness of Multiple Dispatch*. It is a presentation by Stefan Karpinski, recorded at the JuliaCon 2019 conference.

Next, we will look into how function arguments can be parameterized for additional flexibility and expressiveness.

Leveraging parametric methods

Julia's type system and multiple dispatch feature provide a powerful foundation for writing extendable code. As it turns out, we can also use parametric types in function arguments. We can call these parametric methods. Parametric methods provide an interesting way to express what data types may be matched during dispatch.

In the following sections, we will go over how to utilize parametric methods in our game.

Using type parameters

When defining functions, we have an option to annotate each argument with type information. The type of an argument can be a regular abstract type, concrete type, or a parametric type. Let's consider this sample function for exploding an array of game pieces:

```
# explode an array of objects
function explode(things::AbstractVector{Any})
    for t in things
        println("Exploding ", t)
    end
end
```

The `things` argument is annotated with `AbstractVector{Any}`, which means that it can be any `AbstractVector` type that contains any object that is a subtype of `Any` (which is really just everything). To make the method parametric, we can just rewrite it with a `T` type parameter as follows:

```
# explode an array of objects (parametric version)
function explode(things::AbstractVector{T}) where {T}
    for t in things
        println("Exploding ", t)
    end
end
```

Here, the `explode` function can accept any `AbstractVector` with the parameter `T`, which can be any subtype of `Any`. So, if we just pass a vector of `Asteroid` objects—that is, `Vector{Asteroid}`—it should just work. It also works if we pass a vector of symbols—that is, `Vector{Symbol}`. Let's give it a try:

```
julia> explode([a1, a2])
Exploding Asteroid (20,0) 20x20
Exploding Asteroid (0,20) 20x20

julia> explode([:building, :hill])
Exploding building
Exploding hill
```

Note that Vector{Asteroid} is actually a subtype of AbstractVector{Asteroid}. In general, we can say that SomeType{T} is a subtype of SomeOtherType{T} whenever SomeType is a subtype of SomeOtherType. But, if we are unsure, it is easy to check:

```
julia> Vector{Asteroid} <: AbstractVector{Asteroid}
true
```

Perhaps we don't really want the explode function to take a vector of anything. Since this function is written for our space war game, we could restrict the function to accept a vector of any type that is a subtype of Thing. It can be easily achieved as follows:

```
# Same function with a more narrow type
function explode(things::AbstractVector{T}) where {T <: Thing}
    for t in things
        println("Exploding thing => ", t)
    end
end
```

The where notation is used to further qualify the parameter with superclass information. Whenever a type parameter is used in the function signature, we must accompany it with a where clause for the same parameter(s).

Type parameters in function arguments allow us to specify a class of data types that fit within the constraint indicated inside the where clause. The preceding explode function can take a vector containing any subtype of Thing. This means that the function is generic in the sense that it can be dispatched with an unlimited number of types, as long as it satisfies the constraint.

Next, we will explore the use of abstract types as an alternative way to specify function arguments. At first glance, it looks fairly similar to using parametric types; however, there is a slight difference, which we will explain in the next section.

Replacing abstract types with type parameters

In general, we can replace any abstract type with a type parameter in the function signature. When we do this, we will end up with a parametric method that has the same semantics as the original one.

This is not an unimportant observation. Let's see if we can demonstrate this behavior with an example.

Suppose that we are building a `tow` function so that a spaceship can tow away something in the universe, as follows:

```
# specifying abstract/concrete types in method signature
function tow(A::Spaceship, B::Thing)
    "tow 1"
end
```

The `tow` function is currently defined with a concrete `Spaceship` type and an abstract `Thing` type argument. If we want to see the methods defined for this function, we can use the `methods` function to display what is stored in Julia's method table:

```
julia> methods(tow)
# 1 method for generic function "tow":
[1] tow(A::Spaceship, B::Thing) in Main at REPL[67]:2
```

The same method signature comes back perfectly, as expected.

Now, let's define a parametric method where we use a type parameter for the argument B:

```
# equivalent of parametric type
function tow(A::Spaceship, B::T) where {T <: Thing}
    "tow 2"
end
```

We have now defined a new method with a different signature syntax. But is it really a different method? Let's check:

```
julia> methods(tow)
# 1 method for generic function "tow":
[1] tow(A::Spaceship, B::T) where T<:Thing in Main at REPL[69]:2
```

We can see that the methods list still only has one entry, which means that the new method definition has replaced the original one. It should not be too surprising, however. The new method signature, while looking different from the one before, does have the same meaning as the original one. Ultimately, the second argument B still accepts any type that is a subtype of `Thing`.

So, why do we even go through all the trouble to do this? Well, there is no reason to turn this method into a parametric one in this case. But go through the next section, and you will see why doing this can be useful.

Enforcing type consistency in using parameters

One of the most useful features with type parameters is that they can be used to enforce type consistency.

Let's say we want to create a new function that groups two `Thing` objects together. As we don't really care about what concrete types are passed, we can just write a single function that does the work:

```
function group_anything(A::Thing, B::Thing)
    println("Grouped ", A, " and ", B)
end
```

We can also run some trivial tests quickly to ensure that all four combinations of spaceships and asteroids are working:

```
julia> group_anything(s1, s2)
Grouped Spaceship (0,0) 30x5/Missile and Spaceship (10,0) 30x5/Laser

julia> group_anything(a1, a2)
Grouped Asteroid (20,0) 20x20 and Asteroid (0,20) 20x20

julia> group_anything(s1, a1)
Grouped Spaceship (0,0) 30x5/Missile and Asteroid (20,0) 20x20

julia> group_anything(a1, s1)
Grouped Asteroid (20,0) 20x20 and Spaceship (0,0) 30x5/Missile
```

You may wonder how we get such a nice output regarding the specific weapons. As we have learned previously, we can extend the `show` function from the Base package with our types. You can find our implementation of the `show` function in the book's GitHub repository.

Now, all is good, but then we realize that the requirement is slightly different from what we thought originally. Rather than grouping any kind of object, the function should be able to group the same kinds of objects only—that is, it's okay to group spaceship with spaceship and asteroid with asteroid, but not spaceship with asteroid. So what can we do here? An easy solution is to just throw a type parameter in the method signature:

```
function group_same_things(A::T, B::T) where {T <: Thing}
    println("Grouped ", A, " and ", B)
end
```

In this function, we have annotated both arguments with type `T`, and we specify that `T` must be a subtype of `Thing`. Because both arguments use the same type, we are now instructing the system to dispatch to this method only if both arguments have the same type. We can now try the same four test cases as before, as shown in the following code:

```
julia> group_same_things(s1, s2)
Grouped Spaceship (0,0) 30x5/Missile and Spaceship (10,0) 30x5/Laser

julia> group_same_things(a1, a2)
Grouped Asteroid (20,0) 20x20 and Asteroid (0,20) 20x20

julia> group_same_things(s1, a1)
ERROR: MethodError: no method matching group_same_things(::Spaceship, ::Asteroid)
Closest candidates are:
  group_same_things(::T, ::T) where T<:Thing at REPL[76]:2
Stacktrace:
 [1] top-level scope at REPL[79]:1

julia> group_same_things(a1, s1)
ERROR: MethodError: no method matching group_same_things(::Asteroid, ::Spaceship)
Closest candidates are:
  group_same_things(::T, ::T) where T<:Thing at REPL[76]:2
Stacktrace:
 [1] top-level scope at REPL[80]:1
```

Effectively, we can now ensure that the method is only dispatched when the arguments have the same type. This is one of the few reasons why it is a good idea to use type parameters for function arguments.

Next, we will talk about another reason to use type parameters—extracting type information from the method signature.

Extracting type information from the method signature

Sometimes, we want to find out the parameter type within the method body. This is actually very easy to do. As it turns out, all parameters are also bound as a variable that we can access in the method body itself. The implementation of the standard `eltype` function provides a good example for such usage:

```
eltype(things::AbstractVector{T}) where {T <: Thing} = T
```

We can see that the type parameter `T` is referenced in the body. Let's how it works:

```
julia> eltype([s1, s2])
Spaceship

julia> eltype([a1, a2])
Asteroid

julia> eltype([s1, s2, a1, a2])
Thing
```

In the first call, because all objects in the array have the `Spaceship` type, the `Spaceship` type is returned, and likewise for the second call, where `Asteroid` is returned. The third call returns `Thing` because we have a mixed number of `Spaceship` and `Asteroid` objects. These types can be further examined as follows:

```
julia> typeof([s1, s2])
Array{Spaceship,1}

julia> typeof([a1, a2])
Array{Asteroid,1}

julia> typeof([s1, s2, a1, a2])
Array{Thing,1}
```

In summary, we can build more flexible functions by using type parameters in function definitions. From an expressiveness perspective, each type parameter can cover a whole class of data types. We can also use the same type parameter in multiple arguments to enforce type consistency. Finally, we can easily extract type information directly from the method signature.

Now, let's move on and discuss the last topic of this chapter – interfaces.

Working with interfaces

In this section, we will explore how to design and work with interfaces in Julia. Unlike other mainstream programming languages, Julia does not have a formal way to define interfaces. This informality may make some people a little uneasy. Nonetheless, interfaces do exist and are used extensively in many Julia programs.

Designing and developing interfaces

Interfaces are behavioral contracts. A behavior is defined by a set of functions that operates on one or more specific objects). In Julia, the contract is purely conventional and is not formally specified. To illustrate this concept, let's create a module that contains the logic of taking an object anywhere from the galaxy.

Defining the Vehicle interface

We shall first create a module called `Vehicle`. The purpose of this module is to implement our space-travel logic. As we want to keep this module generic, we will design an interface that any object can implement in order to participate in our space-travel program.

The structure of the module consists of four sections, as indicated by the following embedded comments:

```
module Vehicle
# 1. Export/Imports
# 2. Interface documentation
# 3. Generic definitions for the interface
# 4. Game logic
end # module
```

Let's see how the code is actually written in the module:

1. The first section exports a single function called `go!`:

```
# 1. Export/Imports
export go!
```

2. The second code segment is merely documentation:

```
# 2. Interface documentation
# A vehicle (v) must implement the following functions:
#
# power_on!(v) - turn on the vehicle's engine
```

```
# power_off!(v) - turn off the vehicle's engine
# turn!(v, direction) - steer the vehicle to the specified
direction
# move!(v, distance) - move the vehicle by the specified distance
# position(v) - returns the (x,y) position of the vehicle
```

3. The third code segment contains generic definitions of the functions:

```
# 3. Generic definitions for the interface
function power_on! end
function power_off! end
function turn! end
function move! end
function position end
```

4. Finally, the last code segment contains the space-travel logic:

```
# 4. Game logic

# Returns a travel plan from current position to destination
function travel_path(position, destination)
    return round(π/6, digits=2), 1000 # just a test
end

# Space travel logic
function go!(vehicle, destination)
    power_on!(vehicle)
    direction, distance = travel_path(position(vehicle),
destination)
    turn!(vehicle, direction)
    move!(vehicle, distance)
    power_off!(vehicle)
    nothing
end
```

The `travel_path` function calculates the direction and distance to travel from the current position to the final destination. It is expected to return a tuple. For testing purposes, we are just returning hardcoded values.

The `go!` function expects that the vehicle object being passed in the first argument is some kind of space vehicle. Furthermore, the logic also expects the vehicle to exhibit certain behavior, such as being able to turn on the engine, steer in the right direction, move a certain distance, and so on.

If a client program wants to call the `go!` function, it must pass a type that implements the expected interface as assumed by this logic. But how does one know what functions to implement? Well, it is defined as part of the documentation as spelled out in the comment from the *Interface Documentation* code segment:

```
# A vehicle must implement the following functions:

# power_on!(v) - turn on the vehicle's engine
# power_off!(v) - turn off the vehicle's engine
# turn!(v, direction) - steer the vehicle to the specified direction
# move!(v, distance) - move the vehicle by the specified distance
# position(v) - returns the (x,y) position of the vehicle
```

Another clue is that the required functions are defined in the previous code as empty generic functions—that is, functions without any signature or body:

```
function power_on! end
function power_off! end
function turn! end
function move! end
function position end
```

So far, we have written the interface's contractual requirements as comments in the code. It is generally better to do this as Julia doc strings so that the requirements can be generated and published to an online website or printed as hard copy. We could do something like this for every function specified in the interface:

```
"""
Power on the vehicle so it is ready to go.
"""
function power_on! end
```

The `Vehicle` module is now completed, and as part of the source code, we have set certain expectations. If any object wants to participate in our space-travel program, it must implement the five functions—`power_on!`, `power_off!`, `turn!`, `move!`, and `position`.

Next, we will design a new fighter jet line for the space-travel program!

Implementing FighterJet

Now that we understand what to expect from the `Vehicle` interface, we can develop something that actually implements the interface. We will create a new `FighterJets` module and define the `FighterJet` data type as follows:

```
"FighterJet is a very fast vehicle with powerful weapons."
mutable struct FighterJet

    "power status: true = on, false = off"
    power::Bool

    "current direction in radians"
    direction::Float64

    "current position coordinate (x,y)"
    position::Tuple{Float64, Float64}

end
```

To conform to the `Vehicle` interface defined previously, we must first import the generic functions from the `Vehicle` module and then implement the logic for operating the `FighterJet` vehicle. Here is the code for the `power_on` and `power_off` functions:

```
# Import generic functions
import Vehicle: power_on!, power_off!, turn!, move!, position

# Implementation of Vehicle interface
function power_on!(fj::FighterJet)
    fj.power = true
    println("Powered on: ", fj)
    nothing
end

function power_off!(fj::FighterJet)
    fj.power = false
    println("Powered off: ", fj)
    nothing
end
```

Of course, a real fighter jet may be a bit more involved than just setting a Boolean field to either `true` or `false`. For testing purposes, we also print something to the console so that we know what is happening. Let's also define the function to steer the direction:

```
function turn!(fj::FighterJet, direction)
    fj.direction = direction
    println("Changed direction to ", direction, ": ", fj)
    nothing
end
```

Again, the logic for the `turn!` function here is as simple as changing the direction field and printing some text on the console. The `move!` function is a little more interesting:

```
function move!(fj::FighterJet, distance)
    x, y = fj.position
    dx = round(distance * cos(fj.direction), digits = 2)
    dy = round(distance * sin(fj.direction), digits = 2)
    fj.position = (x + dx, y + dy)
    println("Moved (", dx, ",", dy, "): ", fj)
    nothing
end
```

Here, we have used the trigonometric functions `sin` and `cos` to calculate the new position that the fighter jet will be traveling to. Finally, we must implement the `position` function, which returns the current position of the fighter jet:

```
function position(fj::FighterJet)
    fj.position
end
```

Now that the `FighterJet` type fully implements the interface, we can utilize the game logic as expected. Let's give it a spin by creating a new `FighterJet` object and invoke the `go!` function as follows:

```
julia> using Vehicle, FighterJets

julia> fj = FighterJet(false, 0, (0,0))
FighterJet(false, 0.0, (0.0, 0.0))

julia> go!(fj, :mars)
Powered on: FighterJet(true, 0.0, (0.0, 0.0))
Changed direction to 0.52: FighterJet(true, 0.52, (0.0, 0.0))
Moved (867.82,496.88): FighterJet(true, 0.52, (867.82, 496.88))
Powered off: FighterJet(false, 0.52, (867.82, 496.88))
```

In a nutshell, implementing an interface is a fairly simple task. The key is to understand what functions are required to implement an interface and make sure that the custom data type can support those functions. As a professional developer, we should clearly document the interface functions so that there is no confusion about what needs to be implemented.

At this point, we can consider the interface that we just designed as **hard contracts**. They are hard in the sense that all of the functions specified in our interface must be implemented by any object participating in our space-travel program. In the next section, we will go over **soft contracts**, which correspond to interface functions that may be optional.

Handling soft contracts

Sometimes, certain interface contracts are not absolutely required when a default behavior can be assumed by the interface. The functions that are not mandatory may be referred to as soft contracts.

Let's say we want to add a new function for landing a vehicle. Most vehicles have wheels, but some don't, especially high-tech ones! So, as part of the landing procedure, we must engage the wheels only when necessary.

How do we design a soft contract for an interface? In this case, we can assume that most future vehicles have no wheels and therefore the default behavior does not require engaging the wheels. Here, in the `Vehicle` module, we can add the `engage_wheel!` function to document and provide a default implementation, as follows:

```
# 2. Interface documentation
# A vehicle (v) must implement the following functions:
#
# power_on!(v) - turn on the vehicle's engine
# power_off!(v) - turn off the vehicle's engine
# turn!(v, direction) - steer the vehicle to the specified direction
# move!(v, distance) - move the vehicle by the specified distance
# position(v) - returns the (x,y) position of the vehicle
# engage_wheels!(v) - engage wheels for landing. Optional.

# 3. Generic definitions for the interface
# hard contracts
# ...
# soft contracts
engage_wheels!(args...) = nothing
```

The documentation clearly states that the `engage_wheels!` function is optional. Because of this, rather than providing an empty generic function, we have implemented an actual `engage_wheel!` function that does absolutely nothing and just returns a value of `nothing`. The landing logic is then written as follows:

```
# Landing
function land!(vehicle)
    engage_wheels!(vehicle)
    println("Landing vehicle: ", vehicle)
end
```

Now, if the caller provides a vehicle type that implements the `engage_wheels!` function, then it will be used; otherwise, the call to `engage_wheels!` would invoke the generic function and do nothing.

I will leave it to the reader to complete this exercise by creating another vehicle type that implements the `engage_wheel!` function. (Sorry: the vehicle you develop is probably not very *high-tech* since it has wheels.)

A soft contract is a simple way to provide a default implementation for optional interface functions. Next, we will look into a slightly more formal method to declare whether a data type supports certain interface elements. We will call them *traits*.

Using interface traits

Occasionally, you may encounter a situation where you need to determine whether a data type implements an interface. The information about whether a data type exhibits certain behavior is also called a trait.

How do we implement traits for an interface? In the `Vehicle` module, we can add a new function, as follows:

```
# trait
has_wheels(vehicle) = error("Not implemented.")
```

This default implementation simply raises an error, and that's intentional. This trait function is expected to be implemented by any vehicle data types. In the interface code, the landing function can make use of the trait function for a more refined logic:

```
# Landing (using trait)
function land2!(vehicle)
    has_wheels(vehicle) && engage_wheels!(vehicle)
    println("Landing vehicle: ", vehicle)
end
```

Generally speaking, trait functions just need to return a binary answer, `true` or `false`; however, it is entirely up to the developer how to design the trait. For example, it is perfectly reasonable to define the trait function so that it returns the type of landing gear—`:wheels`, `:slider`, or `:none`.

It is a good idea to define traits as simply as possible. As you may recall, the interface that we implemented for our fighter jet in the previous section requires five functions—`power_on!`, `power_off!`, `move!`, `turn!`, and `position`. From a design perspective, we can create different traits:

- `has_power()`: returns `true` if the vehicle needs to be powered on/off
- `can_move()`: returns `true` if the vehicle is able to move
- `can_turn()`: returns `true` if the vehicle can turn in any direction
- `location_aware()`: returns `true` if the vehicle can keep track of its location

Once we have these small building blocks, we can define more complex traits that are composed of these simple ones. For example, we can define a trait called `smart_vehicle` that supports all of the four traits that we listed. In addition, we can define a `solar_vehicle` trait, which is used for vehicles that rely on solar power and is always on.

Using traits is a very powerful technique to model object behaviors. There are some patterns that are built around how to implement traits in practice. We will discuss these more extensively in `Chapter 5`, *Reusability Patterns.*

At this point, you should feel more comfortable about designing interfaces in Julia. They are relatively simple to understand and develop. While Julia does not provide any formal syntax for interface specification, it is not difficult to come up with our own convention. With the help of traits, we can even implement more dynamic behavior for our objects.

We have now concluded all topics in this chapter.

Summary

In this chapter, we started our journey by discussing how to define functions and make use of various types of function arguments, such as positional arguments, keyword arguments, and variable arguments. We talked about how to use splatting to auto assign the elements of an array or tuple to function arguments. We explored first-class functions by assigning them to variables and passing them around in functional calls. We learned how to create anonymous functions and use the do-syntax to make code more readable.

We then discussed Julia's dispatch mechanism and introduced the concept of multiple dispatch. We realized that ambiguity may exist and so we reviewed the standard tools for detecting ambiguities. We have learned how dispatch is dynamic in nature. We looked at parametric methods and how they could be useful in several use cases, such as enforcing type consistency and extracting type information from the type parameters.

We learned how to design interfaces. We realized that there is no formal language syntax for defining interfaces in Julia, but we also recognize defining interfaces is straightforward and easy to do. We came to know that sometimes it is acceptable to have soft contracts so that the developer does not have to implement all interface functions. Finally, we wrapped up the discussion with the concept of traits and how they can be useful for querying whether a data type implements a specific interface.

In the next chapter, we will discuss two more major features in the Julia language—macros and meta programming. Macros are very useful in creating new syntax that makes the code clean and easy to maintain. Just take a deep breath and keep going!

Questions

1. How are positional arguments different from keyword arguments?
2. What is the difference between splatting and slurping?
3. What is the purpose of using the do-syntax?
4. What tool is available for detecting method ambiguities as related to multiple dispatch?
5. How do you ensure that the same concrete type is passed to a function in a parametric method?
6. How are interfaces implemented without any formal language syntax?
7. How do you implement traits, and how are traits useful?

4
Macros and Metaprogramming Techniques

This chapter will discuss two of the most powerful facilities in the Julia programming language: macros and metaprogramming.

In a nutshell, metaprogramming is a technique for writing code that generates code—that's why it has the prefix *meta*. It may sound esoteric, but it is a fairly common practice in many programming languages today. For example, C compiler uses a preprocessor to read source code and produce new source code, and then the new source code is compiled into a binary executable. For example, you can define a MAX macro, as in `#define MAX(a,b) ((a) > (b) ? (a) : (b))`, and this means that every time we use `MAX(a,b)`, it is replaced with `((a) > (b) ? (a) : (b))`. Note that `MAX(a,b)` is much easier to read than the longer form.

The history of metaprogramming is quite long. As far back as the 1970s, it was already popular among the LISP programming language community. Interestingly, the LISP language is designed in such a way that the source code is structured like data—for example, a function call in LISP looks like `(sumprod x y z)`, where the first element is the name of the function and the rest are arguments. Since it is really just a list of four symbols—`sumprod`, `x`, `y`, and `z`—we can take this code and manipulate it in any way—for example, we can expand it so it calculates both the sum and product of the numbers, so the generated code becomes `(list (+ x y z) (* x y z))`.

You may wonder whether we can just write a function for that. The answer is, yes: in both of the examples that we just looked at, there is no need to use a metaprogramming technique. The examples were there only to illustrate how metaprogramming works. In general, we can say that metaprogramming is not needed 99% of the time; however, there is still that remaining 1% of cases where metaprogramming would be very useful. The first section will explore use cases where we would want to use metaprogramming.

In this chapter, we will learn several metaprogramming facilities in Julia. The following topics will be covered in particular:

- Understanding the need for metaprogramming
- Working with expressions
- Developing macros
- Using generated functions

Technical requirements

The sample source code is located at https://github.com/PacktPublishing/Hands-on-Design-Patterns-and-Best-Practices-with-Julia/tree/master/Chapter04.

The code is tested in a Julia 1.3.0 environment.

Understanding the need for metaprogramming

At the beginning of the chapter, we boldly claimed that metaprogramming is not needed 99% of the time. That is indeed not a made-up number. At the JuliaCon 2019 conference, Professor Steven Johnson from MIT delivered a keynote speech regarding metaprogramming. He did some research about the Julia language's own source code. From his study, Julia version 1.1.0 contains 37,000 methods, 138 macros (0.4%), and 14 generated functions (0.04%). So metaprogramming code comprises less than 1% of Julia's own implementation. While this is just one example of metaprogramming's role in one language, it is representative enough that even the smartest software engineers would not use metaprogramming most of the time.

So the next question is: When do you need to use metaprogramming techniques? Generally speaking, there are several reasons for using such techniques:

1. They may allow a solution to be expressed more concisely and in a way that is easier to understand. Writing code without metaprogramming would otherwise look ugly and be difficult to comprehend.
2. It may reduce the development time because the source code can be generated rather than written out; boilerplate code, especially, can be eliminated.
3. It may improve performance because the code is spelled out rather than executed via other higher-level programming constructs, such as looping.

We will now look at some examples of how metaprogramming is used in the real world.

Measuring performance with the @time macro

Julia comes with a useful macro called @time, which measures the time required to execute code. For example, to measure how long it takes to calculate the sum of 10 million random numbers, we can do the following:

```
julia> @time sum(rand(10_000_000))
  0.298792 seconds (171.69 k allocations: 85.020 MiB, 8.64% gc time)
5.000929141615314e6
```

The macro works by inserting code around the code that is being measured. The resulting code may look something like the following:

```
begin
    t1 = now()
    result = sum(rand(10_000_000))
    t2 = now()
    elapsed = t2 - t1
    println("It took ", elapsed)
    result
end
```

The new code uses the now() function to take the current time. Then, it executes the user-provided code and captures the result. It takes the current time again, calculates the elapsed time, prints the timing information to the console, and then it returns the result.

Can this be done without metaprogramming? Perhaps we can give that a try. Let's define a function called timeit as follows:

```
function timeit(func)
    t1 = now()
    result = func()
    t2 = now()
    elapsed = t2 - t1
    println("It took ", elapsed)
    result
end
```

To use this timing facility, we need to wrap the expression in a function.

```
julia> mycode() = sum(rand(10_000_000))
mycode (generic function with 1 method)

julia> timeit(mycode)
It took 252 milliseconds
5.000779720648706e6
```

This function works fairly well, but the problem is that we have to wrap the code in a separate function before we can measure its performance, which is a hugely inconvenient thing to do. Because of this, we can conclude that having a `@time` macro is more appropriate.

Unrolling loops

Another use case of macros is to unroll loops into repeating code fragments. Loop unrolling is a performance optimization technique. The premise behind it is that there is always some overhead that is required to execute code in a loop. The reason is that, every time an iteration is finished, the loop must check for a condition and decide whether it should exit or continue with the next iteration. Now, if we know exactly how many times the loop needs to run the code, then we can *unroll* it by writing out the code in a repeated fashion.

Consider a simple loop as follows:

```
for i in 1:3
    println("hello: ", i)
end
```

We can unroll the loop into three lines of code that do the exact same job:

```
println("hello: ", 1)
println("hello: ", 2)
println("hello: ", 3)
```

But it would be quite a boring and mundane task to have to unroll loops manually. Furthermore, the amount of work grows linearly with the number of iterations required in the loop. With the help of `Unroll.jl`, we can define a function using the `@unroll` macro, as follows:

```
using Unrolled

@unroll function hello(xs)
    @unroll for i in xs
```

```
        println("hello: ", i)
    end
end
```

The code looks as clean as it should be, and the `@unroll` macro is inserted in front of the function as well as the `for` loop. First, we should check that the code works properly:

```
julia> seq = tuple(1:3...)
(1, 2, 3)

julia> hello(seq)
hello: 1
hello: 2
hello: 3
```

Now, we should question whether the `@unroll` macro actually did anything. A good way to check whether the loop was unrolled is to use the `@code_lowered` macro:

```
julia> @code_lowered(hello(seq))
CodeInfo(
    @ /Users/tomkwong/.julia/packages/Unrolled/26uDc/src/Unrolled.jl:128 within
 `hello`
   ┌ @ /Users/tomkwong/.julia/packages/Unrolled/26uDc/src/Unrolled.jl:128 withi
n `macro expansion' @ REPL[11]:2 @ /Users/tomkwong/.julia/packages/Unrolled/26u
Dc/src/Unrolled.jl:47
1 ─│       i@_3 = Base.getindex(xs, 1)
   │       Main.println("hello: ", i@_3)              ◄──── No loop!
   │       i@_4 = Base.getindex(xs, 2)
   │       Main.println("hello: ", i@_4)
   │       i@_5 = Base.getindex(xs, 3)
   │       Main.println("hello: ", i@_5)
   │ @ /Users/tomkwong/.julia/packages/Unrolled/26uDc/src/Unrolled.jl:128 withi
n `macro expansion' @ REPL[11]:2 @ /Users/tomkwong/.julia/packages/Unrolled/26u
Dc/src/Unrolled.jl:48
   │   %7 = Main.nothing
   │ @ /Users/tomkwong/.julia/packages/Unrolled/26uDc/src/Unrolled.jl:128 withi
n `macro expansion'
   └       return %7
   └
)
```

The lowered code clearly contains three `println` statements rather than a single `for` loop.

What is lowered code? The Julia compiler must go through a series of processes before source code is compiled to binaries. The very first step is to parse the code into an **abstract syntax tree** (**AST**) format, which we will learn about in the next session. After that, it goes through a *lowering* process to expand the macros and convert the code into concrete execution steps.

Now that we have seen some examples and know the power of metaprogramming, we shall move forward and learn how to create these macros ourselves.

Working with expressions

Julia represents the source code of any runnable program as a tree structure. This is called an **abstract syntax tree** (**AST**). It is referred to as *abstract* as the tree only captures the structure of the code rather than the real syntax.

For example, the expression x + y can be represented with a tree where the parent node identifies itself as a function call and the child nodes include the operator function + and the x and y arguments. The following is an implementation of this:

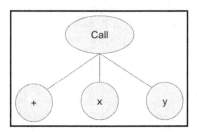

The slightly more complex expression x + 2y + 1 would look like the following diagram. While it was written with two addition operators, the expression is parsed into a single function call to the + function, for which it takes three arguments—x, 2y, and 1. Because 2y is itself an expression, it can be seen as a subtree of the main abstract syntax tree:

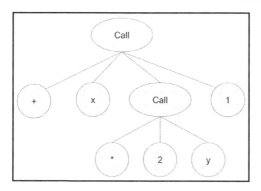

The Julia compiler must first parse source code into an abstract syntax tree, and then it can perform additional transformations and analysis, such as expanding macros, type checking, type inference, and eventually translating the code into machine code.

Experimenting with the parser

Because the abstract syntax tree is just a data structure, we can examine it directly within the Julia REPL environment. Let's just start with a simple expression: x + y:

```
julia> Meta.parse("x + y")
:(x + y)
```

In Julia, every expression is represented as an `Expr` object. We can create an `Expr` object by just parsing a string with the `Meta.parse` function.

Here, the expression object is displayed with a syntax that resembles the original source code so that it is easier to read. We can confirm that the object has the type of `Expr` as follows:

```
julia> Meta.parse("x + y") |> typeof
Expr
```

In order to view the abstract syntax tree, we can use the dump function to print the structure:

```
julia> Meta.parse("x + y") |> dump
Expr
  head: Symbol call
  args: Array{Any}((3,))
    1: Symbol +
    2: Symbol x
    3: Symbol y
```

In Julia, every expression is represented by a head node and an array of arguments.

In this case, the head node contains just a call symbol. The args array contains the + operator and two variables, x and y. Note that everything here is a symbol—that's OK because we are examining the source code itself, which is understandably just a tree of symbols.

Since we have had so much fun here, let's try a few other expressions.

Single-variable expressions

One of the simplest expressions is just a reference to a variable. You can try to parse a numeric or string literal and see what it returns:

```
julia> Meta.parse("x") |> dump
Symbol x
```

Function calls with keyword arguments

Let's try something a little more complex. We will examine a function call that takes a single positional argument and two keyword arguments. Here, we use triple quotes around the code so that we can handle the double quotes inside it properly:

```
julia> Meta.parse("""open("/tmp/test.txt", read = true, write = true)""")
  |> dump
Expr
  head: Symbol call
  args: Array{Any}((4,))
    1: Symbol open
    2: String "/tmp/test.txt"
    3: Expr
      head: Symbol kw
      args: Array{Any}((2,))
        1: Symbol read
        2: Bool true
    4: Expr
      head: Symbol kw
      args: Array{Any}((2,))
        1: Symbol write
        2: Bool true
```

Note that a function call has the `call` symbol as the head node of the expression. Also, the keyword arguments are represented as subexpressions, each with a head node of `kw` and a two-element array for the name and value of the argument.

Nested functions

We may wonder how Julia parses code when functions are nested. We can pick a simple example here that takes the sine of `x+1` and then takes the cosine of the result. The abstract syntax tree is shown as follows:

```
julia> Meta.parse("cos(sin(x+1))") |> dump
Expr
  head: Symbol call
  args: Array{Any}((2,))
    1: Symbol cos
    2: Expr
      head: Symbol call
      args: Array{Any}((2,))
        1: Symbol sin
        2: Expr
          head: Symbol call
          args: Array{Any}((3,))
            1: Symbol +
            2: Symbol x
            3: Int64 1
```

Here, we can clearly see the tree structure. The outermost function, cos, contains a single argument, which is an expression node with a call to the sin function. This expression in turn contains a single argument, which is another expression node with a call to the + operator function with two arguments—the x variable and a value of 1. Now, let's continue with our work on expressions.

Constructing expression objects manually

As an expression is just a data structure, we can easily construct them programmatically. Understanding how to do this is essential for metaprogramming, which involves creating new code structures on the fly.

The Expr constructor has the following signature:

```
Expr(head::Symbol, args...)
```

The head node always carries a symbol. The arguments just contain whatever the head node expects—for example, the simple expression x + y can be created as follows:

```
julia> Expr(:call, :+, :x, :y)
:(x + y)
```

Of course, we can always create a nested expression if we want to:

```
julia> Expr(:call, :sin, Expr(:call, :+, :x, :y))
:(sin(x + y))
```

At this point, you may wonder whether there is an easier way to create expressions without having to construct Expr objects manually. For sure, it can be done as shown below:

```
julia> ex = :(x + y)
:(x + y)

julia> dump(ex)
Expr
  head: Symbol call
  args: Array{Any}((3,))
    1: Symbol +
    2: Symbol x
    3: Symbol y
```

Basically, we can wrap any expression with : (on the left and) on the right. The code that sits inside will not be evaluated, but will instead be parsed into an expression object; however, this way of quoting only works with a single expression—if you try to do this with multiple expressions, an error will be displayed, as shown in the following code:

```
julia> :(x = 1
         y = 2)
ERROR: syntax: missing comma or ) in argument list
```

It does not work because multiple expressions should be wrapped with `begin` and `end` keywords. So it would be fine if we entered the following code block:

```
julia> :(begin
            x = 1
            y = 2
          end)
quote
    #= REPL[39]:2 =#
    x = 1
    #= REPL[39]:3 =#
    y = 2
end
```

The result is a little interesting. As you can see, the code is now wrapped within a `quote`/`end` block rather than a `begin`/`end` block. It actually makes sense because a quoted expression is being displayed rather than the original source code. Remember, this is the abstract syntax tree rather than the original code.

It also turns out that `quote`/`end` can be used directly to create expressions:

```
julia> quote
            x = 1
            y = 2
          end
quote
    #= REPL[40]:2 =#
    x = 1
    #= REPL[40]:3 =#
    y = 2
end
```

We have now learned how to parse source code into an expression object. Next, we will look into more complex expressions so that we are more familiar with the basic code structure of Julia programs.

Playing with more complex expressions

As we said before, any valid Julia program can be represented as an abstract syntax tree. Now that we have the building blocks to create expression objects, let's examine a few more constructs and see what expression objects look like for more complex programs.

Assignment

We will see how it works for assignments first. Consider the following code:

```
julia> :(x = 1 + 1) |> dump
Expr
  head: Symbol =
  args: Array{Any}((2,))
    1: Symbol x
    2: Expr
      head: Symbol call
      args: Array{Any}((3,))
        1: Symbol +
        2: Int64 1
        3: Int64 1
```

From the preceding code, we can see that the variable assignment has a head node of = and two arguments—the variable to be assigned (x, in this case) and another expression object.

Code blocks

A code block is enclosed by the `begin` and `end` keywords. Let's examine what the abstract syntax tree looks like.

```
julia> :(begin
             println("hello")
             println("world")
           end) |> dump
Expr
  head: Symbol block
  args: Array{Any}((4,))
    1: LineNumberNode                    line number
      line: Int64 2                          for
      file: Symbol REPL[43]              debugging
    2: Expr                               purpose
      head: Symbol call
      args: Array{Any}((2,))
        1: Symbol println
        2: String "hello"
    3: LineNumberNode                    Function calls
      line: Int64 3
      file: Symbol REPL[43]
    4: Expr
      head: Symbol call
      args: Array{Any}((2,))
        1: Symbol println
        2: String "world"
```

The head node just contains a `block` symbol. When there are multiple lines in the block, the abstract syntax tree also includes line number nodes. In this example, there is a `LineNumberNode` with line 2 preceding the first call to `println`. Likewise, there is another `LineNumberNode` with line 3 preceding the second call to `println`. The `LineNumberNode` nodes do not do anything, but they are useful for stack traces and debugging.

Conditional

Next up, we'll explore conditional constructs, such as `if-else-end`. Refer to the following code:

```
julia> :(if 2 > 1
            "good"
         else
            "bad"
         end) |> dump
Expr
  head: Symbol if
  args: Array{Any}((3,))
    1: Expr
      head: Symbol call
      args: Array{Any}((3,))
        1: Symbol >          Condition
        2: Int64 2
        3: Int64 1
    2: Expr
      head: Symbol block
      args: Array{Any}((2,))
        1: LineNumberNode          Path #1
          line: Int64 2
          file: Symbol REPL[45]
        2: String "good"
    3: Expr
      head: Symbol block
      args: Array{Any}((2,))          Path #2
        1: LineNumberNode
          line: Int64 4
          file: Symbol REPL[45]
        2: String "bad"
```

The head node contains the `if` symbol. There are three arguments—an expression for the condition, a block expression when the condition is satisfied, and another block expression when the condition is not satisfied.

Loop

We will now move on to looping constructs. Consider a simple `for` loop, as follows:

```
julia> :(for i in 1:5
            println("hello world")
          end) |> dump
Expr
  head: Symbol for
  args: Array{Any}((2,))
    1: Expr
      head: Symbol =
      args: Array{Any}((2,))
        1: Symbol i            ◀──────────  Loop variable
        2: Expr
          head: Symbol call
          args: Array{Any}((3,))
            1: Symbol :
            2: Int64 1          ◀──────────  range
            3: Int64 5
    2: Expr
      head: Symbol block
      args: Array{Any}((2,))
        1: LineNumberNode
          line: Int64 2
          file: Symbol REPL[47]
        2: Expr
          head: Symbol call
          args: Array{Any}((2,))   Function call to println
            1: Symbol println
            2: String "hello world"
```

The head node contains a `for` symbol. There are two arguments: the first one contains the expression about the loop and the second one contains a block expression.

Function definition

Next, we will see the structure for a function definition. Consider the following code:

```
julia> :(function foo(x; y = 1)
            return x + y
        end) |> dump
Expr
  head: Symbol function
  args: Array{Any}((2,))
    1: Expr
      head: Symbol call
      args: Array{Any}((3,))
        1: Symbol foo          Function name
        2: Expr
          head: Symbol parameters  ◄─── Keyword
          args: Array{Any}((1,))           arguments
            1: Expr
              head: Symbol kw
              args: Array{Any}((2,))
                1: Symbol y
                2: Int64 1
        3: Symbol x          ◄─────── Arguments
    2: Expr
      head: Symbol block
      args: Array{Any}((2,))
        1: LineNumberNode
          line: Int64 2
          file: Symbol REPL[48]
        2: Expr
          head: Symbol return    Return value
          args: Array{Any}((1,))
            1: Expr
              head: Symbol call    Function call
              args: Array{Any}((3,))
                1: Symbol +
                2: Symbol x
                3: Symbol y
```

The head node contains a `function` symbol. Then, the first argument contains a `call` expression with the arguments. The second argument is just a block expression.

 The call expression may seem a little odd because we have seen a similar expression object when a function is being called. This is normal because we are currently working at the syntax level. The syntax for function definition is indeed quite similar to the function call itself.

By now, we have seen enough examples. There are obviously many more code constructs that we have not explored. You are encouraged to use the same technique to examine other code structures. Understanding how the abstract syntax tree is structured is essential to writing good metaprogramming code. Next, we will see how we can evaluate these expressions.

Evaluating expressions

We have looked at creating expression objects in great detail. But how are they useful? Remember that an expression object is just an abstract syntax tree representation of a Julia program. At this point, we can ask the compiler to continue translating the expression into executable code and then run the program.

Expression objects can be evaluated by calling the `eval` function. Essentially, the Julia compiler will go through the rest of the compilation process and run the program. Now, let's start a fresh, new REPL and run the following code:

```julia
julia> eval(:(x = 1))
1
```

Clearly, it's just a simple assignment. We can see that the x variable is now defined in the current environment:

```julia
julia> x
1
```

Note that the evaluation of the expression actually happens in the global scope. We can prove this by running `eval` from within a function:

```julia
julia> function foo()
           eval(:(y = 1))
       end
foo (generic function with 1 method)

julia> foo()
1

julia> y
1
```

This is not an unimportant observation! At first glance, we may have expected the y variable to be assigned inside the foo function; however, the variable assignment happened in the global scope instead, so the y variable was defined in the current environment as a side-effect.

 More precisely, the expression is evaluated in the current module. Since we are testing in the REPL, the evaluation was done in the current module, called Main. The expression is designed as such because eval is commonly used for code generation, which can be useful in defining variables or functions within the module.

Next, we will learn how to create expression objects more easily.

Interpolating variables in expressions

It is quite simple to construct expressions from a quote block. But what if we want to dynamically create expressions? This can be done using *interpolation*, which allows us to insert variable values into the expression object with an easy syntax. Interpolation in an expression is very similar to the way that variables can be interpolated in a string. The following screenshot shows an example:

```
julia> x = 2
2

julia> :(sqrt($x))
:(sqrt(2))
```

As expected, the value of 2 is correctly substituted in the expression. Note that splatting is also supported, as shown below:

```
julia> v = [1, 2, 3]
3-element Array{Int64,1}:
 1
 2
 3

julia> quote
            max($(v...))
        end
quote
    #= REPL[69]:2 =#
    max(1, 2, 3)
end
```

We must make sure that the variable that includes the `splatting` operator is interpolated in this case. If we had forgotten to put the parentheses around `v...`, then we would have had a very different result:

```
julia> quote
            max($v...)
        end
quote
        #= REPL[57]:2 =#
        max([1, 2, 3]...)
end
```

Here, splatting does not actually occur during interpolation into the expression. Instead, the splatting operator now becomes part of the expression, so splatting will not occur until the expression is evaluated.

> The order of precedence in an expression such as `$v...` is somewhat unclear. Is the `v` variable bound to the interpolation operation before or after the splatting operation? In a situation like this, it is best to use parentheses around whatever we want to interpolate. As we want the interpolation to happen fully, the syntax should be `$(v...)`. In situations where splatting needs to happen at runtime, we could write `$(v)...` instead.

Interpolation is an important concept for writing macros. We will see more of its usage later in this chapter. Next, we will see how to handle construct expressions with symbol values.

Using QuoteNode for symbols

Symbols are quite special when they appear in expressions. They may appear in the head node of an expression object—for example, the `=` symbol in a variable assignment expression. They may also appear in the arguments of an expression object, in which case they would represent a variable:

```
julia> :(x = y) |> dump
Expr
  head: Symbol =
  args: Array{Any}((2,))
    1: Symbol x
    2: Symbol y
```

Since symbols are already used to represent variables, how would we assign an actual symbol to a variable? To figure out how this works, we can use the same trick that we have learned so far—using the `dump` function to examine the expression object for such a statement:

```
julia> :( x = :hello ) |> dump
Expr
  head: Symbol =
  args: Array{Any}((2,))
    1: Symbol x
    2: QuoteNode
      value: Symbol hello
```

As we can see, an actual symbol must be enclosed in a `QuoteNode` object. Now that we know what is needed, we should try to interpolate an actual symbol into an expression object. The way to achieve this is to create a `QuoteNode` object manually and use the interpolation technique as usual:

```
julia> sym = QuoteNode(:hello)
:(:hello)

julia> :( x = $sym)
:(x = :hello)
```

A common mistake is when you forget to create `QuoteNode`. In this case, the expression object will misinterpret the symbol and treat it as a variable reference. Obviously, the result is very different, and it will not work properly:

```
julia> sym = :hello
:hello

julia> :( x = $sym)
:(x = hello)
```

Not using `QuoteNode` would generate code that assigns the value of one variable to another. In this case, the variable x will be assigned with a value from variable `hello`.

Understanding how `QuoteNode` works is essential creating expressions on the fly. It is common for programmers to interpolate symbols into an existing expression. So next, we will look at how to work with nested expressions.

Interpolating in nested expressions

It is possible to have a quoted expression that contains another quoted expression. This is not a very common practice, unless the programmer needs to write meta-metaprograms. Nonetheless, we should still learn about how to interpolate in such a situation.

First, let's recap what a single-level expression looks like:

```
julia> :(x = 1 + 1) |> dump
Expr
  head: Symbol =
  args: Array{Any}((2,))
    1: Symbol x
    2: Expr
      head: Symbol call
      args: Array{Any}((3,))
        1: Symbol +
        2: Int64 1
        3: Int64 1
```

We can wrap the quoted expression with another quote block in order to see what the structure of a nested expression looks like:

```
julia> :( :( x = 1 ) ) |> dump
Expr
  head: Symbol quote
  args: Array{Any}((1,))
    1: Expr
      head: Symbol =
      args: Array{Any}((2,))
        1: Symbol x
        2: Int64 1
```

Now, let's try to interpolate in such an expression:

```
julia> v = 2
2

julia> :( :( x = $v ) ) |> dump
Expr
  head: Symbol quote
  args: Array{Any}((1,))
    1: Expr
      head: Symbol =
      args: Array{Any}((2,))
        1: Symbol x
        2: Expr
          head: Symbol $
          args: Array{Any}((1,))
            1: Symbol v
```

As we can see, the 2 value did not get into the expression. The expression structure is also entirely different from what we had expected. The solution is to just interpolate the variable twice instead by using two $ signs:

```
julia> :( :( x = $($v) ) )
:($(Expr(:quote, :(x = $(Expr(:$, 2)))))))
```

In general, it is probably not much fun to interpolate more than one-level deep as the logic becomes difficult to work out. It can be useful, however, if you need to generate code for macros. I would definitely not suggest that you go more than two-levels deep and write meta-meta-metaprograms!

By now, you should be more familiar with, and comfortable working with, expressions. From the Julia REPL, it is quite easy to see how an expression is structured as represented as an `Expr` object. You should be able to construct new expressions and interpolate values inside; these are essential skills that will be required for metaprogramming.

In the next section, we will look into a powerful metaprogramming feature in Julia—macros.

Developing macros

Now that we understand how source code is represented as abstract syntax trees, we can start doing more interesting things by writing macros. In this section, we will learn what macros are and how to work with them.

What are macros?

Macros are functions that accept expressions, manipulate them, and return a new expression. This is best understood with a diagram:

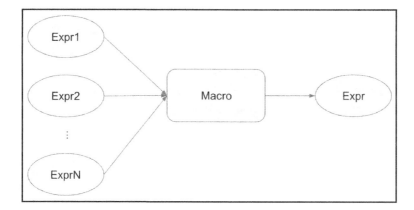

As we know, expressions are just abstract syntax tree representations of source code. So the macro facility in Julia allows you to take any source code and generate new source code. The resulting expression is then executed as if the source code was written directly in place.

At this point, you may wonder why we cannot use regular functions to achieve the same thing. Why could we not write a function that takes expressions, generates a new expression, and then executes the resulting expression?

There are two main reasons:

- Macro expansion happens during compilation. This means that the macro is only executed once from where it is used—for example, when a macro is called from a function, the macro is executed at the time that the function is defined so that the function can be compiled.
- The resulting expression from a macro can be executed within the current scope. At runtime, there is no other way to execute any dynamic code within the function itself because the function, by definition, is already compiled. So, the only way to evaluate any expression is to do so in the global scope.

By the end of this chapter, you should have a better understanding of how macros work and how they differ from functions.

As we now understand what macros are, we will now continue our journey by writing our first macro.

Writing our first macro

Macros are defined in a similar way to how functions are defined, except that the `macro` keyword is used instead of the `function` keyword.

We should also keep in mind that a macro must return expressions. Let's create our first macro. This macro returns an expression object that contains a `for` loop, as follows:

```
macro hello()
    return :(
    for i in 1:3
        println("hello world")
    end
    )
end
```

Invoking the macro is as easy as calling it with the @ prefix. Refer to the following code:

Unlike functions, macros may be called without using parentheses. So we can just do the following:

Fantastic! We have now written our first macro. While it does not look very exciting, because the code being generated is just a static piece of code, we have learned how to define macros and run them.

Next, we will learn how to pass arguments to macros.

Passing literal arguments

Just like functions, macros can also take arguments. In fact, taking an argument is the most common occurrence for a macro. The simplest type of argument is literals, such as numbers, symbols, and strings.

In order to utilize these arguments in the returned expression, we can use the interpolation technique that we learned in the last section. Consider the following code:

```
macro hello(n)
    return :(
    for i in 1:$n
        println("hello world")
    end
    )
end
```

The `hello` macro takes a single argument, n, which is interpolated into the expression when the macro is run. As before, we can just invoke the macro as follows:

```
julia> @hello(2)
hello world
hello world
```

As we learned earlier, parentheses are not required, so we can also call the macro as follows:

```julia
julia> @hello 2
hello world
hello world
```

You can try a similar exercise with string or symbol arguments. Passing literals is easy to understand because it works in the same way as functions. But there is indeed a subtle difference between macros and functions, which we will discuss in detail in the following section.

Passing expression arguments

It is important to emphasize that macro arguments are passed as expressions rather than values. It may look confusing for beginners because macros are invoked similarly to functions, but the behavior is completely different.

Let's make sure that we fully understand what this means. When calling a function with a variable, the value of the variable is passed into the function. Consider the following sample code for a showme function:

```julia
julia> a = 1; b = "hello"; c = :hello;

julia> function showme(x)
           @show x
       end
showme (generic function with 1 method)

julia> showme(a);
x = 1

julia> showme(b);
x = "hello"

julia> showme(c);
x = :hello
```

Now, let's create a `@showme` macro that does nothing but display the argument in the console. We can then compare the results with the preceding code:

```julia
julia> macro showme(x)
              @show x
       end
@showme (macro with 1 method)

julia> @showme(a);
x = :a

julia> @showme(b);
x = :b

julia> @showme(c);
x = :c
```

As we can see, the results from running a macro are totally different than those we get from calling a function. The function argument x really only sees an expression from where the macro was called. From the diagram at the beginning of this section, we can see that macros are supposed to take in expressions and return a single expression as a result. They do not know the value of the arguments as they work at the syntax level.

As we will see in the next section, expressions can even be manipulated when the macro is run. Let's go!

Understanding the macro expansion process

By convention, every macro must return an expression. The process of taking one or more expressions and returning a new one is called **macro expansion**. Sometimes, it helps to see the expression being returned without actually running the code. We can use the `@macroexpand` macro for that purpose. Let's try to use it for the `@hello` macro that we defined earlier in this section:

```julia
julia> @macroexpand @hello 2
:(for var"#67#i" = 1:2
        #= REPL[84]:4 =#
        Main.println("hello world")
    end)
```

There are several things to note from this output:

- The i variable was renamed rather oddly: #67#i. This is done by the Julia compiler to ensure *hygiene*, which we will discuss later in this chapter. Macro hygiene is an important characteristic to keep in mind so that the code being generated does not conflict with other code.
- A comment was inserted into the loop that contains source file and line number information. This is a useful part of the expression when a debugger is used.
- The function call to println is bound to the one in the current environment, Main. This make sense because println is part of the Core package and is automatically brought into scope for every Julia program.

So when does macro expansion happen? Let's go over that next.

Timing of macro expansion

In the REPL, any macro is expanded as soon as we invoke it. Interestingly, when a function containing the macro is defined, the macro is expanded as part of the function definition process.

We can see this in action by developing a simple @identity macro that returns whatever expression is passed into it. Right before the expression is returned, we just dump the object to the screen. The code for the @identity macro is as follows:

```
macro identity(ex)
    dump(ex)
    return ex
end
```

Since this macro returns the same expression that was passed, it should end up executing the original source code that follows the macro.

Now, let's define a function that uses the `@identity` macro:

```
julia> function foo()
            return @identity 1 + 2 + 3
       end
Expr
  head: Symbol call
  args: Array{Any}((4,))
    1: Symbol +
    2: Int64 1
    3: Int64 2
    4: Int64 3
foo (generic function with 1 method)
```

Clearly, the compiler has figured out that the macro is being used in the definition of the `foo` function and, in order to compile the `foo` function, it must understand what the `@identity` macro does. So it expanded the macro and baked that into the function definition. During the macro expansion process, the expression was displayed.

If we use the `@code_lowered` macro against the `foo` function, we can see that the expanded code is now in the body of the `foo` function:

```
julia> @code_lowered foo()
CodeInfo(
1 — %1 = 1 + 2 + 3
  └         return %1
)
```

During development, the programmer may change the definitions of functions, macros, and so on frequently. Because macros are expanded when functions are defined, it is important to redefine the function again if any of the macros being used have been changed; otherwise, the function may continue to use the code generated from the prior macro definition.

The `@macroexpand` utility is an indispensable tool for developing macros, and in particular, is most useful for debugging purposes.

Next, we will try to be a little more creative by manipulating expressions in macros.

Manipulating expressions

Macros are powerful because they allow expressions to be manipulated during the macro expansion process. This is a tremendously useful technique, especially for code generation and designing domain-specific languages. Let's go over some examples to get a taste of what is possible.

Example 1 – Making a new expression

Let's start with a simple one. Suppose that we want to create a macro called `@squared` that takes an expression and just squares it. In other words, if we run `@squared(x)`, then it should be translated into `x * x`:

```
macro squared(ex)
    return :($(ex) * $(ex))
end
```

At first glance, it seems to work fine when we run it from the REPL:

```
julia> @squared 3
9
```

But this macro has a problem with the execution context. The best way to illustrate the problem is by defining a function that uses the macro. So let's define a `foo` function, as follows:

```
function foo()
    x = 2
    return @squared x
end
```

Now, when we call the function, we get the following error:

```
julia> foo()
ERROR: UndefVarError: x not defined
```

Why is that? It is because, during the macro expansion, the x symbol refers to the variable in the module rather than the local variable in the foo function. We can confirm this by using the @code_lowered macro:

```
julia> @code_lowered foo()
CodeInfo(
1 ─        x = 2
│    %2 = Main.x * Main.x
└──       return %2
)
```

Obviously, our intention was to square the local x variable rather than Main.x. The easy fix to this problem is to use the esc function during interpolation in order to place the expression directly in the syntax tree without letting the compiler resolve it. The following is how it can be done:

```
macro squared(ex)
    return :($(esc(ex)) * $(esc(ex)))
end
```

Since the macro was expanded earlier, before foo was defined, we need to define the foo function once again, as follows, for this updated macro to take effect. Alternatively, you can start a new REPL and define the @squared macro and foo function again. Here we go:

```
julia> function foo()
           x = 2
           return @squared x
       end
foo (generic function with 1 method)

julia> foo()
4
```

The foo function works correctly now.

From this example, we have learned how to create a new expression using the interpolation technique. We have also learned that the interpolated variable needs to be escaped using the esc function to avoid it being resolved by the compiler to the global scope.

Example 2 - Tweaking the abstract syntax tree

Let's say we want to design a macro called `@compose_twice` that takes a simple function call expression and calls the same function again with the result—for example, if we run `@compose_twice sin(x)`, then it should be translated to `sin(sin(x))`.

Before we write the macro, let's first get familiar with the abstract syntax tree of the expression:

```
julia> :(sin(x)) |> dump
Expr
  head: Symbol call
  args: Array{Any}((2,))
    1: Symbol sin
    2: Symbol x
```

How does it look for `sin(sin(x))`? Refer to the following:

```
julia> :(sin(sin(x))) |> dump
Expr
  head: Symbol call
  args: Array{Any}((2,))
    1: Symbol sin
    2: Expr
      head: Symbol call
      args: Array{Any}((2,))
        1: Symbol sin
        2: Symbol x
```

No surprise here. The second argument of the top-level call is just another expression that looks like what we saw previously.

We can write the macro as follows:

```
macro compose_twice(ex)
    @assert ex.head == :call
    @assert length(ex.args) == 2
    me = copy(ex)
    ex.args[2] = me
    return ex
end
```

The first two `@assert` statements are used to ensure that the expression represents a function call that takes a single argument. As we want to replace the argument with a similar expression, we just make a copy of the current expression object and assign it to `ex.args[2]`. The macro then returns the resulting expression for evaluation.

We can verify that the macro is working correctly:

```
julia> @compose_twice(sin(1)) == sin(sin(1))
true
```

As you can see, we can translate the source code by manipulating the abstract syntax tree directly rather than interpolating variables into a nice-looking expression.

By now, you can probably appreciate the power of metaprogramming. Compared to using interpolation, manipulating an expression directly is not as easy to understand because the resulting expression is not represented in the code; however, the ability to manipulate expressions provides the ultimate flexibility in translating source code.

Next up, we will go over an important feature of metaprogramming—macro hygiene.

Understanding macro hygiene

Macro hygiene refers to the ability to keep macro-generated code clean. It is referred to as hygiene because the generated code does not get polluted by other parts of the code.

Note that many other programming languages do not provide such a guarantee. The following is a C program that contains a macro called `SWAP`, which is used to exchange the value of two variables:

```c
#include <stdio.h>

#define SWAP(a,b) temp=a; a=b; b=temp;

int main(int argc, char *argv[])
{
    int a = 1;
    int temp = 2;

    SWAP(a,temp);
    printf("a=%d, temp=%d\n", a, temp);
}
```

However, running this C program yields an incorrect result:

```
$ gcc swap.c
$ ./a.out
a=1, temp=1
```

It did not swap the a and temp variables properly because the temp variable is also used as a temporary variable in the body of the macro.

Let's go back to Julia. Consider the following macro, which just runs an ex expression and repeats it n times:

```
macro ntimes(n, ex)
    quote
        times = $(esc(n))
        for i in 1:times
            $(esc(ex))
        end
    end
end
```

Since the times variable is used in the returned expression, what would happen if the same variable name is already used in the call site? Let's try this sample code, which defines a times variable before the macro call and prints the value of the same variable after the macro call:

```
function foo()
    times = 0
    @ntimes 3 println("hello world")
    println("times = ", times)
end
```

If the macro expander took it literally, then the times variable would be modified to 3 after the macro call; however, we can see it working properly in the following code:

```
julia> foo()
hello world
hello world
hello world
times = 0
```

It works because the macro system is able to maintain hygiene by renaming the `times` variable to something different so that there is no conflict. Where is the magic? Well, let's take a look at the expanded code using `@macroexpand`:

```
julia> @macroexpand(@ntimes 3 println("hello world"))
quote
    #= REPL[12]:3 =#
    var"#44#times" = 3
    #= REPL[12]:4 =#
    for var"#45#i" = 1:var"#44#times"
        #= REPL[12]:5 =#
        println("hello world")
    end
end
```

Here, we can see that the `times` variable has turned into `#44#times`. The loop variable `i` has also turned into `#45#i`. These variable names are dynamically generated by the compiler to ensure that macro-generated code does not conflict with other user-written code.

Macro hygiene is an essential feature for macros to function correctly. There is nothing that the programmer needs to do: Julia automatically provides the guarantee.

Next, we will look into a different kind of macro that powers nonstandard string literals.

Developing nonstandard string literals

There is a special kind of macro for defining nonstandard string literals, which look like a literal string but instead a macro is called when it is referenced.

A good example would be Julia's regular expression literal—for example, `r"^hello"`. It is not a standard string literal because of the `r` prefix in front of the double quote. Let's first check the data type of such a literal. We can see that a `Regex` object is created from the string:

```
julia> typeof(r"^hello")
Regex
```

We can also create our own nonstandard string literals. Let's try to work through a fun example together here.

Suppose that, for development purposes, we want to conveniently create sample data frames with different types of columns. The syntax for doing so is a little bit tedious:

```
julia> using DataFrames

julia> DataFrame(x1 = rand(Float64, 100000), x2 = rand(Int16, 100000))
100000×2 DataFrame
 Row │ x1        │ x2     │
     │ Float64   │ Int16  │

 1     │ 0.153125 │ -26112 │
 2     │ 0.516002 │ 19489  │

 99998  │ 0.138176 │ 14862  │
 99999  │ 0.114268 │ -24262 │
 100000 │ 0.57595  │ -9610  │
```

Imagine that we occasionally need to create tens of columns with different data types. The code for creating such a data frame would be very long, and as a programmer, I would be extremely bored typing that all out. So we could design a string literal so that it contains the specification for constructing such a data frame—let's call it a `ndf` (numerical data frame) literal.

The specification on `ndf` just needs to encode the desired number of rows and column types. For instance, the literal `ndf"100000:f64,i16"` can be used to represent the preceding sample data frame, where 100,000 rows are needed, with two columns labeled as the `Float64` and `Int16` columns.

To implement this feature, we just define a macro called `@ndf_str`. The macro takes a string literal and creates the desired data frame accordingly. The following is one way to implement the macro:

```
macro ndf_str(s)
    nstr, spec = split(s, ":")
    n = parse(Int, nstr) # number of rows
    types = split(spec, ",") # column type specifications
    num_columns = length(types)
    mappings = Dict(
    "f64"=>Float64, "f32"=>Float32,
    "i64"=>Int64, "i32"=>Int32, "i16"=>Int16, "i8"=>Int8)
    column_types = [mappings[t] for t in types]
    column_names = [Symbol("x$i") for i in 1:num_columns]
    DataFrame([column_names[i] => rand(column_types[i], n)
        for i in 1:num_columns]...)
end
```

The first few lines parse the string and determine the number of rows (n), as well as the types of the columns (types). Then, a dictionary called mappings is created to map the shorthand to the corresponding numeric types. The column names and types are generated from the type and mapping data. Finally, it calls the DataFrame constructor and returns the result.

Now that we have the macro defined, we can easily create new data frames, as follows:

```
julia> ndf"100000:f64,f32,i16,i8"
100000×4 DataFrame
| Row    | x1        | x2        | x3     | x4   |
|        | Float64   | Float32   | Int16  | Int8 |
|        |           |           |        |      |
| 1      | 0.0857999 | 0.913402  | 32766  | -32  |
| 2      | 0.94144   | 0.467502  | 16344  | -11  |
| 3      | 0.0977344 | 0.0806381 | 26006  | 54   |
| 4      | 0.554632  | 0.74744   | 23622  | -28  |
⋮
| 99996  | 0.693608  | 0.024865  | 10105  | -98  |
| 99997  | 0.151315  | 0.680554  | -20284 | 75   |
| 99998  | 0.525563  | 0.186645  | -20596 | 10   |
| 99999  | 0.475524  | 0.372738  | 11549  | -2   |
| 100000 | 0.0160358 | 0.0794551 | 18773  | 50   |
```

Nonstandard string literals can be quite useful in certain cases. We can see a string specification as a mini domain-specific language that is encoded in the string. As long as the string specification is well defined, it can make the code a lot shorter and more concise.

You may have noticed that the ndf_str macro returns a regular DataFrame object rather than an expression object, as it would normally do with macros. This is perfectly fine because the final DataFrame object will be returned as-is. You may think of an evaluation of a constant as just the constant itself. We can just return a value rather than an expression here because the returned value does not involve any variables from the call site or from the module.

A curious mind might ask - why can't we just create a regular function for this? We can certainly do that for this dummy example. However, using a string literal could improve performance in some cases.

For example, when we use the Regex string literal in a function, the `Regex` object is created at compile-time and so it is executed only once. If we use the `Regex` constructor instead, then the object would be created every single time the function is called.

We have now concluded the topic of macros. We learned how to create macros by taking expressions and generating a new expression. We used the `@macroexpand` macro to debug the macro expansion process. We also learned how to handle macro hygiene. Finally, we took a look at nonstandard string literals and created our own using a macro.

Next, we will look at another metaprogramming facility called generated functions, which can be used to solve a different kind of problem than what regular macros can handle.

Using generated functions

So far, we have explained how to create macros that return expression objects. Since macros work at the syntax level, they can manipulate code only by examining how it *looks*. However, Julia is a dynamic system where data types are determined at runtime. For that reason, Julia provides the ability to create **generated functions**, which allow you to examine data types for a function call and return an expression, just like macros. When an expression is returned, it will be evaluated at the call site.

To understand why generated functions are needed, let's revisit how macros work. Let's say we have created a macro that doubles the value of its arguments. It would look like the following:

```
macro doubled(ex)
    return :( 2 * $(esc(ex)))
end
```

No matter what expression we pass into this macro, it would just blindly rewrite the code so it doubles the original expression. Suppose that one day, a super-duper piece of software is developed that lets us calculate twice the amount of a floating-point number quickly. In this case, we may want the system to switch to that function for floating-point numbers only, instead of using the standard multiplication operator.

So our first attempt might be to try something as follows:

```
# This code does not work. Don't try it.
macro doubled(ex)
    if typeof(ex) isa AbstractFloat
        return :( double_super_duper($(esc(ex))) )
    else
        return :( 2 * $(esc(ex)))
    end
end
```

But unfortunately, it is impossible for macros to do this. Why? Again, macros only have access to the abstract syntax tree. This is at the earlier part of the compilation pipeline and there is no type information available. The ex variable in the preceding code is merely an expression object. This problem can be solved with generated functions. Keep on reading!

Defining generated functions

Generated functions are functions that are prefixed by @generated at the function definition. These functions can return expression objects, just like macros. For example, we can define the doubled function as follows:

```
@generated function doubled(x)
    return :( 2 * x )
end
```

Let's quickly run a test and make sure that it works:

The code works beautifully, as expected.

So defining generated functions is quite similar to defining macros. In both cases, we can create an expression object and return it, and we can expect the expression to be evaluated properly.

We have not, however, exercised the full power of generated functions yet. Next, we will look at how data type information can be made available and how it can be used within generated functions.

Examining generated function arguments

An important point to remember is that arguments of generated functions contain data types, not actual values. The following is a visual representation of how generated functions work:

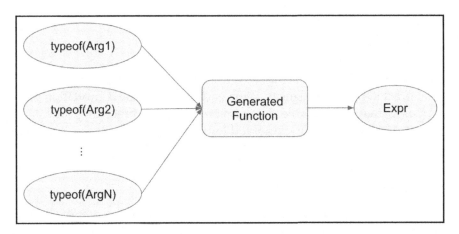

This is in sharp contrast to functions, which accept arguments as values. It is also different from macros, which accept arguments as expressions. Here, generated functions accept arguments as data types. It may seem a little strange, but let's do a simple experiment to confirm that this is indeed the case.

For this experiment, we will define the doubled function again by displaying the argument on screen before returning the expression.

```
@generated function doubled(x)
    @show x
    return :( 2 * x )
end
```

Let's test the function again.

```
julia> doubled(2)
x = Int64
4

julia> doubled(2)
4
```

As it is shown, the value of argument x is Int64 rather than 2 during the execution of the generated function. Furthermore, when the function is called again, it no longer shows the value of x. This is because the function is now compiled after the first call.

Now, let's see what happens if we run it again with a different type:

```
julia> doubled(3.0)
x = Float64
6.0
```

The compiler has kicked in again and compiled a new version based upon the type of Float64. So, technically speaking, we now have two versions of the doubled function for each type of argument.

 You may have realized that the behavior of generated functions is similar to that of regular functions when it comes to specialization. The difference is that we have a chance to manipulate the abstract syntax tree right before the compilation happens.

With this new generated function, we can now take advantage of the hypothetical super-duper software by switching over to the faster double_super_duper function whenever the data type of the argument is a subtype of AbstractFloat, as shown in the following code:

```
@generated function doubled(x)
    if x <: AbstractFloat
        return :( double_super_duper(x) )
    else
        return :( 2 * x )
    end
end
```

Using generated functions, we can specialize the function depending on the type of the argument. When the type is AbstractFloat, the function will resort to the double_super_duper(x) rather than the 2 *x expression.

 As mentioned in the official Julia language reference manual, care must be taken when developing generated functions. The exact limitations are beyond of the scope of this book. You are highly encouraged to refer to the manual if you need to write generated functions for your software.

Generated functions are a useful tool to deal with cases that macros are unable to handle. Specifically, during the macro expansion process, there is no information about the types of the argument. Generated functions allow us to get a little closer to the heart of the compilation process. With the additional knowledge about argument types, we are more flexible when it comes to handling different situations.

As a metaprogramming tool, macros are used much more extensively than generated functions. Nevertheless, it is nice to know that both tools are available.

Summary

In this chapter, we learned how Julia parses expressions into an abstract syntax tree structure. We learned that expressions can be created and evaluated programmatically. We also learned how to interpolate variables into quoted expressions.

Then, we jumped into the topic of macros, which are used to dynamically create new code. We learned that macro arguments are expressions rather than values, and learned how to create new expressions from macros. We had fun creating macros that manipulate the abstract syntax tree to deal with some interesting use cases.

Finally, we looked at generated functions, which can be used to generate code based on the type of the function arguments. We learned how generated functions can be useful for a hypothetical use case.

We have now concluded the introductory part of the book regarding the Julia programming language. In the next chapter, we will start looking at design patterns related to code reusability.

Questions

1. What are the two ways we can use to quote expressions so that the code can be manipulated later?
2. In what environment does the `eval` function execute code?
3. How do you interpolate physical symbols into quoted expressions so that they are not misinterpreted as source code?
4. What is the naming convention for a macro that defines nonstandard string literals?

5. When do you use the `esc` function?

6. How are generated functions different from macros?

7. How do you debug macros?

Section 3: Implementing Design Patterns

3

The aim of this section is to provide you with an inventory of modern Julia-specific design patterns as well as the more traditional object-oriented patterns. You will learn how to apply these patterns to various problems.

This section contains the following chapters:

- Chapter 5, *Reusability Patterns*
- Chapter 6, *Performance Patterns*
- Chapter 7, *Maintainability Patterns*
- Chapter 8, *Robustness Patterns*
- Chapter 9, *Miscellaneous Patterns*
- Chapter 10, *Anti-Patterns*
- Chapter 11, *Traditional Object-Oriented Patterns*

5
Reusability Patterns

In this chapter, we will learn about several patterns related to software reusability. As you may recall from Chapter 1, *Design Patterns and Related Principles*, reusability is one of the four software quality objectives that is required for building large-scale applications. Nobody wants to reinvent the wheel. The ability to reuse an existing software component saves both time and energy—an overall humanity gain! The patterns in this chapter are proven techniques that can help us improve application design, reuse existing code, and reduce overall code size.

In this chapter, we will cover the following topics:

- The delegation pattern
- The holy traits pattern
- The parametric type pattern

Technical requirements

The sample source code for this chapter is located at `https://github.com/PacktPublishing/Hands-on-Design-Patterns-and-Best-Practices-with-Julia/tree/master/Chapter05`.

The code in this chapter has been tested in a Julia 1.3.0 environment.

The delegation pattern

Delegation is a pattern that is commonly applied in software engineering. The primary objective is to leverage the capabilities of an existing component by wrapping it via a *has-a* relationship.

The delegation pattern is widely adopted, even in the object-oriented programming community. In the early days of object-oriented programming, people thought that code reuse could be achieved beautifully using inheritance. However, people came to realize that this promise couldn't be completely fulfilled due to a variety of issues related to inheritance. Since then, many software engineers prefer composition over inheritance. The concept of composition is to wrap one object within another. In order to reuse existing functions, we must delegate functions calls to the wrapped object. This section will explain how delegation can be implemented in Julia.

The concept of composition is to wrap one object within another. In order to reuse existing functions, we must delegate functions calls to the wrapped object.

One way is to enhance an existing component with new features. This may sound good, but it could be challenging in practice. Consider the following situations:

- The existing component comes from a vendor product and the source code is not available. Even if the code is available, the vendor's license may not allow us to make custom changes.
- The existing component is developed and used by another team for a mission-critical system and changes are neither welcome nor applicable for that system.
- The existing component contains a lot of legacy code and new changes may compromise the component's stability and require a lot of testing effort.

If modifying an existing component's source code is not an option, then we should at least be able to use the component via its published programming interface. That is the virtue of the delegation pattern.

Applying the delegation pattern to a banking use case

The delegation pattern is the idea of creating a new object by wrapping an existing one called the *parent* object. In order to reuse the object's features, the functions that have been defined for the new object can be delegated (also known as forwarded) to the parent.

Suppose that we have access to a banking library that provides some basic account management functionality. To understand how it works, let's take a look at the source code.

A bank account has been designed with the following mutable data structure:

```
mutable struct Account
    account_number::String
    balance::Float64
    date_opened::Date
end
```

As part of the programming interface, the library also provides the field accessors (see Chapter 8, *Robustness Patterns*) and functions for making deposits, withdrawals, and transfers, as follows:

```
# Accessors

account_number(a::Account) = a.account_number
balance(a::Account) = a.balance
date_opened(a::Account) = a.date_opened

# Functions

function deposit!(a::Account, amount::Real)
    a.balance += amount
    return a.balance
end

function withdraw!(a::Account, amount::Real)
    a.balance -= amount
    return a.balance
end

function transfer!(from::Account, to::Account, amount::Real)
    withdraw!(from, amount)
    deposit!(to, amount)
    return amount
end
```

Of course, in practice, such a banking library has to be a lot more complex than what is seen here. I suspect that when money goes in and out of a bank account, there are many downstream effects such as logging an audit trail, making the new balance available on a website, sending emails to the customer, and so on.

Let's move on and learn how we can utilize the delegation pattern.

Composing a new type that contains an existing type

As part of a new initiative, the bank wants us to support a new savings account product, which provides daily interest for customers. Since the existing account management's functionality is critical to the bank's business and is maintained by a different team, we have decided to reuse its functionality without touching any of the existing source code.

First, let's create our own `SavingsAccount` data type, as follows:

```
struct SavingsAccount
    acct::Account
    interest_rate::Float64
    SavingsAccount(account_number, balance, date_opened, interest_rate) =
new(
        Account(account_number, balance, date_opened),
        interest_rate
    )
end
```

The first field, `acct`, is used to hold an `Account` object, while the second field, `interest_rate`, contains the interest rate per annum for the account. A constructor is also defined to instantiate the object.

In order to use the underlying `Account` object, we can use a technique called *Delegation*, or *Method Forwarding*. This is where we implement the same API in `SavingsAccount` and forward the call to the underlying `Account` object whenever we want to reuse the existing functions from the underlying object. In this case, we can just forward all the field accessor functions and mutating functions from the `Account` object, as follows:

```
# Forward assessors
account_number(sa::SavingsAccount) = account_number(sa.acct)
balance(sa::SavingsAccount) = balance(sa.acct)
date_opened(sa::SavingsAccount) = date_opened(sa.acct)

# Forward methods
deposit!(sa::SavingsAccount, amount::Real) = deposit!(sa.acct, amount)

withdraw!(sa::SavingsAccount, amount::Real) = withdraw!(sa.acct, amount)

transfer!(sa1::SavingsAccount, sa2::SavingsAccount, amount::Real) =
transfer!(
    sa1.acct, sa2.acct, amount)
```

So far, we have successfully reused the `Account` data type, but let's not forget that we actually want to build new features in the first place. A savings account should accrue interest overnight on a daily basis. So, for the `SavingsAccount` object, we can implement a new accessor for the `interest_rate` field and a new mutating function called `accrue_daily_interest!`:

```
# new accessor
interest_rate(sa::SavingsAccount) = sa.interest_rate

# new behavior
function accrue_daily_interest!(sa::SavingsAccount)
    interest = balance(sa.acct) * interest_rate(sa) / 365
    deposit!(sa.acct, interest)
end
```

At this time, we have created a new `SavingsAccount` object that works just like the original `Account` object, except it has the additional capability of accruing interest!

However, the sheer volume of these forwarding methods makes us feel a little unsatisfied. It would be nice if we didn't have to write all this code manually. Perhaps there's a better way...

Reducing boilerplate code for forwarding methods

You may wonder how it would ever be worth the effort to write so much code just to forward the method calls to the parent object. Indeed, the forwarding methods serve no purpose other than passing the exact same arguments to the parent. If programmers were paid by lines of code, then this would be quite an expensive proposition, wouldn't it?

Fortunately, this kind of boilerplate code can be reduced greatly using macros. There are several open source solutions that can help with this situation. For demonstration purposes, we can utilize the `@forward` macro from the `Lazy.jl` package. Let's replace all the forwarding methods, as follows:

```
using Lazy: @forward

# Forward assessors and functions
@forward SavingsAccount.acct account_number, balance, date_opened
@forward SavingsAccount.acct deposit!, withdraw!

transfer!(from::SavingsAccount, to::SavingsAccount, amount::Real) =
transfer!(
    from.acct, to.acct, amount)
```

The usage of @forward is fairly straightforward. It takes two expressions as arguments. The first argument is the SavingsAccount.acct object that you want to forward to, while the second argument is just a tuple of function names that you wish to forward to, for example, account_number, balance, and date_opened.

Note that we are able to forward mutating functions such as deposit! and withdraw!, but we cannot do the same for transfer!. This is because transfer! requires that we forward its first and second arguments. In this case, we just keep the manual forwarding method. Nevertheless, we were able to forward five out of the six functions using just two lines of code. It's still a pretty good deal!

 It would be possible to make more forwarding macros that take two or three arguments. In fact, there are other open source packages that support such scenarios, such as the TypedDelegation.jl package.

So, how does the @forward macro work? We can examine how the code gets expanded using the @macroexpand macro. The following is the result of the line number nodes being removed. Basically, for each method that is being forwarded (balance and deposit!), it creates the corresponding function definition with all the arguments splatted with the args... notation. It also throws in an @inline node to give the compiler a hint for better performance:

```
julia> @macroexpand @forward SavingsAccount.acct balance, deposit!
quote
    balance(var"#41#x"::SavingsAccount, var"#42#args"...) = begin
            #= /Users/tomkwong/.julia/packages/Lazy/ZAeCx/src/macros.jl:285 =#
            $(Expr(:meta, :inline))
            #= /Users/tomkwong/.julia/packages/Lazy/ZAeCx/src/macros.jl:285 =#
            balance((var"#41#x").acct, var"#42#args"...)
        end
    deposit!(var"#43#x"::SavingsAccount, var"#44#args"...) = begin
            #= /Users/tomkwong/.julia/packages/Lazy/ZAeCx/src/macros.jl:285 =#
            $(Expr(:meta, :inline))
            #= /Users/tomkwong/.julia/packages/Lazy/ZAeCx/src/macros.jl:285 =#
            deposit!((var"#43#x").acct, var"#44#args"...)
        end
    #= /Users/tomkwong/.julia/packages/Lazy/ZAeCx/src/macros.jl:287 =#
    Lazy.nothing
end
```

Inlining is a compiler optimization where a function call is *inlined* as if the code had been interpolated into the current code. It may improve performance by reducing the overhead of allocating a call stack when functions are called repeatedly.

The @forward macro was implemented with only a few lines of code. You are encouraged to take a look at the source code if you are interested in metaprogramming.

You might be wondering why there are several funny variable names such as #41#x or #42#args. We can treat those as if they are normal variables. They are automatically generated by the compiler, and their special naming convention is chosen to avoid conflicts with other variables in the current scope.

Finally, it is important to understand that we may not always want to forward all the function calls to the object. What if we don't want to use 100% of the underlying features? Believe it or not, there are cases like that. For example, let's imagine that we have to support another kind of account, such as a certificate of deposits, also known as CDs. A CD is a short-term investment product that pays a higher interest than a savings account, but the funds cannot be withdrawn during the term of investment. Generally, the term of a CD could be 3 months, 6 months, or longer. Going back to our code, if we create a new CertificateOfDepositAccount object and reuse the Account object again, we wouldn't want to forward the withdraw! and transfer! methods because they are not features of CDs.

You might wonder how delegation differs from class inheritance in object-oriented programming languages. For example, in the Java language, all the public and protected methods from the parent class are inherited automatically. This is analogous to auto-forwarding all the methods from the parent class.

The inability to choose what to inherit is actually one of the reasons why delegation is preferred over inheritance. For a more in-depth discussion, see Chapter 12, *Inheritance and Variance*.

Reviewing some real-life examples

The delegation pattern is used extensively in open source packages. For example, many packages in the JuliaArrays GitHub organization implement the AbstractArray interface. The special array types usually contain a regular AbstractArray object.

Example 1 – the OffsetArrays.jl package

The OffsetArrays.jl package allows us to define arrays with arbitrary indices rather than the standard linear or cartesian style indices. A fun example is to use a zero-based array, just like the ones you may find in other programming languages:

```
julia> using OffsetArrays

julia> y = OffsetArray(rand(3), 0:2)
3-element OffsetArray(::Array{Float64,1}, 0:2) with eltype Float64 with indices 0:2:
 0.886166992999051
 0.045775632545100864
 0.48873087789789316

julia> y[0:2]
3-element Array{Float64,1}:
 0.886166992999051
 0.045775632545100864
 0.48873087789789316
```

To understand how this works, we need to dig into the source code. Let's keep things concise and review just a portion of the code:

```
struct OffsetArray{T,N,AA<:AbstractArray} <: AbstractArray{T,N}
    parent::AA
    offsets::NTuple{N,Int}
end

Base.parent(A::OffsetArray) = A.parent

Base.size(A::OffsetArray) = size(parent(A))
Base.size(A::OffsetArray, d) = size(parent(A), d)

Base.eachindex(::IndexCartesian, A::OffsetArray) =
CartesianIndices(axes(A))
Base.eachindex(::IndexLinear, A::OffsetVector) = axes(A, 1)
```

The OffsetArray data type is composed of the parent and offsets fields. In order to satisfy the AbstractArray interface, it implements some of the basic functions, such as Base.size, Base.eachindex, and so on. Since these functions are simple enough, the code just forwards the call to the parent object manually.

Example 2 – the ScikitLearn.jl package

Let's also take a look at the ScikitLearn.jl package, which defines a consistent API for fitting machine learning models and doing prediction.

The following is how the `FitBit` type is defined:

```
""" `FitBit(model)` will behave just like `model`, but also supports
`isfit(fb)`, which returns true IFF `fit!(model, ...)` has been called """
mutable struct FitBit
    model
    isfit::Bool
    FitBit(model) = new(model, false)
end

function fit!(fb::FitBit, args...; kwargs...)
    fit!(fb.model, args...; kwargs...)
    fb.isfit = true
    fb
end

isfit(fb::FitBit) = fb.isfit
```

Here, we can see that the `FitBit` object contains a `model` object and that it adds a new functionality that keeps track of whether a model has been fitted or not:

```
@forward FitBit.model transform, predict, predict_proba, predict_dist,
get_classes
```

It uses the `@forward` macro to delegate all the major functions, that is, `transform`, `predict`, and so on.

Considerations

You should keep in mind that the delegation pattern introduces a new level of indirection, which can increase code complexity and make the code more difficult to understand. We should consider some factors when deciding to use the delegation pattern.

First, how much code can you reuse from the existing component? Is it 20%, 50%, or 80%? This ought to be the very first question you ask before you consider reusing an existing component. Let's call the amount of reuse the utilization rate. Obviously, the higher the utilization rate, the better it is from a reuse perspective.

Second, how much development effort can be saved by reusing an existing component? If the cost of developing the same functionality is low, then it may not be worth the effort to reuse the component and increase the complexity of extra indirection.

From the opposite angle, we should also review if there is any critical business logic in the existing component. If we decide to not reuse the component, then we could end up implementing the same logic again, violating the **Don't Repeat Yourself (DRY)** principle. This means it can be a maintenance nightmare to not reuse the component.

Given these considerations, we should just to make a good judgment about using the delegation pattern or not.

Next, we will learn how to implement traits in Julia.

The holy traits pattern

The holy traits pattern has an interesting name. Some people also call it the **Tim Holy Traits Trick (THTT)**. As you might have guessed the pattern is named after Tim Holy, who is a long-time contributor to the Julia language and ecosystem.

What are traits? In a nutshell, a trait corresponds to the behavior of an object. For example, birds and butterflies can fly, so they both have the *CanFly* trait. Dolphins and turtles can swim, so they both have the *CanSwim* trait. A duck can fly and swim, so it has both the *CanFly* and *CanSwim* traits. Traits are typically binary – you either exhibit the trait or not – although that is not a mandatory requirement.

Why do we want traits? Traits can be used as a formal contract about how a data type can be used. For example, if an object has the *CanFly* trait, then we would be quite confident that the object has some kind of *fly* method defined. Likewise, if an object has the *CanSwim* trait, then we can probably call some kind of *swim* function.

Let's get back to programming. The Julia language doesn't have any built-in support for traits. However, the language is versatile enough for developers to use traits with the help of the multiple dispatch system. In this section, we will look into how this can be done with the special technique known as holy traits.

Revisiting the personal asset management use case

When designing reusable software, we often create abstractions as data types and associate behaviors with them. One way to model behaviors is to leverage a type hierarchy. Following the Liskov Substitution Principle, we should be able to substitute a type with a subtype when a function is called.

Let's revisit the abstract type hierarchy of managing personal assets from `Chapter 2`, *Modules, Packages, and Type Concepts*:

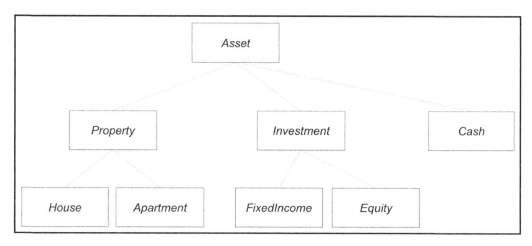

We can define a function called `value` for determining the value of any asset. Such a function can be applied to all the types in the `Asset` hierarchy if we assume that all the asset types have some kind of monetary value attached to them. Following that line of thought, we can say that almost every asset exhibits the *HasValue* trait.

Sometimes, behaviors can only be applied to certain types in the hierarchy. For example, what if we want to define a `trade` function that only works with liquid investments? In that case, we would define `trade` functions for `Investment` and `Cash` but not for `House` and `Apartments`.

 A liquid investment refers to a security instrument that can be traded easily in the open market. The investor can quickly convert a liquid instrument into cash and vice versa. In general, most investors would like a portion of their investment to be liquid in the case of an emergency.

Investments that are not liquid are called illiquid.

Programmatically, how do we know which asset types are liquid? One way is to check the type of the object against a list of types that represent liquid investments. Suppose that we have an array of assets and need to find out which one can be traded quickly for cash. In this situation, the code may look something like this:

```
function show_tradable_assets(assets::Vector{Asset})
    for asset in assets
        if asset isa Investment || asset isa Cash
```

```
            println("Yes, I can trade ", asset)
        else
            println("Sorry, ", asset, " is not tradable")
        end
    end
end
```

The `if` condition in the preceding code is a bit ugly, even in this toy example. If we have more types in the condition, then it gets worse. Of course, we can create a union type to make it a little better:

```
const LiquidInvestments = Union{Investment, Cash}

function show_tradable_assets(assets::Vector{Asset})
    for asset in assets
        if asset isa LiquidInvestments
            println("Yes, I can trade ", asset)
        else
            println("Sorry, ", asset, " is not tradable")
        end
    end
end
```

There are a few issues with this approach:

- The union type has to be updated whenever we add a new liquid asset type. This kind of maintenance is bad from a design perspective because the programmer must remember to update this union type whenever a new type is added to the system.
- This union type is not available for extension. If other developers want to reuse our trading library, then they may want to add new asset types. However, they cannot change our definition of the union type because they do not own the source code.
- The if-then-else logic may be repeated in many places in our source, whenever we need to do things differently for liquid and illiquid assets.

These problems can be solved using the holy traits pattern.

Implementing the holy traits pattern

To illustrate the concept of this pattern, we will implement some functions for the personal asset data types that we developed in `Chapter 2`, *Modules, Packages, and Data Type Concepts*. As you may recall, the abstract types for the asset type hierarchy are defined as follows:

```
abstract type Asset end

abstract type Property <: Asset end
abstract type Investment <: Asset end
abstract type Cash <: Asset end

abstract type House <: Property end
abstract type Apartment <: Property end

abstract type FixedIncome <: Investment end
abstract type Equity <: Investment end
```

The `Asset` type is at the top of the hierarchy and has the `Property`, `Investment`, and `Cash` subtypes. At the next level, `House` and `Apartment` are subtypes of `Property`, while `FixedIncome` and `Equity` are subtypes of `Investment`.

Now, let's define some concrete types:

```
struct Residence <: House
    location
end

struct Stock <: Equity
    symbol
    name
end

struct TreasuryBill <: FixedIncome
    cusip
end

struct Money <: Cash
    currency
    amount
end
```

What do we have here? Let's take a look at these concepts in more detail:

- A `Residence` is a house that someone lives in and has a location.
- A `Stock` is an equity investment, and it is identified by a trading symbol and the name of the company.
- A `TreasuryBill` is a short-term government-issued form of security in the United States, and it is defined with a standard identifier called CUSIP.
- `Money` is just cash, but we want to store the currency and respective amount here.

Note that we have not annotated the types for the fields because they aren't important for illustrating the trait concept here.

Defining the trait type

When it comes to investments, we can distinguish between ones that can be sold for cash easily in the open market and ones that take considerably more effort and time to convert into cash. Things that can easily be converted into cash within several days are known as being *liquid*, while the hard-to-sell ones are known as being *illiquid*. For example, stocks are liquid while a residence is not.

The first thing we want to do is define the traits themselves:

```
abstract type LiquidityStyle end
struct IsLiquid <: LiquidityStyle end
struct IsIlliquid <: LiquidityStyle end
```

Traits are nothing but data types in Julia! The overall concept of the `LiquidityStyle` trait is that it's an abstract type. The specific traits here, `IsLiquid` and `IsIlliquid`, have been set up as concrete types without any fields.

 There is no standard naming convention for traits, but my research seems to indicate that package authors tend to use either `Style` or `Trait` as the suffix for trait types.

Identifying traits

The next step is to assign data types to these traits. Conveniently, Julia allows us to bulk-assign traits to an entire subtype tree using the < : operator in the function signature:

```
# Default behavior is illiquid
LiquidityStyle(::Type) = IsIlliquid()
```

```
# Cash is always liquid
LiquidityStyle(::Type{<:Cash}) = IsLiquid()

# Any subtype of Investment is liquid
LiquidityStyle(::Type{<:Investment}) = IsLiquid()
```

Let's take a look at how we can interpret these three lines of code:

- We have chosen to make all the types illiquid by default. Note that we could have done this the other way around and made everything liquid by default. This decision is arbitrary and depends on the specific use case.
- We have chosen to make all the subtypes of `Cash` liquid, which includes the concrete `Money` type. The notation of `::Type{<:Cash}` indicates all the subtypes of `Cash`.
- We have chosen to make all the subtypes of `Investment` liquid. This includes all the subtypes of `FixedIncome` and `Equity`, which covers `Stock` in this example.

You might be wondering why we don't take `::Type{<: Asset}` as an argument for the default trait function. Doing so makes it more restrictive as the default value would only be available for types that are defined under the `Asset` type hierarchy. This may or may not be desirable, depending on how the trait is used. Either way should be fine.

Implementing trait behavior

Now that we can tell which types are liquid and which are not, we can define methods that take objects with those traits. First, let's do something really simple:

```
# The thing is tradable if it is liquid
tradable(x::T) where {T} = tradable(LiquidityStyle(T), x)
tradable(::IsLiquid, x) = true
tradable(::IsIlliquid, x) = false
```

In Julia, types are first-class citizens. The `tradable(x::T) where {T}` signature captures the type of argument as `T`. Since we have already defined the `LiquidityStyle` function, we can derive whether the passed argument exhibits the `IsLiquid` or `IsIlliquid` trait. So, the first `tradable` method simply takes the return value of `LiquidityStyle(T)` and passes it as the first argument for the other two `tradable` methods. This simple example demonstrates the dispatch effect.

Now, let's look at a more interesting function that exploits the same trait. Since liquid assets are easily tradable in the market, we should be able to discover their market price quickly as well. For stocks, we may call a pricing service from the stock exchange. For cash, the market price is just the currency amount. Let's see how this is coded:

```
# The thing has a market price if it is liquid
marketprice(x::T) where {T} = marketprice(LiquidityStyle(T), x)
marketprice(::IsLiquid, x) = error("Please implement pricing function for
", typeof(x))
marketprice(::IsIlliquid, x) = error("Price for illiquid asset $x is not
available.")
```

The code's structure is the same as the `tradable` function. One method is used to determine the trait, while the other two methods implement different behaviors for the liquid and illiquid instruments. Here, both `marketprice` functions just raise an exception by calling the error function. Of course, that's not what we really want. What we should really have is a specific pricing function for the `Stock` and `Money` types. Okay; let's do just that:

```
# Sample pricing functions for Money and Stock
marketprice(x::Money) = x.amount
marketprice(x::Stock) = rand(200:250)
```

Here, the `marketprice` method for the `Money` type just returns the amount. This is quite a simplification since, in practice, we may calculate the amount in the local currency (for example, US Dollars) from the currency and amount. As for `Stock`, we just return a random number for the purpose of testing. In reality, we would have attached this function to a stock pricing service.

For illustration purposes, we have developed the following test functions:

```
function trait_test_cash()
    cash = Money("USD", 100.00)
    @show tradable(cash)
    @show marketprice(cash)
end

function trait_test_stock()
    aapl = Stock("AAPL", "Apple, Inc.")
    @show tradable(aapl)
    @show marketprice(aapl)
end

function trait_test_residence()
    try
        home = Residence("Los Angeles")
```

```
        @show tradable(home) # returns false
        @show marketprice(home) # exception is raised
    catch ex
        println(ex)
    end
    return true
end

function trait_test_bond()
    try
        bill = TreasuryBill("123456789")
        @show tradable(bill)
        @show marketprice(bill) # exception is raised
    catch ex
        println(ex)
    end
    return true
end
```

Here's the result from the Julia REPL:

```
julia> trait_test_cash();
tradable(cash) = true
marketprice(cash) = 100.0

julia> trait_test_stock();
tradable(aapl) = true
marketprice(aapl) = 244

julia> trait_test_residence();
tradable(home) = false
ErrorException("Price for illiquid asset Residence(\"Los Angeles\") is not available.")

julia> trait_test_bond();
tradable(bill) = true
ErrorException("Please implement pricing function for TreasuryBill")
```

Perfect! The tradable function has correctly identified that cash, stock, and bond are liquid and that residence is illiquid. For cash and stocks, the marketprice function was able to return a value, as expected. Because residence is not liquid, an error was raised. Finally, while treasury bills are liquid, an error was raised because the marketprice function has not been defined for the instrument.

Using traits with a different type of hierarchy

The best part of the holy trait pattern is that we can use it with any object, even when its type belongs to a different abstract type hierarchy. Let's explore the case of literature, where we may define its own type hierarchy as follows:

```
abstract type Literature end

struct Book <: Literature
    name
end
```

Now, we can make it obey the `LiquidityStyle` trait, as follows:

```
# assign trait
LiquidityStyle(::Type{Book}) = IsLiquid()

# sample pricing function
marketprice(b::Book) = 10.0
```

Now, we can trade books, just like other tradable assets.

Reviewing some common usages

The holy traits pattern is commonly used in open source packages. Let's take a look at some examples.

Example 1 – Base.IteratorSize

The Julia Base library uses traits quite extensively. An example of such a trait is `Base.IteratorSize`. Its definition can be found using `generator.jl`:

```
abstract type IteratorSize end
struct SizeUnknown <: IteratorSize end
struct HasLength <: IteratorSize end
struct HasShape{N} <: IteratorSize end
struct IsInfinite <: IteratorSize end
```

This trait is slightly different from what we have learned about so far because it is not binary. The `IteratorSize` trait can be `SizeUnknown`, `HasLength`, `HasShape{N}`, or `IsInfinite`. The `IteratorSize` function is defined as follows:

```
"""
    IteratorSize(itertype::Type) -> IteratorSize
"""
IteratorSize(x) = IteratorSize(typeof(x))
IteratorSize(::Type) = HasLength() # HasLength is the default

IteratorSize(::Type{<:AbstractArray{<:Any,N}}) where {N} = HasShape{N}()
IteratorSize(::Type{Generator{I,F}}) where {I,F} = IteratorSize(I)

IteratorSize(::Type{Any}) = SizeUnknown()
```

Let's focus on the `IsInfinite` trait since it looks quite interesting. A few functions have been defined in `Base.Iterators` that generate infinite sequences. For example, the `Iterators.repeated` function can be used to generate the same value forever, and we can use the `Iterators.take` function to pick up the values from the sequence. Let's see how this works:

```
julia> collect(Iterators.take(Iterators.repeated(1), 5))
5-element Array{Int64,1}:
 1
 1
 1
 1
 1
```

If you look at the source code, you'll see that `Repeated` is the type of the iterator and that it is assigned the `IteratorSize` trait with `IsInfinite`:

```
IteratorSize(::Type{<:Repeated}) = IsInfinite()
```

We can quickly test it out like so:

```
julia> Base.IteratorSize(Iterators.repeated(1))
Base.IsInfinite()
```

Voila! It is infinite, just as we expected! But how is this trait utilized? To find out how, we can look into the `BitArray` from the Base library, which is a space-efficient Boolean array implementation. Its constructor function can take any iterable object, such as an array:

```
julia> BitArray([isodd(x) for x in 1:5])
5-element BitArray{1}:
 1
 0
 1
 0
 1
```

Perhaps it isn't hard to understand that the constructor can't really work with something that is infinite in nature! Therefore, the implementation of the `BitArray` constructor has to take that into account. Because we can dispatch based upon the `IteratorSize` trait, the constructor of `BitArray` happily throws an exception when such an iterator is passed:

```
BitArray(itr) = gen_bitarray(IteratorSize(itr), itr)

gen_bitarray(::IsInfinite, itr) = throw(ArgumentError("infinite-size
iterable used in BitArray constructor"))
```

To see it in action, we can call the `BitArray` constructor with the `Repeated` iterator, like so:

```
julia> BitArray(Iterators.repeated(1))
ERROR: ArgumentError: infinite-size iterable used in BitArray constructor
```

Example 2 – AbstractPlotting.jl ConversionTrait

`AbstractPlotting.jl` is an abstract plotting library that is part of the Makie plotting system. The source code for this library can be found at https://github.com/JuliaPlots/AbstractPlotting.jl.

Let's take a look at a trait that's related to data conversion:

```
abstract type ConversionTrait end

struct NoConversion <: ConversionTrait end
struct PointBased <: ConversionTrait end
struct SurfaceLike <: ConversionTrait end

# By default, there is no conversion trait for any object
```

```
conversion_trait(::Type) = NoConversion()
conversion_trait(::Type{<: XYBased}) = PointBased()
conversion_trait(::Type{<: Union{Surface, Heatmap, Image}}) = SurfaceLike()
```

It defines a `ConversionTrait` that can be used for the `convert_arguments` function. As it stands, the conversion logic can be applied to three different scenarios:

1. No conversion. This is handled by the default trait type of `NoConversion`.
2. `PointBased` conversion.
3. `SurfaceLike` conversion.

By default, the `convert_arguments` function just returns the arguments untouched when conversion is not required:

```
# Do not convert anything if there is no conversion trait
convert_arguments(::NoConversion, args...) = args
```

Then, various `convert_arguments` functions are defined. Here is the function for 2D plotting:

```
"""
    convert_arguments(P, x, y)::(Vector)

Takes vectors `x` and `y` and turns it into a vector of 2D points of the
values
from `x` and `y`.

`P` is the plot Type (it is optional).
"""
convert_arguments(::PointBased, x::RealVector, y::RealVector) =
(Point2f0.(x, y),)
```

Using the SimpleTraits.jl package

The `SimpleTraits.jl` package (`https://github.com/mauro3/SimpleTraits.jl`) may be used to make programming traits a little easier.

Let's try to redo the `LiquidityStyle` example using SimpleTraits. First, define a trait called `IsLiquid`, as follows:

```
@traitdef IsLiquid{T}
```

The syntax may look a little awkward since the T seems to be doing nothing, but it is actually required because the trait is applicable for a specific type T. The next thing is to assign types to this trait:

```
@traitimpl IsLiquid{Cash}
@traitimpl IsLiquid{Investment}
```

Then, a special syntax with four colons can be used to define functions that take objects exhibiting the trait:

```
@traitfn marketprice(x::::IsLiquid) = error("Please implement pricing
function for ", typeof(x))
@traitfn marketprice(x::::(!IsLiquid)) = error("Price for illiquid asset $x
is not available.")
```

The positive case has the argument annotated with x::::IsLiquid, while the negative case has the argument annotated with x::::(!IsLiquid). Note that the parentheses is required so that the code can be parsed correctly. Now, we can test the functions as follows:

```
julia> marketprice(Stock("AAPL", "Apple"))
ERROR: Please implement pricing function for Stock

julia> marketprice(Residence("Los Angeles"))
ERROR: Price for illiquid asset Residence("Los Angeles") is not available.
```

As expected, both default implementations throw an error. Now, we can implement the pricing function for Stock and quickly test again:

```
julia> marketprice(x::Stock) = 123
marketprice (generic function with 4 methods)

julia> marketprice(Stock("AAPL", "Apple"))
123
```

Looks great! As we can see, the SimpleTrait.jl package simplifies the process of creating traits.

Using traits can make your code more extendable. We must keep in mind, however, that it takes some effort to design proper traits. Documentation is also important so that anyone who wants to extend the code can understand how to utilize the predefined traits.

Next, we will go over parametric types, which are commonly used to extends data types easily.

The parametric type pattern

Parametric type is a core language feature that's used to materialize data types with parameters. It is a very powerful technique because the same object structure can be reused for different data types in its fields. In this section, we will demonstrate how parametric types can be applied effectively.

When designing applications, we often create composite types to conveniently hold multiple field elements. In its simplest form, composite types only serve as the containers of fields. As we create more and more composite types, it may become clear that some of these types look almost the same. Furthermore, the functions that operate on these types may be very similar as well. We could end up with a lot of boilerplate code. Wouldn't it be cool to have a template that allows us to customize a general composite type for a specific use?

Consider a trading application that supports buying and selling stocks. In the very first version, we may have the following design:

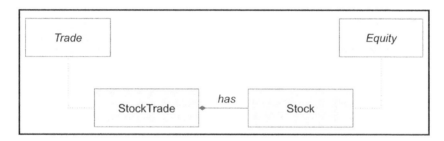

 Please beware that the notation in the preceding diagram may look a lot like **Unified Modeling Language** (**UML**). However, because Julia is not an object-oriented language, we may make certain exceptions when illustrating design concepts with these diagrams.

The corresponding code is as follows:

```
# Abstract type hierarchy for personal assets
abstract type Asset end
abstract type Investment <: Asset end
abstract type Equity <: Investment end

# Equity Instruments Types
struct Stock <: Equity
    symbol::String
    name::String
end
```

```
# Trading Types
abstract type Trade end

# Types (direction) of the trade
@enum LongShort Long Short

struct StockTrade <: Trade
    type::LongShort
    stock::Stock
    quantity::Int
    price::Float64
end
```

The data types we defined in the preceding code are fairly straightforward. The LongShort enum type is used to indicate the direction of trade—buying stock would be long, while selling stock would be short. The @enum macro is conveniently used to define the Long and Short constants.

Now, suppose that we were asked to support stock options in our next version of the software. Naively, we could define more data types, as follows:

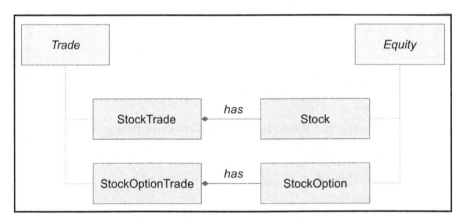

The code is updated with additional data types, like so:

```
# Types of stock options
@enum CallPut Call Put

struct StockOption <: Equity
    symbol::String
    type::CallPut
    strike::Float64
    expiration::Date
end
```

```
struct StockOptionTrade <: Trade
    type::LongShort
    option::StockOption
    quantity::Int
    price::Float64
end
```

You might have noticed that the `StockTrade` and `StockOptionTrade` types are very similar. Such repetition is somewhat unsatisfying. It looks even worse when we define functions for these data types, as follows:

```
# Regardless of the instrument being traded, the direction of
# trade (long/buy or short/sell) determines the sign of the
# payment amount.
sign(t::StockTrade) = t.type == Long ? 1 : -1
sign(t::StockOptionTrade) = t.type == Long ? 1 : -1

# market value of a trade is simply quantity times price
payment(t::StockTrade) = sign(t) * t.quantity * t.price
payment(t::StockOptionTrade) = sign(t) * t.quantity * t.price
```

Both the `sign` and `payment` methods are strikingly similar for both the `StockTrade` and `StockOptionTrade` types. Perhaps it isn't hard to imagine that this cannot scale very well when we add more tradable types to the application. There has to be a better way to do this. This is where the parametric type comes to the rescue!

Utilizing remove text parametric type for the stock trading app

In the trading application we described previously, we could utilize parametric types to simplify the code and make it more reusable when adding future trading instruments.

It is quite clear that `SingleStockTrade` and `SingleStockOptionTrade` are almost the same. In fact, even the function definitions of `sign` and `payment` are identical. In this very simple example, we only have two functions for each type. In practice, we could have many more functions, and it would become quite messy.

Designing parametric types

To simplify this design, we can parameterize the type of the thing being traded. What is the thing? We can leverage the abstract type here. The supertype of `Stock` is `Equity`, while the supertype of `Equity` is `Investment`. Since we want to keep the code generic and buying/selling investment products is similar, we can choose to accept any type that is a subtype of `Investment`:

```
struct SingleTrade{T <: Investment} <: Trade
    type::LongShort
    instrument::T
    quantity::Int
    price::Float64
end
```

Now, we have defined a new type called `SingleTrade`, where the underlying instrument has a type, `T`, where `T` can be any subtype of `Investment`. At this point, we can create trades with different kinds of instruments:

```
julia> stock = Stock("AAPL", "Apple Inc")
Stock("AAPL", "Apple Inc")

julia> option = StockOption("AAPLC", Call, 200, Date(2019, 12, 20))
StockOption("AAPLC", Call, 200.0, 2019-12-20)

julia> SingleTrade(Long, stock, 100, 188.0)
SingleTrade{Stock}(Long, Stock("AAPL", "Apple Inc"), 100, 188.0)

julia> SingleTrade(Long, option, 100, 3.5)
SingleTrade{StockOption}(Long, StockOption("AAPLC", Call, 200.0, 2019-12-20
), 100, 3.5)
```

These objects actually have different types—`SingleTrade{Stock}` and `SingleTrade{StockOption}`. How do they relate to each other? They are also subtypes of `SingleTrade`, as shown in the following screenshot:

```
julia> SingleTrade{Stock} <: SingleTrade
true

julia> SingleTrade{StockOption} <: SingleTrade
true
```

Since both types are subtypes of `SingleTrade`, this allows us to define functions that apply to both types, as we will see in the next section.

Designing parametric methods

In order to fully utilize the compiler's specialization feature, we should define parametric methods that also make use of the parametric type, like so:

```
# Return + or - sign for the direction of trade
function sign(t::SingleTrade{T}) where {T}
    return t.type == Long ? 1 : -1
end

# Calculate payment amount for the trade
function payment(t::SingleTrade{T}) where {T}
    return sign(t) * t.quantity * t.price
end
```

Let's test this out:

```
julia> SingleTrade(Long, stock, 100, 188.0) |> payment
18800.0

julia> SingleTrade(Long, option, 1, 3.50) |> payment
3.5
```

But hey, we just found a little bug. The option of $3.50 seems too good to be true! When looking at buying/selling options, each option contract actually represents 100 shares of the underlying stock. Therefore, the payment amount for stock option trades needs to be multiplied by 100. To fix this, we can just implement a more specific payment method:

```
# Calculate payment amount for option trades (100 shares per contract)
function payment(t::SingleTrade{StockOption})
    return sign(t) * t.quantity * 100 * t.price
end
```

Now, we can test again. Due to this, the new method is only dispatched for option trades:

```
julia> SingleTrade(Long, stock, 100, 188.0) |> payment
18800.0

julia> SingleTrade(Long, option, 1, 3.50) |> payment
350.0
```

Voila! Isn't it beautiful? We will look at a more elaborate example in the next section.

Using multiple parametric type arguments

So far, we're quite happy with our refactoring. However, our boss just called and said we have to support *pair trading* in the next release. This new request is adding yet another twist to our design!

> Pair trading can be used to implement a specific trading strategy, such as market-neutral trades or option strategies such as covered calls.

> **Market neutral** trading involves buying one stock and short-selling another one at the same time. The idea is to neutralize the market's effects so that the investor can focus on picking the stocks that over-perform or under-perform relative to their peers.
>
> **Covered call strategy** involves buying a stock but selling a call option that strikes at a higher price. This allows the investor to earn an additional premium in exchange for the limited upside potential of the underlying stock.

This can be handled easily with parametric types. Let's create a new type called `PairTrade`:

```
struct PairTrade{T <: Investment, S <: Investment} <: Trade
    leg1::SingleTrade{T}
    leg2::SingleTrade{S}
end
```

Note that the two legs from the trade can have different types, `T` and `S`, and that they can be any subtype of `Investment`. Because we expect every `Trade` type to support the `payment` function, we can implement this easily, as follows:

```
payment(t::PairTrade) = payment(t.leg1) + payment(t.leg2)
```

We can reuse the `stock` and `option` objects from the previous session and create a pair trade transaction where we buy 100 shares of the stock and sell 1 option contract. The expected payment amount is $18,800 - $350 = $18,450:

```
julia> stock
Stock("AAPL", "Apple Inc")

julia> option
StockOption("AAPLC", Call, 200.0, 2019-12-20)

julia> pt = PairTrade(SingleTrade(Long, stock, 100, 188.0), SingleTrade(Short, option, 1, 3.5));

julia> payment(pt)
18450.0
```

To appreciate how much parametric types simplified our design, imagine how many functions you would have to write if you had to create separate concrete types. In this example, since we have two possible trades in a pair trade transaction and each trade can be a stock trade or option trade, we have to support 2 x 2 = 4 different scenarios:

- `payment(PairTradeWithStockAndStock)`
- `payment(PairTradeWithStockAndStockOption)`
- `payment(PairTradeWithStockOptionAndStock)`
- `payment(PairTradeWithStockOptionAndStockOption)`

Using parametric types, we only need a single payment function that covers all scenarios.

Real-life examples

You can find the use of parametric types in almost any open source packages. Let's go over some examples.

Example 1 – the ColorTypes.jl package

ColorTypes.jl is a package that defines various data types that represent colors. In practice, there are many ways in which a color can be defined: **Red-Green-Blue (RGB)**, **Hue-Saturation-Value (HSV)**, and so on. Most of the time, a color can be defined using three real numbers. In the case of grayscale, only a single number is required to represent the level of darkness. To support transparent colors, an additional value can be used to store an opacity value. First, let's take a look at the type definitions:

```
"""
`Colorant{T,N}` is the abstract super-type of all types in ColorTypes,
and refers to both (opaque) colors and colors-with-transparency (alpha
channel) information. `T` is the element type (extractable with
`eltype`) and `N` is the number of *meaningful* entries (extractable
with `length`), that is, the number of arguments you would supply to the
constructor.
"""
abstract type Colorant{T,N} end

# Colors (without transparency)
"""
`Color{T,N}` is the abstract supertype for a color (or
grayscale) with no transparency.
"""
abstract type Color{T, N} <: Colorant{T,N} end

"""
`AbstractRGB{T}` is an abstract supertype for red/green/blue color types
that
can be constructed as `C(r, g, b)` and for which the elements can be
extracted as `red(c)`, `green(c)`, `blue(c)`. You should *not* make
assumptions about internal storage order, the number of fields, or the
representation. One `AbstractRGB` color-type, `RGB24`, is not
parametric and does not have fields named `r`, `g`, `b`.
"""
abstract type AbstractRGB{T}        <: Color{T,3} end
```

The Colorant{T,N} type can represent all kinds of colors, with or without transparency. The T parameter represents the type of each individual value in the color definition; for example, Int, Float64, and so on. The N parameter represents the number of values in the color definition, which is usually three.

Color{T,N} is a subtype of Colorant{T,N} and represents non-transparent colors. Finally, AbstractRGB{T} is a subtype of Color{T,N}. Note that the N parameter is no longer needed as a parameter in AbstractRGB{T} because it is already defined with N=3. Now, the concrete parametric type, RGB{T}, is defined as follows:

```
const Fractional = Union{AbstractFloat, FixedPoint}

"""
`RGB` is the standard Red-Green-Blue (sRGB) colorspace. Values of the
individual color channels range from 0 (black) to 1 (saturated). If
you want "Integer" storage types (for example, 255 for full color), use
`N0f8(1)`
instead (see FixedPointNumbers).
"""
struct RGB{T<:Fractional} <: AbstractRGB{T}
    r::T # Red [0,1]
    g::T # Green [0,1]
    b::T # Blue [0,1]
    RGB{T}(r::T, g::T, b::T) where {T} = new{T}(r, g, b)
end
```

The definition of RGB{T <: Fractional} is fairly straightforward. It contains three values of type T, which can be a subtype of Fractional. Since the Fractional type is defined as a union of AbstractFloat and FixedPoint, the r, g, and b fields may be used as any subtype of AbstractFloat, such as Float64 and Float32, or any of the FixedPoint number types.

 FixedPoint is a type that's defined in the FixedPointNumbers.jl package. Fixed-point numbers is a different way to represent real numbers than the floating-point format. More information can be found at https://github.com/JuliaMath/FixedPointNumbers.jl.

If you examine the source code further, you will find that many types are defined in a similar fashion.

Example 2 – the NamedDims.jl package

The NamedDims.jl package adds names to each dimension of a multi-dimensional array. The source code can be found at https://github.com/invenia/NamedDims.jl.

Let's take a look at the definition of `NamedDimsArray`:

```
"""
The `NamedDimsArray` constructor takes a list of names as `Symbol`s,
one per dimension, and an array to wrap.
"""
struct NamedDimsArray{L, T, N, A<:AbstractArray{T, N}} <: AbstractArray{T,
N}
    # `L` is for labels, it should be an `NTuple{N, Symbol}`
    data::A
end
```

Don't be intimidated by the signature. It is actually quite straightforward.

`NamedDimsArray` is a subtype of the abstract array type `AbstractArray{T, N}`. It only contains a single field, `data`, which keeps track of the underlying data. Because `T` and `N` are already parameters in `A`, they also need to be specified in the signature of `NamedDimsArray`. The `L` parameter is used to keep track of the names of the dimensions. Note that `L` is not used in any of the fields but that it is conveniently stored in the type signature itself.

The primary constructor is defined as follows:

```
function NamedDimsArray{L}(orig::AbstractArray{T, N}) where {L, T, N}
    if !(L isa NTuple{N, Symbol})
        throw(ArgumentError(
            "A $N dimensional array, needs a $N-tuple of dimension names.
Got: $L"
        ))
    end
    return NamedDimsArray{L, T, N, typeof(orig)}(orig)
end
```

The function only needs to take an `AbstractArray{T,N}` that is an N-dimensional array with an element type of `T`. First, it checks if `L` contains a tuple of `N` symbols. Because type parameters are first-class, they can be examined in the body of the function. Assuming that `L` contains the right number of symbols, it just instantiates a `NamedDimsArray` using the known parameters `L`, `T`, `N`, as well as the type of the array argument.

It may be easier to see how it's used, so let's take a look:

```julia
julia> using NamedDims

julia> M = reshape(collect(1:9), 3, 3)
3×3 Array{Int64,2}:
 1  4  7
 2  5  8
 3  6  9

julia> nda = NamedDimsArray{(:x, :y)}(M)
3×3 NamedDimsArray{(:x, :y),Int64,2,Array{Int64,2}}:
 1  4  7
 2  5  8
 3  6  9
```

In the output, we can see that the type signature is `NamedDimsArray{(:x, :y),Int64,2,Array{Int64,2}}`. Matching this with the signature of the `NamedDimsArray` type, we can see that `L` is just the two-symbol tuple `(:x, :y)`, `T` is `Int64`, `N` is 2, and the underlying data is of the `Array{Int64, 2}` type.

Let's take a look at the `dimnames` function, which is defined as follows:

```julia
dimnames(::Type{<:NamedDimsArray{L}}) where L = L
```

This function returns the dimensions tuple:

```julia
julia> dimnames(nda)
(:x, :y)
```

Now, things are getting a little more interesting. What is `NamedDimsArray{L}`? Didn't we need four parameters in this type? It is worth noting that a type such as `NamedDimsArray{L, T, N, A}` is actually a subtype of `NamedDimsArray{L}`. We can prove this as follows:

```julia
julia> NamedDimsArray{(:x, :y),Int64,2,Array{Int64,2}} <: NamedDimsArray{(:x, :y)}
true

julia> NamedDimsArray{(:x, :y),Int64,2,Array{Int64,2}} <: NamedDimsArray{(:a, :b)}
false
```

If we really want to see what NamedDimsArray{L} is, we can try the following:

```
julia> NamedDimsArray{(:x, :y)}
NamedDimsArray{(:x, :y),T,N,A} where A<:AbstractArray{T,N} where N where T

julia> NamedDimsArray{(:x, :y), T, N, A} where A<:AbstractArray{T,N} where
N where T
NamedDimsArray{(:x, :y),T,N,A} where A<:AbstractArray{T,N} where N where T

julia> NamedDimsArray{L, T, N, A} where A<:AbstractArray{T,N} where N where
 T where L
NamedDimsArray
```

What seems to be happening is that NamedDimsArray{(:x, :y)} is just shorthand for NamedDimsArray{(:x, :y),T,N,A} where A<:AbstractArray{T,N} where N where T. Because this is a more general type with three unknown parameters, we can see why NamedDimsArray{(:x, :y),Int64,2,Array{Int64,2}} is a subtype of NamedDimsArray{(:x, :y)}.

Using parametric types is very good if we wish to reuse functionalities. We can almost view each type parameter as a "dimension". When a parametric type has two type parameters, we would have many possible subtypes based upon various combinations of each type parameter.

Summary

In this chapter, we have explored several patterns related to reusability. These patterns are highly valuable and can be utilized in many places within an application. In addition, people coming from an object-oriented background will probably find this chapter indispensable when it comes to designing Julia applications.

First, we went into great detail about the delegation pattern, which can be used to create new capabilities and lets us reuse functions from an existing object. The general technique involves defining a new data type that contains a parent object. Then, forwarding functions are defined so that we can reuse the functionalities of the parent object. We learned implementing delegation can be largely simplified by using @forward, which is provided by the Lazy.jl package.

Then, we examined the holy trait pattern, which is a formal way to define the behavior of objects. The idea is to define traits as native types and utilize Julia's built-in dispatch mechanism to call the right method implementation. We realize that traits are useful in making the code more extensible. We also learned that macros from the `SimpleTraits.jl` package can make trait coding easier.

Finally, we looked into the parametric types pattern and how it can be utilized to simplify the design of code. We learned that parametric types can reduce the size of our code. We also saw that parameters can be used in the bodies of parametric functions.

In the next chapter, we will discuss an important subject that attracts a lot of people to the Julia programming language – performance patterns!

Questions

1. How does the delegation pattern work?
2. What is the purpose of traits?
3. Are traits always binary?
4. Can traits be used for objects from a different type hierarchy?
5. What are the benefits of parametric types?
6. How do we store the information of a parametric type?

6
Performance Patterns

This chapter includes patterns related to improving system performance. High performance is a major requirement in scientific computing, artificial intelligence, machine learning, and big data processing. Why is that?

In the past decade, data has grown almost exponentially thanks to the scalability from the cloud. Think about the **Internet of Things** (**IoT**). Sensors are all around us—home security systems, personal assistants, and even room temperature controls are collecting tons of data continuously. Furthermore, the data being collected is stored and analyzed by companies that want to build smarter products. Use cases such as these demand more computing power and speed.

I once debated with a colleague about the use of cloud technologies for solving computationally intensive problems. Computing resources are definitely available in the cloud, but they are not free. It is therefore quite important that computer programs are designed to be more efficient and optimized to avoid unnecessary costs in the cloud.

Fortunately, the Julia programming language allows us to easily utilize CPU resources to the fullest extent. The way to make things fast is not difficult as long as some rules are followed. The online Julia reference manual already contains some tips. This chapter provides further patterns that are used extensively by veteran Julia developers to increase performance.

We will go over the following design patterns:

- Global constant
- Struct of arrays
- Shared arrays
- Memoization
- Barrier function

Let's get started!

Technical requirements

The sample source code is located at `https://github.com/PacktPublishing/Hands-on-Design-Patterns-and-Best-Practices-with-Julia/tree/master/Chapter06`.

The code is tested in a Julia 1.3.0 environment.

The global constant pattern

Global variables are generally considered evil. I'm not kidding—they are evil. If you don't believe me, just google it. There are many reasons why they are bad, but in Julia land, they can also be a contributor to poor application performance.

Why do we want to use global variables? In the Julia language, variables are either in the global or local scope. For example, all variable assignments at the top level of a module are considered global. Variables that appear inside functions are local. Consider an application that connects to an external system—a handle object is typically created upon connection. Such handle objects can be kept in a global variable because all functions in the module can access the variable without having to pass it around as a function argument. That's the convenience factor. Also, this handler object only needs to be created once, and then it can be used at any time for subsequent actions.

Unfortunately, global variables also come with a cost. It may not be obvious at first, but it does hurt performance—indeed, quite badly, in some cases. In this section, we will discuss how bad global variables hurt performance and how the problem can be remedied by using global constants.

Benchmarking performance with global variables

Sometimes, it is convenient to use global variables because they are accessible from anywhere in the code. However, application performance may suffer when using global variables. Let's figure out together how badly performance is affected. Here is a very simple function that just adds two numbers together:

```
variable = 10

function add_using_global_variable(x)
    return x + variable
end
```

To benchmark this code, we will use the great `BenchmarkTools.jl` package, which can repeatedly run the code many times and report back some performance statistics. Let's get started:

```
julia> using BenchmarkTools

julia> @btime add_using_global_variable(10);
  31.350 ns (1 allocation: 16 bytes)
```

It seems a little slow for just adding two numbers. Let's get rid of the global variable and just add the numbers using two function arguments. We can define the new function as follows:

```
function add_using_function_arg(x, y)
    return x + y
end
```

Let's benchmark this new function:

```
julia> @btime add_using_function_arg(10, 10);
  0.031 ns (0 allocations: 0 bytes)
```

That's *unbelievable*! Taking away the reference to the global variable sped up the function by almost 900 times. To understand where the performance hit came from, we can use the built-in introspection tool from Julia to see the generated LLVM code.

Here's the generated code for the faster one. It is clean and contains just a single `add` instruction:

```
julia> @code_llvm add_using_function_arg(10, 10)

;  @ REPL[9]:2 within `add_using_function_arg'
define i64 @julia_add_using_function_arg_17228(i64, i64) {
top:
;  ┌ @ int.jl:53 within `+'
    %2 = add i64 %1, %0
;  └
    ret i64 %2
}
```

On the other hand, the function that uses global variable generated this ugly code:

```
julia> @code_llvm add_using_global_variable(10)

;  @ REPL[6]:2 within 'add_using_global_variable'
define nonnull %jl_value_t addrspace(10)* @julia_add_using_global_variable_17100(i64) {
top:
  %1 = alloca %jl_value_t addrspace(10)*, i32 2
  %gcframe = alloca %jl_value_t addrspace(10)*, i32 4
  %2 = bitcast %jl_value_t addrspace(10)** %gcframe to i8*
  call void @llvm.memset.p0i8.i32(i8* %2, i8 0, i32 32, i32 0, i1 false)
  %3 = call %jl_value_t*** inttoptr (i64 4494723472 to %jl_value_t*** ()*)() #4
  %4 = getelementptr %jl_value_t addrspace(10)*, %jl_value_t addrspace(10)** %gcframe, i32 0
  %5 = bitcast %jl_value_t addrspace(10)** %4 to i64*
  store i64 4, i64* %5
  %6 = getelementptr %jl_value_t**, %jl_value_t*** %3, i32 0
  %7 = load %jl_value_t**, %jl_value_t*** %6
  %8 = getelementptr %jl_value_t addrspace(10)*, %jl_value_t addrspace(10)** %gcframe, i32 1
  %9 = bitcast %jl_value_t addrspace(10)** %8 to %jl_value_t***
  store %jl_value_t** %7, %jl_value_t*** %9
  %10 = bitcast %jl_value_t*** %6 to %jl_value_t addrspace(10)***
  store %jl_value_t addrspace(10)** %gcframe, %jl_value_t addrspace(10)*** %10
  %11 = load %jl_value_t addrspace(10)*, %jl_value_t addrspace(10)** inttoptr (i64 4814001384 to %jl_valu
e_t addrspace(10)**), align 8
  %12 = getelementptr %jl_value_t addrspace(10)*, %jl_value_t addrspace(10)** %gcframe, i32 2
  store %jl_value_t addrspace(10)* %11, %jl_value_t addrspace(10)** %12
  %13 = call %jl_value_t addrspace(10)* @jl_box_int64(i64 signext %0)
  %14 = getelementptr %jl_value_t addrspace(10)*, %jl_value_t addrspace(10)** %gcframe, i32 3
  store %jl_value_t addrspace(10)* %13, %jl_value_t addrspace(10)** %14
  %15 = getelementptr %jl_value_t addrspace(10)*, %jl_value_t addrspace(10)** %1, i32 0
  store %jl_value_t addrspace(10)* %13, %jl_value_t addrspace(10)** %15
  %16 = getelementptr %jl_value_t addrspace(10)*, %jl_value_t addrspace(10)** %1, i32 1
  store %jl_value_t addrspace(10)* %11, %jl_value_t addrspace(10)** %16
  %17 = call nonnull %jl_value_t addrspace(10)* @jl_apply_generic(%jl_value_t addrspace(10)* addrspacecas
t (%jl_value_t* inttoptr (i64 4655294832 to %jl_value_t*) to %jl_value_t addrspace(10)*), %jl_value_t add
rspace(10)** %1, i32 2)
  %18 = getelementptr %jl_value_t addrspace(10)*, %jl_value_t addrspace(10)** %gcframe, i32 1
  %19 = load %jl_value_t addrspace(10)*, %jl_value_t addrspace(10)** %18
  %20 = getelementptr %jl_value_t**, %jl_value_t*** %3, i32 0
  %21 = bitcast %jl_value_t*** %20 to %jl_value_t addrspace(10)**
  store %jl_value_t addrspace(10)* %19, %jl_value_t addrspace(10)** %21
  ret %jl_value_t addrspace(10)* %17
}
```

Why is that? Shouldn't the compiler be smarter? The answer is that the compiler cannot really assume that the global variable is always an integer. Because it is a variable, which means it can be changed at any time, the compiler must generate code that can handle any data type, to stay on the safe side. Well, such additional flexibility introduces a huge overhead in this case.

Enjoying the speed of global constants

To improve performance, let's create a global constant by using the `const` keyword. Then, we can define a new function that accesses the constant, as follows:

```
const constant = 10

function add_using_global_constant(x)
    return constant + x
end
```

Let's benchmark its performance now:

```
julia> @btime add_using_global_constant(10);
  0.032 ns (0 allocations: 0 bytes)
```

This is perfect! If we introspect the function again, we get the following clean code:

```
julia> @code_llvm add_using_global_constant(10)

;   @ REPL[27]:2 within 'add_using_global_constant'
define i64 @julia_add_using_global_constant_17419(i64) {
top:
; ┌ @ int.jl:53 within '+'
    %1 = add i64 %0, 10
; └
    ret i64 %1
}
```

Next, we will discuss how to use a global variable (not a constant) and still make it slightly better.

Annotating variables with type information

It is best when we can just use global constants. But what if the variable *does* need to be changed during the life cycle of the application? For example, maybe it is a global counter that keeps track of the number of visitors on a website.

At first, we may be tempted to do the following, but we quickly realized that Julia does not support annotating global variables with type information:

```julia
julia> variable::Int = 10
ERROR: syntax: type declarations on global variables are not yet supported
```

Instead, what we can do is to annotate the variable type within the function itself, as follows:

```julia
function add_using_global_variable_typed(x)
    return x + variable::Int
end
```

Let's see how it performs:

```julia
julia> variable = 10
10

julia> @btime add_using_global_variable_typed(10);
  5.541 ns (0 allocations: 0 bytes)
```

That's quite a speed boost compared to the untyped version of 31 ns! However, it is still far away from the global constant solution.

Understanding why constants help performance

The compiler has a lot more freedom when dealing with constants because of the following:

- The value does not change.
- The type of the constant does not change.

This will become clear after we look into some simple examples.

Let's take a look at the following function:

```julia
function constant_folding_example()
    a = 2 * 3
    b = a + 1
    return b > 1 ? 10 : 20
end
```

If we just follow the logic, then it is not difficult to see that it always returns a value of 10. Let's just unroll it quickly here:

- The a variable has a value of 6.
- The b variable has a value of a + 1, which is 7.
- Because the b variable is greater than 1, it returns 10.

From the compiler's perspective, the a variable can be inferred as a constant because it is assigned but never changed, and likewise for the b variable.

We can take a look at the code generated by Julia for this:

```
julia> @code_typed constant_folding_example()
CodeInfo(
1 ─     return 10
) => Int64
```

The Julia compiler goes through several stages. In this case, we can use the @code_typed macro, which shows the code that has been generated where all type information has been resolved.

Voila! The compiler has figured it all out and just returns a value of 10 for this function.

We realize that a couple of things have happened here:

- When the compiler saw the multiplication of two constant values (2 * 3), it computed the final value of 6 for a. This process is called **constant folding**.
- When the compiler inferred a as a value of 6, it calculated b as a value of 7. This process is called **constant propagation**.
- When the compiler inferred b as a value of 7, it pruned away the else-branch from the if-then-else operation. This process is called **dead code elimination**.

Julia's compiler optimization is truly state of the art. These are just some of the examples that we can get a performance boost automatically without having to refactor a lot of code.

Passing global variables as function arguments

There is another way to tackle the problem of global variables. In a performance-sensitive function, rather than accessing the global variable directly, we can pass the global variable into the function as an argument.

Let's refactor the code earlier in this section by adding a second argument, as follows:

```
function add_by_passing_global_variable(x, v)
    return x + v
end
```

Now, we can call the function by passing in the variable. Let's benchmark the code as follows:

```
julia> @btime add_by_passing_global_variable(10, $variable);
  0.032 ns (0 allocations: 0 bytes)
```

Fantastic! It's as fast as treating it as a constant. Where's the magic? As it turns out, Julia's compiler automatically generates specialized functions according to the type of its arguments. In this case, when we pass the variable as an integer value, the function is compiled to the most optimized version because the types of the arguments are known. It is fast now for the same reason as using constants.

Of course, you may argue that it defeats the purpose of using global variables. Nonetheless, the flexibility is there and it can be used when you really need to get to the most optimal performance.

When using `BenchmarkTools.jl` macros, we must interpolate global variables using the dollar-sign prefix. Otherwise, the time that it takes to reference the global variable is included in the performance test.

Hiding a variable inside a global constant

Before we conclude this section, there is yet another alternative to keep the flexibility of global variables while not losing too much performance. We can call it a **global variable placeholder**.

As it may have become clear to you by now, Julia can generate highly optimized code whenever the type of a variable is known at compilation time. Hence, one way to solve the problem is to create a constant placeholder and store a value inside the placeholder.

Consider this code:

```
# Initialize a constant Ref object with the value of 10
const semi_constant = Ref(10)

function add_using_global_semi_constant(x)
```

```
        return x + semi_constant[]
    end
```

The global constant is assigned a `Ref` object. In Julia, a `Ref` object is nothing but a placeholder where the type of the enclosed object is known. You can try this in the Julia REPL:

```
julia> Ref(10)
Base.RefValue{Int64}(10)

julia> Ref("abc")
Base.RefValue{String}("abc")
```

As we can see, the value inside `Ref(10)` has a type of `Int64` according to the type signature, `Base.RefValue{Int64}`. Similarly, the type of the value inside `Ref("abc")` is `String`.

To fetch the value inside a `Ref` object, we can just use the index operator with no argument. Hence, in the preceding code, we use `semi_constant[]`.

What would be the performance overhead of this extra indirection? Let's benchmark the code as usual:

```
julia> @btime add_using_global_semi_constant(10);
  2.097 ns (0 allocations: 0 bytes)
```

That's not bad. Although it is far from the optimal performance of using global constant, it is still approximately 15 times faster than using a plain global variable.

Because `Ref` object is just a placeholder, the underlying value can also be assigned:

```
julia> semi_constant[] = 20
20

julia> semi_constant
Base.RefValue{Int64}(20)
```

In summary, the use of `Ref` allows us to simulate global variables without sacrificing too much performance.

Turning to some real-life examples

Global constants are very common among Julia packages. It is not too surprising because constants are also used to avoid hardcoding values directly in functions.

Example 1 – SASLib.jl package

In the `SASLib.jl` package, most constants are defined in the `constants.jl` file located at `https://github.com/tk3369/SASLib.jl/blob/master/src/constants.jl`.

Here's a fragment of the code:

```
# default settings
const default_chunk_size = 0
const default_verbose_level = 1

const magic = [
        b"\x00\x00\x00\x00\x00\x00\x00\x00" ;
        b"\x00\x00\x00\x00\xc2\xea\x81\x60" ;
        b"\xb3\x14\x11\xcf\xbd\x92\x08\x00" ;
        b"\x09\xc7\x31\x8c\x18\x1f\x10\x11" ]

const align_1_checker_value = b"3"
const align_1_offset = 32
const align_1_length = 1
const align_1_value = 4
```

Using these constants allows the file-reading functions to perform well.

Example 2 – PyCall.jl package

The `PyCall.jl` package's documentation suggests the user stores a Python object using the global variable placeholder technique. The following excerpt can be found in its documentation:

"For a type-stable global constant, initialize the constant to `PyNULL()` *at the top level, and then use the* `copy!` *function in your module's __init__ function to mutate it to its actual value."*

A type-stable global constant is generally what we want for high-performance code. Basically, when the module is initialized, this global constant can be initialized with a value of `PyNULL()`. This constant is really just a placeholder object that can be mutated with the actual value later.

This technique is similar to the use of `Ref` as mentioned in the *Hiding a variable inside a global constant* section.

Considerations

If a global variable can be replaced as a global constant, then it should always be done. The reason for doing that is more than performance alone. Constants have the nice property of guaranteeing that their values are unchanged throughout the application life cycle. In general, the fewer global state changes, the more robust the program. Mutating states is traditionally a source of hard-to-find bugs.

At times, we may get into a situation that we cannot avoid using global variables. That's too bad. However, before we feel sad about that, we could also check whether the system performance is materially affected or not.

In the preceding example of adding two numbers, accessing the global variable carries a relatively large cost because the actual operation is so simple and efficient. Hence, more work is done in terms of getting access to the global variable. On the other hand, if we have a more complex function that takes much longer, say, 500 nanoseconds, then the extra 25 nanosecond overhead becomes much less significant. In that case, we may as well ignore the issue as the overhead becomes immaterial.

Finally, we should always watch out when too many global variables are used. The problem multiplies when more global variables are used. How many are too many? It really depends on your situation, but it does not hurt to think about the application design and ask yourself whether the application is designed properly.

In the next section, we will discuss a pattern that helps to improve system performance just by laying out data differently in memory.

The struct of arrays pattern

In recent years, modern CPU architecture has got fancier to meet today's demands. Due to various physical constraints, it is a lot more difficult to attain higher processor speed. Many Intel processors now support a technology called **Single Instruction, Multiple Data (SIMD)**. By utilizing **Streaming SIMD Extension (SSE)** and **Advanced Vector Extensions (AVX)** registers, several mathematical operations can be executed within a single CPU cycle.

That is nice, but one of the pre-requisites of utilizing these fancy CPU instructions is to make sure that the data is located in a contiguous memory block in the first place. That brings us to our topic here. How do we orient our data in a contiguous memory block? You may find the solution in this section.

Working with a business domain model

When designing an application, we often create an object model that mimics business domain concepts. The idea is to clearly articulate data in a form that feels most natural to the programmer.

Let's say we need to retrieve customers' data from a relational database. A customer record may be stored in a CUSTOMER table, and each customer is stored as a row in the table. When we fetch customer data from the database, we can construct a Customer object and push that into an array. Similarly, when we work with NoSQL databases, we may receive data as JSON documents and put them into an array of objects. In both cases, we can see that data is represented as an array of objects. Applications are usually designed to work with objects as defined using the struct statement.

Let's take a look at a use case for analyzing taxi data coming from New York City. The data is publicly available as several CSV files. For illustration purposes, we have downloaded the data for December 2018 and truncated it to 100,000 records.

The full data file can be downloaded from https://data.cityofnewyork.us/Transportation/2018-Yellow-Taxi-Trip-Data/t29m-gskq.

For convenience, a smaller file with 100,000 records is available from our GitHub site at https://github.com/PacktPublishing/Hands-On-Design-Patterns-with-Julia-1.0/raw/master/Chapter06/StructOfArraysPattern/yellow_tripdata_2018-12_100k.csv.

First, we define a type called `TripPayment`, as follows:

```
struct TripPayment
    vendor_id::String
    tpep_pickup_datetime::String
    tpep_dropoff_datetime::String
    passenger_count::Int
    trip_distance::Float64
    fare_amount::Float64
    extra::Float64
    mta_tax::Float64
    tip_amount::Float64
    tolls_amount::Float64
    improvement_surcharge::Float64
    total_amount::Float64
end
```

To read the data into memory, we will take advantage of the `CSV.jl` package. Let's define a function to read the file into a vector:

```
function read_trip_payment_file(file)
    f = CSV.File(file, datarow = 3)
    records = Vector{TripPayment}(undef, length(f))
    for (i, row) in enumerate(f)
        records[i] = TripPayment(row.VendorID,
                                 row.tpep_pickup_datetime,
                                 row.tpep_dropoff_datetime,
                                 row.passenger_count,
                                 row.trip_distance,
                                 row.fare_amount,
                                 row.extra,
                                 row.mta_tax,
                                 row.tip_amount,
                                 row.tolls_amount,
                                 row.improvement_surcharge,
                                 row.total_amount)
    end
    return records
end
```

Now, when we fetch the data, we end up with an array. In this example, we have downloaded 100,000 records, as shown in the following screenshot:

```julia
julia> records = read_trip_payment_file("yellow_tripdata_2018-12_100k.csv")
100000-element Array{TripPayment,1}:
 TripPayment(1, "2018-12-01 00:28:22", "2018-12-01 00:44:07", 2, 2.5, 12.0, 0.5, 0.5
, 3.95, 0.0, 0.3, 17.25)
 TripPayment(1, "2018-12-01 00:52:29", "2018-12-01 01:11:37", 3, 2.3, 13.0, 0.5, 0.5
, 2.85, 0.0, 0.3, 17.15)
 TripPayment(2, "2018-12-01 00:12:52", "2018-12-01 00:36:23", 1, 0.0, 2.5, 0.5, 0.5,
0.0, 0.0, 0.3, 3.8)
 TripPayment(1, "2018-12-01 00:35:08", "2018-12-01 00:43:11", 1, 3.9, 12.5, 0.5, 0.5
, 2.75, 0.0, 0.3, 16.55)
 :

 TripPayment(1, "2018-12-01 11:23:12", "2018-12-01 11:43:25", 1, 1.6, 13.0, 0.0, 0.5
, 3.45, 0.0, 0.3, 17.25)
 TripPayment(1, "2018-12-01 11:45:56", "2018-12-01 11:58:25", 1, 1.7, 10.0, 0.0, 0.5
, 2.7, 0.0, 0.3, 13.5)
 TripPayment(2, "2018-12-01 11:11:12", "2018-12-01 11:27:17", 2, 2.88, 13.5, 0.0, 0.
5, 2.14, 0.0, 0.3, 16.44)
```

Now, suppose that we need to analyze this dataset. In many data analysis use cases, we simply calculate various statistics for some of the attributes in the payment records. For example, we may want to find the average fare amount, as follows:

```julia
julia> mean(r.fare_amount for r in records)
11.985990599999994
```

This should be a fairly fast operation already because it uses a generator syntax and avoids allocation.

 Some Julia functions accept generator syntax, which can be written just like an array comprehension without the square brackets. It is very memory efficient because it avoids allocating memory for the intermediate object.

The only thing is that it needs to access the `fare_amount` field for every record. If we benchmark the function, it shows the following:

```julia
julia> @btime mean(r.fare_amount for r in $records);
  629.761 µs (1 allocation: 16 bytes)
```

How do we know whether it runs at optimal speed? We don't unless we try to do it differently. Because all we are doing is calculating the mean of 100,000 floating-point numbers, we can easily replicate that with a simple array. Let's replicate the data in a separate array:

```
fare_amounts = [r.fare_amount for r in records];
```

Then, we can benchmark the mean function by passing the array as is:

```
julia> @btime mean(fare_amounts);
  27.097 µs (1 allocation: 16 bytes)
```

Whoa! What's happening here? It is 24x faster than before.

In this case, the compiler was able to make use of the more advanced CPU instructions. Because Julia arrays are dense arrays, that is, data is compactly stored in a contiguous block of memory, it enables the compiler to fully optimize the operation.

Converting data into an array seems to be a decent solution. However, just imagine that you have to create these temporary arrays for every single field. It is not much fun anymore as there is a possibility to miss a field while doing so. Is there a better way to solve this problem?

Improving performance using a different data layout

The problem we just saw is caused by the use of an array of structs. What we really want is a struct of arrays. Notice the difference between arrays of structs and structs of arrays?

In an array of structs, to access a field for an object, the program must first index into the object and then find the field via a predetermined offset in memory. For example, the passenger_count field in the TripPayment object is the fourth field of the struct where the preceding three fields are Int64, String, and String types. So, the offset to the fourth field is 24. An array of structs has a row-oriented layout as every row is stored in a contiguous block of memory.

We now introduce the concept of struct of arrays. In a struct of arrays, we take a column-oriented approach. In this case, we only maintain a single object for the entire dataset. Within the object, each field represents an array of a particular field of the original record. For example, the `fare_amount` field would be stored as an array of fare amounts in this object. The column-oriented format is optimized for high-performance computing because the data values in the array all have the same type. In addition, they are also more compact in memory.

 A struct is typically aligned into 8-byte memory blocks in a 64-bit system. For example, a struct that contains just two fields of `Int32` and `Int16` types still consumes 8 bytes even though 6 bytes are enough to store the data. The two extra bytes are used to pad the data structure to an 8-byte boundary.

In the following sections, we will look into how to implement this pattern and confirm that performance has improved.

Constructing a struct of arrays

It is easy and straightforward to construct a struct of arrays. After all, we were able to quickly do that for a single field earlier. For completeness, this is how we can design a new data type for storing the same trip payment data in a column-oriented format. The following code shows that this pattern helps to improve performance:

```
struct TripPaymentColumnarData
    vendor_id::Vector{Int}
    tpep_pickup_datetime::Vector{String}
    tpep_dropoff_datetime::Vector{String}
    passenger_count::Vector{Int}
    trip_distance::Vector{Float64}
    fare_amount::Vector{Float64}
    extra::Vector{Float64}
    mta_tax::Vector{Float64}
    tip_amount::Vector{Float64}
    tolls_amount::Vector{Float64}
    improvement_surcharge::Vector{Float64}
    total_amount::Vector{Float64}
end
```

Notice that every field has been turned into `Vector{T}`, where `T` is the original data type of the particular field. It looks quite ugly but we are willing to sacrifice ugliness here for performance reasons.

The general rule of thumb is that we should just **Keep It Simple** (**KISS**). Under certain circumstances, when we do need higher runtime performance, we could bend a little.

Now, although we have a data type that is more optimized for performance, we still need to populate it with data for testing. In this case, it can be achieved quite easily using array comprehension syntax:

```
columar_records = TripPaymentColumnarData(
    [r.vendor_id for r in records],
    [r.tpep_pickup_datetime for r in records],
    [r.tpep_dropoff_datetime for r in records],
    [r.passenger_count for r in records],
    [r.trip_distance for r in records],
    [r.fare_amount for r in records],
    [r.extra for r in records],
    [r.mta_tax for r in records],
    [r.tip_amount for r in records],
    [r.tolls_amount for r in records],
    [r.improvement_surcharge for r in records],
    [r.total_amount for r in records]
);
```

When we're done, we can prove to ourselves that the new object structure is indeed optimized:

```
julia> @btime mean(columar_records.fare_amount);
  27.202 µs (1 allocation: 16 bytes)
```

Yes, it now has great performance, as we expected.

Using the StructArrays package

The ugliness of the preceding columnar struct left us in a very unsatisfied state. Not only do we need to create a new data type with tons of `Vector` fields, we also have to create a constructor function to convert our array of structs into the new type.

We can recognize the power of Julia when we get to use powerful packages in its ecosystem. To fully implement this pattern, we will introduce the `StructArrays.jl` package, which automates most of the mundane tasks in turning an array of structs into a struct of arrays.

In fact, the usage of StructArrays is embarrassingly simple:

```
using StructArrays
sa = StructArray(records)
```

Let's take a quick look at the content. First of all, we can treat sa just like the original array—for example, we can take the first three elements of the array as before:

```
julia> sa[1:3]
3-element StructArray(::Array{Int64,1}, ::Array{String,1}, ::Array{String,1}, ::Arra
y{Int64,1}, ::Array{Float64,1}, ::Array{Float64,1}, ::Array{Float64,1}, ::Array{Floa
t64,1}, ::Array{Float64,1}, ::Array{Float64,1}, ::Array{Float64,1}, ::Array{Float64,
1}) with eltype TripPayment:
 TripPayment(1, "2018-12-01 00:28:22", "2018-12-01 00:44:07", 2, 2.5, 12.0, 0.5, 0.5
, 3.95, 0.0, 0.3, 17.25)
 TripPayment(1, "2018-12-01 00:52:29", "2018-12-01 01:11:37", 3, 2.3, 13.0, 0.5, 0.5
, 2.85, 0.0, 0.3, 17.15)
 TripPayment(2, "2018-12-01 00:12:52", "2018-12-01 00:36:23", 1, 0.0, 2.5, 0.5, 0.5,
 0.0, 0.0, 0.3, 3.8)
```

If we pick just one record, it comes back with the original TripPayment object:

```
julia> sa[1]
TripPayment(1, "2018-12-01 00:28:22", "2018-12-01 00:44:07", 2, 2.5, 12.0, 0.5, 0.5,
 3.95, 0.0, 0.3, 17.25)
```

Just to make sure that there is no mistake, we can also check the type of the first record:

```
julia> typeof(sa[1])
TripPayment
```

Hence, the new sa object works just like before. Now, the difference comes in when we need to access all of the data from a single field. For example, we can get the fare_amount field as follows:

```
julia> sa.fare_amount
100000-element Array{Float64,1}:
 12.0
 13.0
  ⋮
 10.0
 13.5
```

Because the type is already materialized as a *dense array*, we can expect superb performance when doing numerical or statistical analysis on this field, as follows:

```
julia> @btime mean(sa.fare_amount);
  27.193 µs (1 allocation: 16 bytes)
```

What is a `DenseArray`? It is actually an abstract type for which all elements in the array are allocated in a contiguous block of memory. `DenseArray` is a super-type of array.

Julia supports dynamic arrays by default, which means the size of the array can grow when we push more data into it. When it allocates more memory, it copies existing data over to the new memory location.

To avoid excessive memory reallocation, the current implementation uses a sophisticated algorithm to increase the size of memory allocation—fast enough to avoid excessive reallocation but conservative enough to not over-allocate memory.

Understanding the space versus time trade-off

The `StructArrays.jl` package provides a convenient mechanism to quickly turn an array of structs into a struct of arrays. We must recognize that the price we are paying is an additional copy of the data in memory. Hence, we are once again getting into the classic space versus time trade-off in computing.

Let's quickly look into our use case again. We can use the `Base.summarysize` function in the Julia REPL to see the memory footprint:

```
julia> Base.summarysize(records) / 1024 / 1024
15.068092346191406

julia> Base.summarysize(sa) / 1024 / 1024
14.305671691894531
```

The `Base.summarysize` function returns the size of the object in bytes. We divided the number `1024` twice to arrive at the mega-byte unit. It is interesting to see that the struct of arrays, `sa`, is more memory efficient than the original array of structs, `records`. Nevertheless, we have two copies of data in memory.

Fortunately, we do have some options here if we want to conserve memory. First, we may just discard the original data in the `records` variable if we no longer need the data in that structure. We can even force the garbage collector to run, as follows:

```julia
julia> record = nothing

julia> GC.gc()
```

Second, we can discard the `sa` variable when we are done with the computation.

Handling nested object structures

The preceding sample case works fine for any flat data structure. Nowadays, it is not uncommon to design types that contain other composite types. Let's drill down a little bit deeper to see how we can handle such a nested structure.

First, suppose that we want to separate the fields related to the fare in a separate composite data type:

```julia
struct TripPayment
    vendor_id::String
    tpep_pickup_datetime::String
    tpep_dropoff_datetime::String
    passenger_count::Int
    trip_distance::Float64
    fare::Fare
end

struct Fare
    fare_amount::Float64
    extra::Float64
    mta_tax::Float64
    tip_amount::Float64
    tolls_amount::Float64
    improvement_surcharge::Float64
    total_amount::Float64
end
```

We can adjust the file reader slightly:

```julia
function read_trip_payment_file(file)
    f = CSV.File(file, datarow = 3)
    records = Vector{TripPayment}(undef, length(f))
    for (i, row) in enumerate(f)
```

```
        records[i] = TripPayment(row.VendorID,
                                 row.tpep_pickup_datetime,
                                 row.tpep_dropoff_datetime,
                                 row.passenger_count,
                                 row.trip_distance,
                                 Fare(row.fare_amount,
                                     row.extra,
                                     row.mta_tax,
                                     row.tip_amount,
                                     row.tolls_amount,
                                     row.improvement_surcharge,
                                     row.total_amount))
    end
    return records
end
```

After we read the data, the array of trip payment data would look like the following:

```
julia> records = read_trip_payment_file("yellow_tripdata_2018-12_100k.csv");

julia> records[1]
TripPayment(1, "2018-12-01 00:28:22", "2018-12-01 00:44:07", 2, 2.5, Fare(12.0,
 0.5, 0.5, 3.95, 0.0, 0.3, 17.25))
```

If we just create `StructArray` as before, we cannot extract the `fare_amount` field:

```
julia> sa = StructArray(records);

julia> sa.fare.fare_amount
ERROR: type Array has no field fare_amount
```

To achieve the same result at a level deeper, we can use the `unwrap` option:

```
julia> sa = StructArray(records, unwrap = t -> t <: Fare);
```

The value of the `unwrap` keyword argument is basically a function that accepts a data type for a particular field. If the function returns `true`, then that particular field will be constructed with a nested `StructArray`.

We can now access the `fare_amount` field with another level of indirection as follows:

```
julia> sa.fare.fare_amount
100000-element Array{Float64,1}:
  12.0
  13.0
   2.5
   ⋮
  10.0
  13.5
```

Using the `unwrap` keyword argument, we can easily walk through the entire data structure and create a `StructArray` object that allows us to access any data element in a compact array structure. From this point on, application performance can be improved.

Considerations

When designing applications, we ought to determine what is the most important thing that is valued by our users. Similarly, when working on data analysis or data science projects, we should think about what we care about the most. A customer-first approach is essential in any decision-making process.

Let's assume that our priority is to achieve better performance. Then, the next question is which part of the system requires optimization? If the part is slowed down due to the use of an array of structs, how much do we gain in speed when we employ the struct of arrays pattern? Is the performance gain noticeable—is it measured in milliseconds, minutes, hours, or days?

Further, we need to consider system constraints. We like to think that the sky is the limit. But then coming back to reality, we are limited in system resources all over the place—the number of CPU cores, available memory, and disk space, as well other limits imposed by our system administrators, such as, maximum number of opened files and processes.

While struct of arrays can improve performance, there is an overhead in allocating memory for the new arrays. If the data size is large, the allocation and data copy operation will take some time as well.

In the next section, we will look into another pattern that helps to conserve memory and allows distributed computing— shared arrays.

The shared array pattern

Modern operating systems can handle many concurrent processes and fully utilize all processor cores. When it comes to distributed computing, a larger task is typically broken down into smaller ones such that multiple processes can execute the tasks concurrently. Sometimes, the results of these individual executions may need to be combined or aggregated for final delivery. This process is called **reduction**.

This concept is reincarnated in various forms. For example, in functional programming, it is common to implement data processes using map-reduce. The mapping process takes a list and applies a function to each element, and the reduction process combines the results. In big data processing, Hadoop uses a similar form of map-reduce, except that it runs across multiple machines in a cluster. The `DataFrames` package contains functions that perform the Split-Apply-Combine pattern. These all present pretty much the same concept.

Sometimes, parallel worker processes need to communicate with each other. In general, processes can talk to each other by passing data via some form of **Inter-Process Communication** (**IPC**). There are many ways to do that—sockets, Unix domain sockets, pipes, named pipes, message queues, shared memory, and memory maps.

Julia ships with a standard library called `SharedArrays`, which interfaces with the operating system's shared memory and memory map interface. This facility allows Julia processes to communicate with each other by sharing a central data source.

In this section, we will take a look at how `SharedArrays` can be used for high-performance computing.

Introducing a risk management use case

In a risk management use case, we want to estimate the volatility of portfolio returns using a process called Monte Carlo simulation. The concept is pretty simple. First, we develop a risk model based on historical data. Second, we use the model to predict the future in 10,000 ways. Finally, we look at the distribution of security returns in the portfolio and gauge how much the portfolio gains or losses in each of those scenarios.

Portfolios are often measured against benchmarks. For example, a stock portfolio may be benchmarked against the S&P 500 Index. The reason is that portfolio managers are typically rewarded for earning *alpha*, a term for describing the excess return that is over and above the benchmark's return. In other words, the portfolio manager is rewarded for their skills in picking the right stocks.

In the fixed income market, the problem is a little more challenging. Unlike the stock market, typical fixed income benchmarks are quite large, up to 10,000 bonds. In assessing portfolio risk, we often want to analyze the sources of return. Did the value of a portfolio go up because it was riding the wave in a bull market, or did it go down because everyone is selling? The risk that correlates to market movement is called **systematic risk**. Another source of return relates to the individual bond. For example, if the issuer of the bond is doing well and making good profit, then the bond has a lower risk and the price goes up. This kind of movement due to the specific individual bond is called **idiosyncratic risk**. For a global portfolio, some bonds are exposed to **currency risk** as well. From a computational complexity perspective, to estimate the returns of the benchmark index 10,000 ways, we have to perform *10,000 future scenarios x 10,000 securities x 3 sources of returns = 300 million* pricing calculations.

Coming back to our simulation example, we can generate 10,000 possible future scenarios of the portfolio, and the results are basically a set of returns across all such scenarios. The returns data is stored on disk and is now ready for additional analysis. Here comes the problem—an asset manager has to analyze over 1,000 portfolios, and each portfolio may require access to returns data varying between 10,000 to 50,000 bonds depending on the size of the benchmark index. Unfortunately, the production server is limited in memory but has plenty of CPU resources. How can we fully utilize our hardware to perform the analysis as quickly as possible?

Let's quickly summarize our problem:

- Hardware:
    - 16 vCPU
    - 32 GB RAM
- Security returns data:
    - Stored in 100,000 individual files
    - Each file contains a 10,000 x 3 matrix (10,000 future states and 3 return sources)
    - Total memory footprint is ~22 GB
- Task:
    - Calculate statistical measures (standard deviation, skewness, and kurtosis) for all security returns across the 10,000 future states.
    - Do that as quickly as possible!

The naive way to just load all of the files sequentially. Needless to say, loading 100,000 files one by one is not going to be very fast no matter how small the files are. We are going to use the Julia distributed computing facility to get it done.

Preparing data for the example

To follow the subsequent code for this pattern, we can prepare some test data. Before you run the code here, make sure that you have enough disk space for the test data. You will need approximately 22 GB of free space.

Rather than putting 100,000 files in a single directory, we can split them into 100 sub-directories. So, let's just create the directories first. A simple function is created for that purpose:

```
function make_data_directories()
    for i in 0:99
        mkdir("$i")
    end
end
```

We can assume that every security is identified by a numerical index value between 1 and 100,000. Let's define a function that generates the path to find the file:

```
function locate_file(index)
    id = index - 1
    dir = string(id % 100)
    joinpath(dir, "sec$(id).dat")
end
```

The function is designed to hash the file into one of the 100 sub-directories. Let's see how it works:

```
julia> locate_file.(vcat(1:2, 100:101))
4-element Array{String,1}:
 "0/sec0.dat"
 "1/sec1.dat"
 "99/sec99.dat"
 "0/sec100.dat"
```

So, the first 100 securities are located in directories called 0, 1, ..., 99. The 101st security starts wrapping and goes back to directory 0. For consistency reasons, the filename contains the security index minus 1.

Now we are ready to generate the test data. Let's define a function as follows:

```
function generate_test_data(nfiles)
    for i in 1:nfiles
        A = rand(10000, 3)
        file = locate_file(i)
        open(file, "w") do io
            write(io, A)
```

```
          end
       end
   end
```

To generate all test files, we just need to call this function by passing `nfiles` with a value of 100,000. By the end of this exercise, you should have test files scattered in all 100 sub-directories. Note that the `generate_test_data` function will take a few minutes to generate all the test data. Let's do that now:

```julia
julia> folder = joinpath(ENV["HOME"], "julia_book_ch06_data")
"/home/ubuntu/julia_book_ch06_data"

julia> make_data_directories(folder)

julia> cd(folder)

julia> generate_test_data(100_000)
```

When it is done, let's quickly take a look at our data files in a Terminal:

```
[$ pwd
/home/ubuntu/julia_book_ch06_data
[$ ls
0    14   2    25   30   36   41   47   52   58   63   69   74   8    85   90   96
1    15   20   26   31   37   42   48   53   59   64   7    75   80   86   91   97
10   16   21   27   32   38   43   49   54   6    65   70   76   81   87   92   98
11   17   22   28   33   39   44   5    55   60   66   71   77   82   88   93   99
12   18   23   29   34   4    45   50   56   61   67   72   78   83   89   94
13   19   24   3    35   40   46   51   57   62   68   73   79   84   9    95
[$ ls -l 0 | tail -6
-rw-rw-r-- 1 ubuntu ubuntu 240000 Dec  8 18:36 sec99400.dat
-rw-rw-r-- 1 ubuntu ubuntu 240000 Dec  8 18:36 sec99500.dat
-rw-rw-r-- 1 ubuntu ubuntu 240000 Dec  8 18:36 sec99600.dat
-rw-rw-r-- 1 ubuntu ubuntu 240000 Dec  8 18:36 sec99700.dat
-rw-rw-r-- 1 ubuntu ubuntu 240000 Dec  8 18:36 sec99800.dat
-rw-rw-r-- 1 ubuntu ubuntu 240000 Dec  8 18:36 sec99900.dat
```

We're now ready to tackle the problem using the shared array pattern. Let's get started.

Overview of a high-performance solution

The beauty of `SharedArrays` is that the data is maintained as a single copy, and multiple processes can have both read and write access. It is a perfect solution to our problem.

In this solution, we will do the following:

1. The master program creates a shared array.
2. Using a distributed `for` loop, the master program commands worker processes to read each individual file into a specific segment of the array.
3. Again, using a distributed `for` loop, the master program commands worker process to perform statistical analysis.

As we have 16 vCPUs, we can utilize all of them.

> In practice, we should probably utilize fewer vCPUs so that we can leave some room for the operating system itself. Your mileage may vary depending on what else is running on the same server. The best approach is to test various configurations and determine the optimal settings.

Populating data in the shared array

The security return files are distributed and stored in 100 different directories. Where it gets stored is based upon a simple formula: *file index **modulus** 100*, where the *file index* is the numerical identifier for each security, numbered between 1 to 100,000.

Each data file is in a simple binary format. The upstream process has calculated three source returns for 10,000 future states, as in a 10,000 x 3 matrix. The layout is column-oriented, meaning that the first 10,000 numbers are used for the first return source, the next 10,000 numbers are for the second return source, and so on.

Before we start using distributed computing functions, we must spawn worker processes. Julia comes with a convenient command-line option (`-p`) that the user can specify the number of worker processes up front as follows:

```
$ julia -p 16
               _
   _       _ _(_)_       |  Documentation: https://docs.julialang.org
  (_)     | (_) (_)      |
   _ _   _| |_  __ _     |  Type "?" for help, "]?" for Pkg help.
  | | | | | | |/ _` |    |
  | | |_| | | | (_| |    |  Version 1.3.0 (2019-11-26)
 _/ |\__'_|_|_|\__'_|    |  Official https://julialang.org/ release
|__/                     |

julia> nworkers()
16
```

When the REPL comes up, we would already have 16 processes running and ready to go. The `nworkers` function confirms that all 16 worker processes are available.

Let's look into the code now. First, we must load `Distributed` and `SharedArrays` packages:

```
using Distributed
using SharedArrays
```

To make sure that the worker processes know where to find the files, we have to change directory on all of them:

```
@everywhere cd(joinpath(ENV["HOME"], "julia_book_ch06_data"))
```

The `@everywhere` macro executes the statement on all worker processes.

The main program looks like this:

```
nfiles = 100_000
nstates = 10_000
nattr = 3
valuation = SharedArray{Float64}(nstates, nattr, nfiles)
load_data!(nfiles, valuation)
```

In this case, we are creating a 3-dimensional shared array. Then, we call the `load_data!` function to read all 100,000 files and shovel the data into the valuation matrix. How does the `load_data!` function work? Let's take a look:

```
function load_data!(nfiles, dest)
    @sync @distributed for i in 1:nfiles
        read_val_file!(i, dest)
    end
end
```

It's a very simple `for` loop that just calls the `read_val_file!` function with an index number. Notice the use of two macros here—`@distributed` and `@sync`. First, the `@distributed` macro does the magic by sending the body of the `for` loop to the worker processes. In general, the master program here does not wait for the worker processes to return. However, the `@sync` macro blocks until all jobs are completely finished.

How does it actually read the binary file? Let's see:

```
# Read a single data file into a segment of the shared array `dest`
# The segment size is specified as in `dims`.
@everywhere function read_val_file!(index, dest)
    filename = locate_file(index)
    (nstates, nattrs) = size(dest)[1:2]
```

```
open(filename) do io
    nbytes = nstates * nattrs * 8
    buffer = read(io, nbytes)
    A = reinterpret(Float64, buffer)
    dest[:, :, index] = A
end
end
```

Here, the function first locates the path of the data file. Then, it opens the file and reads all the binary data into a byte array. Since the data is just 64-bit floating pointer numbers, we use the `reinterpret` function to parse the data into an array of `Float64` values. We do expect 30,000 `Float64` values here in each file, representing 10,000 future states and 3 source returns. When the data is ready, we just save them into the array for the particular index.

We also use the `@everywhere` macro to ensure that the function is defined and made available to all worker processes. The `locate_file` function is a little less interesting. It is included here for completeness:

```
@everywhere function locate_file(index)
    id = index - 1
    dir = string(id % 100)
    return joinpath(dir, "sec$(id).dat")
end
```

To load the data files in parallel, we can define a `load_data!` function as follows:

```
function load_data!(nfiles, dest)
    @sync @distributed for i in 1:nfiles
        read_val_file!(i, dest)
    end
end
```

Here, we just put the `@sync` and `@distributed` macros in front of a `for` loop. Julia automatically schedules and distributes the call among all work processes. Now that everything is set up, we can run the program:

```
nfiles = 100_000
nstates = 10_000
nattr = 3
valuation = SharedArray{Float64}(nstates, nattr, nfiles)
```

We simply create a valuation `SharedArray` object. Then, we pass it to the `load_data!` function for processing:

```
julia> @time load_data!(nfiles, valuation);
180.645677 seconds (1.26 M allocations: 63.418 MiB, 0.00% gc time)
```

It only took about three minutes to load 100,000 files into memory using 16 parallel processes. *That's pretty good!*

If you try to run the program in your own environment but encounter an error, it may be due to system constraints. Refer to the later section, *Configuring system settings for shared memory usage*, for more information.

It turns out that this exercise is still IO-bound. CPU utilization hovered just around 5% during the load process. Should the problem demand incremental computation, we could possibly leverage the remaining CPU resource by spawning other asynchronous processes that operate on data and just got loaded into memory.

Analyzing data directly on a shared array

Using shared arrays allows us to perform parallel operations on the data from a single memory space. As long as we do not mutate the data, then these operations can run independently without conflicts. This type of problem is called *embarrassingly parallel*.

To illustrate the power of multi-processing, let's first benchmark a simple function that calculates the standard deviation of the returns across all securities:

```julia
using Statistics: std

# Find standard deviation of each attribute for each security
function std_by_security(valuation)
    (nstates, nattr, n) = size(valuation)
    result = zeros(n, nattr)
    for i in 1:n
        for j in 1:nattr
            result[i, j] = std(valuation[:, j, i])
        end
    end
    return result
end
```

The value of `n` represents number of securities. The value of `nattr` represents number of sources of return. Let's see how much time it takes for a single process. The best timing was 5.286 seconds:

```
julia> @benchmark std_by_security($valuation) seconds=30
BenchmarkTools.Trial:
  memory estimate:  22.38 GiB
  allocs estimate:  600002
  --------------
  minimum time:     5.286 s (3.20% GC)
  median time:      5.305 s (3.30% GC)
  mean time:        5.679 s (3.74% GC)
  maximum time:     6.586 s (4.73% GC)
  --------------
  samples:          6
  evals/sample:     1
```

The `@benchmark` macro provides some statistics about the performance benchmark. Sometimes, it is useful to see the distribution and have an idea about how much GC impacts performance.

The `seconds=30` parameter was specified because this function takes seconds to run. The default parameter value is 5 seconds, and that would not allow the benchmark to collect enough samples for reporting.

We are now ready to run the program in parallel. First, we need to make sure that all child processes have the dependent packages loaded:

```
@everywhere using Statistics: std
```

Then, we can define a distributed function, as follows:

```
function std_by_security2(valuation)
    (nstates, nattr, n) = size(valuation)
    result = SharedArray{Float64}(n, nattr)
    @sync @distributed for i in 1:n
        for j in 1:nattr
            result[i, j] = std(valuation[:, j, i])
        end
    end
    return result
end
```

This function looks very similar to the previous one, with some exceptions:

1. We have allocated a new shared array, `result`, to store the computed data. This array is 2-dimensional because we are reducing the third dimension into a single standard deviation value. This array is accessible by all worker processes.
2. The `@distributed` macro in front of the `for` loop is used to automatically distribute the work, in other words, the body of the `for` loop, to the worker processes.
3. The `@sync` macro in front of the `for` loop makes the system wait until all of the work is done.

We can now benchmark the performance of this new function using the same 16 worker processes:

```
julia> @benchmark std_by_security2($valuation) seconds=30
BenchmarkTools.Trial:
  memory estimate:  227.22 KiB
  allocs estimate:  4948
  --------------
  minimum time:     842.373 ms (0.00% GC)
  median time:      875.328 ms (0.00% GC)
  mean time:        864.056 ms (0.00% GC)
  maximum time:     884.748 ms (0.00% GC)
  --------------
  samples:          35
  evals/sample:     1
```

Compared to the performance of a single process, this is approximately 6x faster than before.

Understanding the overhead of parallel processing

Have you noticed something interesting here? Since we have 16 worker processes, we would have expected that the parallel processing function to be close to 16 times faster. But the result came in at around 6 times, which is somewhat less than we expected. Why is that?

The answer is that it is just a matter of scale. There is some performance overhead to use the parallel processing facility. Typically, this overhead can be ignored because it is immaterial when compared to the amount of work being performed. In this particular example, calculating standard deviation is a really trivial computation. So, in relative terms, the overhead of coordinating remote function calls and collecting results overshadows the actual work itself.

Perhaps we should prove it. Let's just do a little more work and calculate skewness and kurtosis in addition to standard deviation:

```
using Statistics: std, mean, median
using StatsBase: skewness, kurtosis

function stats_by_security(valuation, funcs)
    (nstates, nattr, n) = size(valuation)
    result = zeros(n, nattr, length(funcs))
    for i in 1:n
        for j in 1:nattr
            for (k, f) in enumerate(funcs)
                result[i, j, k] = f(valuation[:, j, i])
            end
        end
    end
    return result
end
```

The parallel processing version is similar:

```
@everywhere using Statistics: std, mean, median
@everywhere using StatsBase: skewness, kurtosis

function stats_by_security2(valuation, funcs)
    (nstates, nattr, n) = size(valuation)
    result = SharedArray{Float64}((n, nattr, length(funcs)))
    @sync @distributed for i in 1:n
        for j in 1:nattr
            for (k, f) in enumerate(funcs)
                result[i, j, k] = f(valuation[:, j, i])
            end
        end
    end
    return result
end
```

Let's compare their performance now:

```
julia> funcs = (std, skewness, kurtosis);

julia> @time result = stats_by_security(valuation, funcs);
  21.099982 seconds (3.60 M allocations: 67.156 GiB, 3.27% gc time)

julia> @time result = stats_by_security2(valuation, funcs);
   2.329082 seconds (5.06 k allocations: 242.359 KiB)
```

The parallel process is now 9x faster, as shown in the preceding. If we continue on this path and do more non-trivial computation, then we would expect a higher impact up to somewhere closer to 16x difference.

Configuring system settings for shared memory usage

The magic of `SharedArrays` come from the use of memory map and shared memory facilities in the operating system. When dealing with large amounts of data, we may need to configure the system to handle the volume.

Adjusting system kernel parameters

The Linux operating system has a limit on the size of shared memory. To find out what that is, we can use the `ipcs` command:

```
$ ipcs -lm --human

------ Shared Memory Limits --------
max number of segments = 4096
max seg size = 16E
max total shared memory = 16E
min seg size = 1B
```

The E unit may look a little unfamiliar. It's in exabytes, which basically mean 18 zeros: kilo, mega, giga, tera, peta, and exa. Get it? So, we're in luck here, because the limit is so high that we will probably never reach. However, if you see a small number, then you may need to reconfigure the system. The three kernel parameters are as follows:

- Maximum number of segments (SHMMNI)
- Maximum segment size (SHMMAX)
- Maximum total shared memory (SHMALL)

We can find out the actual values using the sysctl command:

```
$ sysctl kernel.shmmni kernel.shmall kernel.shmmax
kernel.shmmni = 4096
kernel.shmall = 18446744073692774399
kernel.shmmax = 18446744073692774399
```

To adjust the values, we can again use the sysctl command. For example, to set the maximum segment size (shmmax) to 128 GiB, we can do the following:

```
$ sudo sysctl -w kernel.shmmax=137438953472
kernel.shmmax = 137438953472
```

We can see that the kernel setting is now updated.

Configuring a shared memory device

It is not enough to just change the system limits as shown in the preceding section. The Linux kernel actually uses the /dev/shm device as an in-memory backing store for shared memory. We can find out the size of the device using the regular df command:

```
$ df -h
Filesystem       Size  Used Avail Use% Mounted on
udev             16G     0   16G   0% /dev
tmpfs            3.1G  796K  3.1G   1% /run
/dev/nvme0n1p1   39G    25G   15G  63% /
shmfs            16G     0   16G   0% /dev/shm
tmpfs            5.0M    0  5.0M   0% /run/lock
tmpfs            16G     0   16G   0% /sys/fs/cgroup
/dev/loop0       18M    18M     0 100% /snap/amazon-ssm-agent/1480
/dev/loop1       90M    90M     0 100% /snap/core/7713
tmpfs            3.1G    0  3.1G   0% /run/user/1000
```

At the current state, the `/dev/shm` device is unused as shown in the preceding. The overall size of the block device is 16 GiB. As an exercise, let's now open a Julia REPL and create `SharedArray`:

```julia
julia> using SharedArrays

julia> A = SharedArray{Float64}(10000,10000);

julia> A[:] = rand(10000, 10000);

julia> varinfo(Main, r"A")
  name          size summary
  ----          ---- --------------------------------
  A       762.940 MiB 10000×10000 SharedArray{Float64,2}
```

Re-running the `df` command, we can see that `/dev/shm` is now used:

```
$ df -h | egrep '(Used|shm)'
Filesystem      Size  Used Avail Use% Mounted on
shmfs           16G   763M  16G   5% /dev/shm
```

Now that we know `SharedArray` uses the `/dev/shm` device, how can we increase the size to accommodate our problem, which requires more than 22 GiB? It can be done using the `mount` command with a new size:

```
$ sudo mount -t tmpfs shmfs -o size=28g /dev/shm
$
$ df -h | egrep '(Used|shm)'
Filesystem      Size  Used Avail Use% Mounted on
shmfs           28G    0    28G   0% /dev/shm
```

The size of `/dev/shm` is now clearly shown as `28G`.

Debugging the shared memory size issue

What happens if we exceed the size of the shared memory device if we have forgotten to increase the size as described earlier? Let's say we need to allocate 20 GiB but there is only 16 GiB:

```
julia> using SharedArrays

julia> A = SharedArray{UInt8}(20 * 1024 * 1024 * 1024);

julia> varinfo(Main, r"A")
  name         size summary
  ----   ---------- -----------------------------------------
  A      20.000 GiB 21474836480-element SharedArray{UInt8,1}
```

There is no error even though we have exceeded the limit! Are we getting a free ride? The answer is no. It turns out that Julia does not know the limit has been breached. We can even work with the array *up close and personal* to the 16 GiB mark:

```
julia> 15 * 1024 * 1024 * 1024
16106127360

julia> A[1:16106127360] .= 0x01;
```

The preceding code simply sets the first 15 GiB of memory to `0x01`. No error is shown so far. Going back to the shell, we can check the size of /dev/shm again. Clearly, 15 GiB is in use:

```
$ df -h | egrep '(Used|shm)'
Filesystem      Size  Used Avail Use% Mounted on
shmfs            16G   15G  1.0G  94% /dev/shm
```

Now, if we continue to assign values to the later part of the array, we get an ugly **Bus error** and a long stack trace:

```
julia> A[16106127361:end]

signal (7): Bus error
in expression starting at REPL[21]:1
getindex at ./array.jl:744 [inlined]
getindex at /buildworker/worker/package_linux64/build/usr/share/julia/stdlib/v1.3
/SharedArrays/src/SharedArrays.jl:508 [inlined]
```

You may wonder why Julia cannot be smarter and tell you up front that you do not have enough shared memory space. As it turns out, it's the same behavior if you had used the underlying operating system's `mmap` function. Honestly, Julia just does not have any more information about the system constraint.

Sometimes, a C function's manual page can be useful and provide some hints. For example, the documentation about the `mmap` call indicates that a SIGBUS signal will be thrown when the program attempts to access an unreachable portion of the memory buffer. The manual page can be found at `https://linux.die.net/man/2/mmap`.

Ensuring worker processes have access to code and data

When developing parallel computation, a beginner often runs into the following issues:

- **Functions not defined in the worker processes:** This can be a symptom of a library package not being loaded, or a function that was only defined in the current process but not defined in the worker processes. Both issues can be resolved by using the `@everywhere` macro as shown in the preceding examples.
- **Data not available in the worker processes:** This can be a symptom of the data being stored as a variable in the current processes but not passed to the worker processes. `SharedArray` is convenient because it is automatically made available to worker processes. For other cases, the programmer generally has two options:
  - Explicitly pass the data via function arguments.
  - If the data is in a global variable, then it can be transferred using the `@everywhere` macro, as follows:

```
@everywhere my_global_var = whatever_value
```

For more advanced use cases, the `ParallelDataTransfer.jl` package provides several helpful functions to facilitate data transfer among the master process and worker processes.

Avoiding race conditions among parallel processes

`SharedArrays` provides an easy conduit for sharing data across multiple processes. At the same time, a `SharedArray` is by design a global variable across all worker processes. As a general rule of thumb for every parallel program, extreme care should be given when the array is mutated. If the same memory address needs to be written by multiple processes, then these operations must be synchronized or the program could crash easily.

The best option is to avoid mutation whenever possible.

An alternative is to assign each worker a mutually exclusive set of slots in the array so that they do not collide with each other.

Working with the constraints of shared arrays

Elements in a `SharedArray` must be *bits type*. What does that mean? The formal definition of bits type can be summarized as follows:

- The type is immutable.
- The type contains only primitive types or other bits types.

The following `OrderItem` type is a bits type because all fields are primitive types:

```
struct OrderItem
    order_id::Int
    item_id::Int
    price::Float64
    quantity::Int
end
```

The following `Customer` type is not a bits type because it contains a reference to `String`, which is neither a primitive type nor a bits type:

```
struct Customer
    name::String
    age::Int
end
```

Let's try to create `SharedArray` for a bits type. The following code confirms that it works properly:

```
julia> @everywhere struct Point{T <: Real}
           x::T
           y::T
       end

julia> A = SharedArray{Point{Float64}}(3);

julia> A .= [Point(rand(), rand()) for in in 1:length(A)]
3-element SharedArray{Point{Float64},1}:
 Point{Float64}(0.691831981451819, 0.04122373427955228)
 Point{Float64}(0.34750583216758857, 0.48636218254669883)
 Point{Float64}(0.38570823722796876, 0.15871901377125908)
```

If we try to create `SharedArray` with a non-bits type such as a mutable struct type, an error will result:

```
julia> @everywhere mutable struct MutablePoint{T <: Real}
           x::T
           y::T
       end

julia> B = SharedArray{MutablePoint{Float64}}(3);
ERROR: ArgumentError: type of SharedArray elements must be bits types,
 got MutablePoint{Float64}
```

In summary, Julia's shared array is a great way to distribute data to multiple parallel processes for high-performance computing. The programming interface is also very easy to use.

In the next section, we will look into a pattern that improves performance by exploiting the space-time trade-off.

The memoization pattern

In 1968, an interesting article was published—it envisioned that computers should be able to learn from experience during execution and improve their own efficiency.

In developing software, we often face a situation where the speed of execution is constrained by many factors. Maybe a function needs to read a large amount of historical data from disk (also known as I/O-bound). Or a function just needs to perform some complex calculation that takes a lot of time (also known as CPU-bound). When these functions are called repeatedly, application performance can suffer greatly.

Memoization is a powerful concept to address these problems. In recent years, it has become more popular as functional programming is becoming more mainstream. The idea is really simple. When a function is called for the first time, the return value is stored in a cache. If the function is called again with the exact same argument as before, we can look up the value from the cache and return the result immediately.

As you will see later in this section, memoization is a specific form of caching where the return data of a function call is cached according to the arguments being passed to the function.

Introducing the Fibonacci function

In functional programming, recursion is a common technique for computation. Sometimes, we may fall into a performance pitfall unknowingly. A classic example is the generation of a Fibonacci sequence, which is defined as follows:

```julia
julia> fib(n) = n < 3 ? 1 : fib(n-1) + fib(n-2);

julia> fib.(1:10)
10-element Array{Int64,1}:
  1
  1
  2
  3
  5
  8
 13
 21
 34
 55
```

It works well functionally but it is not very efficient. Why? It is because the function is recursively defined, and the same function is called multiple times with the same arguments. Let's take a look at the computation graph when finding the sixth Fibonacci number, where each f(n) node represents a call to the fib function:

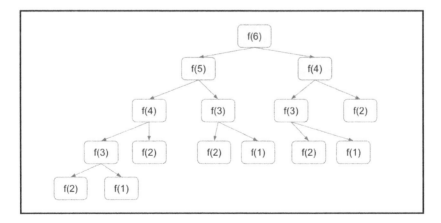

As you can see, the function is called many times, especially for those that are at the beginning part of the sequence. To calculate fib(6), we end up calling the function 15 times! And this is like a snowball, getting worse very quickly.

Improving the performance of the Fibonacci function

First, let's analyze how bad the performance is by revising the function to keep track of the number of executions. The code is as follows:

```
function fib(n)
    if n < 3
        return (result = 1, counter = 1)
    else
        result1, counter1 = fib(n - 1)
        result2, counter2 = fib(n - 2)
        return (result = result1 + result2, counter = 1 + counter1 +
counter2)
    end
end
```

Every time the `fib` function is called, it keeps tracks a counter. If the value of n is smaller than 3, then it returns the count of 1 along with the result. If n is a larger number, then it aggregates the counts from the recursive calls to `fib` function.

Let's run it several times with various input values:

```
julia> fib(6)
(result = 8, counter = 15)

julia> fib(10)
(result = 55, counter = 109)

julia> fib(20)
(result = 6765, counter = 13529)
```

This simple example just illustrated how quickly it turns into a disaster when the computer has no memory about what it did before. A high school student would be able to calculate `fib(20)` manually with just 18 additions, discounting the first two numbers of the sequence. Our nice little function calls itself over 13,000 items!

Let's now put back the original code and benchmark the function. To illustrate the problem, I will start with `fib(40)`:

```
julia> fib(n) = n < 3 ? 1 : fib(n-1) + fib(n-2);

julia> using BenchmarkTools

julia> @btime fib(40);
  426.559 ms (0 allocations: 0 bytes)
```

For this task, the function should really return instantly. The 430 millisecond feels like an eternity in computer time!

We can use memoization to solve this problem. Here is our first attempt:

```
const fib_cache = Dict()

_fib(n) = n < 3 ? 1 : fib(n-1) + fib(n-2)

function fib(n)
    if haskey(fib_cache, n)
        return fib_cache[n]
    else
        value = _fib(n)
        fib_cache[n] = value
        return value
    end
end
```

First of all, we have created a dictionary object called `fib_cache` to store the results of previous calculations. Then, the core logic for the Fibonacci sequence is captured in this private function, `_fib`.

The `fib` function works by first looking up the input argument from the `fib_cache` dictionary. If the value is found, it returns the value. Otherwise, it invokes the private function, `_fib`, and updates the cache before returning the value.

The performance should be much better now. Let's test it quickly:

```
julia> @btime fib(40);
  31.777 ns (0 allocations: 0 bytes)
```

We should be must happier with the performance result by now.

We have used a `Dict` object to cache calculation results here for demonstration purposes. In reality, we can optimize it further by using an array as a cache. The lookup from an array should be a lot faster than a dictionary key lookup.

Note that an array cache works well for the `fib` function because it takes a positive integer argument. For more complex functions, a `Dict` cache would be more appropriate.

Automating the construction of a memoization cache

While we are quite happy with the result in the preceding implementation, it feels a little unsatisfactory because we have to write the same code every time we need to memoize a new function. Wouldn't it be nice if the cache is automatically maintained? Realistically, we just need one cache for each function that we want to memoize.

So, let's do it a little differently. The thought is that we should be able to build a higher-order function that takes an existing function and return a memoized version of it. Before we get there, let's first redefine our `fib` function as an anonymous function, as follows:

```
fib = n -> begin
    println("called")
    return n < 3 ? 1 : fib(n-1) + fib(n-2)
end
```

For now, we have added a `println` statement just so that we can validate the correctness of our implementation. If it works properly, `fib` should not be called millions of times. Moving on, we can define a `memoize` function as follows:

```
function memoize(f)
    memo = Dict()
    x -> begin
        if haskey(memo, x)
            return memo[x]
        else
            value = f(x)
            memo[x] = value
            return value
        end
    end
end
```

The `memoize` function first creates a local variable called `memo` for storing previous return values. Then, it returns an anonymous function that captures the `memo` variable, performs cache lookup, and calls `f` functions when it is needed. This coding style of capturing a variable in an anonymous function is called a **closure**. Now, we can use the `memoize` function to build a cache-aware `fib` function:

```
fib = memoize(fib)
```

Let's also prove that it does not call the original `fib` function too many times. For example, running `fib(6)` should be no more than 6 calls:

```
julia> fib(6)
called with n = 6
called with n = 5
called with n = 4
called with n = 3
called with n = 2
called with n = 1
8
```

That looks satisfactory. If we run the function again with any input less than or equal to 6, then the original logic should not be called at all, and all results should be returned straight from the cache. However, if the input is larger than 6, then it calculates the ones above 6. Let's try that now:

```
julia> fib(5)
5

julia> fib(10)
called with n = 10
called with n = 9
called with n = 8
called with n = 7
55
```

We cannot conclude what we did is good enough until we benchmark the new code. Let's do it now.

```
julia> fib = n -> n < 3 ? 1 : fib(n-1) + fib(n-2);

julia> fib = memoize(fib);

julia> @btime fib(40)
  46.617 ns (0 allocations: 0 bytes)
102334155
```

The original function took 433 ms to compute `fib(400)`. This memoized version only takes 50 ns. This is a huge difference.

Understanding the constraint with generic functions

One drawback of the preceding method is that we must define the original function as an anonymous function rather than a generic function. That seems to be a major constraint. The question is why doesn't it work with generic function?

Let's do a quick test by starting a new Julia REPL, defining the original `fib` function again, and wrapping it with the same `memoize` function:

```
julia> fib(n) = n < 3 ? 1 : fib(n-1) + fib(n-2);

julia> fib = memoize(fib)
ERROR: invalid redefinition of constant fib
```

The problem is that `fib` is already defined as a generic function, and it cannot be bound to a new anonymous function, which is what is being returned from the `memoize` function. To work around the issue, we may be tempted to assign the memoized function with a new name:

```
fib_fast = memoize(fib)
```

However, it does not really work because the original `fib` function makes a recursive call to itself rather than the new memoized version. To see it more clearly, we can unroll a call as follows:

1. Call the function as `fib_fast(6)`.
2. In the `fib_fast` function, it checks whether the cache contains a key that equals 6.
3. The answer is no, so it calls `fib(5)`.
4. In the `fib` function, since n is 5 and is greater than 3, it calls `fib(4)` and `fib(3)` recursively.

As you can see, the original `fib` function got called rather than the memoized version, so we are back to the same problem before. Hence, if the function being memoized uses recursion, then we must write the function as an anonymous function. Otherwise, it would be okay to create a memoized function with a new name.

Supporting functions that take multiple arguments

In practice, we would probably encounter functions that are more complex than this. For example, the function that requires speed-up probably requires multiple arguments and possibly keyword arguments as well. Our memoize function in the previous section assumes a single argument, so it would not work properly.

A simple way to fix this is illustrated as follows:

```
function memoize(f)
    memo = Dict()
    (args...; kwargs...) -> begin
        x = (args, kwargs)
        if haskey(memo, x)
            return memo[x]
        else
            value = f(args...; kwargs...)
            memo[x] = value
            return value
        end
    end
end
```

The anonymous function being returned now covers any number of positional arguments and keyword arguments as specified in the splatted arguments, args... and kwargs.... We can quickly test this with a dummy function as follows:

```
# Simulate a slow function with positional arguments and keyword arguments
slow_op = (a, b = 2; c = 3, d) -> begin
    sleep(2)
    a + b + c + d
end
```

Then, we can create the fast version as follows:

```
op = memoize(slow_op)
```

Let's test the memoized function with a few different cases:

```
julia> @time op(2, d = 5);
  2.425834 seconds (474.05 k allocations: 23.989 MiB, 7.40% gc time)

julia> @time op(2, d = 5);
  0.000023 seconds (14 allocations: 480 bytes)

julia> @time op(1, c = 4, d = 5);
  2.142616 seconds (240.63 k allocations: 11.878 MiB)

julia> @time op(1, c = 4, d = 5);
  0.000022 seconds (16 allocations: 624 bytes)
```

It's working great!

Handling mutable data types in the arguments

So far, we did not pay much attention to the arguments or keyword arguments being passed to the function. Care must be taken when any of those arguments are mutable. Why? Because our current implementation uses the arguments as the key of the dictionary cache. If we mutate the key of a dictionary, it could lead to unexpected results.

Suppose that we have a function that takes 2 seconds to run:

```
# This is a slow implementation
slow_sum_abs = (x::AbstractVector{T} where {T <: Real}) -> begin
    sleep(2)
    sum(abs(v) for v in x)
end
```

Knowing that it's quite slow, we happily memoize it as usual:

```
sum_abs = memoize(slow_sum_abs)
```

Initially, it seems to work perfectly, as it has always been:

```
julia> x = [1, -2, 3, -4, 5]
5-element Array{Int64,1}:
  1
 -2
  3
 -4
  5

julia> sum_abs = memoize(slow_sum_abs);

julia> @time sum_abs(x)
  2.212859 seconds (474.49 k allocations: 23.549 MiB)
15

julia> @time sum_abs(x)
  0.000008 seconds (6 allocations: 192 bytes)
15
```

However, we are shocked by the following observation:

```
julia> push!(x, -6)
6-element Array{Int64,1}:
  1
 -2
  3
 -4
  5
 -6

julia> @time sum_abs(x)
  0.000008 seconds (6 allocations: 192 bytes)
15
```

Bummer! Rather than returning a value of 21, it returns the previous result as if -6 were not inserted to the array. Out of curiosity, let's push one more value to the array and try again:

```
julia> push!(x, 7)
7-element Array{Int64,1}:
  1
 -2
  3
 -4
  5
 -6
  7

julia> @time sum_abs(x)
  2.001202 seconds (14 allocations: 368 bytes)
28
```

It's working again. Why is that happening? To understand that, let's recap how the memoize function was written:

```
function memoize(f)
    memo = Dict()
    (args...; kwargs...) -> begin
        x = (args, kwargs)
        if haskey(memo, x)
            return memo[x]
    ...
```

As you can see, we are caching the data using the (args, kwargs) tuple as the key of the dictionary object. The problem is that the argument being passed to the memoized sum_abs function is a mutable object. The dictionary object gets *confused* when the key is mutated. In that case, it may or may not locate the key anymore.

When we added -6 to the array, it found the same object in the dictionary and returned the cached result. When we added 7 to the array, it could not find the object. Hence, the function does not work 100% of the time.

To fix this issue, we need to make sure that the content of the arguments are considered, not just the memory address of the container. A common practice is to apply a hash function to the thing that we wish to use as a key to the dictionary. Here's one implementation:

```
function hash_all_args(args, kwargs)
    h = 0xed98007bd4471dc2
    h += hash(args, h)
    h += hash(kwargs, h)
    return h
end
```

The initial value of the h variable is randomly selected. On a 64-bit system, we can generate it with a call to rand(UInt64). The hash function is a generic function defined in the Base module. We will keep it simple here for illustration purposes. In reality, a better implementation would support a 32-bit system as well.

The `memoize` function can now be rewritten to utilize such a hashing scheme:

```julia
# Adjust memoize function
function memoize(f)
    memo = Dict()
    (args ... ; kwargs ... ) → begin
        key = hash_all_args(args, kwargs)
        if haskey(memo, key)
            return memo[key]
        else
            value = f(args ... ; kwargs ... )
            memo[key] = value
            return value
        end
    end
end
```

We can test it again more extensively. Let's redefine the `sum_abs` function again using the new `memoize` function. Then, we run a loop and capture the calculation result and timing.

The result is shown as follows:

```julia
julia> sum_abs = memoize(slow_sum_abs);

julia> x = [1, -2, 3, -4, 5];

julia> for i in 6:10
           push!(x, i * (iseven(i) ? -1 : 1))
           ts = @elapsed val = sum_abs(x)
           println(i, ": ", x, " -> ", val, " (", round(ts, digits=1), "s)")
           ts = @elapsed val = sum_abs(x)
           println(i, ": ", x, " -> ", val, " (", round(ts, digits=1), "s)")
       end
6: [1, -2, 3, -4, 5, -6] -> 21 (2.0s)
6: [1, -2, 3, -4, 5, -6] -> 21 (0.0s)
7: [1, -2, 3, -4, 5, -6, 7] -> 28 (2.0s)
7: [1, -2, 3, -4, 5, -6, 7] -> 28 (0.0s)
8: [1, -2, 3, -4, 5, -6, 7, -8] -> 36 (2.0s)
8: [1, -2, 3, -4, 5, -6, 7, -8] -> 36 (0.0s)
9: [1, -2, 3, -4, 5, -6, 7, -8, 9] -> 45 (2.0s)
9: [1, -2, 3, -4, 5, -6, 7, -8, 9] -> 45 (0.0s)
10: [1, -2, 3, -4, 5, -6, 7, -8, 9, -10] -> 55 (2.0s)
10: [1, -2, 3, -4, 5, -6, 7, -8, 9, -10] -> 55 (0.0s)
```

Fast and correct

Fantastic! It now returns the correct result even though the input data has been mutated.

Memoizing generic functions with macros

Earlier, we discussed that generic functions cannot be supported by the `memoize` function. It would be most awesome if we can just annotate the functions as memoized while they are being defined. For example, the syntax would be like this:

```
@memoize fib(n) = n < 3 ? 1 : fib(n-1) + fib(n-2)
```

It turns out that there's already an awesome package called `Memoize.jl` that does the exact same thing. It is indeed quite convenient:

```
julia> using Memoize

julia> @memoize fib(n) = n < 3 ? 1 : fib(n-1) + fib(n-2);

julia> @time fib(40)
  0.012276 seconds (7.45 k allocations: 374.536 KiB)
102334155

julia> @time fib(40)
  0.000005 seconds (7 allocations: 208 bytes)
102334155

julia> @time fib(39)
  0.000004 seconds (7 allocations: 208 bytes)
63245986
```

Here, we can observe the following:

1. The first call to `fib(40)` was quite fast already, which is an indication that the cache is utilized.
2. The second call to `fib(40)` was almost instant, which means that the result was just a cache lookup.
3. The third call to `fib(39)` was almost instant, which means that the result was just a cache lookup.

 You should be advised that `Memoize.jl` does not support mutable data as arguments either. It carries the same problem that we described in the preceding section because it uses the objects' memory addresses as the key to the dictionary.

Turning to real-life examples

Memoization is used in some open source packages. The actual usage may be more common in private applications and data analysis. Let's see some use cases for memoization in the following sections.

Symata.jl

The `Symata.jl` package provides support for Fibonacci polynomials. As we may have realized, the implementation of Fibonacci polynomials is also recursive just like the Fibonacci sequence problem we discussed earlier in this section. `Symata.jl` uses the `Memoize.jl` package to create the `_fibpoly` function as follows:

```
fibpoly(n::Int) = _fib_poly(n)

let myzero = 0, myone = 1, xvar = Polynomials.Poly([myzero,myone]), zerovar
= Polynomials.Poly([myzero]), onevar = Polynomials.Poly([myone])
    global _fib_poly
    @memoize function _fib_poly(n::Int)
        if n == 0
            return zerovar
        elseif n == 1
            return onevar
        else
            return xvar * _fib_poly(n-1) + _fib_poly(n-2)
        end
    end
end
```

Omega.jl

The `Omega.jl` package implements its own memoization cache. Interestingly, it ensures proper return type from the cache lookup using the `Core.Compiler.return_type` function. It is done to avoid type instability problems. In *The barrier function pattern* section later in this chapter, we will discuss more the problem of type instability and how to deal with the issue. Check out the following code example:

```
@inline function memapl(rv::RandVar, mω::TaggedΩ)
  if dontcache(rv)
    ppapl(rv, proj(mω, rv))
  elseif haskey(mω.tags.cache, rv.id)
    mω.tags.cache[rv.id]::(Core.Compiler).return_type(rv,
typeof((mω.taggedω,)))
  else
```

```
        mω.tags.cache[rv.id] = ppapl(rv, proj(mω, rv))
    end
end
```

Considerations

Memoization can only be applied to *pure* functions.

What is a pure function? A function is called pure when it always returns the same value given the same input. It may seem intuitive for every function to behave that way but in practice, it is not that straightforward. Some functions are not pure due to reasons such as these:

- A function uses a random number generator and is expected to return random results.
- A function relies on data from an external source that produces different data at different times.

Because the memoization pattern uses function arguments as the key of the in-memory cache, it will always return the same result for the same key.

Another consideration is that we should be aware of the extra memory overhead due to the use of a cache. It is important to choose the right cache invalidation strategy for the specific use case. Typical cache invalidation strategies include **Least Recently Used (LRU)**, **First-In, First-Out (FIFO)**, and time-based expiration.

Utilizing the Caching.jl package

There are several packages that can make memoization easier. Some are mentioned here:

- `Memoize.jl` provides a `@memoize` macro. It's very easy to use.
- `Anamnesis.jl` provides a `@anamnesis` macro. It has more functionalities than `Memoize.jl`.
- `Caching.jl` was created with the ambition to provide more functionalities such as persistence to disk, compression, and cache size management.

Here, we can take a look at `Caching.jl` as it is developed more recently and has great features.

Let's build a memoized CSV file reader as follows:

```
julia> using Caching, CSV, DataFrames

julia> @cache function read_csv(filename::AbstractString)
           println("Reading file: ", filename)
           @time df = CSV.File(filename) |> DataFrame
           return df
       end
read_csv (cache with 0 entries, 0 in memory 0 on disk)
```

The `@cache` macro makes a memoized version of the `read_csv` function. To confirm that a file is read only once, we inserted a `println` statement and timed the file read operation.

For demonstration purposes, we have downloaded a copy of the film permits file from the City of New York. The file is available from `https://catalog.data.gov/dataset/film-permits`. Let's read the data file now:

```
julia> df = read_csv("Film_Permits.csv");
Reading file: Film_Permits.csv
 10.485855 seconds (11.47 M allocations: 606.323 MiB, 2.00% gc time)

julia> size(df)
(61920, 14)

julia> df_again = read_csv("Film_Permits.csv");

julia> df === df_again
true
```

Here, we can see that the file is read only once. If we call `read_csv` again with the same filename, then the same object is returned instantly.

We can examine the cache. Before doing that, let's see what properties `read_csv` supports:

```
julia> propertynames(read_csv)
(:name, :filename, :func, :cache, :offsets, :history, :max_size)
```

Without looking at the manual, we can guess that the `cache` property represents the cache. Let's take a quick look:

```
julia> read_csv.cache
Dict{UInt64,Any} with 1 entry:
  0x602537e6ffb4d3f0 => 61920×14 DataFrame. Omitted printing of 11 colum…
```

We can also persist the cache to disk. Let's examine the name and size of the cache file:

```
julia> read_csv.filename
"/Users/tomkwong/Downloads/_5f33edd2ce0e7123_.bin"

shell> ls -1s /Users/tomkwong/Downloads/_5f33edd2ce0e7123_.bin
ls: /Users/tomkwong/Downloads/_5f33edd2ce0e7123_.bin: No such file or dir
ectory                                     Save cached
                                           content to disk
julia> @persist! read_csv  ◄──
read_csv (cache with 1 entry, 1 in memory 1 on disk)

shell> ls -1s /Users/tomkwong/Downloads/_5f33edd2ce0e7123_.bin
45408 /Users/tomkwong/Downloads/_5f33edd2ce0e7123_.bin
```

The location of the cache file is found in the `filename` property. The file does not exist until the `@persist!` macro was used to persist data to disk. We can also see how many objects are present in memory or on disk by just examining the function `itself` from the REPL:

```
julia> read_csv
read_csv (cache with 1 entry, 1 in memory 1 on disk)
```

The `@empty!` macro can be used to purge the in-memory cache:

```
julia> @empty! read_csv
read_csv (cache with 1 entry, 0 in memory 1 on disk)
```

Interestingly, because the on-disk cache still exists, we can still utilize it without having to re-populate the memory cache:

```
julia> df = read_csv("Film_Permits.csv");

julia> size(df)                    Does not display "Reading file:"
(61920, 14)                        so it must be reading from cache

julia> read_csv
read_csv (cache with 1 entry, 0 in memory 1 on disk)
```

Finally, we can synchronize the memory and disk caches:

```
julia> @syncache! read_csv "disk"
read_csv (cache with 1 entry, 1 in memory 1 on disk)
```

The `Caching.jl` package has more functionalities that are not shown here. Hopefully, we have got an idea of what it is capable of already.

Next, we will look into a pattern that can be used to address the type-instability problem, which is a common issue causing performance problems.

The barrier function pattern

While Julia is designed as a dynamic language, it also aims for high performance. The magic comes from its state-of-the-art compiler. When the type of variables is known in a function, the compiler can generate highly optimized code. However, when the type of a variable is unstable, the compiler has to compile more generic code that works with any data types. In some sense, Julia can be forgiving—it never fails on you even when it comes with a cost against runtime performance.

What makes the type of a variable *unstable*? It means that in some circumstances the variable may be one type, and in other circumstances, it may be another type. This section will discuss such a type instability problem, how it may arise, and what we can do about it.

Barrier function is a pattern that can be used to solve performance problems due to type instability. So, let's see how to achieve that.

Identifying type-unstable functions

In Julia, there is no need to specify the type of variables. In fact, to be more precise, variables are not typed. Variables are merely bindings to values, and values are typed. That is what makes Julia programs dynamic. However, such flexibility comes with a cost. Because the compiler must generate code that supports all possible types that may come up during runtime, it is unable to generate optimized code.

Consider a simple function that just returns an array of random numbers:

```
random_data(n) = isodd(n) ? rand(Int, n) : rand(Float64, n)
```

If the n argument is odd, then it returns an array of random Int values. Otherwise, it returns an array of random Float64 values.

This innocent function is actually type-unstable. We can use the @code_warntype facility to check:

```
julia> @code_warntype random_data(3)
Variables
  #self#::Core.Compiler.Const(random_data, false)
  n::Int64

Body::Union{Array{Float64,1}, Array{Int64,1}}
1 ─ %1 = Main.isodd(n)::Bool
  └──      goto #3 if not %1
2 ─ %3 = Main.rand(Main.Int, n)::Array{Int64,1}
  └──      return %3
3 ─ %5 = Main.rand(Main.Float64, n)::Array{Float64,1}
  └──      return %5
```

The @code_warntype macro displays an **Intermediate Representation** (IR) of the code. An IR is generated by the compiler after it understand the flow and data type of every line in that code. For our purpose here, we do not need to understand everything printed on screen but we can pay attention to the highlighted text as related to the data types generated from the code. In general, when you see red text, it would also be a red flag.

In this case, the compiler has figured that the result of this function can be an array of Float64 or an array of Int64. Hence, the return type is just Union{Array{Float64,1}, Array{Int64,1}}.

> In general, more red signs from the `@code_warntype` output indicates more type instability problems in the code.

The function does exactly what we want to do. But when it's used in the body of another function, the type instability problem further affects runtime performance. We can use a barrier function to solve this problem.

Understanding performance impact

When a function is called, the type of its arguments are known and then the function is compiled with the exact data types from its arguments. This is called *specialization*. What exactly is a barrier function? It simply exploits Julia's function specialization to *stabilize* the type of variable as part of a function call. We will continue the preceding example to illustrate the technique.

First, let's create a simple function that makes use of the type unstable function, as mentioned earlier:

```
function double_sum_of_random_data(n)
    data = random_data(n)
    total = 0
    for v in data
        total += 2 * v
    end
    return total
end
```

The `double_sum_of_random_data` function is just a simple function that returns the sum of doubled random numbers generated by the `random_data` function. If we just benchmark the function with either an odd or an even number argument, it comes back with the following results:

```
julia> @btime double_sum_of_random_data(100000);
  347.050 μs (2 allocations: 781.33 KiB)

julia> @btime double_sum_of_random_data(100001);
  179.623 μs (2 allocations: 781.39 KiB)
```

The timing is better for the call with an input value of 100001, most likely because the random number generator for Int is better than the one for Float64. Let's see what @code_warntype comes back for this function:

```
julia> @code_warntype double_sum_of_random_data(100000);
Variables
  #self#::Core.Compiler.Const(double_sum_of_random_data, false)
  n::Int64
  data::Union{Array{Float64,1}, Array{Int64,1}}
  total::Union{Float64, Int64}
  @_5::Union{Nothing, Tuple{Union{Float64, Int64},Int64}}
  v::Union{Float64, Int64}

Body::Union{Float64, Int64}
1 ─        (data = Main.random_data(n))
  │        (total = 0)
  │   %3  = data::Union{Array{Float64,1}, Array{Int64,1}}
  │        (@_5 = Base.iterate(%3))
  │   %5  = (@_5 === nothing)::Bool
  │   %6  = Base.not_int(%5)::Bool
  └        goto #4 if not %6
2 ─ %8  = @_5::Tuple{Union{Float64, Int64},Int64}::Tuple{Union{Float64, I
nt64},Int64}
  │        (v = Core.getfield(%8, 1))
  │   %10 = Core.getfield(%8, 2)::Int64
  │   %11 = total::Union{Float64, Int64}
  │   %12 = (2 * v)::Union{Float64, Int64}
  │        (total = %11 + %12)
  │        (@_5 = Base.iterate(%3, %10))
  │   %15 = (@_5 === nothing)::Bool
  │   %16 = Base.not_int(%15)::Bool
  └        goto #4 if not %16
3 ─        goto #2
4 ─        return total
```

As you can see, there are tons of red marks around. The type instability issue of a single function has a larger impact on other functions that use it.

Developing barrier functions

A barrier function involves refactoring a piece of logic from an existing function into a new, separate function. When it's done, all data required by the new function will be passed as function arguments. Continuing with the preceding example, we can factor out the logic that calculates the doubled sum of data as follows:

```
function double_sum(data)
    total = 0
    for v in data
    total += 2 * v
    end
    return total
end
```

Then, we just modify the original function to make use of this function:

```
function double_sum_of_random_data(n)
    data = random_data(n)
    return double_sum(data)
end
```

Does it really improve performance? Let's run the test:

```
julia> @btime double_sum_of_random_data(100000);
  245.044 μs (2 allocations: 781.33 KiB)

julia> @btime double_sum_of_random_data(100001);
  180.454 μs (2 allocations: 781.39 KiB)
```

It turns out to have a huge difference for the `Float64` case—the elapsed time went from 347 to 245 microseconds. Comparing the floating-point sum versus integer sum cases, the result also makes perfect sense because summing integers is generally faster than summing floating-point numbers.

Dealing with a type-unstable output variable

What we haven't noticed is another type instability problem concerning the accumulator. In the preceding example, the `double_sum` function has a `total` variable that keeps track of the doubled numbers. The problem is that the variable was defined as an integer, but then the array may contain floating-pointer numbers instead. This problem can be easily revealed by running `@code_warntype` against both scenarios.

Here is the output of `@code_warntype` for when an array of integers is passed into the function:

```
julia> @code_warntype double_sum(rand(Int, 3))
Variables
  #self#::Core.Compiler.Const(double_sum, false)
  data::Array{Int64,1}
  total::Int64
  @_4::Union{Nothing, Tuple{Int64,Int64}}
  v::Int64

Body::Int64
1 ─         (total = 0)
    %2  = data::Array{Int64,1}
            (@_4 = Base.iterate(%2))
    %4  = (@_4 === nothing)::Bool
    %5  = Base.not_int(%4)::Bool
            goto #4 if not %5
2 ─ %7  = @_4::Tuple{Int64,Int64}::Tuple{Int64,Int64}
            (v = Core.getfield(%7, 1))
    %9  = Core.getfield(%7, 2)::Int64
    %10 = total::Int64
    %11 = (2 * v)::Int64
            (total = %10 + %11)
            (@_4 = Base.iterate(%2, %9))
    %14 = (@_4 === nothing)::Bool
    %15 = Base.not_int(%14)::Bool
            goto #4 if not %15
3 ─         goto #2
4 ─         return total
```

Compare it with the output when an array of `Float64` is passed:

```
julia> @code_warntype double_sum(rand(Float64, 3))
Variables
  #self#::Core.Compiler.Const(double_sum, false)
  data::Array{Float64,1}
  total::Union{Float64, Int64}
  @_4::Union{Nothing, Tuple{Float64,Int64}}
  v::Float64

Body::Union{Float64, Int64}
1 ─       (total = 0)
    %2  = data::Array{Float64,1}
          (@_4 = Base.iterate(%2))
    %4  = (@_4 === nothing)::Bool
    %5  = Base.not_int(%4)::Bool
          goto #4 if not %5
2 ┄ %7  = @_4::Tuple{Float64,Int64}::Tuple{Float64,Int64}
          (v = Core.getfield(%7, 1))
    %9  = Core.getfield(%7, 2)::Int64
    %10 = total::Union{Float64, Int64}
    %11 = (2 * v)::Float64
          (total = %10 + %11)
          (@_4 = Base.iterate(%2, %9))
    %14 = (@_4 === nothing)::Bool
    %15 = Base.not_int(%14)::Bool
          goto #4 if not %15
3 ─       goto #2
4 ─       return total
```

If we call the function with an array of integers, then the type is stable. If we call the function with an array of floats, then we see the type instability issue.

How do we fix this? Well, there are standard `Base` functions for creating type-stable zeros or ones. For example, rather than hardcoding the initial value of `total` to be an integer zero, we can do the following instead:

```
function double_sum(data)
    total = zero(eltype(data))
    for v in data
        total += 2 * v
    end
    return total
end
```

If we look into the @code_warntype output of the double_sum_of_random_data function, it is much better than before. I will let you do this exercise and compare the @code_warntype output with the prior one.

A similar solution makes use of the parametric method:

```
function double_sum(data::AbstractVector{T}) where {T <: Number}
    total = zero(T)
    for v in data
        total += v
    end
    return total
end
```

The T type parameter is used to initialize the total variable to the properly typed value of zero.

This kind of performance gotcha is sometimes difficult to catch. To ensure optimized code is generated, it is always a good practice to use the following functions for an accumulator or an array that stores output values:

- zero and zeros create a value of 0 or an array of 0s for the desired type.
- one and ones create a value of 1 or an array of 1s for the desired type.
- similar creates an array of the same type as the array argument.

For example, we can create a value of 0 or an array of 0s for any numeric types as follows:

```
julia> zero(Int)
0

julia> zeros(Float64, 5)
5-element Array{Float64,1}:
 0.0
 0.0
 0.0
 0.0
 0.0
```

Likewise, the `one` and `ones` functions work the same way:

```
julia> one(UInt8)
0x01

julia> ones(UInt8, 5)
5-element Array{UInt8,1}:
 0x01
 0x01
 0x01
 0x01
 0x01
```

If we want to create an array that looks like another one (in other words, has the same type, shape, and size), then we can use the `similar` function:

```
julia> A = rand(3,4)
3x4 Array{Float64,2}:
 0.222531   0.401065  0.117088  0.983905
 0.71607    0.987111  0.500108  0.782027
 0.0305057  0.870299  0.56723   0.380603

julia> B = similar(A)
3x4 Array{Float64,2}:
 2.34095e-314  2.34095e-314  2.34095e-314  2.14919e-321
 2.34238e-314  4.94066e-324  2.34095e-314  6.22523e-322
 2.34095e-314  2.34095e-314  1.4822e-323   2.26291e-314
```

Note that the `similar` function does not zero out the content of the array.

The `axes` function may come in handy when we need to create an array of zeros that matches the same dimensions of another array:

```
julia> zeros(axes(A))
3x4 Array{Float64,2}:
 0.0  0.0  0.0  0.0
 0.0  0.0  0.0  0.0
 0.0  0.0  0.0  0.0
```

Next, we will look into a way to debug type instability issues.

Using the @inferred macro

Julia comes with a handy macro in the Test package that can be used to check whether the return type of a function matches the *inferred* return type of the function. The inferred return type is simply the type that we see from the @code_warntype output before.

For example, we can check the notorious random_data function from the beginning of this section:

```
julia> @inferred random_data(1)
ERROR: return type Array{Int64,1} does not match inferred return type Uni
on{Array{Float64,1}, Array{Int64,1}}
Stacktrace:
 [1] error(::String) at ./error.jl:33
 [2] top-level scope at REPL[31]:1

julia> @inferred random_data(2)
ERROR: return type Array{Float64,1} does not match inferred return type U
nion{Array{Float64,1}, Array{Int64,1}}
Stacktrace:
 [1] error(::String) at ./error.jl:33
 [2] top-level scope at REPL[32]:1
```

The macro reports an error whenever the actual returned type differs from the inferred return type. It could be a useful tool to validate the type instability problem as part of an automated test suite in the continuous integration pipeline.

The primary reason to use a barrier function is to improve performance where the type instability problem exists. If we think about it more deeply, it also has the side benefit of forcing us to create smaller functions. Smaller functions are easier to read and debug and perform better.

We have now concluded all patterns in this chapter.

Summary

In this chapter, we explored several patterns related to performance.

First, we discussed how global variables hurt performance and the technique of the global constant pattern. We looked into how the compiler optimizes performance by doing constant folding, constant propagation, and dead branch elimination. We also learned how to create a constant placeholder for wrapping a global variable.

We discussed how to utilize the struct of arrays pattern to turn an array of structs into a struct of arrays. The new layout of the data structure allows better CPU optimization and, hence, better performance. We took advantage of a very useful package, `StructArrays`, for automating such data structure transformation. We reviewed a financial services use case where a large amount of data needs to be loaded into memory and used by many parallel processes. We implemented the shared array pattern and went over some tricks to configure shared memory properly in the operating system.

We learned about the memoization pattern for caching function call results. We did a sample implementation using a dictionary cache and made it work with functions taking various arguments and keyword arguments. We also found a way to support mutable objects as function arguments. Finally, we discussed the barrier function pattern. We saw how performance can be degraded by type-unstable variables. We learned that splitting logic into a separate function allows the compiler to produce more optimal code.

In the next chapter, we will examine several patterns that improve system maintainability.

Questions

1. Why does the use of global variables impact performance?
2. What would be a good alternative to using a global variable when it cannot be replaced by a constant?
3. Why does a struct of arrays perform better than an array of structs?
4. What are the limitations of `SharedArray`?
5. What is an alternative to multi-core computation instead of using parallel processes?
6. What care must be taken when using the memoization pattern?
7. What is the magic behind barrier functions in improving performance?

7
Maintainability Patterns

This chapter will cover several patterns that are related to improving code readability and the ease of maintenance. These aspects are sometimes overlooked because programmers always think that they know what they are doing. In reality, programmers do not always write code that is readable to others. Sometimes, the code could be too cluttered and difficult to follow, or the files may not be very well organized. These problems can often be mitigated by refactoring.

Metaprogramming can be a good way to further improve readability and maintainability. In some cases, there are existing macros that we can utilize today. It would be a shame if we do not explore such opportunities. We know good programmers always have the relentless desire for achieving excellence, so learning these techniques would be a rewarding exercise. In the subsequent sections, we will look into the following patterns:

- Sub-module pattern
- Keyword definition pattern
- Code generation pattern
- Domain-specific language pattern

By the end of this chapter, you will have learned how to organize your code better. You will be able to reduce clutter and write very concise code. In addition, if you are working on a problem with a specific industry domain, you can build your own **domain-specific language (DSL)** to further express your problem clearly in your own syntax.

Let's go!

Technical requirements

The sample source code is located at https://github.com/PacktPublishing/Hands-on-Design-Patterns-and-Best-Practices-with-Julia/tree/master/Chapter07.

The code is tested in a Julia 1.3.0 environment.

Sub-module pattern

When a module becomes too large, it can be difficult to manage and comprehend. Generally, it can happen organically when the programmer keeps adding more and more functionalities to an application. So, how large is too large? It is difficult to say as it varies and depends on the programming language, the problem domain, and even the skillsets of the application maintainers. Nevertheless, it is mostly agreed upon by professionals that smaller modules are easier to manage, especially when the code is maintained by multiple developers.

In this section, we will explore the idea of splitting the source code of a large module into separately managed sub-modules. We will discuss how to make that decision and how to do that properly. As part of our journey, we will look into some examples and see how other experts do it in their packages.

Understanding when sub-module is needed

When should we consider creating sub-modules? There are several factors to consider:

- First, we could consider the size of the application. Size is an abstract concept and can be measured in several ways, some of which are mentioned here:
  - **Number of lines of code**: This is the simplest measure to understand the size of an application. The more lines of code in the source files, the larger the application. This is analogous to the number of pages in a book. It takes more time for you to read and understand the content for a book that has more pages.
  - **Number of functions**: When there are too many functions in a single module, it is more difficult to understand and learn all those functions. When there are too many functions, the number of interactions between functions naturally increase, making the application more prone to messy spaghetti code.
  - **Number of data types**: Every data type represents a kind of an object. It is more difficult for a developer to comprehend all the functions operating on a large number of data types because the human brain cannot handle too many concepts at the same time.

- The second thing we should consider is separation of concern. As we look into an application that comprises various components, we may logically think of them as separate things that can be managed independently. Humans are an excellent species that know how to work on items that are small and organized.
- Lastly, we can consider the complexity of matter. Sometimes, you look at the source code and realize that the logic is difficult to grasp. Perhaps it's the domain knowledge. Or, it could be a complex algorithm. While the size of the application is not large, it may still make sense to split the code into separate files physically.

So far, we have not set any concrete threshold for any of the preceding factors. That is because the decision to call something large or complex is quite subjective. A common way to do that is to have a discussion among several software engineers and make a group decision. Doing that allows us to overcome the *original developer bias*, where the person already knows everything by heart, and therefore, the person would tend to believe that the application is not too large nor too complex.

Suppose that you are ready to take the plunge and split part of your code into sub-modules. The next challenge is to figure out how to do it properly. The work can be part art and part science. To formalize the process for splitting source code into sub-modules, we will first discuss the concept of coupling.

Understanding afferent and efferent coupling

Before splitting code into separate components, the first step is to analyze the existing code structure. Are there any high-level domain concepts that stand on their own? For example, a banking application may involve account management, deposit/withdrawal, balance transfer, customer notification, and so on. Each of these domain concepts can potentially be split into separate components.

We must also understand how components interact with each other. Here, we will talk about two concepts that originated from object-oriented programming:

- Afferent coupling – number of external entities that depend on the current entity
- Efferent coupling – number of external entities that the current entity depends upon

Let's take a look at this diagram:

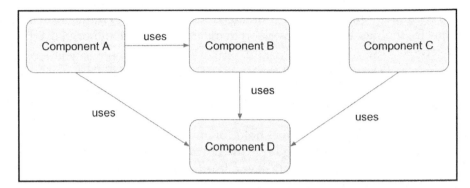

In this example, we can arrive at the following observations:

- Component A has two efferent couplings.
- Component B has one afferent coupling and one efferent coupling.
- Component C has one efferent coupling.
- Component D has three afferent couplings.

So, if a component is *used by* many external components, then this component has high afferent coupling. On the other hand, if a component *uses* many external components, then it has high efferent coupling.

These coupling characteristics help us to understand the stability requirement of a component. A component having high afferent coupling needs to be as stable as possible because making changes in this component may have a higher risk of breaking other components. That would be the case for Component D in the preceding example.

Similarly, a component having high efferent coupling means that it may be more unstable due to many possible changes from the components that it depends on. That would be the case for the preceding Component A. Hence, it would be best to reduce coupling whenever possible, whether it's afferent or efferent. A decoupled system tends to have a minimum number of afferent and efferent couplings.

The same concepts apply when designing sub-modules. When we split code into separate sub-modules, it would be most ideal if afferent/efferent couplings are minimized. Now, we will first take a look at the best practice of organizing files for sub-modules.

Organizing sub-modules

There are generally two patterns for organizing sub-module files. Let's take a look at each:

- The first one involves a simpler situation where each sub-module is fully contained in a single source file, as follows:

```
module MyPackage
include("sub_module1.jl")
include("sub_module2.jl")
include("sub_module3.jl")
end
```

- The second one involves larger sub-modules where there could be several source files for each sub-module. In that case, the source code of a sub-module resides in a subdirectory:

```
# MyPackage.jl
module MyPackage
include("sub_module1/sub_module1.jl")
include("sub_module2/sub_module2.jl")
include("sub_module3.jl")
end
```

- Of course, the sub module's directory may include multiple files. In the preceding example, sub_module1 may contain several more source files, which are shown in the following code snippet:

```
# sub_module1.jl
module SubModule1
include("file1.jl")
include("file2.jl")
include("file3.jl")
end
```

Next, we will look into how to reference symbols and functions between the modules and these sub-modules.

Referencing symbols and functions between modules and sub-modules

A module can access its sub-modules using the regular `using` or `import` statements. In fact, a sub-module does not work any differently than an external package, except how it is being referenced.

Perhaps we can recall the example from Chapter 2, *Modules, Packages, and Type Concepts*. Back then, we created a `Calculator` module that defines two interest rate-related functions and a `Mortgage` sub-module that defines a payment calculator function. The `Calculator` module file has the following source code:

```
# Calculator.jl
module Calculator

include("Mortgage.jl")

export interest, rate

function interest(amount, rate)
    return amount * (1 + rate)
end

function rate(amount, interest)
    return interest / amount
end

end # module
```

Furthermore, the sub-module contains the following code:

```
# Mortgage.jl
module Mortgage

function payment(amount, rate, years)
    # TODO code to calculate monthly payment for the loan
    return 100.00
end

end # module
```

Let's look into how to reference functions and symbols from a sub-module and vice versa.

Referencing symbols defined in sub-modules

To begin, we can finish our implementation of the Mortgage sub-module with a real implementation of the payment function.

Let's see how this works:

1. The payment function takes a loan amount, an annual interest rate, the number of years for the loan, and calculates the monthly payment of the loan, as shown in the following code:

```
# Mortgage.jl
module Mortgage

function payment(amount, rate, years)
    monthly_rate = rate / 12.0
    factor = (1 + monthly_rate) ^ (years * 12.0)
    return amount * (monthly_rate * factor / (factor - 1))
end

end # module
```

2. At this point, the Calculator module should be able to use the Mortgage sub-module as if it's yet another module, except that the notation to get access to the sub-module requires a relative path that is prefixed with a dot notation:

```
# Calculator.jl
module Calculator

# include sub-modules
include("Mortgage.jl")
using .Mortgage: payment

# functions for the main module
include("funcs.jl")

end # module
```

Here, we have brought the payment function into the current scope of the sub-module via using .Mortgage: payment.

3. In order to organize our code better, we have also moved the functions into a separate file called `funcs.jl`. The code is shown as follows:

```
# funcs.jl - common calculation functions

export interest, rate, mortgage

function interest(amount, rate)
    return amount * (1 + rate)
end

function rate(amount, interest)
    return interest / amount
end

# uses payment function from Mortgage.jl
function mortgage(home_price, down_payment, rate, years)
    return payment(home_price - down_payment, rate, years)
end
```

As we can see, the new `mortgage` function can use the `payment` function from the Mortgage sub-module now.

Referencing symbols from the parent module

If the sub-module needs access to any symbol from the parent module, then the sub-module may use the `import` or `using` statement while adding `..` as a prefix to the name of the parent module. This is shown with the following code:

```
# Mortgage.jl
module Mortgage

# access to parent module's variable
using ..Calculator: days_per_year

end # module
```

Now, the `Mortgage` sub-module has access to the `days_per_year` constant from the parent module.

Having the ability to reference symbols and functions between modules and sub-modules allows us to just reorganize code into various sub-modules and keep it working as before. However, the reason for separating code into sub-modules in the first place is to allow the developer to work in each module independently. In addition, having bidirectional references could lead to confusion and messy spaghetti code.

Next, we will discuss how to reduce such coupling among modules and sub-modules.

Removing bidirectional coupling

When we have a module (or sub-module) referencing another sub-module and vice versa, it increases coupling between these components. Generally speaking, it is best to avoid bidirectional dependency between the parent module and the sub-module because it introduces tight coupling and makes the code difficult to understand and debug. How can we fix this? Let's explore this next.

Passing data as function arguments

The first solution is to pass the required data as a function argument. Suppose that the `payment` function from the `Mortgage` sub-module can take a `days_per_year` keyword argument, then the `Calculator` module can just pass the value as follows:

```
# Calculator.jl
module Calculator

const days_per_year = 365

include("Mortgage.jl")
using .Mortgage: payment

function do_something()
    return payment(1000.00, 3.25, 5; days_per_year = days_per_year)
end

end # module
```

Hence, the `Mortgage` sub-module does not really need to reference the `days_per_year` symbol from `Calculator` anymore, reducing any unnecessary dependency.

Factoring common code as another sub-module

Another solution is to split the dependent member into a separate sub-module and have both existing modules depend on the new sub-module.

Suppose that we have two sub-modules set up in a way that they use functions from each other. Consider the scenario depicted in the diagram as follows:

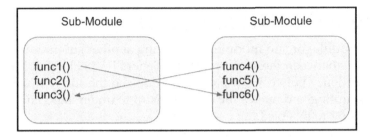

The func1 function from the first sub-module uses func6 from the other sub-module. And, the func4 function from the other sub-module needs to call the func3 function from the first module. Clearly, there is a high coupling between these two modules.

Considering the dependencies between these modules, it looks like a cycle as the first sub-module depends on the second sub-module and vice versa. To fix that, we can introduce a new sub-module to break the cycle as follows:

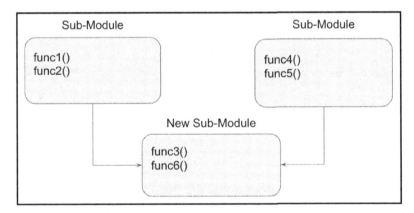

Breaking the cycle has the benefit of a cleaner dependency graph. It also makes the code easier to understand.

Considering splitting into top-level modules

If we are already considering creating sub-modules, it may be a good time to consider splitting the code into top-level modules. These top-level modules can be put together as separate Julia packages.

Let's take a look at the benefits and potential issues for making new top-level modules:

The benefits of having separate top-level modules are as follows:

- Each package can have its own release life cycle and version. It is possible to make changes to a package and release only that portion.
- Version compatibility is enforced by Julia's `Pkg` system. A new version of the package may be released, and it may be used by another package as long as the package versions are compatible.
- Packages are more reusable because they can be utilized by other applications.

Potential issues with top-level modules are as follows:

- There is more management overhead because each package will be maintained and released independently.
- Deployment may be more difficult since multiple packages have to be installed and inter dependent packages must obey version compatibility requirements.

Understanding the counterarguments of using sub-modules

You are advised to avoid this pattern under the following conditions:

- When the existing code base is not large enough, splitting into sub-modules too early hinders the speed of development. We should avoid doing this prematurely.
- When there is a high coupling in the source code, it can be difficult to split the code. In that case, try to refactor the code to reduce coupling and then reconsider splitting code into sub-modules later.

The idea of creating sub-modules does force the programmer to think about code dependencies. It is a necessary step when the application eventually grows bigger.

Next, we will discuss the keyword definition pattern, which allows us to construct objects with more readable code.

Keyword definition pattern

In Julia, you can create an object using the default constructor, which accepts a list of positional arguments for each of the fields defined for the struct. For small objects, this should be simple and straightforward. For larger objects, it becomes confusing because it is hard to remember which argument corresponds to which field without referring to the struct's definition every time we write code to create such objects.

In 1956, George Miller, a psychologist, published research that involved figuring out how many random digits a person could remember at any time, so the Bell System could decide how many numbers to use for the format of a telephone number. He found that most people can only remember five to nine digits at any time.

If remembering digits is difficult enough, it should be even more difficult to remember fields that come with different names and types.

We will discuss how to reduce such stress when developing Julia code, and how it can be done using the `@kwdef` macro so that the code is easy to read and maintain.

Revisiting struct definitions and constructors

Let's first take a look at how a struct is defined and what constructor is provided. Consider the use case of text style configuration for a text editing application.

We may define a struct as follows:

```julia
struct TextStyle
    font_family
    font_size
    font_weight
    foreground_color
    background_color
    alignment
    rotation
end
```

By default, Julia provides a constructor with positional arguments for all fields in the same order as how they are defined in the struct. So, the only way to create a TextStyle object is to do the following:

```julia
style = TextStyle("Arial", 11, "Bold", "black", "white", "left", 0)
```

There is nothing wrong here, but we could argue that the code is not very readable. Every time we have to write code to create a TextStyle object, we must ensure that all arguments are specified in the right order. In particular, as a developer, I must remember that the first three arguments represent font settings, then followed by two colors where the foreground color comes first, and so on. In the end, I just give up and go back to revisit the struct definition again.

Another issue is that we may want to have default values for some fields. For example, we want the alignment field to have a value of "left" and the rotation field to have 0 by default. The default constructor does not provide an easy way to do that.

A more sensible syntax for creating objects with so many arguments is to use keyword arguments in the constructor. Let's try to implement that next.

Using keyword arguments in constructors

We can always add new constructor functions to make it easier for creating objects. Using keyword arguments solves the following two problems:

- Code readability
- Ability to specify default values

Let's go ahead and define a new constructor as follows:

```
function TextStyle(;
        font_family,
        font_size,
        font_weight = "Normal",
        foreground_color = "black",
        background_color = "white",
        alignment = "left",
        rotation = 0)
    return TextStyle(
        font_family,
        font_size,
        font_weight,
        foreground_color,
        background_color,
        alignment,
        rotation)
end
```

Here, we have elected to provide default values for most of the fields except `font_family` and `font_size`. It is simply defined as a function that provides keyword arguments for all fields in the struct. Creating the `TextStyle` object is much easier and the code is more readable now. In fact, we have obtained an additional benefit that the arguments can be specified in any order, as shown here:

```
style = TextStyle(
    alignment = "left",
    font_family = "Arial",
    font_weight = "Bold",
    font_size = 11)
```

This is, indeed, quite a simple recipe. We can just create this kind of constructor for every struct and the problem is solved. Right? Well, yes and no. While it is fairly easy to create these constructors, it is a hassle to do that for every struct everywhere.

In addition, the constructor definition must specify all field names in the function arguments, and these fields repeat in the body of the function. So, it becomes quite difficult to develop and maintain. Next, we will introduce a macro to simplify our code.

Simplifying code with the @kwdef macro

Given that the keyword definition pattern addresses a fairly common use case, there is already a macro provided by Julia to help define structs along with constructors accepting keyword arguments. The macro is currently not exported, but you can use it directly as follows:

```
Base.@kwdef struct TextStyle
    font_family
    font_size
    font_weight = "Normal"
    foreground_color = "black"
    background_color= "white"
    alignment = "center"
    rotation = 0
end
```

Basically, we can just place the `Base.@kwdef` macro in front of the type definition. As a part of the type definition, we can also provide default values. The macro automatically defines the struct and the corresponding constructor function with keyword arguments. We can see that by using the `methods` function as follows:

```
julia> methods(TextStyle)
# 2 methods for generic function "(::Type)":
[1] TextStyle(; font_family, font_size, font_weight, foreground_colo
r, background_color, alignment, rotation) in Main at util.jl:723
[2] TextStyle(font_family, font_size, font_weight, foreground_color,
 background_color, alignment, rotation) in Main at REPL[41]:2
```

From the output, we can see that the first method is the one that accepts keyword arguments. The second method is the default construct that requires positional arguments. Now, creating new objects is as convenient as we would like:

```
julia> style = TextStyle(
            alignment = "left",
            font_family = "Arial",
            font_weight = "Bold",
            font_size = 11)
TextStyle("Arial", 11, "Bold", "black", "white", "left", 0)
```

We should note that the preceding definition did not specify any default values for font_family and font_size. So, those fields are mandatory when creating a TextStyle object:

```
julia> TextStyle()
ERROR: UndefKeywordError: keyword argument font_family not assigned
Stacktrace:
 [1] TextStyle() at ./util.jl:723
 [2] top-level scope at REPL[45]:1

julia> TextStyle(font_family = "Arial")
ERROR: UndefKeywordError: keyword argument font_size not assigned
Stacktrace:
 [1] (::getfield(Core, Symbol("#kw#Type")))(::NamedTuple{(:font_family
,),Tuple{String}}, ::Type{TextStyle}) at ./none:0
 [2] top-level scope at REPL[46]:1
```

Using this macro can greatly simplify object construction and make the code more readable. There is no reason not to use it everywhere.

As of Julia version 1.3, the `@kwdef` macro is not exported. There is a feature request to export it. Should you feel uncomfortable using non-exported features, consider using the `Parameters.jl` package instead.

Next, we will discuss code generation pattern, which allows us to create new functions dynamically so as to avoid writing repeated boilerplate code.

Code generation pattern

New Julia programmers are often amazed by the conciseness of the language. Surprisingly, some of the very popular Julia packages are written with very little code. There are multiple reasons for that, but one major contributing factor is the ability to generate code dynamically in Julia.

In certain use cases, code generation can be extremely helpful. In this section, we will look into some code generation examples and try to explain how it can be done properly.

Introducing the file logger use case

Let's consider a use case for building a file logging facility.

Suppose that we want to provide an API for logging messages to files based upon a set of logging levels. By default, we will support three levels: info, warning, and error. A logger facility is provided so that a message will be directed to a file, as long as it comes with a high enough logging level.

The functional requirements can be summarized as follows:

- An info-level logger accepts messages with info, warning, or error levels.
- A warning-level logger accepts messages with warning or error levels only.
- An error-level logger accepts messages with an error level only.

To implement the file logger, we will first define some constants for the three logging levels:

```
const INFO    = 1
const WARNING = 2
const ERROR   = 3
```

These constants are designed to be in numerical order, so we can easily determine when a message has a logging level as high as what the logger can accept. Next, we define the `Logger` facility as follows:

```
struct Logger
    filename    # log file name
    level       # minimum level acceptable to be logged
    handle      # file handle
end
```

A `Logger` object carries the filename of the log file, the minimum level for which messages can be accepted by the logger, and a file handle that is used for saving data. We can provide a constructor for `Logger` as follows:

```
Logger(filename, level) = Logger(filename, level, open(filename, "w"))
```

The constructor automatically opens the specified file for writing. Now, we can develop the first logging function for info-level messages:

```
using Dates

function info!(logger::Logger, args...)
    if logger.level <= INFO
        let io = logger.handle
            print(io, trunc(now(), Dates.Second), " [INFO] ")
            for (idx, arg) in enumerate(args)
                idx > 0 && print(io, " ")
                print(io, arg)
            end
            println(io)
            flush(io)
        end
    end
end
```

This function is designed to write the message into the file only if the `INFO` level is high enough to be accepted by the logger. It also prints the current time using the `now()` function and an `[INFO]` label in the log file. Then, it writes all the arguments separated by spaces and finally flushes the I/O buffer.

We can quickly test the code so far. First, we will use `info_logger`:

```julia
julia> info_logger = Logger("/tmp/info.log", INFO);

julia> info!(info_logger, "hello", 123)

julia> readlines("/tmp/info.log")
1-element Array{String,1}:
 "2019-11-18T15:34:38 [INFO]  hello 123"
```

The message is correctly logged in the `/tmp/info.log` file. What happens if we send an info-level message to an error-level logger? Let's take a look:

```julia
julia> error_logger = Logger("/tmp/error.log", ERROR);

julia> info!(error_logger, "hello", 123)

julia> readlines("/tmp/error.log")
0-element Array{String,1}
```

Now, this is a little more interesting. As expected, because the error-level logger only accepts a message with an ERROR level or higher, it did not pick up the info-level message.

At this point, we may be tempted to quickly finish the two other functions: `warning!` and `error!` and call it the day. If we were determined to do that, the `warning!` function would look just like `info!`, with just a few small changes:

```julia
function info!(logger::Logger, args...)
    if logger.level <= INFO
        let io = logger.handle
            print(io, trunc(now(), Dates.Second), " [INFO] ")
            for (idx, arg) in enumerate(args)
                idx > 0 && print(io, " ")
                print(io, arg)
            end
            println(io)
            flush(io)
        end
    end
end
```

```julia
function warning!(logger::Logger, args...)
    if logger.level <= WARNING
        let io = logger.handle
            print(io, trunc(now(), Dates.Second), " [WARNING]
            for (idx, arg) in enumerate(args)
                idx > 0 && print(io, " ")
                print(io, arg)
            end
            println(io)
            flush(io)
        end
    end
end
```

What are the differences between these two logging functions? Let's take a look:

- The function names are different: `info!` versus `warning!`.
- The logging level constants are different: `INFO` versus `WARNING`.
- The labels are different: `[INFO]` versus `[WARNING]`.

Other than these, both functions shared the exact same code. Of course, we can just keep going and wrap up the project by writing `error!` the same way. However, this is not the best solution. Imagine that if the core logging logic needs to be changed, for example, the formatting of log messages, then we have to make the same change in three different functions. Worse yet, if we forget to modify all of these functions, then we end up with inconsistent logging formats. After all, we have violated the **Don't Repeat Yourself** (DRY) principle.

Code generation for function definitions

Code generation is one way to tackle this problem, as mentioned in the preceding section. What we will do is to build up the syntax of defining the function and then throw that into a loop to define all three logging functions. Here is how the code may look:

```
for level in (:info, :warning, :error)
    lower_level_str = String(level)
    upper_level_str = uppercase(lower_level_str)
    upper_level_sym = Symbol(upper_level_str)

    fn = Symbol(lower_level_str * "!")
    label = " [" * upper_level_str * "] "

    @eval function $fn(logger::Logger, args...)
        if logger.level <= $upper_level_sym
            let io = logger.handle
                print(io, trunc(now(), Dates.Second), $label)
                for (idx, arg) in enumerate(args)
                    idx > 0 && print(io, " ")
                    print(io, arg)
                end
                println(io)
                flush(io)
            end
        end
    end
end
```

The explanation for the preceding code is as follows:

- As we need to define functions for three logging levels, we have created a loop that goes through a list of symbols: :info, :warning, and :error.
- Inside the loop, we can see the function name as fn, the label as label, and the constant for log level comparison (such as INFO, WARN, or ERROR) as upper_level_sym.
- We use the @eval macro to define the logging function, where the fn variables, label, and upper_level_sym are interpolated into the function body.

After running the code in the Julia REPL, all three functions: info!, warning!, and error! should be defined already. For testing, we can call these with three different kinds of loggers.

Let's try info_logger first:

```
julia> info_logger = Logger("/tmp/info.log", INFO);

julia> info!(info_logger, "hello", 123);

julia> warning!(info_logger, "hello", 456);

julia> error!(info_logger, "hello", 789);

julia> readlines("/tmp/info.log")
3-element Array{String,1}:
 "2019-11-18T15:37:37 [INFO]   hello 123"
 "2019-11-18T15:37:40 [WARNING]   hello 456"
 "2019-11-18T15:37:43 [ERROR]   hello 789"
```

As expected, all messages are logged to the file because info_logger can take messages at any level. Next, let's test error_logger:

```
julia> error_logger = Logger("/tmp/error.log", ERROR);

julia> info!(error_logger, "hello", 123);

julia> warning!(error_logger, "hello", 456);

julia> error!(error_logger, "hello", 789);

julia> readlines("/tmp/error.log")
1-element Array{String,1}:
 "2019-11-18T15:39:00 [ERROR]  hello 789"
```

In this case, only the error-level message was written to the log file. The
error_logger code effectively filtered out any message that is lower than the error level.

Although we are quite satisfied with the resulting code, do we know what actually
happened behind the scenes? How do we debug the code that we cannot even see? Let's
take a look at this next.

Debugging code generation

Given that the code is generated behind the scene, it may feel a little awkward when we
cannot even see what the generated code will look like. How can we guarantee that the
generated code is exactly what we expect after all those interpolations of variables?

Fortunately, there is a package called CodeTracking that can make debugging code
generation easier. We will see how it works here.

From the previous section, we should have generated three functions: info!, warning!,
and error!. As these are defined as generic functions, we can examine what methods are
defined for each. Let's take error! as an example:

```
julia> methods(error!)
# 1 method for generic function "error!":
[1] error!(logger::Logger, args...) in Main at REPL[14]:10
```

In this case, we only have a single method. We can get to the method object itself using the `first` function:

```
julia> methods(error!) |> first
error!(logger::Logger, args...) in Main at REPL[14]:10
```

Once we have a reference of the method object, we can lean on `CodeTracking` to reveal the source code of the generated function. In particular, we can use the `definition` function, which takes a method object and returns an expression object. In order to use this function, we also need to load the `Revise` package. Enough said, let's try the following:

```
julia> using Revise, CodeTracking

julia> methods(error!) |> first |> definition
:(function error!(logger::Logger, args...)
      #= REPL[14]:10 =#
      if logger.level <= ERROR
          #= REPL[14]:11 =#
          let io = logger.handle
              #= REPL[14]:12 =#
              print(io, trunc(now(), Dates.Second), " [ERROR] ")
              #= REPL[14]:13 =#
              for (idx, arg) = enumerate(args)
                  #= REPL[14]:14 =#
                  idx > 0 && print(io, " ")
                  #= REPL[14]:15 =#
                  print(io, arg)
              end
              #= REPL[14]:17 =#
              println(io)
              #= REPL[14]:18 =#
              flush(io)
          end
      end
  end)
```

Here, we can clearly see that the variables are interpolated correctly; the `logger.level` variable is compared with the `ERROR` constant, and the logging label correctly contains the `[ERROR]` string.

We can also see that line numbers are included in the output. Since we defined the functions from the REPL, the line numbers are less useful. If we would have generated the functions from a module that is stored in a file, the filename and line number information would be much more interesting.

The line number nodes seem to be a bit too distracting here, though. We can easily remove them using the `rmlines` function from the `MacroTools` package:

```julia
julia> using MacroTools

julia> MacroTools.postwalk(rmlines, definition(first(methods(error!))))
:(function error!(logger::Logger, args...)
        if logger.level <= ERROR
            let io = logger.handle
                print(io, trunc(now(), Dates.Second), " [ERROR] ")
                for (idx, arg) = enumerate(args)
                    idx > 0 && print(io, " ")
                    print(io, arg)
                end
                println(io)
                flush(io)
            end
        end
    end)
```

The `MacroTools.postwalk` function is used to apply the `rmlines` function to every node in the abstract syntax tree. The `postwalk` function is necessary because the `rmlines` function only works with the current node.

Now that we understand how to do code generation properly, let's turn around and ask ourselves—is code generation really necessary? Are there any other alternatives? Let us see in the next section.

Considering options other than code generation

Throughout this section, we have been focusing on code generation techniques. The premise is that we can easily add a new function that works just like an existing one but a little differently. In practice, code generation is not the only option we have on hand.

Let's continue our discussion with the same example. As we recall, we wanted to add the `warning!` and `error!` functions after defining the logic for `info!`. If we take a step back, we can generalize the `info!` function and make it handle different logging levels. This can be done as follows:

```
function logme!(level, label, logger::Logger, args...)
    if logger.level <= level
        let io = logger.handle
            print(io, trunc(now(), Dates.Second), label)
            for (idx, arg) in enumerate(args)
```

```
                    idx > 0 && print(io, " ")
                    print(io, arg)
                end
                println(io)
                flush(io)
            end
        end
    end
```

The `logme!` function looks exactly like `info!` before, except that it takes two extra arguments: `level` and `label`. These variables are taken and used in the body of the function. Now we can define all three logging functions as follows:

```
info!   (logger::Logger, msg...) = logme!(INFO,    " [INFO] ",    logger,
msg...)
warning!(logger::Logger, msg...) = logme!(WARNING, " [WARNING] ", logger,
msg...)
error!  (logger::Logger, msg...) = logme!(ERROR,   " [ERROR] ",   logger,
msg...)
```

As we can see, we have solved the original problem using a regular structured programming technique, and we have minimized as much repetitive code as possible.

In this case, the only variation between these functions are simple types: a constant and a string. In another situation, we may need to call different functions within the body. That is okay as well because functions are first-class in Julia, and so we could just pass around a reference of the function.

Can we do better? Yes. The code can be simplified a little more using closure technique. To illustrate the concept, let's define a new `make_log_func` function as follows:

```
function make_log_func(level, label)
    (logger::Logger, args...) -> begin
        if logger.level <= level
            let io = logger.handle
                print(io, trunc(now(), Dates.Second), " [", label, "] ")
                for (idx, arg) in enumerate(args)
                    idx > 0 && print(io, " ")
                    print(io, arg)
                end
                println(io)
                flush(io)
            end
        end
    end
end
```

This function takes the `level` and `label` arguments and returns an anonymous function that contains the main logging logic. The `level` and `label` arguments are captured in a closure and used inside the anonymous function. So, we can now define the logging functions more easily as follows:

```
info!    = make_log_func(INFO,    "INFO")
warning! = make_log_func(WARNING, "WARNING")
error!   = make_log_func(ERROR,   "ERROR")
```

So, three anonymous functions are defined here: `info!`, `warning!`, and `error!` and they all work equally well.

> In computer science terms, closure is a first-class function that captures variables from an enclosing environment.
>
> Technically speaking, there is a non-trivial difference between the structured programming solution and closure. The former technique defines generic functions that are named functions within the module that can be extended. In contrast, anonymous functions are unique and cannot be extended.

In this section, we have learned how to do code generation in Julia and how to debug this code. We have also discussed how to restructure code to achieve the same effect without having to use code generation technique. Both options are available.

Next, we will discuss DSLs, which is a technique for building syntax for specific domain usage, thereby making the code much easier to read and write.

Domain-specific language pattern

Julia is a general purpose programming language that can be used effectively for any domain problem. However, Julia is also one of the few programming languages that allows the developer to build new syntax to fit a specific domain usage.

So, a DSL is an example of **Structured Query Language (SQL)**. SQL is designed to process data in a two-dimensional table structure. It is very powerful, and yet it is only appropriate when you need to handle data in tables.

There are a few prominent areas in the Julia ecosystem where a DSL is used extensively. The one that stood out the most is the `DifferentialEquations` package, which allows you to write differential equations in a form that is very close to their original mathematical notation. For example, consider the Lorenz system equations as follows:

$$\frac{dx}{dt} = \sigma(y - x) \qquad (1)$$
$$\frac{dy}{dt} = x(\rho - z) - y \qquad (2)$$
$$\frac{dz}{dt} = xy - \beta z \qquad (3)$$

The code to define these equations can be written as follows:

```
@ode_def begin
    dx = σ * (y - x)
    dy = x * (ρ - z) - y
    dz = x * y - β * z
end σ ρ β
```

As we can see, the syntax almost matches with the mathematical equations.

After this, in the next section, we will explore how to build our own DSL for a practical use case in computer graphics called L-System.

Introducing the L-System

An **L-System**, also known as **Lindenmayer System**, is a formal syntax for describing how organisms evolve by way of simple patterns. It was first introduced in 1968 by Aristid Lindenmayer, a Hungarian biologist and botanist. An L-System can generate interesting patterns that mimic real-life shape and form. A well-known example is the growth of a specific algae, which can be modeled as follows:

```
Axiom: A
  Rule: A -> AB
  Rule: B -> A
```

Here is how it works. We always start with the axiom, in this case, the character A. For each generation, we apply the rules to every character in the string. If the character is A, then it is replaced with AB. Similarly, if the character is B, it is replaced with A. Let's work through the first five iterations:

- A
- AB

- ABA
- ABAAB
- ABAABABA

You may wonder, how does it even look like an algae? Here's a visualization of the growth from the first generation to the fifth generation:

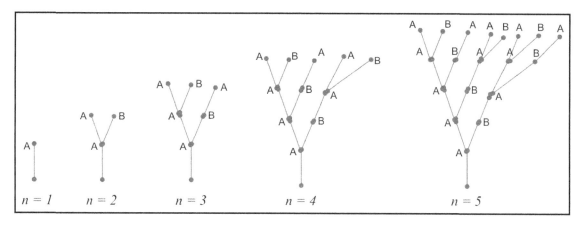

There are many softwares that can produce interesting graphical visualizations based on L-Systems. An example is **My Graphics**, an iOS app developed by me. The application can produce several kinds of patterns such as the preceding algae example. An interesting sample called a **Koch** curve is shown as follows:

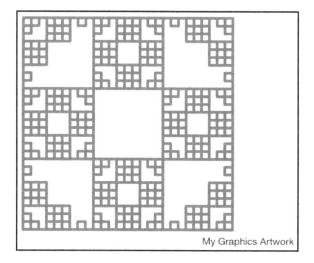

My Graphics Artwork

Enough said. From what we know so far, the concept is fairly simple. What we are going to do next is design a DSL for the L-System.

Designing DSL for L-System

The characteristics of a DSL are that the source code should look like the original representation of the domain concept. In this case, the domain concept is described by an axiom and a set of rules. Using the algae growth example, it needs to look like the following:

```
Axiom: A
   Rule: A -> AB
   Rule: B -> A
```

If we try to write them in plain Julia language, we may end up with code like this:

```
model = LModel("A")
add_rule!(model, "A", "AB")
add_rule!(model, "B", "A")
```

As we can see, this is not ideal. While the code is neither long nor difficult to read, it does not look as clean as the L-System grammar. What we really want is to build a DSL that lets us specify the model as follows:

```
model = @lsys begin
    axiom : A
    rule  : A → AB
    rule  : B → A
end
```

This will be the target syntax for our DSL.

Reviewing the L-System core logic

As part of this example, we will develop an L-System package together. Before we jump into the DSL implementation, let's take a quick detour and understand how the core logic works. Knowledge of the API allows us to design and test DSL properly.

Developing the LModel object

To develop the LModel object, perform the following steps:

1. Let's first create a type called LModel to keep track of the axiom and the set of rules. The struct can be defined as follows:

```
struct LModel
    axiom
    rules
end
```

2. Then, we can add a constructor that populates the axiom field and initializes the rules field:

```
"Create a L-system model."
LModel(axiom) = LModel([axiom], Dict())
```

3. By design, the axiom is an array of a single element. The rules are captured in a dictionary for fast lookups. An add_rule! function is also written to append new rules to the model:

```
"Add rule to a model."
function add_rule!(model::LModel, left::T, right::T) where {T <:
AbstractString}
    model.rules[left] = split(right, "")
    return nothing
end
```

We have used the split function to convert a string into an array of single-character strings.

4. Lastly, we add a Base.show function just so we can display a model nicely on Terminal:

```
"Display model nicely."
function Base.show(io::IO, model::LModel)
    println(io, "LModel:")
    println(io, " Axiom: ", join(model.axiom))
    for k in sort(collect(keys(model.rules)))
        println(io, " Rule: ", k, " → ", join(model.rules[k]))
    end
end
```

Having defined these functions, we can quickly verify our code as follows:

```
julia> algae_model = LModel("A");

julia> add_rule!(algae_model, "A", "AB");

julia> add_rule!(algae_model, "B", "A");

julia> algae_model
LModel:
    Axiom: A
    Rule:  A → AB
    Rule:  B → A
```

Next, we will work on the core logic that takes a model and keeps track of the current state of the iteration.

Developing the state object

To simulate the growth of an L-System model, we can develop an LState type that keeps track of the current state of the growth. It's a simple type that just keeps a reference to the model, the current iteration of growth, and the current result. For this, consider the following code:

```
struct LState
    model
    current_iteration
    result
end
```

The constructor just needs to take the model as the only argument. It defaults current_iteration to 1 and defaults result to the axiom of the model, as shown here:

```
"Create a L-system state from a `model`."
LState(model::LModel) = LState(model, 1, model.axiom)
```

We need a function to advance to the next stage of the growth. So, we just provide a next function:

```
function next(state::LState)
    new_result = []
    for el in state.result
        # Look up `el` from the rules dictionary and append to
`new_result`.
```

```
    # Just default to the element itself when it is not found
    next_elements = get(state.model.rules, el, el)
    append!(new_result, next_elements)
  end
  return LState(state.model, state.current_iteration + 1, new_result)
end
```

Basically, given the current state, it iterates all the elements of the current result and expands each element using the rules from the model. The `get` function looks up the element in the dictionary. If it is not found, it defaults to itself. The expanded elements are just appended to the `new_results` array.

At the end, a new `LState` object is created with the next iteration number and the new result. For a better display in Terminal, we can add a `Base.show` method for `LState` as follows:

```
"Compact the result suitable for display"
result(state::LState) = join(state.result)

Base.show(io::IO, s::LState) =
    print(io, "LState(", s.current_iteration, "): ", result(s))
```

The `result` function just combines all the elements of the array into a single string. The `show` function displays both the current iteration number and the result string.

We should have a fully functional system now. Let's try to simulate the growth of the algae:

```
julia> state = LState(algae_model)
LState(1): A

julia> state = next(state)
LState(2): AB

julia> state = next(state)
LState(3): ABA

julia> state = next(state)
LState(4): ABAAB

julia> state = next(state)
LState(5): ABAABABA
```

Wonderful! Now that the functionalities are built, we can move on to the interesting part of this chapter—how to create a DSL with the L-System syntax.

Implementing a DSL for L-System

Recall from the previous section that we want to have a clean syntax for defining an L-System model. From a metaprogramming perspective, we just need to translate the code from one abstract syntax tree to another. The following diagram shows graphically what kind of translation is required:

It turns out that the translation is quite straightforward. When we encounter an axiom, we translate the code to construct a new `LModel` object. When we encounter a rule, we translate the code to an `add_rule!` function call.

While it seems easy enough, this kind of source-to-source translation can be greatly simplified using pre-existing tools. In particular, the MacroTools package contains some very useful macros and functions for handling these cases. Let's first learn about the tool and then we can utilize them in developing our DSL.

Using the @capture macro

The `MacroTools` package provides a macro called `@capture` that can be used to match an expression against a pattern. As part of the matching process, it also assigns variables for which the developer wishes to capture the matched values.

The `@capture` macro accepts two arguments; the first one is an expression that needs to be matched, and the second one is a pattern used for matching. Consider the following example:

```julia
julia> using MacroTools

julia> @capture( :( x = 1 ), x = val_)
true
```

The macro returns `true` when the pattern can be matched, or else it just returns `false`. When the pattern is matched, the variables ending with an underscore will be assigned in the current environment, with the underscore stripped away from the variable name. In the preceding example, because `x = 1` matches `x = val_`, it has returned `true`:

```
julia> val
1
```

Because the pattern was matched successfully, a `val` variable was also assigned with the value of `1`.

Matching axiom and rule statements

We can use the same trick to extract useful information from the `axiom` and rule statements. Let's do a quick experiment for the `axiom` statement, which consists of the word axiom, a colon, and a symbol. Matching it with the `@capture` macro is pretty slick as follows:

```
julia> ex = :( axiom : A )
:(axiom:A)

julia> match_axiom = @capture(ex, axiom : sym_)
true

julia> sym
:A
```

Matching a `rule` statement is just as easy. The only difference is that we want to match the original symbol and the corresponding replacement symbol, as shown here:

```
julia> ex = :( rule : A → AB)
:(rule:A → AB)

julia> @capture(ex, rule : original_ → replacement_)
true

julia> original
:A

julia> replacement
:AB
```

Once matched, the `original` and `replacement` variables are assigned with the corresponding symbols from the rule. We can also observe that the matched variables are symbols rather than strings. As the `LModel` programming interface requires strings, we will have to perform an additional data conversion from the symbol in the `walk` function, which will be presented in the *Developing the macro for a DSL* section.

Using the postwalk function

In order to traverse the whole abstract syntax tree, we can use the MacroTool's `postwalk` function. To understand how it works, we can play with a simple example, as outlined in the following steps:

1. Let's create an expression object as follows:

```
julia> ex = quote
           x = 1
           y = x^2 + 3
       end |> rmlines
quote
    x = 1
    y = x ^ 2 + 3
end
```

   Here, we have used the `rmlines` function to remove the line number nodes since we do not need them in this exercise.

2. Then, we can use the `postwalk` function to traverse the tree and display everything that it has ever encountered:

```
julia> MacroTools.postwalk(x -> @show(x), ex)
x = :x
x = 1
x = :(x = 1)
x = :y
x = :+
x = :^
x = :x
x = 2
x = :(x ^ 2)
x = 3
x = :(x ^ 2 + 3)
x = :(y = x ^ 2 + 3)
x = quote
    x = 1
    y = x ^ 2 + 3
end
quote
    x = 1
    y = x ^ 2 + 3
end
```

The `postwalk` function accepts a function as its first argument and an expression as the second argument. As it traverses the tree, it calls the function with the sub-expression being visited. We can see that it considered every single leaf node (for example, `:x`) as well as every sub-tree from the expression such as `:(x = 1)`. It also includes the top-level expression as we can see at the bottom of the output.

> If we pay a little more attention to the order of the traversal, we realize that the `postwalk` function works from the bottom up, starting from the leaf nodes.

> MacroTools also provides a `prewalk` function that also traverses the tree. The difference between `prewalk` and `postwalk` is that `prewalk` would work from the top down rather than bottom up. You are encouraged to try that out and learn how they differ.

> For our use case, we can use either one.

Now that we know how to match expressions and traverse the tree, we have everything in our toolbox to develop our DSL. That's the fun part. *Let's go!*

Developing the macro for a DSL

To support the `LModel` syntax, we have to match both the axiom and rule statements to how they are written in the model.

Let's get started by creating the `lsys` macro, as follows:

```
macro lsys(ex)
    return MacroTools.postwalk(walk, ex)
end
```

The macro simply uses `postwalk` to traverse the abstract syntax tree. The resulting expression is returned as is. The main translation logic actually resides in the `walk` function as follows:

```
function walk(ex)
    match_axiom = @capture(ex, axiom : sym_)
    if match_axiom
        sym_str = String(sym)
        return :( model = LModel($sym_str) )
    end
    match_rule = @capture(ex, rule : original_ → replacement_)
    if match_rule
        original_str = String(original)
```

```
        replacement_str = String(replacement)
        return :(
            add_rule!(model, $original_str, $replacement_str)
        )
    end

    return ex
end
```

Let's dissect the preceding code one portion at a time.

The `walk` function uses the `@capture` macro to match the `axiom` and `rule` patterns. When there is a match, the corresponding symbols are converted to a string and then interpolated into the corresponding expression, and the final expression is returned. Consider this line of code:

```
match_axiom = @capture(ex, axiom : sym_)
```

The `@capture` macro call tries to match the expression with the `axiom : sym_` pattern, which is an `axiom` symbol, followed by a colon, and then followed by another symbol. Since the `sym_` target symbol ends with an underscore, if the match is successful, the `sym` variable would be assigned with the matched value. In the `algae` model example of the *Developing the state object* section, we would expect `sym` to be assigned with the `:A` symbol. Once matched, the following code is executed:

```
if match_axiom
    sym_str = String(sym)
    return :( model = LModel($sym_str) )
end
```

The target expression simply constructs an `LModel` object and assigns it to the `model` variable. With the algae model, we can expect that the translated expression will look like this:

```
model = LModel("A")
```

Similarly, the `rule` statement can be matched using the pattern as follows:

```
match_rule = @capture(ex, rule : original_ → replacement_)
```

The `original` and `replacement` variables are assigned, converted to a string, and interpolated into an `add_rule!` statement in the target expression.

From the `lsys` macro, the `walk` function is called by the `postwalk` function many times—once for each node and sub-tree of the abstract syntax tree. To see how `postwalk` generates the code, we can test it from the REPL:

```
julia> ex = quote
               axiom : A
               rule : A → AB
               rule : B → A
           end;

julia> MacroTools.postwalk(walk, ex) |> rmlines
quote
    model = LModel("A")
    add_rule!(model, "A", "AB")
    add_rule!(model, "B", "A")
end
```

As it turns out, we are not completely done yet because the translated statements sit inside a `quote` block and the return value of the block would come from the block's last expression, which is zero as the `add_rule!` function does not return any meaningful value.

This final change is actually the simple part. Let's modify the `@lsys` macro again as follows:

```
macro lsys(ex)
    ex = MacroTools.postwalk(walk, ex)
    push!(ex.args, :( model ))
    return ex
end
```

The `push!` function was used to add the `:( model )` expression at the end of the block. Let's test the macro expansion and see what it looks like:

```
julia> @macroexpand(@lsys begin
               axiom : A
               rule : A → AB
               rule : B → A
           end) |> rmlines
quote
    #44#model = LSystem.LModel("A")
    LSystem.add_rule!(#44#model, "A", "AB")
    LSystem.add_rule!(#44#model, "B", "A")
    #44#model
end
```

It's good now! Finally, we can just use the macro as follows:

```
julia> algae_model = @lsys begin
            axiom : A
            rule  : A → AB
            rule  : B → A
        end
LModel:
  Axiom: A
  Rule:  A → AB
  Rule:  B → A
```

Awesome! The `algae_model` example can now be constructed using our little DSL. As it turns out, developing a DSL is not difficult at all. Given excellent tools such as MacroTools, we can quickly come up with a set of translation patterns and manipulate an abstract syntax tree into whatever we want.

A DSL is a great way to simplify the code and make it easier to maintain. It can be very useful in specific domain areas.

Summary

In this chapter, we have looked at several patterns related to improving the readability and maintainability of an application.

First, we learned about when a module becomes too large and when it should be considered for reorganization. We realized that coupling is an important consideration when splitting code into separate modules. Next, we discussed the problem of constructing objects that have many fields. We determined that using a keyword-based constructor can make the code more readable and can provide additional flexibility of supporting default values. We learned that the Julia Base module already provides a macro.

Then we explored how to do code generation, which is a convenient technique for dynamically defining many similar functions without having to repeat the code. We picked up a utility from `CodeTracking` to review the generated source code.

Finally, we went over details about how to develop DSLs. It is a good way to simplify code by mimicking the syntax with the original form of the domain concepts. We used an L-System as an example for developing a DSL. We picked up several utilities from the MacroTools package, where we can transform our source code by matching patterns. We learned how to use the `postwalk` function to examine and transform source code. And, pleasantly, we were able to complete the exercise with very little code.

In the next chapter, we will go over a set of patterns related to code safety. *Enjoy reading!*

Questions

1. What is the difference between afferent and efferent coupling?
2. Why are bidirectional dependencies bad from a maintainability perspective?
3. What is an easy way to generate code on the fly?
4. What would be an alternative to code generation?
5. When and why should you consider building a DSL?
6. What are the tools available for developing a DSL?

8
Robustness Patterns

This chapter will cover several patterns that can be used to improve software robustness. By robustness, we are referring to the quality aspects, that is, can the software perform its functions correctly? Are all possible scenarios handled properly? This is an extremely important factor to consider when writing code for mission-critical systems.

Based on the **Principle of Least Privilege** (**POLP**), we would consider hiding unnecessary implementation details to the client of the interface. However, Julia's data structure is transparent – all fields are automatically exposed and accessible. This poses a potential problem because any improper usage or mutation can break the system. Additionally, by accessing the fields directly, the code becomes more tightly coupled with the underlying implementation of an object. So, what if a field name needs to be changed? What if a field needs to be replaced by another one? Therefore, there is a need to apply abstraction and decouple object implementation from its official interface. We should adopt the more general definition – not only do we want to cover as many lines of code as possible but also every possible scenario as well. An increase in code coverage would give us more confidence about the correctness of our code.

We have classified these techniques into the following sections:

- Accessor patterns
- Property patterns
- Let block patterns
- Exception handling patterns

By the end of this chapter, you will be able to encapsulate data access by developing your own accessor functions and property functions. You will also be able to hide away global variables from unexpected access outside of the module. Finally, you will also know about various exception handling techniques and understand how to retry failed operations.

Let's get started!

Technical requirements

The example source code for this chapter can be found at `https://github.com/PacktPublishing/Hands-on-Design-Patterns-and-Best-Practices-with-Julia/tree/master/Chapter08`.

The code is tested in a Julia 1.3.0 environment.

Accessor patterns

Julia objects are transparent. What does that mean? Well, currently, the Julia language does not have the ability to apply access control over the fields of an object. Therefore, people coming from a C++ or Java background may find it a little uneasy. In this section, we will explore a number of ways in which to make the language more acceptable for those users who are seeking more access control.

So, perhaps we should define our requirements first. While we write up the requirements, we will also ask ourselves why we want to have them in the first place. Let's just consider any object in a Julia program:

- **Some fields need to be hidden from the outside world**: Some fields are considered to be part of the public interface and are, therefore, fully documented and supported. Other fields are considered implementation details, and they may not be used because they are subject to change in the future.
- **Some fields require validation before being mutated**: Some fields may only accept a range of values. For example, an `age` field of a `Person` object may reject anything less than 0 or greater than 120! Avoiding invalid data is paramount to building robust systems.
- **Some fields require a trigger before they can be read**: Some fields may be lazily loaded, which means they are not loaded until the value is read. Another reason is that some fields may contain sensitive data, and the use of such fields must be logged for audit purposes.

We will now discuss how to address these requirements.

Recognizing the implicit interface of an object

Before we dive into the specific patterns, let's first take a quick detour and discuss how and why we have a problem in the first place.

Suppose that we have defined a data type called `Simulation` to keep track of some scientific experiment data and related statistics. The syntax for it is as follows:

```
mutable struct Simulation{N}
    heatmap::Array{Float64, N}
    stats::NamedTuple{(:mean, :std)}
end
```

A `Simulation` object contains an N-dimensional array of floating-point values and a named tuple of statistical values. For demonstration purposes, we will create a simple function to perform a simulation and create an object, as follows:

```
using Distributions

function simulate(distribution, dims, n)
    tp = ntuple(i -> n, dims)
    heatmap = rand(distribution, tp...)
    return Simulation{dims}(heatmap, (mean = mean(heatmap), std =
std(heatmap)))
end
```

The simulation data called `heatmap` is generated using the `rand` function based on a distribution provided by the user. The `dims` argument represents the number of dimensions in the array, and the value of `n` represents the size of each dimension. Here's how to simulate a normally distributed 2-dimensional heatmap of size 1000 x 1000:

```
sim = simulate(Normal(), 2, 1000);
```

At this point, we can easily access the `heatmap` and `stats` fields of the object as follows:

```
julia> sim.heatmap
1000×1000 Array{Float64,2}:
 -0.0245684  -0.516914  -0.724059   …  -0.689534  0.81001     0.39468
 -0.373427   -0.949831  -1.03348       -3.00237   0.773453    0.611133
  0.186331   -2.23334   -0.594446      -0.277771  0.352053    2.35161
  ⋮                                ⋱
 -0.596433    0.69343    0.120265       1.15336   1.48342     0.113038
  0.0407504  -0.690448   0.606609       0.446669  0.355279   -0.885373
 -0.476229   -0.919225   2.42769       -0.687196  0.0981667  -0.840961

julia> sim.stats
(mean = 0.00011828545617957905, std = 0.9997327420929258)
```

Let's pause for a second. Is it OK to access the fields directly? We can argue here that it is not. The primary reason is that there is an implicit assumption that the field names represent the public interface of the object.

Unfortunately, such an assumption can be a little brittle in reality. As any seasoned programmer would have pointed out, software is always subject to change. *Always to change.* The world is not static, and requirements are not set in stone. For example, here are some possible changes that will certainly break our programming interface:

- Changing the field name of `heatmap` to `heatspace` because the new name is better suited for 3-dimensional or higher-dimensional data
- Changing the data type of `stats` from a named tuple to a new `struct` type because it has grown to include more complex statistical measures and we want to develop new functions along with that
- Removing the `stats` field altogether and computing it on the fly

As you can see, the programming interface cannot be taken lightly. In order to build software that lasts, we need to be clear about every single interface and understand how to support them in the future.

One way to provide an interface to an object is to create assessor functions, which are sometimes called getters and setters in other programming languages. So, in the next sections, let's look at how to use them.

Implementing getter functions

In mainstream object-oriented languages, we often implement getters for accessing the fields of an object. In Julia, we can also create getter functions. When implementing getter functions, we can choose which fields to expose as part of the **application programming interface (API)**. For our example, we will implement getter functions for both fields, as follows:

```
get_heatmap(s::Simulation) = s.heatmap
get_stats(s::Simulation) = s.stats
```

Our choice of function names here is somewhat non-idiomatic for the Julia language. A better convention is to use the nouns directly:

```
heatmap(s::Simulation) = s.heatmap
stats(s::Simulation) = s.stats
```

So, when we read the code that uses the `heatmap` function, we can read it as the *heatmap of the simulation*. Likewise, we can read it as the *statistics of the simulation* when the `stats` function is used.

These getter functions serve the purpose of defining a formal data retrieval interface for the object. If we ever need to change the names (or even the types) of the underlying fields, it would be fine as long as the public interface does not change. Furthermore, we could even remove the `stats` field and implement the statistical calculation directly in the `stats` function. Backward compatibility can now be easily maintained for any program that uses this object.

Next, we will look at write access for objects.

Implementing setter functions

For mutable types, we may implement setters. The scope would include fields that can only ever be mutated. For our simulation project, suppose that we want to allow the client program to do some transformation of the heatmap and put it back to the object. We can support that use case easily, as shown in the following code snippet:

```
function heatmap!(
        s::Simulation{N},
        new_heatmap::AbstractArray{Float64, N}) where {N}
    s.heatmap = new_heatmap
    s.stats = (mean = mean(new_heatmap), std = std(new_heatmap))
    return nothing
end
```

The setter function, `heatmap!`, accepts a `Simulation` object and a new heatmap array. Because the `stats` field contains the statistics of the underlying heatmap, we must maintain consistency within the object by recalculating the statistics and updating the field. Note that such a guarantee for consistency is only possible when we provide a setter function. Otherwise, the object would be in an inconsistent state if we ever to allow users to directly mutate the `heatmap` field in the object.

An additional benefit is that we can perform data validation in the setter function. For example, we can control the size of the map and throw an error when the size of the heatmap contains odd shapes:

```
function heatmap!(
            s::Simulation{N},
            new_heatmap::AbstractArray{Float64, N}) where {N}
    if length(unique(size(new_heatmap))) != 1
```

```
        error("All dimensions must have same size")
    end
    s.heatmap = new_heatmap
    s.stats = (mean = mean(new_heatmap), std = std(new_heatmap))
    return nothing
end
```

Here, we first determine the size of `new_heatmap`, which should be returned as a tuple. Then, we find out how many unique values are in this tuple. If there is only a single unique number in the tuple, then we know that the array is square, cubic, and so on. Otherwise, we just throw an error back to the caller.

Just like getter functions, setter functions serve as a public interface where the data of an object may be mutated. After we have both getter and setter functions, we can expect the caller to go through the interfaces. But the original fields can still be accessed directly. So, how do we stop that from happening? Let's explore that next.

Discouraging direct field access

While getter and setter functions are convenient, it is easy to forget about these functions and so the program ends up accessing the fields directly. That would be too bad, as we have just spent all that effort creating getter and setter functions and they end up getting bypassed.

A possible solution is to discourage direct field access by renaming the fields to something that looks obviously private. A common convention is to prepend the field names with underscores.

For our example, we can redefine the struct as follows:

```
mutable struct Simulation{N}
    _heatmap::Array{Float64, N}
    _stats::NamedTuple{(:mean, :std)}
end
```

These oddly named fields will then only be used within the implementation of the `Simulation` type, and all external usages will avoid them. Such a convention discourages the programmer from making the mistake of accessing the fields directly.

However, some of us may not be very satisfied with this solution because the use of a coding convention is a very weak method for enforcing the proper use of the programming interface. Such concern is very valid especially when we hold ourselves to a higher standard of software robustness. So, in the next section, we will explore a stronger technique that will allow us to control access programmatically.

Property patterns

In this section, we will take a deep dive and learn how to enforce more granular control over the fields of an object by using the property interface. Julia's property interface allows you to provide a custom implementation for the dot notation used in field access. By overriding the standard behavior, we can apply any kind of access control and validation against the field being referenced or assigned. To illustrate this concept, we will tackle a new use case here – implementing a lazy file loader.

Introducing the lazy file loader

Suppose that we are developing a file loading facility that supports lazy loading. By lazy, we are talking about not loading a file until the content is required. Let's take a look at the following code:

```
mutable struct FileContent
    path
    loaded
    contents
end
```

The `FileContent` struct contains three fields:

- `path`: The location of the file
- `loaded`: A Boolean value that indicates whether the file has been loaded into memory
- `contents`: A byte array that contains the contents of the file

Here's the constructor for the same struct:

```
function FileContent(path)
    ss = lstat(path)
    return FileContent(path, false, zeros(UInt8, ss.size))
end
```

As with our current design, we pre-allocate memory for the file but we do not read the file content until later. The size of the file is determined by a call to the `lstat` function. When creating the `FileContent` object, we initialize the `loaded` field with a `false` value – an indication that the file has not been loaded into memory.

Eventually, we must load the file content, so we just provide a separate function that reads the file into the pre-allocated byte array:

```
function load_contents!(fc::FileContent)
    open(fc.path) do io
        readbytes!(io, fc.contents)
        fc.loaded = true
    end
    nothing
end
```

Let's run a quick test to see how it works:

```
julia> fc = FileContent("/etc/hosts")
FileContent("/etc/hosts", false, UInt8[0x00, 0x00, 0x00, 0x00, 0x00,
0x00, 0x00, 0x00, 0x00, 0x00  …  0x00, 0x00, 0x00, 0x00, 0x00, 0x00,
0x00, 0x00, 0x00, 0x00])

julia> fc.loaded
false
```

Here, we have just created a new `FileContent` object. Clearly, the `loaded` field contains a `false` value because we have not read the file yet. The `content` field is also full of zeros.

Let's load the file content now:

```
julia> load_contents!(fc)

julia> fc.loaded
true

julia> fc.contents
359-element Array{UInt8,1}:
 0x23
 0x23
 0x0a
 0x23
```

Now, the `contents` field contains some real data, and the `loaded` field has the value of `true`. Of course, we are just babysitting and running the code manually for now. The idea is to implement lazy loading. We need a way to intercept any *read* operation into the `contents` field so that the file content can be loaded just in time. Ideally, this should happen whenever someone uses the `fc.contents` expression. In order to *hijack* the call to get `fc.contents`, we must first understand how Julia's dot notation works. Let's take a detour and go over that now.

Understanding the dot notation for field access

In general, whenever we need to access a specific field of an object, we can conveniently write it as `object.fieldname`. As it turns out, this notation is really *syntactic sugar*, that is, some *sweet* syntax, for the `getproperty` function call. To be clear, whenever we write the code in the following format:

```
object.fieldname
```

It is translated to a function call to `getproperty`:

```
getproperty(object, :fieldname)
```

For our lazy file loader example, `fc.path` is really the same as `getproperty(fc, :path)`.

All that magic is performed automatically by the Julia compiler. A great thing about Julia is that this kind of magic is quite transparent. We can actually see what the compiler did by using the `Meta.lower` function, as follows:

```
julia> Meta.lower(Main, :( fc.path ))
:($(Expr(:thunk, CodeInfo(
    @ none within `top-level scope'
1 ─     %1 = Base.getproperty(fc, :path)
  └──          return %1
))))
```

Similarly, when we assign a value to a field of an object, the same kind of translation takes place:

```
julia> Meta.lower(Main, :( fc.path = "/etc/hosts"))
:($(Expr(:thunk, CodeInfo(
    @ none within `top-level scope'
1 ─    Base.setproperty!(fc, :path, "/etc/hosts")
  └    return "/etc/hosts"
))))
```

From the preceding result, we can see when the code assigns a string to fc.path, it is just translated to a setproperty!(fc, :path, "/etc/hosts") function call.

Let's not stop there. What do the getproperty and setproperty! functions do? Well, they happen to be plain Julia functions defined in the Base module. The best place to understand how they work is by examining the Julia source code itself. From the Julia REPL, we can easily bring up the source code as follows:

```
julia> @edit fc.path
```

From the preceding code, we can see that the @edit macro is used to locate the source code of the function being called – in this case, getproperty. From the REPL terminal, it should open your editor and display the code as follows:

```
 Base.jl    ×

cations > Julia-1.2.app > Contents > Resources > julia > share > julia > base >  Base.jl > {} Base >  getproperty
   19
   20    getproperty(Core.@nospecialize(x), f::Symbol) = getfield(x, f)
   21    setproperty!(x, f::Symbol, v) = setfield!(x, f, convert(fieldtype(typeof(x), f), v))
   22
```

Aha! We see that the getproperty function just forwards the call to getfield, which is used to extract the data from the object. The next line in the same source file shows the definition of setproperty!. The implementation of setproperty! is a bit more interesting. Besides using the setfield! function to mutate the field in the object, it also converts the v value to the type of the field in object x, which is determined by a call to fieldtype.

The `getfield` function is a built-in function for getting any field value from an existing object. It takes two arguments – an object and a symbol. For example, to get the path from a `FileContent` object, we can use `getfield(fc, :path)`. Likewise, the `setfield!` function is used to update any field of an existing object. Both `getfield` and `setfield!` are low-level functions in the Julia implementation.

 Type conversion is convenient, especially for numerical types. For example, it is quite common for an object to store a `Float64` field but the code happens to pass an integer instead. Of course, the conversion logic is more general than just numeric types. For custom types, the same auto-conversion process would work fine as long as a `convert` function is defined.

Now that we understand how the dot notation is translated to the `getproperty` and `setproperty!` function calls, we can develop the lazy loading feature for our file loader.

Implementing read access and lazy loading

In order to implement lazy loading, we can extend the `getproperty` function. During the call, we can check whether the file content has been loaded yet. If not, we just load the file content right before returning the data back to the caller.

Extending the `getproperty` function is as easy as simply defining it with the `FileContent` type and a symbol as the arguments of the function. The following code shows this:

```
function Base.getproperty(fc::FileContent, s::Symbol)
    direct_passthrough_fields = (:path, )
    if s in direct_passthrough_fields
        return getfield(fc, s)
    end
    if s === :contents
        !getfield(fc, :loaded) && load_contents!(fc)
        return getfield(fc, :contents)
    end
    error("Unsupported property: $s")
end
```

It is important that we define the function for `Base.getproperty` rather than just `getproperty`. That is because the compiler will translate the dot notation to `Base.getproperty` rather than the `getproperty` function in your own module. If this is unclear, you are encouraged to revisit the namespace concept from the *Understanding namespaces, modules, and packages* section in Chapter 2, *Modules, Packages, and Data Type Concepts*.

We have chosen to put `Base` as a prefix to the function name in the definition. This style of coding is preferred because it is clear from the function definition that we are extending the `getproperty` function from the `Base` package.

Another way to extend functions from another package is to first import the third-party package. For the preceding example, we could have written it as follows. This coding style is not recommended because it is less obvious that the `getproperty` function being defined is an extension of the function from `Base`:

```
import Base: getproperty

function getproperty(fc::FileContent, s::Symbol)
    ....
end
```

By contrast, the `getproperty` function must handle all possible property names. Let's first consider the following section of code:

```
# extend Base.getproperty to redefine the meaning of dot notation
function Base.getproperty(fc::FileContent, s::Symbol)
    direct_passthrough_fields = (:path, )
    if s in direct_passthrough_fields
        return getfield(fc, s)
    end
    if s == :contents
        getfield(fc, :loaded) || load_contents!(fc)
        return getfield(fc, :contents)
    end
    error("Unsupported property: $s")
end
```

In this case, we must support `:path` and `:contents`. If the s symbol is one of those fields that we want to pass through directly, then we just forward the call to the `getfield` function.

Now, let's consider the next section of code:

```
# extend Base.getproperty to redefine the meaning of dot notation
function Base.getproperty(fc::FileContent, s::Symbol)
    direct_passthrough_fields = (:path, )
    if s in direct_passthrough_fields
        return getfield(fc, s)
    end
    if s === :contents
        getfield(fc, :loaded) || load_contents!(fc)
        return getfield(fc, :contents)
    end
    error("Unsupported property: $s")
end
```

If the symbol is `:contents`, then we check the value of the `loaded` field. If the `loaded` field contains `false`, then we call the `load_contents!` function to load the file content into memory.

Note that we have used `getfield` all over the place in this function. If we had written the code using the normal dot syntax, for example, `fc.loaded`, then it would start calling the `getproperty` function again and we could end up with infinite recursion.

If the field name is not one of the supported ones, then we just raise an exception, as follows:

```
# extend Base.getproperty to redefine the meaning of dot notation
function Base.getproperty(fc::FileContent, s::Symbol)
    direct_passthrough_fields = (:path, )
    if s in direct_passthrough_fields
        return getfield(fc, s)
    end
    if s === :contents
        getfield(fc, :loaded) || load_contents!(fc)
        return getfield(fc, :contents)
    end
    error("Unsupported property: $s")
end
```

One interesting observation is that we have decided to support two property names only – path and contents – and we have dropped the support for the loaded property. The reason for this is that the loaded field is really used as an internal state of the object. There is no reason to expose it as part of the public programming interface. As we talk about software robustness in this chapter, we can also appreciate developing code that only exposes necessary information.

 An analogy is that data is always *classified* but can be released only on a *need-to-know basis*, which is how government officials usually like to describe highly sensitive data.

We are almost done. The only remaining piece of work is to refactor the load_content! function to use getfield and setfield! instead of the dot notation:

```
# lazy load
function load_contents!(fc::FileContent)
    open(getfield(fc, :path)) do io
        readbytes!(io, getfield(fc, :contents))
        setfield!(fc, :loaded, true)
    end
    nothing
end
```

We can now test the lazy loading functionality:

```
julia> fc = FileContent("/etc/hosts")
FileContent("/etc/hosts", false, UInt8[0x00, 0x00, 0x00, 0x00, 0x00, 0
x00, 0x00, 0x00, 0x00, 0x00 …  0x00, 0x00, 0x00, 0x00, 0x00, 0x00, 0x
00, 0x00, 0x00, 0x00])

julia> fc.contents
359-element Array{UInt8,1}:
 0x23
 0x23
    ⋮
 0x6d
 0x0a

julia> fc.path
"/etc/hosts"
```

Both references to the path and contents fields are working properly. In particular, a reference to fc.contents triggered the file load and then returned the proper content. So, what happened to the loaded field? Let's try it:

```
julia> fc.loaded
ERROR: Unsupported property: loaded
```

Voila! We have successfully prevented the `loaded` field from being accessed directly.

The property interface has enabled us to manage read access and implement the lazy loading feature. Next, we will look at how to manage write access as well.

Controlling write access to object fields

In order to manage write access to the fields of an object, we can extend the `setproperty!` function, in a similar way to how we did for read access.

Let's recall how the `FileContent` data type was designed:

```
mutable struct FileContent
    path
    loaded
    contents
end
```

Suppose that we want to allow the user to switch to a different file by mutating the `path` field with a new file location. In addition to this, we want to prevent the `loaded` and `contents` fields from being changed directly using dot notation. To achieve that, we can extend the `setproperty!` function as follows:

```
function Base.setproperty!(fc::FileContent, s::Symbol, value)
    if s === :path
        ss = lstat(value)
        setfield!(fc, :path, value)
        setfield!(fc, :loaded, false)
        setfield!(fc, :contents, zeros(UInt8, ss.size))
        println("Object re-initialized for $value (size $(ss.size))")
        return nothing
    end
    error("Property $s cannot be changed.")
end
```

To extend the `setproperty!` function, we must use `setfield!` in the function definition whenever we need to change any field in the object.

In this case, when the user tries to assign a value to the `path` field, we can just reinitialize the object like how we did in the constructor function. This involves setting the values of the `path` and `loaded` fields, as well as pre-allocating memory space for the file content. Let's go ahead and test it now:

```
julia> fc.path
"/etc/profile"

julia> fc.path = "/etc/profile"
Object re-initialized for /etc/profile (size 189)
"/etc/profile"
```

If the user tries to assign a value to any other field, an error is thrown:

```
julia> fc.contents = []
ERROR: Property contents cannot be changed.
```

By extending the `setproperty!` function, we have successfully controlled write access to any field for any object.

> While individual field access can be controlled, we cannot prevent additional changes to the underlying data of a field. For example, the `contents` property is just an array of bytes and the programmer should be able to change the elements in the array. If we want to protect the data from being modified, we can return a copy of the `contents` byte array from the `getproperty` call.

By now, we know how to implement the `getproperty` and `setproperty!` functions so that we can control access to the individual fields of an object. Next, we will look at how to document what properties are available.

Reporting accessible fields

A development environment can often help a programmer to enter field names correctly. In the Julia REPL, when I press the *Tab* key twice after entering the dot character, it will try to autocomplete and display the available field names:

```
julia> fc.                                press Tab key twice
contents loaded      path
```

Now that we have implemented the `getproperty` and `setproperty!` functions, the list is no longer accurate. More specifically, the `loaded` field should not be displayed because it can neither be accessed nor changed. In order to fix this, we can simply extend the `propertynames` function, as follows:

```
function Base.propertynames(fc::FileContent)
    return (:path, :contents)
end
```

The `propertynames` function just needs to return a tuple of valid symbols. After the function is defined, the REPL will only display the valid field names, as follows:

```
julia> fc.                              press Tab key twice
contents path
```

In this section, we have learned how to leverage Julia's property interface to control both read and write access to any field of an object. It is an essential technique to write robust programs.

While the use of the property interface seems to address most of the requirements we set forth earlier, it is not bulletproof.

For example, there is nothing that prevents the program from calling the `getfield` and `setfield!` functions directly on any object. It would not be possible to completely hide that from the programmer unless the language is updated to support granular field access controls. Such a feature may be available in the future.

Next, we will look at some patterns related to limiting the scope of variables so that we can minimize the exposure of private variables to the outside world.

Let block patterns

The recurring theme in this chapter is to learn how to improve and gain more control over the visibility and accessibility of data and functions in the public API. By enforcing the access of the programming interface, we can guarantee how the program is utilized. Additionally, we can focus on testing the interface as *advertised*.

Currently, Julia provides little help in encapsulating implementation details within a module. While we can use the `export` keyword to expose certain functions and variables to the other modules, it is not designed to be an access control or data encapsulation feature. You can always *peek* into a module and access any variable or function even when they are not exported.

In this section, we will continue the trend and go over some strategies that we can use to limit access to variables or functions in a module. Here, we will use a web crawler use case to illustrate the problem and a possible solution.

Introducing the web crawler use case

Suppose that we have to build a web crawler that can be used to index content from various websites. The process of doing that involves setting up a list of target sites and then kicking off the crawler. Let's create a module with the structure, as follows:

```
module WebCrawler

using Dates

# public interface
export Target
export add_site!, crawl_sites!, current_sites, reset_crawler!

# == insert global variables and functions here ==

end # module
```

Our programming interface is quite simple. Let's see how to do this:

1. `Target` is a data type that represents the website being crawled. Then, we can use the `add_site!` function to add new target sites to the list.
2. When ready, we just call the `crawl_sites!` function to visit all sites.
3. For convenience, the `current_sites` function can be used to review the current list of target sites and their crawling status.
4. Finally, the `reset_crawler!` function can be used to reset the state of the web crawler.

Let's take a look at the data structure now. The `Target` type is used to maintain the URL of the target website. It also contains a Boolean variable regarding the status and the time it finished crawling. The struct is defined as follows:

```
Base.@kwdef mutable struct Target
    url::String
    finished::Bool = false
    finish_time::Union{DateTime,Nothing} = nothing
end
```

In order to keep track of the current target sites, a global variable is used:

```
const sites = Target[]
```

To complete the web crawler implementation, we have the following functions defined in the module:

```
function add_site!(site::Target)
    push!(sites, site)
end

function crawl_sites!()
    for s in sites
        index_site!(s)
    end
end

function current_sites()
    copy(sites)
end

function index_site!(site::Target)
    site.finished = true
    site.finish_time = now()
    println("Site $(site.url) crawled.")
end

function reset_crawler!()
    empty!(sites)
end
```

To use the web crawler, first, we can add some sites, as follows:

```julia
julia> using Main.WebCrawler

julia> add_site!(Target(url = "http://cnn.com"));

julia> add_site!(Target(url = "http://yahoo.com"));

julia> current_sites()
2-element Array{Target,1}:
 Target("http://cnn.com", false, nothing)
 Target("http://yahoo.com", false, nothing)
```

Then, we can just run the crawler and retrieve the results afterward:

```julia
julia> crawl_sites!()
current_sites()
Site http://cnn.com crawled.
Site http://yahoo.com crawled.

julia> current_sites()
2-element Array{Target,1}:
 Target("http://cnn.com", true, 2019-12-08T17:24:30.631)
 Target("http://yahoo.com", true, 2019-12-08T17:24:30.637)
```

The current implementation is not bad, but it has the following two access-related issues:

1. The global variable, `sites`, is visible to the outside world, which means that anyone can get a handle of the variable and mess it up, for example, by inserting a malicious website.
2. The `index_site!` function should be considered a private function and should not be included as part of the public API.

Now that we have set the stage, we will demonstrate how to address these problems in the next section.

Using closure to hide private variables and functions away

Our goal is to hide the global constant, `sites`, and the helper function, `index_site!`, such that they are not visible in the public API. To achieve that, we can utilize `let` blocks.

In the body of the module, we can wrap all of the functions inside a `let` block, as follows:

```
let sites = Target[]

    global function add_site!(site :: Target)
        push!(sites, site)
    end

    global function crawl_sites!()
        for s in sites
            index_site!(s)
        end
    end

    global function current_sites()
        copy(sites)
    end

    function index_site!(site :: Target)
        site.finished = true
        site.finish_time = now()
        println("Site $(site.url) crawled.")
    end

    global function reset_crawler!()
        empty!(sites)
    end

end # let
```

Now, let's see what has been changed:

- The `sites` constant has been replaced by a bound variable at the beginning of the `let` block. The variables in a `let` block are bound only in the scope of the block and are not visible to the outside world.
- The functions that need to be exposed to the API are prefixed with the `global` keyword. This includes `add_site!`, `crawl_sites!`, `current_sites`, and `reset_crawler!`. The `index_site!` function is left as-is so that it is not exposed.

The `global` keyword allows us to expose the function names to the global scope of the module, which can be exported and made accessible from the public API.

After reloading the module, we can confirm that neither `sites` nor `index_site!` are available from the API, as shown in the following output:

```
julia> Main.WebCrawler.index_site!()
ERROR: UndefVarError: index_site! not defined
Stacktrace:
 [1] getproperty(::Module, ::Symbol) at ./Base.jl:13
 [2] top-level scope at REPL[8]:1

julia> Main.WebCrawler.sites
ERROR: UndefVarError: sites not defined
```

As you can see, a `let` block is an effective way to control access to global variables or functions in a module. We have the ability to encapsulate functions or variables that we want to prevent access from outside of the module.

There may be a performance overhead when wrapping functions within a `let` block. You may want to run a performance test before using this pattern in any performance-critical section of your code.

As `let` blocks are quite useful in limiting the scope, we can often use it in longer scripts and functions. Next, we will look at how it is used in practice.

Limiting the variable scope for long scripts or functions

Another usage of the let block is to limit the scope of variables in a long Julia script or function. In a long script or function, the code could be difficult to follow if we declare a variable at the top and use it throughout the body. Instead, we can write a series of let blocks, which operate independently with their own bound variables. By limiting the bounded variables in smaller blocks, we can follow the code more easily.

While writing long script/functions is not a generally recommended practice, we can find them occasionally in testing code, which tends to be quite repetitive. In test scripts, we may have many test cases that are grouped in the same test set. Here is an example from the `GtkUtilities` package:

```
# Source: GtkUtilities.jl/test/utils.jl

let c = Canvas(), win = Window(c, "Canvas1")
    Gtk.draw(c) do widget
```

```
            fill!(widget, RGB(1,0,0))
        end
        showall(win)
end
let c = Canvas(), win = Window(c, "Canvas2")
        Gtk.draw(c) do widget
            w, h = Int(width(widget)), Int(height(widget))
            randcol = reshape(reinterpret(RGB{N0f8}, rand(0x00:0xff, 3, w*h)),
w, h)
            copy!(widget, randcol)
        end
        showall(win)
end
let c = Canvas(), win = Window(c, "Canvas3")
        Gtk.draw(c) do widget
            w, h = Int(width(widget)), Int(height(widget))
            randnum = reshape(reinterpret(N0f8, rand(0x00:0xff, w*h)),w,h)
            copy!(widget, randnum)
        end
        showall(win)
end
```

We have a few observations here from the preceding code:

- The c variable is bound to a new Canvas object every time.
- The win variable is bound to a new Window object having a different title every time.
- The w, h, randcol, and randnum variables are local variables that do not escape from their respective let blocks.

By using let blocks, it does not matter how long the test script is. Every let block maintains its own scope and nothing should leak from one block to the next. This kind of programming style immediately provides some comfort to the programmer when it comes to the quality of testing code, as each testing unit is independent from each other.

Next, we will go over some exception handling techniques. Although it is more fun doing programming projects, exception handling is not something that we want to overlook. So, let's take a look at it next.

Exception handling patterns

Robust software requires robust error handling practice. The fact is that an error can be raised at any time, sometimes, unexpectedly. As a responsible programmer, we need to ensure that every path of computation is taken care of, including both the *happy paths* and *unhappy paths*. Happy paths refer to program execution that runs normally as expected. Unhappy paths refer to an unexpected outcome due to error conditions.

In this section, we will explore several ways about to catch exceptions and recover from failures effectively.

Catching and handling exceptions

A general technique to catch exceptions is to enclose any logic in a try-catch block. This is the easiest way to ensure that unexpected errors are handled:

```
try
    # do something that may possible raise an error
catch ex
    # recover from failure depending on the type of condition
end
```

A common question, however, is where this `try-catch` block should be placed. Of course, we could have just wrapped every single line of code but that would be impractical. After all, not every line of code would throw an error.

We do want to be smart about choosing where to catch exceptions. We know that adding exception handling increases the code size. Additionally, every line of code requires maintenance. Ironically, the less code we write, the less chance of introducing bugs. After all, we should not introduce more problems by trying to catch problems, right?

Next, we will look at what kind of scenarios we should consider doing error handling for.

Dealing with various types of exceptions

The most obvious places to wrap a try-catch block are in the code blocks that we need to acquire network resources, for example, querying a database or connecting to a web server. Whenever the network is involved, there is a much higher chance of encountering an issue than doing something locally on the same computer.

It is important to understand what kind of errors can be thrown. Suppose that we continue developing the web crawler use case from the previous section. The `index_sites!` function is now implemented using the HTTP library as follows:

```
function index_site!(site::Target)
    response = HTTP.get(site.url)
    site.finished = true
    site.finish_time = now()
    println("Site $(site.url) crawled. Status=", response.status)
end
```

The `HTTP.get` function is used to retrieve the content from the website. The code looks pretty innocent but it does not handle any error condition. For example, what happens if the site's URL is wrong or if the site is down? In those cases, we would run into a runtime exception, such as the following:

```
julia> add_site!(Target(url = "https://this-site-does-not-exist-haha.com"))
1-element Array{Target,1}:
 Target("https://this-site-does-not-exist-haha.com", false, nothing)

julia> crawl_sites!()
ERROR: IOError(Base.IOError("connect: connection refused (ECONNREFUSED)", -61)
during request(https://this-site-does-not-exist-haha.com))
```

So, at a minimum, we should handle `IOError`. It turns out that the HTTP library actually does more than that. If the remote site returns any HTTP status code in the 400- or 500-series, then it also wraps the error code and raises a `StatusError` exception, as follows:

```
julia> reset_crawler!()
0-element Array{Target,1}

julia> add_site!(Target(url = "https://www.google.com/this-page-does-not-exist"
))
1-element Array{Target,1}:
 Target("https://www.google.com/this-page-does-not-exist", false, nothing)

julia> crawl_sites!()
ERROR: HTTP.ExceptionRequest.StatusError(404, "GET", "/this-page-does-not-exist
", HTTP.Messages.Response:
"""
HTTP/1.1 404 Not Found
```

So, how do we know for sure what kind of errors can ever be thrown? Well, we can always *read the fine manual* or so-called RTFM. From the HTTP package's documentation, we can see that the following exceptions may be thrown when making HTTP requests:

- `HTTP.ExceptionRequest.StatusError`
- `HTTP.Parsers.ParseError`
- `HTTP.IOExtras.IOError`
- `Sockets.DNSError`

In Julia, the try-catch block catches all exceptions regardless of the type of exception. So, we should have the ability to handle any other exception even when it is unknown to us. Here is an example of a function that handles exceptions properly:

```julia
function try_index_site!(site::Target)
    try
        index_site!(site)
    catch ex
        println("Unable to index site: $site")
        if ex isa HTTP.ExceptionRequest.StatusError
            println("HTTP status error (code = ", ex.status, ")")
        elseif ex isa Sockets.DNSError
            println("DNS problem: ", ex)
        else
            println("Unknown error:", ex)
        end
    end
end
```

We can see from the preceding code that, in the body of the `catch` block, we can check the type of exception and handle it appropriately. The `else` part of the block ensures that all types of exceptions are caught, whether we know about them or not. Let's hook up the `crawl_site!` function to this new function:

```julia
global function crawl_sites!()
    for s in sites
        try_index_site!(s)
    end
end
```

We can test out the error handling code now:

```
julia> add_site!(Target(url = "https://www.google.com/this-page-does-not-exist"
))
1-element Array{Target,1}:
 Target("https://www.google.com/this-page-does-not-exist", false, nothing)

julia> crawl_sites!()
Unable to index site: Target("https://www.google.com/this-page-does-not-exist",
 false, nothing)
HTTP status error (code = 404)
```

This works well!

So, this is one instance; what other places do we want to inject exception handling logic? Let's explore this next.

Handling exceptions at the top level

Another place where you would normally handle exceptions is at the very top level of the program. Why? One reason is that we may want to avoid the program from crashing due to an uncaught exception. The top level of the program is the very last gate to catch anything, and the program has an option to either recover from the failure (such as doing a *soft reset*) or gracefully close all the resources and shut down.

When a computer program finishes execution, it normally returns an exit status back to the shell where the program was invoked. In Unix, the usual convention is to indicate successful termination with a zero status and unsuccessful termination with a nonzero status.

Consider the following pseudocode:

```
try
    # 1. do some work related to reading writing files
    # 2. invoke an HTTP request to a remote web service
    # 3. create a status report in PDF and save in a network drive
catch ex
    if ex isa FileNotFoundError
        println("Having trouble with reading local file")
        exit(1)
    elseif ex isa HTTPRequestError
        println("Unable to communicate with web service")
        exit(2)
    elseif ex isa NetworkDriveNotReadyError
```

```
                println("All done, except that the report cannot be saved")
                exit(3)
        else
                println("An unknown error has occurred, please report. Error=", ex)
                exit(255)
        end
    end
end
```

We can see from the previous code that, by design, we can exit the program with a specific status code for different error conditions so that the calling program can handle the exception properly.

Next, we will take a look at how to determine where an exception was originally raised from a deeply nested execution frame.

Walking along the stack frames

Often, an exception is raised from a function but it is not handled in the right away. The exception then travels to the parent calling function. If that function does not catch the exception either, it again travels to the next parent calling function. This process continues until a try-catch block catches the exception. At this point, the program's current *stack frame* – an execution context of where the code is currently running – handles the exception.

It would be tremendously useful if we can see where the exception was originally raised. To do that, let's first try to understand how to retrieve a stack trace that is an array of stack frames. Let's create a simple set of nested function calls such that they throw an error at the end. Consider the following code:

```
function foo1()
    foo2()
end

function foo2()
    foo3()
end

function foo3()
    throw(ErrorException("bad things happened"))
end
```

Now, if we execute the `foo1` function, we should get an error, as follows:

```
julia> foo1()
ERROR: bad things happened
Stacktrace:
 [1] foo3() at ./REPL[12]:2
 [2] foo2() at ./REPL[11]:2
 [3] foo1() at ./REPL[10]:2
 [4] top-level scope at REPL[13]:1
```

As you can see, the stack trace shows the execution sequence in reversed order. At the top of the stack trace is the `foo3` function. Because we're doing this in the REPL, we do not see a source filename; however, the number 2, as in `REPL[17]:2`, indicates that an error was thrown from line 2 of the `foo3` function.

Let's introduce the `stacktrace` function now. This function is part of the `Base` package and it can be used to obtain the current stack trace. As the `stacktrace` function returns an array of `StackFrame`, it would be nice if we could create a function to display it nicely. We can define a function to print the stack trace, as follows:

```
function pretty_print_stacktrace(trace)
    for (i,v) in enumerate(trace)
        println(i, " => ", v)
    end
end
```

As we want to handle exceptions properly, we will now update the `foo1` function by wrapping the call to `foo2` with a `try-catch` block. In the `catch` block, we will also print the stack trace so that we can further debug the issue:

```
function foo1()
    try
        foo2()
    catch
        println("handling error gracefully")
        pretty_print_stacktrace(stacktrace())
    end
end
```

Let's run the foo1 function now:

```
julia> foo1()
handling error gracefully
1 => foo1() at REPL[15]:7
2 => top-level scope at REPL[16]:1
3 => eval(::Module, ::Any) at boot.jl:330
4 => eval_user_input(::Any, ::REPL.REPLBackend) at REPL.jl:86
5 => macro expansion at REPL.jl:118 [inlined]
6 => (::REPL.var"#26#27"{REPL.REPLBackend})() at task.jl:333
```

Oops! What happened to foo2 and foo3? The exception was thrown from foo3 but we can no longer see them in the stack trace. This is because we have caught the exception, and from Julia's perspective, it is already handled and the current execution context is in foo1 already.

In order to address this issue, there is another function in the Base package called catch_backtrace. It gives us the backtrace of the current exception so we know where the exception was originally raised. We just need to update the foo1 function as follows:

```
function foo1()
    try
        foo2()
    catch
        println("handling error gracefully")
        pretty_print_stacktrace(stacktrace(catch_backtrace()))
    end
end
```

Then, if we run foo1 again, we get the following results, where foo3 and foo2 are back to the stack trace:

```
julia> foo1()
handling error gracefully
1 => foo3() at REPL[12]:2
2 => foo2() at REPL[11]:2
3 => foo1() at REPL[17]:3
4 => top-level scope at REPL[18]:1
5 => eval(::Module, ::Any) at boot.jl:330
6 => eval_user_input(::Any, ::REPL.REPLBackend) at REPL.jl:86
7 => macro expansion at REPL.jl:118 [inlined]
8 => (::REPL.var"#26#27"{REPL.REPLBackend})() at task.jl:333
```

Note that the use of `catch_backtrace` must be within the `catch` block. If it is called outside of a `catch` block, it would return an empty backtrace.

Next, we will look at a different aspect of exception handling – performance impact.

Understanding the performance impact of exception handling

There is actually a performance overhead to use a try-catch block. In particular, if the application is doing something in a tight loop, it would be a bad idea to catch exceptions inside the loop. To understand the impact, let's try a simple example.

Consider the following code that simply calculates the sum of the square root of every number in an array:

```
function sum_of_sqrt1(xs)
    total = zero(eltype(xs))
    for i in eachindex(xs)
        total += sqrt(xs[i])
    end
    return total
end
```

Knowing that `sqrt` may throw `DomainError` for negative numbers, our first attempt may be to catch such exceptions inside the loop:

```
function sum_of_sqrt2(xs)
    total = zero(eltype(xs))
    for i in eachindex(xs)
        try
            total += sqrt(xs[i])
        catch
            # ignore error intentionally
        end
    end
    return total
end
```

What would be the performance impact of doing that? Let's use the BenchmarkTools package to measure the performance for both functions:

```
julia> @btime sum_of_sqrt1($x);
  482.808 µs (0 allocations: 0 bytes)

julia> @btime sum_of_sqrt2($x);
  2.478 ms (0 allocations: 0 bytes)
```
5x slower!

It turns out that just wrapping the code around a try-catch block has made the loop 5 times slower! Perhaps that is not a very good deal. So, what should we do in this case? Well, we can always proactively check the number before calling the sqrt function and avoid the problem with negative values. Let's write a new sum_of_sqrt3 function as follows:

```
function sum_of_sqrt3(xs)
    total = zero(eltype(xs))
    for i in eachindex(xs)
        if xs[i] >= 0.0
            total += sqrt(xs[i])
        end
    end
    return total
end
```

Let's measure the performance again:

```
julia> @btime sum_of_sqrt3($x);
  482.810 µs (0 allocations: 0 bytes)
```

Fantastic! We have now restored the performance. The moral of the story is that we should be smart about using try-catch blocks, especially when performance is a concern. If there is any way to avoid a try-catch block, then it would certainly be a better option whenever a higher performance is needed.

Next, we will explore how to perform retries, a commonly-used strategy for recovering from failures.

Retrying operations

Sometimes, exceptions are thrown due to unexpected outages or so-called *hiccups*. It is not an uncommon scenario for a system that is highly integrated with other systems or services. For example, the trading system in a stock exchange may need to publish trade execution data to a messaging system for downstream processing. But if the messaging system experiences just a momentary outage, then the operation could fail. In that case, the most common approach is to sleep for a while and then come back and try again. If the retry fails again, then the operation will be retried again later, until the system fully recovers.

Such retry logic is not difficult to write. Here, we will play with an example. Suppose that we have a function that fails randomly:

```julia
using Dates

function do_something(name::AbstractString)
    println(now(), " Let's do it")
    if rand() > 0.5
        println(now(), " Good job, $(name)!")
    else
        error(now(), " Too bad :-(")
    end
end
```

On a good day, we would see this lovely message:

```
julia> do_something("John")
2020-01-07T21:58:39.602 Let's do it
2020-01-07T21:58:39.602 Good job, John!
```

On a bad day, we would get this instead:

```
julia> do_something("John")
2020-01-07T21:59:14.153 Let's do it
ERROR: 2020-01-07T21:59:14.154 Too bad :-(
```

Naively, we can develop a new function that incorporates the retry logic:

```julia
function do_something_more_robustly(name::AbstractString;
        max_retry_count = 3,
        retry_interval = 2)
    retry_count = 0
    while true
        try
```

```
            return do_something(name)
        catch ex
            sleep(retry_interval)
            retry_count += 1
            retry_count > max_retry_count && rethrow(ex)
        end
    end
end
```

This function just calls the `do_something` function. If it encounters an exception, it will wait 2 seconds as specified in the `retry_interval` keyword argument and try again. It keeps a track of a counter in `retry_count`, and so it will just retry up to 3 times by default, as indicated by the `max_retry_count` keyword argument:

```
julia> do_something_more_robustly("John")
2020-01-07T21:59:59.055 Let's do it
2020-01-07T22:00:01.059 Let's do it
2020-01-07T22:00:03.062 Let's do it
2020-01-07T22:00:03.063 Good job, John!
```

Of course, this code is fairly straightforward and easy to write. But we will get bored quickly if we do this over and over again for many functions. It turns out that Julia comes with a `retry` function that solves this problem nicely. We can achieve the exact same functionality with a single line of code:

```
retry(do_something, delays=fill(2.0, 3))("John")
```

The `retry` function takes a function as the first argument. The `delays` keyword argument can be any object that supports the iteration interface. In this case, we have provided an array of 3 elements, each containing the number of 2.0. The return value of the `retry` function is an anonymous function that takes any number of arguments. Those arguments will be *fed* into the original function that needs to be called, in this case, `do_something`. Here is how it looks using the `retry` function:

```
julia> retry(do_something, delays=fill(2.0, 3))("John")
2020-01-07T22:00:36.522 Let's do it
2020-01-07T22:00:38.527 Let's do it          2 seconds delay
2020-01-07T22:00:40.529 Let's do it          up to 3 retries
2020-01-07T22:00:40.53 Good job, John!
```

Since the `delays` argument can contain any number, we could utilize a different strategy that comes back with a different waiting time. A common usage is that we would want to retry quickly (that is, sleep less) in the beginning but slow down over time. When connecting to a remote system, it is possible that the remote system is just having a short hiccup, or perhaps it is undergoing an extended outage. In the latter scenario, it does not make sense to flood the system with quick requests as it would be a waste of system resources and get the water muddier when it is already in a mess.

In fact, the default value for the `delays` argument is `ExponentialBackOff`, which iterates by exponentially increasing the delay time. On a very unlucky day, using `ExponentialBackOff` yields the following pattern:

```
julia> retry(do_something, delays=ExponentialBackOff(; n = 10))("John")
2020-01-07T22:05:16.633 Let's do it
2020-01-07T22:05:16.685 Let's do it
2020-01-07T22:05:16.937 Let's do it          Incrementally wait more time
2020-01-07T22:05:18.106 Let's do it           for the next retry.  Max wait
2020-01-07T22:05:23.814 Let's do it          time is 10 seconds.  Retry up to
2020-01-07T22:05:33.82 Let's do it                    10 times.
2020-01-07T22:05:43.827 Let's do it
2020-01-07T22:05:53.829 Let's do it
2020-01-07T22:05:53.83 Good job, John!
```

Let's pay attention to the wait time between retries. The result should match the default setting of `ExponentialBackOff` as seen from its signature:

```
ExponentialBackOff(; n=1, first_delay=0.05, max_delay=10.0, factor=5.0,
jitter=0.1)
```

The keyword argument, `n`, indicates the number of retries, for which we used the value of 10 in the preceding code. The first retry comes after 0.05 seconds. Then, for every retry, the time of delay grows by a factor of 5 up until it hits a maximum of 10 seconds. The growth rate may be jittered by 10%.

The `retry` function is often overlooked but it is a very convenient and powerful way to make the system more robust.

It is easy to throw an exception when something goes wrong. But that's not the only way to handle error conditions. In the next section, we will discuss the concepts of exceptions versus normal negative conditions.

Choosing nothing over exceptions

Given the powerful features of a try-catch block, it is sometimes tempting to handle all negative scenarios with `Exception` types. In practice, we want to be very clear about what is truly an exception and what is a normal negative case.

We can turn to the `match` function as an example. The `match` function from the `Base` package can be used to match a regular expression against a string. If there is a match, then it returns a `RegexMatch` object, which contains the captured results. Otherwise, it returns `nothing`. The following example illustrates this effect:

```julia
julia> match(r"\.com$", "google.com") |> typeof
RegexMatch

julia> match(r"\.com$", "w3.org") |> typeof
Nothing
```

The first `match` function call returned a `RegexMatch` object because it found that `google.com` ends with `.com`. The second call could not find any match and so it returned `nothing`.

By design, the `match` function does not throw any exception. Why not? One reason for this is that the function is frequently used for checking whether a string contains another string and then the program decides what to do either way. Doing that would require a simple `if` statement; for instance, refer to the following code:

```julia
url = "http://google.com"
if match(r"\.com$", url) !== nothing
    # do something about .com sites
elseif match(r"\.org$", url) !== nothing
    # do something about .org sites
else
    # do something different
end
```

If it were to throw an exception instead, then our code would have to look different, as follows:

```julia
url = "http://google.com"
try
    match(r"\.com$", url)
    # do something about .com sites
catch ex1
    try
```

```
        match(r"\.org$", url)
        # do something about .org sites
    catch ex2
        # do something different
    end
  end
end
```

As you can see, the code can get very ugly very quickly using a try-catch block.

When designing a programming interface, we should always think about whether an exception is truly an exception or whether it could be just a negative status. In the case of the match function, a negative case is effectively represented by nothing.

In this section, we learned where to place try-catch blocks in our code. Now we should be able to properly catch exceptions and examine the stack frames.

We have come to understand better how performance may be impacted by the exception-handling code. Based on our understanding, we should be able to design and develop more robust software.

Summary

In this chapter, we have learned about the various patterns and techniques for building robust software. While Julia is a great language for quick prototypes and research projects, it has all the features to build robust, mission-critical systems.

We began our journey with the idea of encapsulating data with accessor functions, which allow us to design a formal API that we can support. We also discussed a naming convention that discourages people from accessing the internal state of the object.

We looked at Julia's property interface, which allows us to implement new *meanings* whenever the field access dot notation is used. By extending the getproperty and setproperty! functions, we are able to control both read and write access to the fields of an object.

We also learned how to hide specific variables or functions defined in a module. This strategy can be utilized whenever we want to have tighter control of the visibility of variables and functions of a module.

Finally, we wanted to *take exception handling seriously!* We know robust software needs to be able to handle all kinds of exceptions. We dived deep into the try-catch process and learned how to determine the stack trace properly. We have proved that performance can be negatively impacted by the use of a try-catch block, so we need to be diligent about where to apply exception handling logic. We also learned how to use the standard `retry` function as a recovery strategy.

In the next chapter, we will go over a few more miscellaneous patterns commonly used in the Julia programs.

Questions

1. What are the benefits of developing assessor functions?
2. What would be an easy way to discourage the use of internal fields of an object?
3. Which functions may to be extended as part of the property interface?
4. How can we capture the stack trace from a catch block after an exception has been caught?
5. What is the best way to avoid the performance impact of a try-catch block for a system that requires optimal performance?
6. What is the benefit of using the retry function?
7. How do we hide away global variables and functions that are used internally in a module?

Miscellaneous Patterns

9

This chapter will cover a few miscellaneous design patterns that are quite useful in building larger applications. These patterns provide additional tools that we can leverage apart of the major patterns that we have seen so far from previous chapters. In a nutshell, we will explore three patterns, as follows:

- The singleton type dispatch pattern
- The stubbing/mocking pattern
- The functional pipes pattern

The singleton type dispatch pattern leverages Julia's multiple dispatch feature, which allows you to add new functionalities without having to modify existing code.

The stubbing/mocking pattern can be utilized to test software components in isolation. It's also possible to test external dependencies without actually using them. It makes automated testing a lot easier.

The functional pipes pattern makes use of the pipe operator to represent a linear flow of execution. It is a way of programming that is adopted in many data processing pipelines. Some people find this concept of linear execution more intuitive. We will explore some examples about they may well with this pattern.

Let's get started!

Technical requirements

The sample source code for this chapter is located at `https://github.com/PacktPublishing/Hands-on-Design-Patterns-and-Best-Practices-with-Julia/tree/master/Chapter09`.

The code in this chapter has been tested in a Julia 1.3.0 environment.

Singleton type dispatch pattern

Julia supports dynamic dispatch, which is a specific feature of its multiple dispatch system. Dynamic dispatch allows the program to dispatch to the proper function based on the type of the function arguments at runtime. If you are familiar with polymorphism in terms of object-oriented programming languages, then this concept is similar. In this section, we will explain what singleton types are and how they can be used to implement dynamic dispatch.

To begin, let's consider a desktop application use case where the system responds to user click events. Here is what the **graphical user interface (GUI)** may look like:

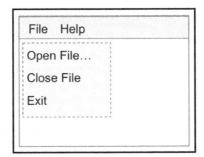

We will try to implement the processing function with simple logic first and then see how it can be improved using the singleton type dispatch pattern.

Developing a command processor

Our first attempt to implement a command process that may look similar to the following:

```
function process_command(command::String, args)
    if command == "open"
        # open a file
    elseif command == "close"
        # close current file
    elseif command == "exit"
        # exit program
    elseif command == "help"
        # pops up a help dialog
    else
        error("bug - this should have never happened.")
    end
end
```

The `process_command` function simply takes the command as a string. Then, depending on the value of the string, it will call the respective function. The `args` argument may be passed by the GUI code for additional information; for example, the path of the file that is being opened or closed.

There is nothing wrong with this code from a logical perspective, but it can be improved, as follows:

- The code contains a list of if-then-else statements. In this example, we only have to support four functions. In practice, we will probably have to handle many more functions. Having such a large if-then-else block makes the code very ugly and hard to maintain.
- Whenever we need to add a new command, we have to modify this function to include a new condition.

Fortunately, we can make it better using singleton types and dynamic dispatch. We'll go over that next.

Understanding singleton types

A singleton type is just a data type that is designed to have a single instance. In Julia, it can be implemented easily by defining a type without any field:

```
struct OpenCommand end
```

To create a single instance of such a data type, we can use the following default constructor:

```
OpenCommand()
```

Unlike in some object-oriented programming languages, this constructor returns exactly the same instance, even if you call it multiple times. In other words, it is already a singleton. We can prove this like so:

```
julia> oc1 = OpenCommand()
OpenCommand()

julia> oc2 = OpenCommand()
OpenCommand()

julia> oc1 === oc2
true
```

After creating two instances of OpenCommand, we compare them using the === operator, which tells us that these two instances are indeed referring to the same object. Hence, we have achieved the creation of a singleton.

Moving on, we can take the same approach and create a singleton types for each command, that is, CloseCommand, ExitCommand, HelpCommand, and so on. Furthermore, we can also create a new abstract type called AbstractCommand, which can serve as the supertype for all these command types.

It seems exhaustively verbose that we have to create a new type for each command. A better way to handle this situation is to use parametric types. Since it's a fairly common use case, Julia predefines a type called Val. Let's take a look at it.

Using the Val parametric data type

Val is a parametric data type that is defined in the Julia Base package. Its purpose is to provide us with an easy way to dispatch using singleton types. The Val type is defined as follows:

```
struct Val{x} end
```

How do we create a singleton object? We can use the Val constructor and pass it any value. For example, we can create a singleton type that embeds a value of 1, as follows:

```
julia> Val(1)
Val{1}()
```

Let's confirm the data type of such an object:

```
julia> Val(1) |> typeof
Val{1}

julia> Val(2) |> typeof
Val{2}
```

Here, we can see that Val(1) and Val(2) have their own types – Val{1} and Val{2}, respectively. Interestingly, the value being passed to the constructor ends up in the type signature. Again, we can prove that these are indeed singletons by calling the Val constructor twice and comparing their identities:

```
julia> Val(1) === Val(1)
true

julia> Val(:foo) === Val(:foo)
true
```

As you can see, the `Val` constructor function can also accept a symbol as an argument. Note that `Val` can only accept data that is a bit type because it goes to the type signature. Most use cases involve the `Val` type with integers and symbols in the type parameter. If we try to create new `Val` objects with non-bits type, then we get an error, as follows:

```
julia> Val("julia")
ERROR: TypeError: in Type, in parameter, expected Type, got String
```

You may be wondering why we go through so much to talk about singleton types. This is because singleton types can be used for dynamic dispatch. Now that we know how to create singletons, let's learn how to utilize them for dispatch.

Using singleton types with dynamic dispatch

In Julia, function calls are dispatched according to the type of the arguments when the function is called. For a quick introduction to this mechanism, please refer to Chapter 3, *Designing Functions and Interfaces.*

Let's recall the use case that we presented earlier in this chapter about a command processor function. With a naive implementation, we have a large if-then-else block that dispatch to different functions according to the command string. Let's try to implement the same feature using singleton types.

For each command, we can define a function that takes a singleton type. For example, the signatures of the functions for the `Open` and `Close` events are as follows:

```
function process_command(::Val{:open}, filename)
    println("opening file $filename")
end

function process_command(::Val{:close}, filename)
    println("closing file $filename")
end
```

We didn't have to specify any name for the first argument because we don't need to use it. However, we do specify the type of the first argument to be `Val{:open}` or `Val{:close}`. Given such a function signature, we can handle the `Open` event as follows:

```
julia> process_command(Val(:open), "julia.pdf")
opening file julia.pdf
```

Basically, we create a singleton and pass it to the function. Because the type signature matches, Julia will dispatch to the function we just defined in the preceding screenshot. Now, assuming that we have defined all other functions, we can write the code for the main dispatcher as follows:

```
function process_command(command::String, args...)
    process_command(Val(Symbol(command)), args...)
end
```

Here, we simply convert the command into a symbol and then create a singleton type object by passing it to the `Val` constructor. At runtime, the proper `process_command` functions will be dispatched accordingly. Let's quickly test that out:

```
julia> process_command("open", "julia.pdf")
opening file julia.pdf

julia> process_command("close", "julia.pdf")
closing file julia.pdf
```

Fabulous! Now, let's pause for a moment and think about what we have just achieved. In particular, we can make two observations:

- The main dispatcher function in the preceding screenshot no longer has an if-then-else block. It just utilizes dynamic dispatch to figure out which underlying function to call.
- Whenever we need to add a new command, we can just define a new `process_command` function with a new `Val` singleton. There is no change to the main dispatcher function anymore.

It is possible to create your own parametric type rather than using the standard `Val` type. This can be achieved quite simply, as follows:

```
# A parametric type that represents a specific command
struct Command{T} end

# Constructor function to create a new Command instance from a string
Command(s::AbstractString) = Command{Symbol(s)}()
```

The constructor function takes a string and creates a `Command` singleton object with a `Symbol` type parameter that is converted from the string. Having such a singleton type, we can define our dispatcher function and corresponding actions as follows:

```
# Dispatcher function
function process_command(command::String, args...)
    process_command(Command(command), args...)
end

# Actions
function process_command(::Command{:open}, filename)
    println("opening file $filename")
end

function process_command(::Command{:close}, filename)
    println("closing file $filename")
end
```

This style of code is fairly idiomatic in Julia programming – there is no conditional branch anymore since it is replaced by function dispatch. In addition, you also extend the functionality of a system by defining new functions, without the need to modify any existing code. This is a fairly useful characteristic when we need to extend functions from a third-party library.

Next, we will do some experiments and measure the performance of dynamic dispatch.

Understanding the performance benefits of dispatch

Using a singleton type is nice because we can avoid writing conditional branches. Another side benefit is that performance can be greatly improved. An interesting example can be found in the `ntuple` function from Julia's Base package.

The `ntuple` function is used to create a tuple of N elements by applying a function over the sequence of 1 to N. For example, we can create a tuple of even numbers as follows:

```
julia> ntuple(i -> 2i, 10)
(2, 4, 6, 8, 10, 12, 14, 16, 18, 20)
```

The first argument is an anonymous function that doubles the value. Since we specified 10 in the second argument, it mapped over the range of 1 to 10 and gave us 2, 4, 6, ... 20. If we take a peek into the source code, we will find this interesting definition:

```
function ntuple(f::F, n::Integer) where F
    t = n == 0 ? () :
        n == 1 ? (f(1),) :
        n == 2 ? (f(1), f(2)) :
        n == 3 ? (f(1), f(2), f(3)) :
        n == 4 ? (f(1), f(2), f(3), f(4)) :
        n == 5 ? (f(1), f(2), f(3), f(4), f(5)) :
        n == 6 ? (f(1), f(2), f(3), f(4), f(5), f(6)) :
        n == 7 ? (f(1), f(2), f(3), f(4), f(5), f(6), f(7)) :
        n == 8 ? (f(1), f(2), f(3), f(4), f(5), f(6), f(7), f(8)) :
        n == 9 ? (f(1), f(2), f(3), f(4), f(5), f(6), f(7), f(8), f(9)) :
        n == 10 ? (f(1), f(2), f(3), f(4), f(5), f(6), f(7), f(8), f(9),
f(10)) :
            _ntuple(f, n)
    return t
end
```

While the code is indented quite nicely, we can clearly see that it supports up to 10 elements by hard coding the short-circuit branches with the ? and : ternary operators. If it's more than 10, then it calls another function to create the tuple:

```
function _ntuple(f, n)
    @_noinline_meta
    (n >= 0) || throw(ArgumentError(string("tuple length should be ≥ 0, got
", n)))
    ([f(i) for i = 1:n]...,)
end
```

This _ntuple function is expected to perform poorly because it creates an array using comprehension and then the result is splatted into a new tuple. You may be very surprised by the performance benchmarking result when we compare the case of creating a 10-element tuple versus an 11-element tuple:

```
julia> using BenchmarkTools

julia> @btime ntuple(i->2i, 10);
  0.031 ns (0 allocations: 0 bytes)

julia> @btime ntuple(i->2i, 11);
  820.195 ns (4 allocations: 336 bytes)
```

The `ntuple` function is designed to perform optimally when the number of elements is small, that is, for 10 or fewer elements. It would be possible to change the `ntuple` function to hardcode more, but it would be too tedious to write the code, and the resulting code would be extremely ugly.

Perhaps a little more surprisingly, Julia actually comes with another variation of the same function while using the `Val` singleton type, as shown in the following screenshot:

```
julia> @btime ntuple(i->2i, Val(10));
  0.032 ns (0 allocations: 0 bytes)

julia> @btime ntuple(i->2i, Val(11));
  0.031 ns (0 allocations: 0 bytes)

julia> @btime ntuple(i->2i, Val(100));
  17.301 ns (0 allocations: 0 bytes)
```

There is literally no difference between 10 and 11 elements. In fact, even with 100 elements, the performance is quite reasonable (17 nanoseconds) compared to the non-`Val` version (820 nanoseconds). Let's take a look at how it is implemented. The following has been taken from the Julia source code:

```
# Using singleton type dynamic dispatch
# inferrable ntuple (enough for bootstrapping)
ntuple(f, ::Val{0}) = ()
ntuple(f, ::Val{1}) = (@_inline_meta; (f(1),))
ntuple(f, ::Val{2}) = (@_inline_meta; (f(1), f(2)))
ntuple(f, ::Val{3}) = (@_inline_meta; (f(1), f(2), f(3)))

@inline function ntuple(f::F, ::Val{N}) where {F,N}
    N::Int
    (N >= 0) || throw(ArgumentError(string("tuple length should be ≥ 0, got
", N)))
    if @generated
        quote
            @nexprs $N i -> t_i = f(i)
            @ncall $N tuple t
        end
    else
        Tuple(f(i) for i = 1:N)
    end
end
```

From the preceding code, we can see that there are a few functions being defined for tuples that have fewer than four elements. After that, the function uses a meta-programming technique to generate code on the fly. In this case, it uses a special construct that allows the compiler to choose between code generation and its generic implementation, which is represented in if-blocks and else-blocks in the code. Looking at how the `@generated`, `@nexprs`, and `@ncalls` macros work is out of the scope of this section, but you are encouraged to find out more from the Julia reference manual.

According to our preceding performance test, calling `ntuple` with `Val(100)` was quite fast, so it appears that the compiler has chosen the code generation path.

To summarize, we have learned how to use parametric types to create new singletons and create functions that are dispatched by these singleton types. We can apply this pattern whenever we need to handle such conditional branches.

Next, we will learn how to develop automated testing code effectively using stubs and mocks.

Stubbing/Mocking pattern

Julia comes with excellent tools for building automated unit tests. When the programmer follows good design patterns and best practices, the software is likely going to be composed of many small functions that can be tested individually.

Unfortunately, certain test cases are more difficult to handle. They usually involve testing components that have specific dependencies that are awkward to be included in automated tests. Common issues include the following:

- **Performance**: The dependency may be a time-consuming process.
- **Cost**: The dependency may incur a financial cost every time it is invoked.
- **Randomness**: The dependency may produce a different result every time it is invoked.

Stubbing/Mocking is a common strategy to address these issues. In this section, we will look into how to apply stubs and mocks while testing Julia code.

What are testing doubles?

Before we get into the specifics about stubbing/mocking, it would be helpful to go over some industry-standard terminology. First of all, there is the concept of *testing doubles*. Interestingly, the term comes from a movie-making technique that's related to how stunts are filmed. When performing dangerous acts, a stuntman or stuntwoman replaces the actor or actress to perform the job. From a viewer's perspective, it would look like the original actor or actress was performing. Testing doubles are the same in the sense that a fake component is used in place of the real thing during testing.

There are multiple types of testing doubles, but the most useful ones are *stubs* and *mocks*, which we will focus on in this section. In object-oriented programming, these concepts are expressed in terms of classes and objects. In Julia, we will leverage the same terminology for functions. One benefit of working with functions is that we can focus all of our effort on testing a single thing.

A **stub** is a fake function that imitates the real function, also known as the *collaborator function*. Depending on what is required from the testing objectives, they can be as dumb as returning the same result all the time, or they can be a little smarter and return different values, depending on the input arguments. Regardless of how smart they are, return values are almost always hardcoded for consistency reasons. During testing, stubs replace the collaborator function when the **function under test** (**FUT**) is being exercised. When the FUT finishes its execution, we can determine the correctness of the returned value. This is called *state verification*. The interaction between these functions can be depicted as follows:

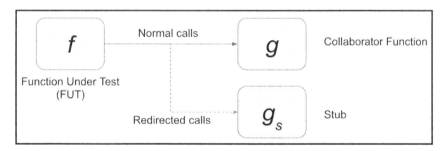

A **mock** is also a fake function that imitates the collaborator function. The difference between mocks and stubs is that a mock focuses on behavior verification. Rather than just examining the state of the FUT, mocks keep track of all the calls being made. It can be used to verify behavior, such as how many times the mock is expected to be called, the types and values of the arguments that the mock expected to be passed, and so on. This is called *behavior verification*. At the end of their execution, we can perform both state verification and behavior verification. This is depicted as follows:

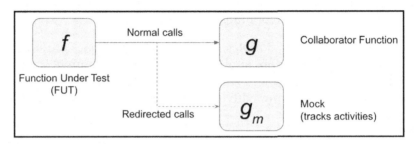

In the upcoming sections, we will focus on how to apply stubs and mocks in testing.

Introducing the credit approval use case

In this section, we'll introduce a sample use case related to credit approval. Suppose that you are developing a system that has the ability to open a new credit card account for a customer upon a successful background check. You may create a Julia module that has the following structure:

```julia
module CreditApproval

# primary function to open an account
function open_account(first_name, last_name, email) end

# supportive functions
function check_background(first_name, last_name) end
function create_account(first_name, last_name, email) end
function notify_downstream(account_number) end

end
```

Now, let's implement each of the functions. We'll start with the `check_background` function, which just logs the event and returns true, meaning that the background check is successful. Consider the following code:

```
# Background check.
# In practice, we would call a remote service for this.
# For this example, we just return true.
function check_background(first_name, last_name)
    println("Doing background check for $first_name $last_name")
    return true
end
```

The `create_account` function is similar to this. In this case, the expected behavior is to return an account number, that is, an integer value that refers to the account that has just been created. For this example, we just return a hardcoded value of 1, as follows:

```
# Create an account.
# In practice, we would actually create a record in database.
# For this example, we return an account number of 1.
function create_account(first_name, last_name, email)
    println("Creating an account for $first_name $last_name")
    return 1
end
```

The `notify_customer` function is supposed to send an email to the customer. For testing purposes, we will just log the event; nothing needs to be returned:

```
# Notify downstream system by sending a message.
# For this example, we just print to console and returns nothing.
function notify_downstream(account_number)
    println("Notifying downstream system about new account
$account_number")
    return nothing
end
```

Finally, the `open_account` function is as follows:

```
# Open a new account.
# Returns `:success` if account is created successfully.
# Returns `:failure` if background check fails.
function open_account(first_name, last_name, email)
    check_background(first_name, last_name) || return :failure
    account_number = create_account(first_name, last_name, email)
    notify_downstream(account_number)
    return :success
end
```

This is the FUT in our example. The logic involves checking the background for a customer and creating an account and notifying downstream about the new account if the background check is successful.

Let's think about how to test the `open_account` function. The obvious thing that needs our attention is the background check code. More specifically, we expect two possible execution paths – when the background check is successful and when the background check fails. If we need to cover both cases, then we need to be able to simulate the different return values of the `check_background` function. We will do that next with a stub.

Performing state verification using stubs

Our goal is to test the `open_account` function with two scenarios, where the `check_background` function returns either true or false. When a background check is successful, we expect `open_account` to return `:success`. Otherwise, it should return `:failure`.

Using our terminology, `open_account` is the function under test, while `check_background` is the collaborator function. It is a bit unfortunate that we can't really control how the collaborator function behaves. In practice, this function may even reach out to a background check service, the working of which we have little influence on. As a matter of fact, we would not want to call the remote service every single time that we test our software.

Now that we have copied from the original `CreditApproval` module to a new module called `CreditApprovalStub`, we can move on.

Since we are smart programmers, we can just create a stub that replaces the collaborator function. As functions are first-class in Julia, we can refactor the `open_account` function so that it can take any background check function from a keyword argument, as follows:

```julia
function open_account(first_name, last_name, email; checker =
check_background)
    checker(first_name, last_name) || return :failure
    account_number = create_account(first_name, last_name, email)
    notify_downstream(account_number)
    return :success
end
```

The new `checker` keyword argument takes a function that is used to perform a background check for a customer. We have set the default value to the original `check_background` function, so it should behave the same as before. Now, the function is more testable.

In our test suite, we can now exercise both execution paths, as follows:

```
@testset "CreditApprovalStub.jl" begin

    # stubs
    check_background_success(first_name, last_name) = true
    check_background_failure(first_name, last_name) = false

    # testing
    let first_name = "John", last_name = "Doe", email = "jdoe@julia-is-
awesome.com"
        @test open_account(first_name, last_name, email, checker =
check_background_success) == :success
        @test open_account(first_name, last_name, email, checker =
check_background_failure) == :failure
    end
```

Here, we have created two stubs for background checks: `check_background_success` and `check_background_failure`. They return true and false to simulate a successful and failed background check, respectively. Then, when we need to test the `open_account` function, we can just pass these stub functions via the `checker` keyword argument.

Let's run the test now:

```
(CreditApprovalStub) pkg> test
   Updating registry at `~/.julia/registries/General`
   Updating git-repo `https://github.com/JuliaRegistries/General.git`
   Testing CreditApprovalStub
 Resolving package versions...
[ Info: No changes
Creating an account for John Doe
Notifying downstream system about new account 1
Test Summary:    | Pass  Total
CreditApproval.jl |    2      2
   Testing CreditApprovalStub tests passed
```

At this point, we have only enabled the `check_background` function for stubbing in the `open_account` function. What if we want to do the same for the `create_account` and `notify_downstream` functions? It would be just as easy if we created two more keyword arguments and called it done. This isn't a bad option. However, you may not be very satisfied with the fact that we need to keep changing the code to make new tests. Furthermore, these keyword arguments were added merely for the sake of testing, rather than being a part of the call interface.

In the next section, we will explore the use of the Mocking package, which is an excellent tool for applying stubs and mocks without messing too much with the source code.

Implementing stubs with the Mocking package

A good alternative to implementing stubs is the Mocking package. This package is fairly straightforward to use. We will quickly go over how to use Mocking to apply the same stubs that we applied earlier.

In order to follow this exercise, you can copy the code from the original `CreditApproval` module to a new module called `CreditApprovalMockingStub`. Now, follow these steps:

1. First, make sure that the Mocking package is installed. Then, modify the function under test, as follows:

   ```
   using Mocking

   function open_account(first_name, last_name, email)
       @mock(check_background(first_name, last_name)) || return
   :failure
       account_number = create_account(first_name, last_name, email)
       notify_downstream(account_number)
       return :success
   end
   ```

   The `@mock` macro creates an injection point where a stub can be applied, replacing the existing call to the collaborator function, that is, `check_background`. Under normal execution conditions, the `@mock` macro simply calls the collaborator function.

2. During testing, however, a stub can be applied. To achieve such behavior, we need to activate mocking at the top of the test script, as follows:

```
using Mocking
Mocking.activate()
```

3. Next, we can define stub functions using the @patch macro:

```
check_background_success_patch =
    @patch function check_background(first_name, last_name)
        println("check_background stub ==> simulating success")
        return true
    end

check_background_failure_patch =
    @patch function check_background(first_name, last_name)
        println("check_background stub ==> simulating failure")
        return false
    end
```

The @patch macro can be placed right in front of a function definition. The function name must match the original collaborator function name. Likewise, the function arguments should match as well.

4. The @patch macro returns an anonymous function that can be applied to the call site in the FUT. To apply a patch, we use the apply function, as follows:

```
# test background check failure case
apply(check_background_failure_patch) do
    @test open_account("john", "doe", "jdoe@julia-is-awesome.com")
== :failure
end

# test background check successful case
apply(check_background_success_patch) do
    @test open_account("peter", "doe", "pdoe@julia-is-awesome.com")
== :success
end
```

5. The `apply` function takes the stub and applies it to everywhere that the collaborator function is called, as identified by the `@mock` macro in the function under test. Let's run the test from the REPL:

```
(CreditApprovalMockingStub) pkg> test
    Testing CreditApprovalMockingStub
 Resolving package versions...
check_background stub ==> simulating failure
check_background stub ==> simulating success
Creating an account for peter doe
Notifying downstream system about new account 1
Test Summary: | Pass  Total
Stubs         |    2      2
    Testing CreditApprovalMockingStub tests passed
```

6. Now, let's make sure that the stubs are not applied under normal execution conditions. From the REPL, we can call the function directly:

```
julia> open_account("John", "Doe", "jdoe@julia-is-awesome.com")
Doing background check for John Doe
Creating an account for John Doe
Notifying downstream system about new account 1
:success
```

Fabulous! From the preceding output, we can see that the original collaborator function, `check_background`, was called.

Next, we will expand on the same idea and apply multiple stubs to the same function.

Applying multiple stubs to the same function

In our example, the `open_account` function calls several dependent functions. It performs background checks for a customer, creates the account, and notifies downstream systems. Practically speaking, we may want to create stubs for all of them. How do we apply multiple stubs? The Mocking package supports this feature.

As usual, we would need to decorate the open_account function with a @mock macro for every function that we want to apply to our stubs. The following code shows this:

```
function open_account(first_name, last_name, email)
    @mock(check_background(first_name, last_name)) || return :failure
    account_number = @mock(create_account(first_name, last_name, email))
    @mock(notify_downstream(account_number))
    return :success
end
```

Now, we're all set to create more stubs. For demonstration purpose, we will define another stub for the create_account function, as follows:

```
create_account_patch =
    @patch function create_account(first_name, last_name, email)
        println("create_account stub is called")
        return 314
    end
```

As part of its design, this stub function must return an account number. Therefore, we are just returning a fake value of 314. To test the scenario where both check_background_success_patch and create_account_patch are applied, we can pass them as an array to the apply function:

```
apply([check_background_success_patch, create_account_patch]) do
    @test open_account("peter", "doe", "pdoe@julia-is-awesome.com") ==
:success
end
```

Note that we have not provided any stub for the notify_downstream function. When a stub is not provided, the original collaborator function is used. Hence, we have all the flexibility we want in applying stub functions in our test suite. In the open_account function, since we have placed @mock in three different injection points, we can technically test eight different scenarios, for which each stub is enabled or disabled.

> The complexity of tests for the FUT increases exponentially by the number of branches and functions that are used inside the function. This is also one of the reasons why we want to write small functions. Due to this, it is a good idea to break down large functions into smaller ones so that they can be tested independently.

Using stubs, we can easily verify the expected return value for a function. A different approach is mocking, which shifts the focus to verifying the behavior of the FUT and its collaboration functions. We will look into that next.

Performing behavior verification using mocks

Mocks are different from stubs – rather than just testing the return value of a function, we focus on testing expectations from the collaborator functions' perspective. What kind of activities does a collaborator function expect? Here are some examples for our use case:

- From the `check_background` function's perspective, was it called only once for each `open_account` call?
- From the `create_account` function's perspective, was it called when a background check was successful?
- From the `create_account` function's perspective, was it not called when the background check failed?
- From the `notify_account` function's perspective, was it called with an account number that is greater than 0?

The process to set up a mock-enabled test involves four main steps:

1. Set up the mock functions that will be used during the test.
2. Establish the expectations for the collaborator functions.
3. Run the tests.
4. Verify the expectations that we set earlier.

Now, let's try to develop our own mock test. Here, we will exercise the success path for opening a new account. In this case, we can expect the `check_background`, `create_account`, and `notify_downstream` functions to be called exactly once. Also, we can expect that the account number being passed to the `notify_downstream` function should be a number greater than 1. Keeping this information in mind, we will create a let-block with bound variables to track everything that we want to test against our expectations:

```
let check_background_call_count  = 0,
    create_account_call_count    = 0,
    notify_downstream_call_count = 0,
    notify_downstream_received_proper_account_number = false

    # insert more code here...
end
```

The first three variables will be used to track the number of calls to the three mocks that we are about to create. Also, the last variable will be used to record whether the `notify_downstream` function received a proper account number during the test. Within this let-block, we will implement the four steps we outlined previously. Let's define the mock functions first:

```
check_background_success_patch =
    @patch function check_background(first_name, last_name)
        check_background_call_count += 1
        println("check_background mock is called, simulating success")
        return true
    end
```

Here, we just increment the `check_background_call_count` counter within the mock function so that we can keep track of how many times the mock function is called. Similarly, we can define the `create_account_patch` mock function in the same way:

```
create_account_patch =
    @patch function create_account(first_name, last_name, email)
        create_account_call_count += 1
        println("create account_number mock is called")
        return 314
    end
```

The last mock function, `notify_downstream_patch`, covers two expectations. Not only does it keep track of the number of calls, but it also verifies that the account number being passed is proper and, if so, updates the Boolean flag. The following code shows this:

```
notify_downstream_patch =
    @patch function notify_downstream(account_number)
        notify_downstream_call_count += 1
        if account_number > 0
            notify_downstream_received_proper_account_number = true
        end
        println("notify downstream mock is called")
        return nothing
    end
```

The second step is to establish our expectation formally. This can be defined as a simple function, as follows:

```
function verify()
    @test check_background_call_count   == 1
    @test create_account_call_count     == 1
    @test notify_downstream_call_count == 1
    @test notify_downstream_received_proper_account_number
end
```

The `verify` function includes a set of expectations, formally defined as regular Julia tests. Now, we are ready to exercise our test by applying all three mock functions:

```
apply([check_background_success_patch, create_account_patch,
notify_downstream_patch]) do
    @test open_account("peter", "doe", "pdoe@julia-is-awesome.com") ==
:success
end
```

Finally, as the very last step, we will test against our expectation. It is simply a call to the `verify` function that we defined earlier:

```
verify()
```

Now, we are ready to run the mock test. The respective results are as follows:

```
(CreditApprovalMockingStub) pkg> test
    Testing CreditApprovalMockingStub
 Resolving package versions...
check_background mock is called, simulating success
create account_number mock is called
notify downstream mock is called
Test Summary: | Pass  Total
Mocking       |   5      5
    Testing CreditApprovalMockingStub tests passed
```

The result statistics show five test cases in total and all of them passed. Four out of the five tests came from the `verify` function for behavior verification, while one came from the state verification for the return value of the `open_account` function.

As you can see, mocks are quite different from stub because they are used to perform both behavior and state verifications.

Next, we will look into a pattern that's related to how data pipelines can be built more intuitively.

Functional pipes pattern

Sometimes, when building an application, we face a large problem that requires complex calculations and data transformation. Using structured programming techniques, we can often break down the large problem into medium-sized problems and then break these down further into small-sized problems. When a problem is small enough, we can write functions to tackle each problem individually.

Of course, these functions do not work in isolation – it is more likely that the results of one function will feed into another function. In this section, we will explore the functional pipes pattern, which allows data to be passed seamlessly through a data pipeline. This is not uncommon in functional programming languages but is seen less in Julia. Nevertheless, we will take a look and see how it can be done.

First, we will go over a sample use case related to downloading recent Hacker News stories for analysis. Then, we will progressively refactor the code into using the functional pipes pattern. Let's go!

Introducing the Hacker News analysis use case

Hacker News is a popular online forum that's used by software developers. The topics on this forum are usually related to technology, but not always. The stories are ranked according to the number of votes by users, respective timeliness, and other factors. Every story has a score associated with it.

In this section, we will develop a program that retrieves the top stories from Hacker News and calculates an average score of those stories. More information about the Hacker News API can be found in the following GitHub repository: `https://github.com/HackerNews/API`. Here, you can quickly go over the process of retrieving stories and details about each story.

Fetching top story IDs on Hacker News

First, we will create a module called `HackerNewsAnalysis`. The very first function is going to retrieve the top stories from Hacker News. The code for this is as follows:

```
using HTTP
using JSON3

function fetch_top_stories()
    url = "https://hacker-news.firebaseio.com/v0/topstories.json"
    response = HTTP.request("GET", url)
    return JSON3.read(String(response.body))
end
```

How does it work? Let's try it out:

```julia
julia> using HackerNewsAnalysis

julia> fetch_top_stories()
495-element JSON3.Array{Int64,Base.CodeUnits{UInt8,JSON3.VectorString{A
rray{UInt8,1}}},Array{UInt64,1}}:
 21676252
 21676933
 21677389
 21674752
 21675456
 21676027
    ⋮
 21662367
 21666888
```

Let's take several steps and dissect the logic in this function. The top stories can be retrieved from a fixed URL. Here, we have used the HTTP package for fetching data from web services. The `HTTP.request` function call, if successful, returns an `HTTP.Message.Response` object. It is easy to verify from the REPL:

```julia
julia> using HTTP

julia> url = "https://hacker-news.firebaseio.com/v0/topstories.json";

julia> response = HTTP.request("GET", url);

julia> typeof(response)
HTTP.Messages.Response
```

So, how do we get the content from the `Response` object? It is available from the `body` field. As it turns out, the `body` field is just a byte array. To understand what the data means, we can convert it into a `String`, as follows:

```julia
julia> response.body
4438-element Array{UInt8,1}:
 0x5b
 0x32
    ⋮
 0x36
 0x5d

julia> String(response.body)
"[21676252,21676933,21675456,21677389,21676027,21676923,21676606,2167
4599,21674752,21675498,21674729,21671304,21676543,21669530,21675894,2
1676384,21674610,21675030,21675228,21675280,21667223,21675148,2167580
```

Judging from the output, we can see that it is in JSON format. We can also verify the same by visiting the web URL from a browser. From the API documentation, we know that the numbers represent story IDs from Hacker News. To parse the data into usable Julia data types, we can leverage the JSON3 package:

```
julia> using JSON3

julia> response = HTTP.request("GET", url);

julia> JSON3.read(String(response.body))
493-element JSON3.Array{Int64,Base.CodeUnits{UInt8,String},Array{UInt
64,1}}:
 21676252
 21676933
 21677389
     ⋮
 21659963
 21654501
 21666086
```

The JSON3.Array object is a lazy version of an array. By design, JSON3 does not extract the value until you ask for it. We can use it as if it were a regular Julia array. For more information, you are encouraged to visit JSON3's documentation on GitHub: https://github.com/quinnj/JSON3.jl/blob/master/README.md.

Now that we have an array of story IDs, we will develop the function for retrieving detailed information about a Hacker News story.

Fetching details about a story

Given a story ID, we can retrieve information about the story using the item endpoint of the Hacker News API. Before we write the function, let's define a type to store the data:

```
struct Story
    by::String
    descendants::Union{Nothing,Int}
    score::Int
    time::Int
    id::Int
    title::String
    kids::Union{Nothing,Vector{Int}}
    url::Union{Nothing,String}
end
```

The fields of a `Story` are designed according to the JSON schema documented on the Hacker News API website. Sometimes, a field may be unavailable for certain story types, in which case we will leave them as `nothing` in the object. These optional fields include `descendants`, `kids`, and `url`. Lastly, every story comes with a unique identifier `id`.

We need a constructor to create `Story` objects. Because JSON3 returns a dictionary-like object, we can just extract individual fields and pass them to the constructor. The constructor's function can be defined as follows:

```
# Construct a Story from a Dict (or Dict-compatible) object
function Story(obj)
    value = (x) -> get(obj, x, nothing)
    return Story(
        obj[:by],
        value(:descendants),
        obj[:score],
        obj[:time],
        obj[:id],
        obj[:title],
        value(:kids),
        value(:url))
end
```

Generally, we can extract the field from a `Dict` object using the index operator (square brackets). However, we need to handle the fact that some fields may be unavailable in the object. To avoid an unexpected `KeyError`, we can define a closure function called `value` for extracting a field or returning `nothing` when the key is not found in the object.

Now, let's take a look at the function for retrieving the details of a single story:

```
function fetch_story(id)
    url = "https://hacker-news.firebaseio.com/v0/item/$(id).json"
    response = HTTP.request("GET", url)
    return Story(JSON3.read(response.body))
end
```

Again, we retrieve the data using `HTTP.request`. After we receive the response, we can parse the data using JSON3 and construct a `Story` object accordingly. Here's how it works:

```
julia> fetch_story(21676252)
Story("kkm", 372, 517, 1575218518, 21676252, "The world needs more sear
ch engines", [21676507, 21676549, 21676457, 21676352, 21677053, 2167679
0, 21676616, 21676315, 21676385, 21677210 … 21676442, 21676505, 21676
858, 21676598, 21676736, 21677029, 21676919, 21676853, 21676397, 216767
03], "https://www.0x65.dev/blog/2019-12-01/the-world-needs-cliqz-the-wo
rld-needs-more-search-engines.html")
```

Next, we will go over the main program for calculating the average score for the top N stories from Hacker News.

Calculating the average score for the top N stories

Now that we have the ability to find the top stories and retrieve details about each story, we can create a new function to calculate an average score from the top N stories.

The `average_score` function is as follows:

```
using Statistics: mean

function average_score(n = 10)
    story_ids = fetch_top_stories()
    println(now(), " Found ", length(story_ids), " stories")

    top_stories = [fetch_story(id) for id in story_ids[1:min(n,end)]]
    println(now(), " Fetched ", n, " story details")

    avg_top_scores = mean(s.score for s in top_stories)
    println(now(), " Average score = ", avg_top_scores)

    return avg_top_scores
end
```

There are three parts to this function:

1. The first part finds the story IDs for top stories using the `fetch_top_stories` function.
2. Then, it retrieves details of the first n stories using the `fetch_story` function.
3. Finally, it calculates the average score from just those stories. Then, the average score is returned to the caller.

In order to get the top n story IDs, we have chosen to use the index operator with the range `1:min(n,end)`. The `min` function is used to handle the case when n is greater than the size of the array.

Let's run the function and see what happens:

```
julia> average_score()
2019-12-01T12:29:44.24 Found 495 stories
2019-12-01T12:29:46.079 Fetched 10 story details
2019-12-01T12:29:46.128 Average score = 125.4
125.4
```

From the result, we can see that the top n stories from Hacker News have an average score of 125.4. Note that you may get a different result since this number changes in real time as Hacker News users vote on their favorite stories.

Now that the use case has been established, we will leap forward and experiment with a different way of writing the same program. We call this style of programming *functional pipes*.

Understanding functional pipes

In Julia, there is a pipe operator that can be used to pass data from one function to another. The concept is very simple. First, let's take a look at some examples.

In the previous section, we developed a `fetch_top_stories` function that's used to retrieve the current top stories from Hacker News. The return value is a `JSON3.Array` object that looks like an array of integers. Let's say we want to find the first story ID from the array. To do this, we can create a pipe operation, as follows:

```julia
julia> fetch_top_stories() |> first
21676252
```

The pipe operator `|>` is actually defined as a regular function in Julia, just like how + is defined as a function. Note that the preceding code is syntactically equivalent to the following:

```julia
julia> first(fetch_top_stories())
21676252
```

In addition, we can use multiple pipe operators in an expression. For example, we can retrieve the details of the first story by appending the `fetch_story` function at the end of the pipe:

```julia
julia> fetch_top_stories() |> first |> fetch_story
Story("kkm", 375, 522, 1575218518, 21676252, "The world needs more sear
ch engines", [21676507, 21676549, 21676457, 21676352, 21677053, 2167679
0, 21676616, 21676315, 21676385, 21677210 … 21676442, 21676505, 21676
858, 21676598, 21676736, 21677029, 21676919, 21676853, 21676397, 216767
03], "https://www.0x65.dev/blog/2019-12-01/the-world-needs-cliqz-the-wo
rld-needs-more-search-engines.html")
```

Because the data naturally flows from left to right, this is called a functional pipe pattern. This can be seen in the following diagram:

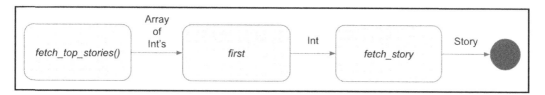

Note that every function that follows the piping operator must accept a single argument. In the preceding example, we can see the following:

- The `first` function takes an array and returns the first element.
- The `fetch_story` function takes an integer of the story ID and returns a `Story` object.

This is a very important point, so let me say this once again – *a functional pipe only feeds data to single-argument functions.*

We will learn about how to deal with this constraint later. For now, we will talk about a similar pattern where the syntax is written in reverse compared to functional pipes. This concept is called composability, and is a design technique that leads to highly reusable code.

Designing composable functions

Sometimes, you may hear other Julia programmers talk about composability. What does that mean?

Composability is used to describe how easily functions can be assembled in different ways to achieve different results. Let's look at an analogy. I would say that Lego has a highly composable design. This is because almost every piece of Lego can be combined with any other piece of Lego, even if they have different shapes. For that reason, any kid can use Lego to build almost anything imaginable.

When it comes to system design, we can also keep composability in mind. If we could build our functions so that they can be composed easily, then we would have the flexibility to build many different things as well. In Julia, we can compose functions quite easily.

Let's use the same example from the previous section. We will create a new function called `top_story_id` that retrieves the first story ID from Hacker News:

```
julia> top_story_id = first ∘ fetch_top_stories
#58 (generic function with 1 method)
```

From the preceding code, we can see that the `top_story_id` function is defined as an anonymous function. The Unicode circle symbol (∘, input as `\circ`) is the compose operator in Julia. Unlike the pipe operator, we read the order of composed functions from right to left. In this case, we apply the `fetch_top_stories` function first and then apply the `first` function. Intuitively, we can use the `top_story_id` function as usual:

```
julia> top_story_id()
21676252
```

We can also compose multiple functions. To get the top story details, we can compose a new function called `top_story`, as follows:

```
julia> top_story = fetch_story ∘ first ∘ fetch_top_stories
#58 (generic function with 1 method)

julia> top_story()
Story("kkm", 380, 525, 1575218518, 21676252, "The world needs more sear
ch engines", [21676507, 21676549, 21676457, 21676352, 21677053, 2167679
0, 21676616, 21676315, 21676385, 21677210 … 21676442, 21676505, 21676
858, 21676598, 21676736, 21677029, 21676919, 21676853, 21676397, 216767
03], "https://www.0x65.dev/blog/2019-12-01/the-world-needs-cliqz-the-wo
rld-needs-more-search-engines.html")
```

This is great! We have taken three random Lego blocks and built a new thing out of them. The `top_story` function is a new thing that is composed of three smaller blocks:

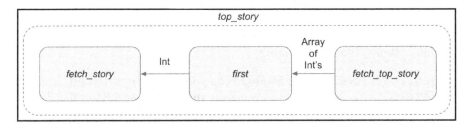

Let's go one step further and create a new function to retrieve the title of the top story. Now, we run into a little trouble. No function that returns the story title from a Story object has been defined. However, we can solve this problem by utilizing the Accessors Pattern, which we described in Chapter 8, *Robustness Patterns*.

Let's define an accessor for the title field and then compose a new top_story_title function, as follows:

```julia
julia> title(s::Story) = s.title
title (generic function with 1 method)

julia> top_story_title = title ∘ fetch_story ∘ first ∘ fetch_top_stories
#58 (generic function with 1 method)
```

This new function works beautifully, as expected:

```julia
julia> top_story_title()
"The world needs more search engines"
```

The compose operator allows us to create a new function that is composed of several other functions. It is slightly more convenient than the pipe operator in the sense that the composed function doesn't need to be executed right away.

Similar to functional pipes, the compose operator also expects single-argument functions. Having said that, it is also the reason why single-argument functions are more composable.

Next, we will go back and revisit the Hacker News average_score function and see how we can refactor the code into the functional pipe style.

Developing a functional pipe for the average score function

First, let's recap on how the average_score function was written:

```julia
function average_score(n = 10)
    story_ids = fetch_top_stories()
    println(now(), " Found ", length(story_ids), " stories")

    top_stories = [fetch_story(id) for id in story_ids[1:min(n,end)]]
    println(now(), " Fetched ", n, " story details")

    avg_top_scores = mean(s.score for s in top_stories)
```

```
        println(now(), " Average score = ", avg_top_scores)

        return avg_top_scores
    end
```

Although the code looks quite decent and simple to understand, let me point out some potential issues:

- The top stories are retrieved via array comprehension syntax. The logic is a little busy and we won't be able to test this part of the code independently from the `average_score` function.
- The `println` function is used for logging, but we seem to be replicating the code to display the current timestamp.

Now, we will refactor the code. The logic is largely linear, which makes it a good candidate for functional pipes. Conceptually, this is what we think about the computation:

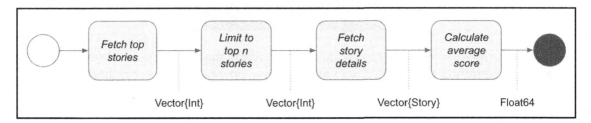

It would be nice to design a function that works like this:

```
average_score2(n = 10) =
    fetch_top_stories() |>
    take(n) |>
    fetch_story_details |>
    calculate_average_score
```

This is our second version of the same function, so we have named it `average_score2`.

For now, we just ignore the logging aspect to keep it simple. We will come back to this later. Since we have already defined the `fetch_top_stories` function, we just have to develop the other three functions, as follows:

```
take(n::Int) = xs -> xs[1:min(n,end)]

fetch_story_details(ids::Vector{Int}) = fetch_story.(ids)

calculate_average_score(stories::Vector{Story}) = mean(s.score for s in
stories)
```

From the preceding code, we can see the following:

- The `take` function takes an integer, n, and returns an anonymous function that returns the first n elements from an array.
- The `min` function is used to ensure that it will take no more than the actual size of the array.
- The `fetch_story_details` function takes an array of story IDs and broadcasts the `fetch_story` function over them using the dot notation.
- The `calculate_average_score` function takes an array of `Story` objects and calculates the mean of the scores.

As a quick reminder, all of these functions accept a single argument as input so that they can participate in the functional pipe operation.

Now, let's get back to logging. Logging plays a funny role in functional pipes. It is designed to produce side effects and do not affect the result of computation. It is *slippery* in the sense that it just returns the same data that it received from its input. Since the standard `println` function returns nothing, we cannot use it directly in a piping operation. Instead, we must create a logging function that is smart enough to print what we want and yet returns the same data that it was passed.

In addition, we want to be able to format the output using the data that passes through the system. For that reason, we can utilize the `Formatting` package. It contains a flexible and efficient formatting facility. Let's build our own logging function, as follows:

```
using Formatting: printfmtln

logx(fmt::AbstractString, f::Function = identity) = x -> begin
    let y = f(x)
        print(now(), " ")
        printfmtln(fmt, y)
    end
    return x
end
```

The `logx` function takes a format string and a possible transformer function, `f`. It returns an anonymous function that passes the transformed value to the `printfmln` function. It also automatically prefixes the log with the current timestamp. Most importantly, this anonymous function returns the original value of the argument.

To see how this logging function works, we can play with a few examples:

```
julia> "John" |> logx("Hello, {}")
2019-12-01T12:49:36.947 Hello, John
"John"

julia> [1,2,3] |> logx("Array size is {}", length)
2019-12-01T12:49:40.099 Array size is 3
3-element Array{Int64,1}:
 1
 2
 3
```

In the first example shown in the preceding screenshot, the `logx` function was called with just a format string, so the input coming via the pipe will be used as-is in the log. The second example passes the `length` function as the second argument of `logx`. The `length` function is then used to transform the input value for logging purposes.

Putting this all together, we can introduce logging to our functional pipe in our new `average_score3` function, as follows:

```
average_score3(n = 10) =
    fetch_top_stories()                           |>
    logx("Number of top stories = {}", length)    |>
    take(n)                                        |>
    logx("Limited number of stories = $n")        |>
    fetch_story_details                           |>
    logx("Fetched story details")                 |>
    calculate_average_score                       |>
    logx("Average score = {}")
```

Occasionally, functional pipes can make the code easier to understand. Because conditional statements are not allowed in a piping operation, the logic is always linear.

You may be wondering how to handle conditional logic in functional pipe design. We'll learn about this in the next section.

Implementing conditional logic in functional pipes

Since the logical flow is quite linear, how do we deal with conditional logic?

Suppose we want to determine the hotness of top stories by checking the average score against a threshold. If the average score is higher than 100, then it would be considered high; otherwise, it would be considered low. So, literally, we need an if-statement that determines what to execute next.

We can use dynamic dispatch to solve this problem. We are going to build this function from the bottom-up, as follows.

1. Create the `hotness` function, which determines the hotness of the Hacker News site by score. It returns an instance of the `Val{:high}` or `Val{:low}` parametric type. The built-in `Val` data type is a convenient way to create new parametric types that can be used for dispatch purposes:

   ```
   hotness(score) = score > 100 ? Val(:high) : Val(:low)
   ```

2. Create two `celebrate` functions with respect to the `Val` parametric types. They simply use the `logx` function to print some text. We call it with the value of `v` so that the hotness argument is passed downstream if we ever want to do more work after celebration:

   ```
   celebrate(v::Val{:high}) = logx("Woohoo! Lots of hot topics!")(v)
   celebrate(v::Val{:low}) = logx("It's just a normal day...")(v)
   ```

3. Build the `check_hotness` function, which uses a functional pipe pattern. It uses the `average_score3` function to calculate the average score. Then, it uses the `hotness` function to determine how to change the execution path. Finally, it calls the `celebrate` function via the multiple dispatch mechanism:

   ```
   check_hotness(n = 10) =
       average_score3(n) |> hotness |> celebrate
   ```

Let's test this out:

```
julia> HackerNewsAnalysis.check_hotness(10)
2019-12-01T13:33:58.384 Number of top stories = 496
2019-12-01T13:33:58.385 Limited number of stories = 10
2019-12-01T13:34:00.343 Fetched story details
2019-12-01T13:34:00.343 Average score = 64.9
2019-12-01T13:34:00.343 It's just a normal day...
Val{:low}()
```

This simple example demonstrates how conditional logic can be implemented in functional pipe design. Of course, in reality, we would have more complex logic than just printing something to the screen.

An important observation is that functional pipes only handle linear execution. Hence, whenever the execution splits conditionally, we would form a new pipe for each possible path. The following diagram depicts how an execution path may be designed with functional pipes. Each split of execution is enabled by dispatching over the type of a single argument:

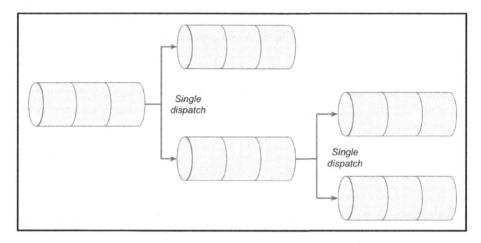

Functional pipes look fairly simple and straightforward from a conceptual point of view. However, they are sometimes criticized for having to pass intermediate data between each component in the pipe, causing unnecessary memory allocation and slowness. In the next section, we will go over how to use broadcasting to overcome this issue.

Broadcasting along functional pipes

In a data processing pipeline, we may encounter a situation where the functions can be fused together into a single loop. This is called *broadcasting* and it can be conveniently enabled by using the dot notation. Using broadcasting may make a huge performance difference for data-intensive applications.

Consider the following scenario, where two vectorized functions have already been defined, as follows:

```
add1v(xs) = [x + 1 for x in xs]
mul2v(xs) = [2x for x in xs]
```

The `add1v` function takes a vector and increments all the elements by 1. Likewise, the `mul2v` function takes a vector and multiplies every element by 2. Now, we can combine the functions to create a new one that takes a vector and sends it down the pipe to `add1v` and subsequently `mul2v`:

```
add1mul2v(xs) = xs |> add1v |> mul2v
```

However, the `add1mul2v` function is not optimal from a performance perspective. The reason for this is that each operation must be fully completed and then passed to the next function. The intermediate result, while only needed temporarily, must be allocated in memory:

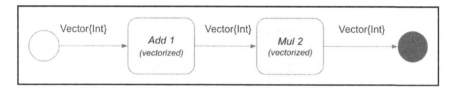

As depicted in the preceding diagram, besides the input vector and the output vector, an intermediate vector must be allocated to hold the results from the `add1v` function.

In order to avoid the allocation of the intermediate results, we can utilize broadcasting. Let's create another set of functions that operate on individual elements rather than arrays, as follows:

```
add1(x) = x + 1
mul2(x) = 2x
```

Our original problem still requires taking a vector, adding 1, and multiplying by 2 for every element. So, we can define such a function using the dot notation, as follows:

```
add1mul2(xs) = xs .|> add1 .|> mul2
```

The dot character right before the pipe operator indicates that the elements in xs will be broadcast to the add1 and mul2 functions, fusing the whole operation into a single loop. The data flow now looks more like the following:

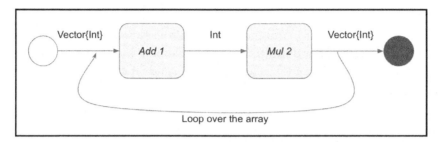

Here, the intermediate result becomes a single integer, eliminating the need for the temporary array. To appreciate the performance improvement we get from broadcasting, we can run a performance benchmark for the two functions, as shown in the following screenshot:

```
julia> using BenchmarkTools

julia> xs = collect(1:10000);

julia> @btime add1mul2v($xs);
  15.354 μs (4 allocations: 156.41 KiB)

julia> @btime add1mul2($xs);
  7.530 μs (2 allocations: 78.20 KiB)
```

As you can see, the broadcasting version ran twice as fast as the vectorized version in this scenario.

In the next section, we will review some considerations about using functional pipes.

Considerations about using functional pipes

Before you get too excited about functional pipes, let's make sure that we understand the pros and cons of using functional pipes.

From a readability perspective, functional pipes can possibly make the code easier to read and easier to follow. This is because the logic has to be linear. On the contrary, some people may find it less intuitive and harder to read because the direction of computation is reversed as compared to nested function calls.

Functional pipes require single-argument functions, for which they can be easily composed with other functions. When it comes to functions that require multiple arguments, the general solution is to create *curried functions* – higher-order functions that fix an argument. Previously, we defined a `take` function that takes the first few elements from a collection:

```
take(n::Int) = xs -> xs[1:min(n,end)]
```

The `take` function is a curried function made out of the `getindex` function (with a convenient syntax of using square brackets). The `getindex` function takes two arguments: a collection and a range. Because the number of arguments has been reduced to 1, it can now participate in the functional pipe.

On the flip side, we cannot utilize multiple dispatch for single-argument functions. This could be a huge disadvantage when you are handling logic that requires consideration of multiple arguments.

While functions can only accept single arguments, it is possible to work around the issue by using tuples. Tuples have a composite type signature that can be used for dispatch. However, it's not recommended because it is quite awkward to define functions that take a single tuple argument rather than multiple arguments.

Nevertheless, functional pipes can be a useful pattern under certain circumstances. Any data-processing task that fits into a linear process style could be a good fit.

Summary

In this chapter, we learned about several patterns that can be quite useful in application design.

We started with the singleton type dispatch pattern. Using a command processor example, we successfully refactored the code from using if-then-else conditional statements to utilizing dynamic dispatch. We learned how to create new singleton types using the standard `Val` type or rolling our own parametric type.

Then, we switched gears and discussed how to implement automated testing effectively using the stubbing/mocking pattern. We took a simple use case of a credit approval process and experimented with a simple way to inject stubs using keyword arguments. We weren't very satisfied with the need to change the API for testing, so we leaned on the Mocking package for a more seamless approach. We then learned how to replace function calls with stubs and mocks in our test suite and how they work differently.

Finally, we learned about the functional pipes pattern and how it can make the code easier to read and follow. We learned about composability and how the compose operator works similarly to the pipe operator. We went over how to develop efficient code using functional pipes and broadcasting. Finally, we discussed the pros and cons of using functional pipes and other related considerations.

In the next chapter, we will turn around and look at some anti-patterns of Julia programming.

Questions

1. What predefined data type can be used to conveniently create new singleton types?
2. What are the benefits of using singleton type dispatch?
3. Why do we want to create stubs?
4. What is the difference between mocking and stubbing?
5. What does composability mean?
6. What is the primary constraint of using functional pipes?
7. How are functional pipes useful?

10
Anti-Patterns

Over the last five chapters, we have looked in great detail at reusability, performance, maintainability, safety, and some miscellaneous design patterns. These patterns are extremely useful and can be applied to various situations for different types of applications. While it is important to know what the best practices are, it is also beneficial to understand what pitfalls to avoid. To do this, we are going to cover several **anti-patterns** in this chapter.

Anti-patterns are bad practices that programmers may do unintentionally. Sometimes, these problems are not severe enough to cause trouble; however, it is possible that an application may become unstable or have degraded performance due to improper design. In this chapter, we will cover the following topics:

- Piracy anti-pattern
- Narrow argument types anti-pattern
- Nonconcrete field types anti-pattern

By the end of this chapter, you will have learned how to avoid developing pirate functions. You will also be more conscious and smart about the level of abstraction when specifying the type of function arguments. Finally, you will be able to leverage more parametric types in your design for your own composite types for high-performance applications.

Let's start with the most interesting topic—piracy!

Technical requirements

The sample source code is located at `https://github.com/PacktPublishing/Hands-on-Design-Patterns-and-Best-Practices-with-Julia/tree/master/Chapter10`.

The code is tested in a Julia 1.3.0 environment.

Piracy anti-pattern

In Chapter 2, *Modules, Packages and Data Type Concepts*, we learned how to create new namespaces using modules. As you may recall, modules are used to define functions so that they are logically separated. It is possible, then, that we can define two different functions—one in module X and another in module Y, with both having exactly the same name. In fact, these functions do not even need to mean the same thing. For example, in a mathematics package, we can define a trace function for matrices. In a computer graphics package, we can define a trace function for doing ray tracing work. These two trace functions perform different things, and they do not interfere with each other.

On the other hand, a function can also be designed to be extended from another package. For example, in the Base package, the AbstractArray interface is designed to be extended. Here's an example:

```
# My own array-like type for tracking scores
struct Scores <: AbstractVector{Float64}
    values::Vector{Float64}
end

# implement AbstractArray interface
Base.size(s::Scores) = (length(s.values),)
Base.getindex(s::Scores, i::Int) = s.values[i]
```

Here, we have extended the size and getindex functions from the Base package so that they can work with our own data types. This is a perfectly good usage of the Julia language; however, it can be problematic when we do not extend functions from other packages correctly. In particular, *piracy* refers to the situation in which a third-party function is replaced or extended in a bad way. This is an anti-pattern because it may cause system behavior to become nondeterministic. For convenience, we can define three different kinds of piracy:

- **Type I piracy**: Function is redefined
- **Type II piracy**: Function is extended without using your own types in any of the arguments
- **Type III piracy**: Function is extended but used for a different purpose

We will now drill down into each one in more detail.

Type I – Redefining a function

Type I piracy refers to the situation where a programmer redefines a third-party function from their own module. Perhaps you did not like the original implementation in the third-party module and replaced the function with your own implementation.

The worst form of Type I piracy is when you replace the function without conforming to the original function's interface. Let's do an experiment and see what could happen. We will use the + function from `Base` as an example. As you know, when the + function is passed with two `Int` arguments, it should return an `Int` value as a result. What would happen if we replace the function so that it returns a string? Let's open up a REPL and give it a try:

```julia
julia> Base.:(+)(x::Int, y::Int) = "hello world"

Error: Error in the keymap
    exception =
    MethodError: no method matching Int64(::String)
    Closest candidates are:
      Int64(::Union{Bool, Int32, Int64, UInt32, UInt64, UInt8, Int128, Int16, Int8, UInt128, UInt16}) at boot.jl:710
      Int64(::Ptr) at boot.jl:720
      Int64(::Float32) at float.jl:700
      ...
```

Boom! The Julia REPL crashed immediately as soon as the function was defined. That is because the return value of this + function is expected to be an integer. When we return a string, it violates the contract of this function and all functionalities that rely on the + function are negatively impacted. Given that + is a commonly used function, it crashes the system immediately.

Why does Julia even allow us to do that? For some situations, the ability to do this can be useful. Say that you found a bug for a specific function in a third-party package—you can inject a fix immediately without having to wait for the bug fix upstream. Likewise, you can replace a slow function with a more performant version. Ideally, these changes should be sent upstream, but you have the flexibility to implement the change immediately.

The only requirement is that the function being replaced should adhere to the same contract that was originally intended. Therefore, it requires an intimate understanding about how the third-party package is designed. In reality, it is even better if you can contact the original author and discuss the change before applying piracy.

With great power comes great responsibility. Great care must be taken if we ever want to make use of Type I piracy.

Next, we will look into Type II piracy, which is more common across packages in the Julia ecosystem.

Type II piracy – Extending without your own types

Type II piracy is commonly known as *type piracy* by the Julia developer community. It refers to the situation where a third-party function is extended without using the programmer's own types in any of the function arguments. It usually happens when you want to extend the third-party package by injecting your own code. Let's go through a hypothetical example.

Suppose that you want to mimic the same behavior in JavaScript of adding a string and a number together, where the values concatenate as if they are both strings:

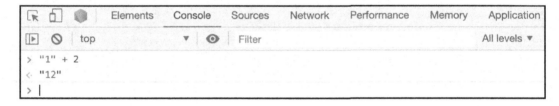

To make it happen in Julia, we would be tempted to do the following in `MyModule`:

```
module MyModule
    import Base.+
    (+)(s::AbstractString, n::Number) = "$s$n"
end
```

We can paste the preceding code in the REPL and do a quick test:

```
julia> using .MyModule

julia> "1" + 2
"12"
```

This seems to be working great! But there are some hidden issues with this approach. Let's look at why it is still a bad idea.

Conflicting with another pirate

Now that we are using the enhanced version of the + function, can we rely on the fact that the function will always do exactly what we have made it do? Perhaps surprisingly, the answer is no.

Let's say we have found an open source package called AnotherModule, and we want to use it in our MyModule module. The AnotherModule module happens to do the same kind of type II piracy; however, the author decided to do the *right* thing—instead of concatenating the arguments as if they are strings, the string argument is parsed into a number and then the two numbers are added together. The code is as follows:

```
module AnotherModule
    import Base: +, -, *, /
    (+)(s::AbstractString, n::T) where T <: Number = parse(T, s) + n
    (-)(s::AbstractString, n::T) where T <: Number = parse(T, s) - n
    (*)(s::AbstractString, n::T) where T <: Number = parse(T, s) * n
    (/)(s::AbstractString, n::T) where T <: Number = parse(T, s) / n
end
```

If we go back to the REPL and define this module, then we get the new definition:

```
julia> using .AnotherModule

julia> "1" + 2
3
```

We now have two implementations of the same function with exactly the same signature, and they return different results. Who is going to win? Is it the one defined in MyModule or the one in AnotherModule? Only one of them can be in effect. That means that either AnotherModule or MyModule is going to break. This problem can lead to a disastrous situation and hard-to-find bugs.

Another reason to avoid type II piracy is the future-proofing problem. We will discuss this next.

Future-proofing your code

Say that we have extended the + function in `Base` as follows:

```
module MyModule
    import Base.+
    (+)(s::AbstractString, n::Number) = "$s$n"
end
```

It may seem to be a great addition today; however, there is no guarantee that the same function will not be implemented in a future version of Julia. It is conceivable (which is not to say that it's likely or unlikely) that the + function will be enhanced to work with strings in the future.

In addition, these kinds of changes would be considered nonbreaking, meaning that the Julia dev team can add this feature with just a minor release. Unfortunately, your application now breaks for a nonbreaking Julia upgrade. That's not something that we normally expect.

If you want to future-proof your code, then do not be a pirate!

Avoiding type piracy

Type II piracy can be mitigated by creating your own types and using them in the function argument. In this case, perhaps we should consider creating a wrapper type to hold the string and using this new type for dispatch:

```
module MyModule
    export @str_str
    import Base: +, show

    struct MyString
        value::AbstractString
    end

    macro str_str(s::AbstractString)
        MyString(s)
    end

    show(io::IO, s::MyString) = print(io, s.value)
    (+)(s::MyString, n::Number) = MyString(s.value * string(n))
    (+)(n::Number, s::MyString) = MyString(string(n) * s.value)
    (+)(s::MyString, t::MyString) = MyString(s.value * t.value)
end
```

Here, we have redefined the module with a new `MyString` type that holds a string. Then, we can still extend the + function to concatenate `MyString` with any number. For completeness, we have defined three variations of the + function for accepting `MyString` and `Number` arguments in any order and another one that accepts two `MyString` arguments. We have also defined a `str_str` macro for convenience. The new module works properly as follows:

```julia
julia> using .MyModule

julia> str"I am " + 25 + str" years old!"
I am 25 years old!
```

By using your own type in the function argument, we can avoid any conflict with other dependent packages, as well as future-proofing our code for Julia upgrades.

The last kind of piracy is somewhat less severe but still worth a look. Let's take a look at that next.

Type III piracy – Extending with your own type, but for a different purpose

Type III piracy refers to the situation where a function is extended, but is used for a different purpose. It is the right procedure of extending code, but done in a bad way. This kind of piracy is also called a *pun* by the Julia developers. To understand what it is, let's consider a fun example here.

Suppose that we are developing a simple party registration application. The type definition and constructor are shown here:

```
# A Party just contains a title and guest names
struct Party
    title::String
    guests::Vector{String}
end

# constructor
Party(title) = Party(title, String[])
```

The `Party` type contains just a title and an array of guest names. The constructor just takes the title and initializes the guest array as an empty array. Now, just to be cute, we can define a function for joining a party as follows:

```
Base.join(name::String, party::Party) = push!(party.guests, name)
```

This is an extension to the `join` method from `Base`. Why would we want to do that? Well, if we create the `join` function in our own namespace, then we can get into a naming conflict with the standard `join` function. To avoid handling that conflict, maybe it is easier to just extend the function from `Base`.

At first glance, it would work as expected:

```
julia> party = Party("Halloween 2019")
Party("Halloween 2019", String[])

julia> join("Tom", party)
1-element Array{String,1}:
 "Tom"

julia> join("Kevin", party)
2-element Array{String,1}:
 "Tom"
 "Kevin"
```

However, there is a hidden trap. If we were to let multiple people join the party at the same time, then we could get into trouble easily:

```
julia> join(["Bob", "Jeff"], party)
"BobParty(\"Halloween 2019\", [\"Tom\", \"Kevin\"])Jeff"
```

What happened? Let's take a look at the original meaning of the `join` function, as shown in the `help` screen:

```
help?> join

  join([io::IO,] strings, delim, [last])
```

The purpose of the `join` function is to take multiple strings and put them together separated by some kind of delimiter. So the call to the `join` function in the preceding code ended up using the `Party` object as a delimiter.

Let's think a little bit about how we got into trouble. When we defined the function using our own type (`Party`), we did not expect our function to be used by any other code except our own. However, that is not true here. Our function was clearly utilized by the string concatenation logic from the `Base` package.

It turns out that we are an unfortunate victim of *duck typing*. If you look into the source code of Julia, you will find that some `join` functions are defined without specifying any type in the arguments. So, when we pass a `Party` object to the `join` function, it leaks into the original `join` logic. Worse yet, no error was thrown because everything just *worked*.

It is best to avoid type III piracy altogether. In the preceding example, we could have defined the `join` function in our own module rather than extending the one from `Base`. If we are bothered by the name conflict issue, we can also choose a different function name—for example, `register`. We have to realize that the meaning of joining a party is not the same as joining strings together.

All three types of piracy are bad, and they can cause bugs that are surprisingly difficult to find or debug. We should avoid them as much as possible.

Next, we will go over another anti-pattern related to specifying argument types in function definitions.

Narrow argument types anti-pattern

When designing functions in Julia, we have many options about whether and how to provide the type of arguments. The narrow argument types anti-pattern refers to the situation in which the types of the arguments are too narrowly specified, causing the function to be less useful unnecessarily.

Let's consider a simple example function that is used for computing the sum of the products of two vectors:

```
function sumprod(A::Vector{Float64}, B::Vector{Float64})
    return sum(A .* B)
end
```

There is nothing wrong with this design, except that the function can only be used when the arguments are vectors of `Float64` values. What are the other possible options? Let's take a look at that next.

Considering various options for argument types

Julia's dispatch mechanism can select the right function to call as long as the type of the arguments being passed matches the signature of the function. Based upon the type hierarchy, we can possibly specify abstract types and the function still gets selected properly.

Such flexibility gives us many options. We can consider any of the following:

- `sumprod(A::Vector{Float64}, B::Vector{Float64})`
- `sumprod(A::Vector{Number}, B::Vector{Number})`
- `sumprod(A::Vector{T}, B::Vector{T}) where T <: Number`
- `sumprod(A::Vector{S}, B::Vector{T}) where {S <: Number, T <: Number}`
- `sumprod(A::Array{S,N}, B::Array{T,N}) where {N, S <: Number, T <: Number}`
- `sumprod(A::AbstractArray{S,N}, B::AbstractArray{T,N}) where {N, S <: Number, T <: Number}`
- `sumprod(A, B)`

Which one is the most appropriate option for our function? We're not sure yet, but we can always revisit our requirements and perform some testing before drawing a conclusion.

Let's first define what scenarios we plan to support. As we expect, this is just a numeric calculation: we would like to support any numeric container that supports broadcasting. Broadcasting is required because we use dot notation when calculating the product of A and B in the preceding code.

Our test scenarios involve the following combinations of arguments:

Scenario	Argument 1	Argument 2
1	`Array{Float64, 1}`	`Array{Float64, 1}`
2	`Array{Int64, 1}`	`Array{Int64, 1}`
3	`Array{Int, 1}`	`Array{Float64, 1}`
4	`Array{Float64, 2}`	`Array{Float64, 2}`
5	`Array{Number,1}`	`Array{Number,1}`

To test these scenarios for various function signature options, we can build a test harness function, as follows:

```
function test_harness(f, scenario, args...)
    try
        f(args...)
        println(f, " #$(scenario) success")
    catch ex
        if ex isa MethodError
            println(f, " #$(scenario) failure (method not selected)")
        else
            println(f, " #$(scenario) failure (unknown error $ex)")
        end
    end
end
```

The test harness applies function `f` with the provided arguments `args` for a specific `scenario`. If the function is dispatched, it displays a success message in the console; otherwise, it displays a failure message. As we want to test the preceding listed scenarios, we can define just one more function so that we can execute our tests easily:

```
function test_sumprod(f)
    test_harness(f, 1, [1.0,2.0], [3.0, 4.0]);
    test_harness(f, 2, [1,2], [3,4]);
    test_harness(f, 3, [1,2], [3.0,4.0]);
    test_harness(f, 4, rand(2,2), rand(2,2));
    test_harness(f, 5, Number[1,2.0], Number[3.0, 4]);
end
```

The `test_sumprod` function takes a function and executes the five preceding test cases.

Now we are all set. Let's dissect each option and see how well they work for us.

Option 1 – Vectors of Float64 values

The first option is what we started with at the beginning of this section. It has the most specific types of arguments. The drawback is that it can only work with a vector of `Float64` values.

Let's define our function as follows so that we can pass it to the testing function:

```
sumprod_1(A::Vector{Float64}, B::Vector{Float64}) = sum(A .* B)
```

We can try our test harness now:

```
julia> test_sumprod(sumprod_1)
sumprod_1 #1 success
sumprod_1 #2 failure (method not selected)
sumprod_1 #3 failure (method not selected)
sumprod_1 #4 failure (method not selected)
sumprod_1 #5 failure (method not selected)
```

As expected, this function can work with the first scenario when both arguments are vectors of Float64 values. So it does not satisfy all of our requirements. Let's try the next option.

Option 2 – Vectors of instances of Number

The second option is a little more interesting. We have switched the type parameter from Float64 to Number, which is the topmost abstract type in the numeric type hierarchy:

```
sumprod_2(A::Vector{Number}, B::Vector{Number}) = sum(A .* B)
```

Let's test it now:

```
julia> test_sumprod(sumprod_2)
sumprod_2 #1 failure (method not selected)
sumprod_2 #2 failure (method not selected)
sumprod_2 #3 failure (method not selected)
sumprod_2 #4 failure (method not selected)
sumprod_2 #5 success
```

At first glance, it may appear that using Number as a type parameter would make it more generic. It turns that out that it can only accept an array of Number types, which means that it has to be a heterogenous array where each element can be a different type as long as all element types are subtypes of Number. For that reason, a vector of Float64 values is not a subtype of a vector of Number values. Check the following code snippet:

```
julia> Vector{Float64} <: Vector{Number}
false
```

For that reason, none of the scenarios was successful except the last one, which takes vectors of Number exactly as arguments. So this option is not a great one either. Let's move on!

Option 3 – Vectors of type T where T is a subtype of Number

The third option is to take vectors of type T, where T is just a subtype of Number.

The function can be defined as follows:

```
sumprod_3(A::Vector{T}, B::Vector{T}) where T <: Number = sum(A .* B)
```

Let's try it first:

```
julia> test_sumprod(sumprod_3)
sumprod_3 #1 success
sumprod_3 #2 success
sumprod_3 #3 failure (method not selected)
sumprod_3 #4 failure (method not selected)
sumprod_3 #5 success
```

As the type parameter T can be any subtype of Number, this function comfortably handles vectors of Float64, Int64, and even Number types. Unfortunately, it cannot handle arguments of different types, but we should be able to improve it further. Let's try the next option.

Option 4 – Vectors of type S and T where S and T are subtypes of Number

This option differs from option 3 only in the way that the types of arguments are separately specified. Thus, the function can accept different types for the first and second arguments. The function is defined as follows:

```
sumprod_4(A::Vector{S}, B::Vector{T}) where {S <: Number, T <: Number} =
sum(A .* B)
```

We can try it now:

```
julia> test_sumprod(sumprod_4)
sumprod_4 #1 success
sumprod_4 #2 success
sumprod_4 #3 success
sumprod_4 #4 failure (method not selected)
sumprod_4 #5 success
```

We have definitely addressed the issue with mixed argument types by now. We're getting close to the final destination. Scenario 4 is the case where the arguments are matrices rather than vectors. For sure we know how to fix this, so let's do that next.

Option 5 – Arrays of type S and type T where S and T are subtypes of Number

Since Julia arrays support broadcasting, we can generalize the function arguments from a `Vector{T}` to an `Array{T,N}` signature in order to support multidimensional arrays. Let's now define the function as follows:

```
sumprod_5(A::Array{S,N}, B::Array{T,N}) where {N, S <: Number, T <: Number}
=
    sum(A .* B)
```

We have pretty good confidence that this would work. Let's test it now:

```
julia> test_sumprod(sumprod_5)
sumprod_5 #1 success
sumprod_5 #2 success
sumprod_5 #3 success
sumprod_5 #4 success
sumprod_5 #5 success
```

Fabulous! We have finally satisfied all the requirements as listed in the test scenarios. Are we done? Maybe not. For the sake of argument, we may want to support other types of containers that are not necessarily a dense array. What if the input is sparse matrices? Let's improve the function once again.

Option 6 – Abstract arrays

The `AbstractArray` is the abstract type for all Julia array containers. Many Julia packages implement the array interface and are made to be subtypes of `AbstractArray`. It would be a shame if we go so far to make the `sumprod` function versatile enough, and yet we cannot support sparse matrices or other types of array-type containers. To make it more general, let's turn our function definition from `Array` to `AbstractArray` as follows:

```
sumprod_6(A::AbstractArray{S,N}, B::AbstractArray{T,N}) where
    {N, S <: Number, T <: Number} = sum(A .* B)
```

The signature is the same as the previous option, except that the function can be dispatched with any `AbstractArray` container types. Let's make sure that the function works as expected:

```
julia> test_sumprod(sumprod_6)
sumprod_6 #1 success
sumprod_6 #2 success
sumprod_6 #3 success
sumprod_6 #4 success
sumprod_6 #5 success
```

The function is working properly for our existing cases. Let's just try it once again using the sparse matrix type:

```
julia> using SparseArrays

julia> A = sparse([1,10,100], [1,10,100], [1,2,3])
100×100 SparseMatrixCSC{Int64,Int64} with 3 stored entries:
  [1  ,   1]  =  1
  [10 ,  10]  =  2
  [100, 100]  =  3

julia> B = sparse([1,10,100], [1,10,100], [4,5,6])
100×100 SparseMatrixCSC{Int64,Int64} with 3 stored entries:
  [1  ,   1]  =  4
  [10 ,  10]  =  5
  [100, 100]  =  6

julia> sumprod_6(A, B)
32
```

Bravo! It is working great now, even with a non-dense array type. We are almost done. Let's look at our last option—duck typing.

Option 7 – Duck typing

Our last option basically skips the types in the function arguments. This is also called duck typing, as the function will be dispatched as long as two arguments are provided. Julia will specialize and compile a new version for different variations of the argument types. The function is simply defined as follows:

```
sumprod_7(A, B) = sum(A .* B)
```

For completeness, we will run the test again:

```
julia> test_sumprod(sumprod_7)
sumprod_7 #1 success
sumprod_7 #2 success
sumprod_7 #3 success
sumprod_7 #4 success
sumprod_7 #5 success
```

The benefit of this option is that the function is free of type information in the signature, so it looks very clean. However, the drawback is that the function can be dispatched for any type—not even an array or for numeric values. When garbage is passed into the function, garbage comes out, or the function just throws an error when the objects being passed do not have the * operator function defined.

Now that we have considered all the options and performed the respective tests, let's summarize what we have done so far and what we would want to do next.

Summarizing all options

Let's now summarize all the options that we have considered so far:

Option	Signature	Passed all tests?
1	sumprod(A::Vector{Float64}, B::Vector{Float64})	No
2	sumprod(A::Vector{Number}, B::Vector{Number})	No
3	sumprod(A::Vector{T}, B::Vector{T}) where T <: Number	No

Option	Signature	Passed all tests?
4	`sumprod(A::Vector{S}, B::Vector{T}) where {S <: Number, T <: Number}`	No
5	`sumprod(A::Array{S,N}, B::Array{T,N}) where {N, S <: Number, T <: Number}`	Yes
6	`sumprod(A::AbstractArray{S,N}, B::AbstractArray{T,N}) where {N, S <: Number, T <: Number}`	Yes
7	`sumprod(A, B)`	Yes

Technically speaking, options 5, 6, or 7 could work for all array types. Options 6 and 7 support other array containers, such as sparse matrix. Option 7 works with non-`AbstractArray` types, as long as the type is broadcasting multiplication as well as summation.

Before we draw our conclusion, let's do one last test from a performance perspective. Do you wonder whether making the function accept more general types would sacrifice performance? The only way to know this is to prove it with real experiments. Let's do that next.

Evaluating performance

Do we sacrifice performance when we make the functions accept more general types in their arguments? Let's do some benchmarking tests and see how they perform.

Here, we will benchmark the functions for options 1, 5, 6, and 7 using exactly the same input: two `Float64` vectors with 10,000 elements:

```
using BenchmarkTools

A = rand(10_000);
B = rand(10_000);

@btime sumprod_1($A, $B);
@btime sumprod_5($A, $B);
@btime sumprod_6($A, $B);
@btime sumprod_7($A, $B);
```

Here are the test results:

```
julia> @btime sumprod_1($A, $B);
  12.126 µs (2 allocations: 78.20 KiB)

julia> @btime sumprod_5($A, $B);
  11.742 µs (2 allocations: 78.20 KiB)

julia> @btime sumprod_6($A, $B);
  11.925 µs (2 allocations: 78.20 KiB)

julia> @btime sumprod_7($A, $B);
  11.706 µs (2 allocations: 78.20 KiB)
```

As you can see, there is no material difference between these options. How the argument types are specified does not affect the runtime performance of the function.

In summary, what we have learned about this anti-pattern is that the function argument should not be made too narrow unnecessarily. A function can be much more useful when the *net* is cast wide. A function that can accept and support more input types is automatically more reusable.

Our next anti-pattern relates to how field types should be chosen when designing data types. This is an extremely important topic as it can dramatically affect system performance.

Nonconcrete field types anti-pattern

The nonconcrete field types anti-pattern is an anti-pattern in which a struct field is not concrete. The main problem with nonconcrete types for fields is that they can cause major performance problems. To understand why, let's take a look at the memory layout for composite types that have nonconcrete versus concrete types, then design and compare the two.

Understanding the memory layout of composite data types

Let's first take a look at a simple example for a composite type for tracking the coordinates of a point:

```
struct Point
    x
    y
end
```

When the field type is not specified, it is implicitly interpreted as `Any`, the super type of all types, hence the preceding code is syntactically equivalent to the following (except that we have renamed the type name as `Point2` to avoid confusion):

```
struct Point2
    x::Any
    y::Any
end
```

The fields `x` and `y` have the `Any` type, meaning that they can be anything: `Int64`, `Float64`, or any other data type. To compare the memory layout and utilization, it is worth creating a new point type that uses a small concrete type, such as `UInt8`:

```
struct Point3
    x::UInt8
    y::UInt8
end
```

As we know, `UInt8` should occupy a single byte of storage. Having both `x` and `y` fields should consume only two bytes of storage. Perhaps we should just prove it to ourselves. Check the following code:

```
julia> Point3(0x01, 0x01) |> sizeof
2
```

Clearly, a single `Point3` object only occupies two bytes. Let's do the same with the original `Point` object:

```
julia> Point(0x01, 0x01) |> sizeof
16
```

The `Point` object takes 16 bytes, even though we want to store just two bytes. As we know, the `Point` object can take any data type in the `x` and `y` fields. Now, let's do the same exercise with a larger data type, such as `Int128`:

```
julia> Point(Int128(1), Int128(1)) |> sizeof
16
```

An `Int128` is a 128-bit integer, which occupies 16 bytes in memory. Interestingly, even though we are carrying two `Int128` fields in `Point`, the size of the object remains as 16 bytes.

Why? It is because `Point` actually stores two 64-bit pointers, each occupying eight bytes of storage. We can visualize the memory of a `Point` object as follows:

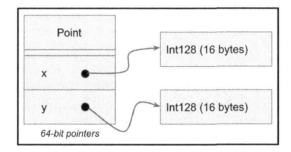

When the field types are concrete, the Julia compiler knows exactly what the memory layout looks like. With two `UInt8` fields, it is compactly represented with two bytes. With two `Int128` fields, it will occupy 32 bytes. Let's try that in REPL:

```
julia> Point4(Int128(1), Int128(1)) |> sizeof
32
```

The memory layout of `Point4` is compact, as shown in the following diagram:

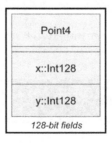

Now that we know the difference in memory layout, we can immediately see the benefits of using concrete types. Every time we need to access the x or y field, if it is a concrete type, then the data is right there. If the fields are just pointers, then we have to dereference the pointer to find the data. Furthermore, the physical memory locations of x and y may not even be adjacent to each other, which may cause hardware cache misses, further hurting performance.

So, do we just follow the rule of using concrete types directly in the field definitions? Not necessarily. There are other options that we can consider, which we will do in the following sections.

Designing composite types with concrete types in mind

Perhaps the reason why we use abstract types in the fields in the first place is to support different types of data in the field. Taking the Point type in the previous section, we can see that the type can be useful in the context of computer games, where the coordinates are identified by integer pixel positions on the screen. On the other hand, we also think that the same type may be useful for storing coordinates of shapes in architectural diagrams, in which case, we would want floating-point values.

If we want to be flexible, we would want to support Point fields with any subtype of the Real type. Conceptually, we want something like this:

```
struct Point
    x::Real
    y::Real
end
```

However, since Real is an abstract type, we would expect poor performance, just like we would with Any. In order to utilize concrete types without sacrificing the flexibility of supporting other numeric types, we can turn Point into a parametric type. Let's restart the REPL and define the new Point type, as follows:

```
struct Point{T <: Real}
    x::T
    y::T
end
```

Making it a parametric type has the benefit of being concrete. We can check this out easily from the REPL. The following is a basic syntax implementation:

```
julia> p = Point(0x01, 0x01)
Point{UInt8}(0x01, 0x01)

julia> sizeof(p)
2
```

The following code shows another example:

```
julia> p = Point(Int128(1), Int128(1))
Point{Int128}(1, 1)

julia> sizeof(p)
32
```

So far, we have been assuming that concrete types would outperform nonconcrete types in `struct` fields. It would be nice to get an idea of how much difference it makes. Let's try that now.

Comparing performance between concrete versus nonconcrete field types

We can run a performance test with these two different types, depicted here:

Our benchmark test function will compute the center of all points from an array, as follows:

```
using Statistics: mean

function center(points::AbstractVector{T}) where T
    return T(
        mean(p.x for p in points),
        mean(p.y for p in points))
end
```

In addition, we will also define a function that can be used to make an array of points for whatever type we want:

```
make_points(T::Type, n) = [T(rand(), rand()) for _ in 1:n]
```

Let's start with a `PointAny` type.

We will generate 100,000 points and use `BenchmarkTools` to measure the time:

```
julia> points = make_points(PointAny, 100_000);

julia> @btime center($points)
  5.221 ms (200007 allocations: 3.05 MiB)
PointAny(0.5004320956272242, 0.49907908658144426)
```

Next, we will run the performance test for the `Point` type:

```
julia> points = make_points(Point, 100_000);

julia> @btime center($points)
  207.244 µs (2 allocations: 32 bytes)
Point{Float64}(0.4979919250808648, 0.5010439178246113)
```

As we can see, there is a huge difference between the two. Using the parametric `Point` type is approximately 25 times faster than the one that uses `Any` as a field type.

What we have learned from this anti-pattern is that we should use concrete types for fields defined in composite types. It is quite easy to *factor out* the abstract type we want into a type parameter. Doing this allows us to gain performance benefits from concrete types without sacrificing the ability to support other data types.

Summary

In this chapter, we learned about several anti-patterns in Julia programming. When we went over details for each anti-pattern, we also figured out how to apply alternative design solutions.

We began with the piracy anti-pattern, which refers to bad practices as related to extending functions from a third-party module. For convenience, we classified piracy anti-patterns into three different types—type I, II, and III. Each type poses a different problem in causing the system to become unstable or potentially invite problems in the future.

Next, we looked into the narrow argument types anti-pattern. When function arguments are too narrowly specified, they become less reusable. Because Julia can specialize the function for various argument types, it is more beneficial to make argument types as general as possible, utilizing abstract types. We went through several design options in great detail, and concluded that the most general types can be used without sacrificing performance.

Finally, we reviewed the nonconcrete field types anti-pattern. We proved that having nonconcrete types poses a performance problem because of the resulting inefficient memory layout structure. We figured that the problem can be solved easily by using parametric types, specifying concrete types as part of the type parameters.

In the next chapter, we will turn our attention to traditional object-oriented design patterns and see how they can be applied in Julia programming. *Fasten your seat belt: if you used to be an OOP programmer, your ride may be a little bumpy!*

Questions

1. What are the risks and potential benefits of type I piracy?
2. What kind of problems can arise from type II piracy?
3. How does type III piracy cause trouble?
4. What should we watch out for when specifying function arguments?
5. How is system performance affected by using abstract function arguments?
6. How is system performance affected by using abstract field types for composite types?

11
Traditional Object-Oriented Patterns

By now, we have already learned about the many design patterns that we need to know in order to be an effective Julia programmer. The cases presented in the previous chapters included various problems that we can solve by writing *idiomatic* Julia code. Some might ask, after all these years, I have learned and adapted to the **object-oriented programming (OOP)** paradigm; how do I apply the same concepts in Julia? The general answer is, you won't solve the problem the same way. The solution written in Julia will look different, reflecting a different programming paradigm. Nevertheless, it is still an interesting exercise to think about how to adopt some of the OOP techniques in Julia.

In this chapter, we will cover all 23 design patterns from the classic **Gang of Four (GoF)** *Design Patterns* book. We will keep the tradition and organize the topics in the following sections:

- Creational patterns
- Behavioral patterns
- Structural patterns

By the end of this chapter, you will have an idea of how each of these patterns may be applied in Julia, as compared to an OOP approach.

Technical requirements

The sample source code is located at `https://github.com/PacktPublishing/Hands-on-Design-Patterns-and-Best-Practices-with-Julia/tree/master/Chapter11`.

The code is tested in a Julia 1.3.0 environment.

Creational patterns

Creational patterns refer to the various ways of constructing and instantiating objects. Since OOP groups data and behavior together, and since a class may inherit the structure and behavior from an ancestor class, there are additional levels of complexity involved when building a large-scale system. By design, Julia has already gotten rid of many issues by not allowing fields to be declared in abstract types and not allowing creating new subtypes from concrete types. Nevertheless, some of these patterns could be helpful in certain situations.

The creational patterns include the factory method, abstract factory, singleton, builder, and prototype patterns. We shall discuss them in detail in the following sections.

The factory method pattern

The idea of the **factory method** pattern is to provide a single interface to create different types of objects that conform to an interface while hiding the actual implementation from the client. This abstraction decouples the client from the underlying implementation of the feature provider.

For example, a program might need to format some numbers in the output. In Julia, we might want to use the `Printf` package to format numbers, as follows:

```julia
julia> using Printf

julia> @sprintf("%d", 1234)
"1234"

julia> @sprintf("%.2f", 1234.567)
"1234.57"
```

Perhaps we do not want to couple with the `Printf` package because we want to switch and use a different formatting package in the future. In order to make the application more flexible, we can design an interface where numbers can be formatted according to their types. The following interface is described in the doc string:

```
"""
    format(::Formatter, x::T) where {T <: Number}

Format a number `x` using the specified formatter.
Returns a string.
"""
function format end
```

The `format` function takes a `formatter` and a numeric value, `x`, and returns a formatted string. The `Formatter` type is defined as follows:

```
abstract type Formatter end
struct IntegerFormatter <: Formatter end
struct FloatFormatter <: Formatter end
```

Then, the factory methods basically create singleton types for dispatch purposes:

```
formatter(::Type{T}) where {T <: Integer} = IntegerFormatter()
formatter(::Type{T}) where {T <: AbstractFloat} = FloatFormatter()
formatter(::Type{T}) where T = error("No formatter defined for type $T")
```

The default implementation may look like the following, utilizing the `Printf` package:

```
using Printf
format(nf::IntegerFormatter, x) = @sprintf("%d", x)
format(nf::FloatFormatter, x) = @sprintf("%.2f", x)
```

Putting everything in a `FactoryExample` module, we can run the following testing code:

```
function test()
    nf = formatter(Int)
    println(format(nf, 1234))
    nf = formatter(Float64)
    println(format(nf, 1234))
end
```

The output is as follows:

```
julia> FactoryExample.test()
1234
1234.00
```

Should we ever want to change the formatter in the future, we just need to provide a new implementation with format functions defined for the numeric types that we want to support. This is handy when we have a lot of number-formatting code lying around. The switch to a different formatter involves literally two lines of code changes (in this example).

Let's look at the abstract factory pattern next.

The abstract factory pattern

The **abstract factory** pattern is used for creating objects via a set of factory methods, which are abstracted away from the concrete implementation. The abstract factory pattern can be viewed as a factory of factories.

We can explore the example of building a multiplatform GUI library that supports Microsoft Windows and macOS. As we want to develop code that is cross-platform, we can leverage this design pattern. This design is described in the following UML diagram:

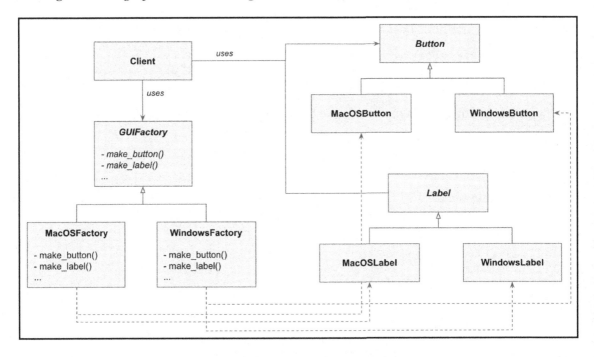

In a nutshell, we have presented two types of GUI objects here: `Button` and `Label`. The concept is the same for both Microsoft Windows and macOS platforms. The client does not care how these objects are instantiated; instead, it asks an abstract factory `GUIFactory` to return factories (either `MacOSFactory` or `WindowsFactory`) that support multiple factory methods for creating platform-dependent GUI objects.

The Julia implementation can simply be modeled with the appropriate abstract and concrete types. Let's start at the OS level:

```
abstract type OS end
struct MacOS <: OS end
struct Windows <: OS end
```

We intended to use `MacOS` and `Windows` as singleton types for dispatch purposes later. For now, let's continue and define the abstract types `Button` and `Label` as follows. Additionally, we have defined `show` methods for each type respectively:

```
abstract type Button end
Base.show(io::IO, x::Button) =
    print(io, "'$(x.text)' button")

abstract type Label end
Base.show(io::IO, x::Label) =
    print(io, "'$(x.text)' label")
```

We do need to provide concrete implementation for these GUI objects. Let's define them now:

```
# Buttons
struct MacOSButton <: Button
    text::String
end

struct WindowsButton <: Button
    text::String
end

# Labels
struct MacOSLabel <: Label
    text::String
end

struct WindowsLabel <: Label
    text::String
end
```

For the sake of simplicity, we just hold on to a text string, whether it's a button or a label. As factory methods are platform-dependent, we can leverage the OS trait and multiple dispatch to call the right `make_button` or `make_label` functions:

```
# Generic implementation using traits
current_os() = MacOS() # should get from system
make_button(text::String) = make_button(current_os(), text)
make_label(text::String) = make_label(current_os(), text)
```

For testing, we have hardcoded the `current_os` function to return `MacOS()`. In reality, this function should return either `MacOS()` or `Windows()` by examining whatever system variable is appropriate to identify the platform. Finally, we need to implement the specific functions for each platform as follows:

```
# MacOS implementation
make_button(::MacOS, text::String) = MacOSButton(text)
make_label(::MacOS, text::String) = MacOSLabel(text)

# Windows implementation
make_button(::Windows, text::String) = WindowsButton(text)
make_label(::Windows, text::String) = WindowsLabel(text)
```

Our simple test just involves calling the `make_button` function:

```
julia> button = make_button("Click me")
'Click me' button
```

Using multiple dispatch, we can easily extend to new platforms or new GUI objects by simply defining new functions for the specific OS.

Next, we will look into the singleton pattern.

The singleton pattern

The **singleton** pattern is used to create a single instance of an object and reuse it from anywhere. A singleton object is typically constructed when the application starts, or it can be created lazily on the first use of the object. An interesting requirement for the singleton pattern arises for multithreaded applications because the instantiation of the singleton object must happen only once. It can be a challenge if the object creation function is called lazily from many threads.

Suppose that we want to create a singleton called `AppKey` that is used for encryption in the application:

```
# AppKey contains an app id and encryption key
struct AppKey
    appid::String
    value::UInt128
end
```

Initially, we may be tempted to use a global variable. Given that we have learned about the performance impact of global variables, we can apply the global constant pattern that we learned in Chapter 6, *Performance Patterns*. Essentially, a `Ref` object is created as a placeholder, as follows:

```
# placeholder for AppKey object.
const appkey = Ref{AppKey}()
```

The `appkey` global constant is first created without being assigned with any value, but then it can be updated when the singleton is instantiated. The construction of singleton can be done as follows:

```
function construct()
    global appkey
    if !isassigned(appkey)
        ak = AppKey("myapp", rand(UInt128))
        println("constructing $ak")
        appkey[] = ak
    end
    return nothing
end
```

This code works fine as long as there is a single thread. If we test it with multiple threads, then the `isassigned` check is problematic. For example, two threads might check whether the key is assigned at the same time, and both threads might think that the singleton object needs to be instantiated. In this case, we end up constructing the singleton twice.

The testing code is shown as follows:

```
function test_multithreading()
    println("Number of threads: ", Threads.nthreads())
    global appkey
    Threads.@threads for i in 1:8
        construct()
    end
end
```

We can demonstrate the problem below. Let's start the Julia REPL with four threads:

```
$ JULIA_NUM_THREADS=4 julia --project=.
                  _
      _       _ _(_)_     |  Documentation: https://docs.julialang.org
     (_)     | (_) (_)    |
      _ _   _| |_  __ _   |  Type "?" for help, "]?" for Pkg help.
     | | | | | | |/ _` |  |
     | | |_| | | | (_| |  |  Version 1.3.0 (2019-11-26)
    _/ |\__'_|_|_|\__'_|  |  Official https://julialang.org/ release
   |__/                   |

julia> Threads.nthreads()
4
```

Then, we can run the testing code:

```
julia> SingletonExample.test_multithreading()
Number of threads: 4
constructing AppKey("myapp", 0xd04169b66cda2e7ec8d3207357a3e4e9)
constructing AppKey("myapp", 0x345ea51c3f16bf5a5b543aeea2165038)
constructing AppKey("myapp", 0x39d0fcb993802a1d443a8a32468d50f7)
constructing AppKey("myapp", 0xd73f2bf060fa925699b8cfce1fdd9d91)
```

As you can see, the singleton being constructed twice here.

So how do we solve this problem? We can use a lock to synchronize the singleton construction logic. Let's first create another global constant to hold the lock:

```
const appkey_lock = Ref(ReentrantLock())
```

To use the lock, we can modify the `construct` function as follows:

```
# change construct() function to acquire lock before
# construction, and release it after it's done.
function construct()
    global appkey
    global appkey_lock
    lock(appkey_lock[])              ◀━━━━━━━━  Acquire lock
    try
        if !isassigned(appkey)
            ak = AppKey("myapp", rand(UInt128))
            println("constructing $ak")
            appkey[] = ak
        else
            println("skipped construction")
        end
    finally
        unlock(appkey_lock[])        ◀━━━━━━━━  Release lock
        return appkey[]
    end
end
```

We must first acquire the lock before checking whether `appkey[]` is already assigned. When we are done constructing the singleton (or skipping it, if it has already been created), we release the lock. Note that we have wrapped the critical section of the code in a `try` block, and we placed the `unlock` function in the `finally` block. This is done to ensure that the lock is released regardless of whether the construction of the singleton is successful or not.

Our new test shows that the singleton is constructed only once:

```
julia> SingletonExample2.test_multithreading()
Number of threads: 4
constructing Main.SingletonExample2.AppKey("myapp", 0x08f07d791fffab
d448555d11384fe040)
skipped construction
skipped construction
skipped construction
skipped construction
skipped construction
skipped construction
skipped construction
```

The singleton pattern is useful when we need to hold on to a single object. Practical use cases include database connections or other references to external resources. Next, we will take a look at the builder pattern.

The builder pattern

The **builder** pattern is used to build a complex object by incrementally building simpler parts of it. We can imagine that a factory assembly line would work in a similar fashion. In that case, a product is assembled step-by-step with more and more parts, and at the end of the assembly line, the product is finished and ready to go.

One benefit of this pattern is that the builder code looks like a linear data flow and is easier for some people to read. In Julia, we may want to write something like this:

```
car = Car() |>
    add(Engine("4-cylinder 1600cc Engine")) |>
    add(Wheels("4x 20-inch wide wheels")) |>
    add(Chassis("Roadster Chassis"))
```

Essentially, this is the exact functional pipe pattern described in Chapter 9, *Miscellaneous Patterns*. For this example, we can develop higher-order functions for building each part (such as the wheels, engine, and chassis). The following code illustrates how to create a curry (higher-order) function for creating wheels:

```
function add(wheels::Wheels)
    return function (c::Car)
```

```
            c.wheels = wheels
            return c
      end
end
```

The `add` function just returns an anonymous function that takes a `Car` object as input and returns an enhanced `Car` object. Likewise, we can develop similar functions for the `Engine` and `Chassis` types. Once these functions are ready, we can build a car by simply chaining these function calls together.

Next, we will discuss the prototype pattern.

The prototype pattern

The **prototype** pattern is used to create new objects by cloning fields from an existing object, or the prototype object. The idea is that some objects are difficult or time-consuming to construct, so it would be useful to make a copy of the object and call it a new one by making small modifications.

As Julia keeps data and logic separate, making copies of objects is really the same as duplicating the content. That sounds easy, but we should not overlook the difference between a shallow copy and a deep copy.

A **shallow copy** of an object is merely an object with all the fields copied from another object. A **deep copy** of an object is created by recursively going into the fields of the object and copying their underlying fields as well. As such, a shallow copy may not be desirable because some data can be shared with the original object.

To illustrate this, let's consider the following struct definitions for a bank account example:

```
mutable struct Account
    id::Int
    balance::Float64
end

struct Customer
    name::String
    savingsAccount::Account
    checkingAccount::Account
end
```

Now, suppose that we have an array of `Customer` objects that are returned from this function:

```
function sample_customers()
    a1 = Account(1, 100.0)
    a2 = Account(2, 200.0)
    c1 = Customer("John Doe", a1, a2)
    a3 = Account(3, 300.0)
    a4 = Account(4, 400.0)
    c2 = Customer("Brandon King", a3, a4)

    return [c1, c2]
end
```

The `sample_customer` function returns an array of two customers. For testing purposes, let's build a test harness to update the balance for the first customer as follows:

```
function test(copy_function::Function)
    println("--- testing ", string(copy_function), " ---")
    customers = sample_customers()
    c = copy_function(customers)
    c[1].checkingAccount.balance += 500
    println("orig: ", customers[1].checkingAccount.balance)
    println("new: ", c[1].checkingAccount.balance)
end
```

If we exercise the test harness with built-in `copy` and `deepcopy` functions, we get the following results:

```
julia> PrototypeExample.test(copy)
--- testing copy ---
orig: 700.0
new:  700.0

julia> PrototypeExample.test(deepcopy)
--- testing deepcopy ---
orig: 200.0
new:  700.0
```

Unexpectedly, we got the wrong result in the `orig` output since we should be adding $500 to the new customer. Why do we have the same balance for both the original customer record and the new customer record instead? This is because a shallow copy was made from the customer array when the `copy` function was used. When this happens, the customer records are essentially shared between the original array and the new array. This means that mutating the new record also affected the original record.

In the second part of the result, only the new copy of the customer record was changed. This is because the `deepcopy` function was used. By definition, the prototype pattern requires making changes to the copy. It is probably safer to make a deep copy should this pattern be applied.

We have covered all five creational patterns. These patterns allow us to build new objects in an effective manner.

Next, we're going to cover a set of behavioral design patterns.

Behavioral patterns

Behavioral patterns refer to how objects are designed to collaborate and communicate with each other. There are 11 GoF patterns from the OOP paradigm. We will cover all of them here with some interesting hands-on examples.

The chain-of-responsibility pattern

The **chain-of-responsibility (CoR)** pattern is used to process the request using a chain of request handlers, whereas each handler has its own distinct and independent responsibility.

This pattern is quite common in many applications. For example, web servers usually handle HTTP requests using so-called middleware. Each piece of middleware is responsible for performing a specific task—for example, authenticating requests, maintaining cookies, validating requests, and performing business logic. A specific requirement about the CoR pattern is that any part of the chain can be broken at any time, resulting in an early exit of the process. In the preceding web server example, the authentication middleware may have decided that the user has not been authenticated, and that therefore, the user should be redirected to a separate website for login. This means that the rest of the middleware is skipped unless the user gets past the authentication step.

How do we design something like this in Julia? Let's look at a simple example:

```
mutable struct DepositRequest
    id::Int
    amount::Float64
end
```

A DepositRequest object contains an amount that a customer wants to deposit in their account. Our marketing department wants us to provide a thank-you note to the customer if the deposit amount is greater than $100,000. To process such a request, we have designed three functions, as follows:

```
@enum Status CONTINUE HANDLED

function update_account_handler(req::DepositRequest)
    println("Deposited $(req.amount) to account $(req.id)")
    return CONTINUE
end

function send_gift_handler(req::DepositRequest)
    req.amount > 100_000 &&
        println("=> Thank you for your business")
    return CONTINUE
end

function notify_customer(req::DepositRequest)
    println("deposit is finished")
    return HANDLED
end
```

What is the responsibility of these functions?

- The update_account_handler function is responsible for updating the account with the new deposit.
- The send_gift_handler function is responsible for sending a thank-you note to the customer for a large deposit amount.
- The notify_customer function is responsible for informing the customer after the deposit is made.

These functions also return an enum value, either CONTINUE or HANDLED, to indicate whether the request should be passed on to the next handler when the current one is finished.

It should be quite clear that these functions run in a specific order. In particular, the notify_customer function should run at the end of the transaction. For that reason, we can establish an array of functions:

```
handlers = [
    update_account_handler,
    send_gift_handler,
    notify_customer
]
```

We can also have a function to execute these handlers in order:

```
function apply(req::DepositRequest, handlers::AbstractVector{Function})
    for f in handlers
        status = f(req)
        status == HANDLED && return nothing
    end
end
```

As part of this design, the loop will end immediately if any handler returns a value of HANDLED. Our test code for testing the function of sending the thank-you note to a premier customer is shown as follows:

```
function test()
    println("Test: customer depositing a lot of money")
    amount = 300_000
    apply(DepositRequest(1, amount), handlers)

    println("\nTest: regular customer")
    amount = 1000
    apply(DepositRequest(2, amount), handlers)
end
```

Running the test gives us this result:

```
julia> ChainOfResponsibilityExample.test()
Test: customer depositing a lot of money
Deposited 300000.0 to account 1
=> Thank you for your business
deposit is finished

Test: regular customer
Deposited 1000.0 to account 2
deposit is finished
```

I will leave it as an exercise for you to build another function in this chain to perform an early exit. But for now, let's move on to the next pattern—the mediator pattern.

The mediator pattern

The **mediator** pattern is used to facilitate communication between different components in an application. This is done in such a way that individual components are decoupled from each other. In most applications, changes in one component can affect another. Sometimes, there are also cascading effects. A mediator can take the responsibility of getting notified when one component is changed, and it can notify other components about the event so that further downstream updates can be made.

As an example, we can consider the use case of a **graphical user interface** (**GUI**). Suppose that we have a screen that contains three fields for our favorite banking application:

- **Amount**: Current balance in the account.
- **Interest Rate**: Current interest rate expressed as a percentage.
- **Interest Amount**: Interest amount. This is a read-only field.

How do they interact with each other? If the amount is changed, then the interest amount needs to be updated. Likewise, if the interest rate is changed, then the interest amount needs to be updated as well.

To model the GUI, we can define the following types for the individual GUI objects onscreen:

```
abstract type Widget end

mutable struct TextField <: Widget
    id::Symbol
    value::String
end
```

The `Widget` is an abstract type and it can be used as the supertype for all GUI objects. This application only needs text fields, so we just define a `TextField` widget. A text field is identified by an `id`, and it contains a `value`. In order to extract and update the value in the text field widget, we can define functions as follows:

```
# extract numeric value from a text field
get_number(t::TextField) = parse(Float64, t.value)

# set text field from a numeric value
function set_number(t::TextField, x::Real)
    println("* ", t.id, " is being updated to ", x)
    t.value = string(x)
    return nothing
end
```

From the preceding code, we can see that the `get_number` function gets the value from the text field widget and returns it as a floating-point number. The `set_number` function populates the text field widget with the provided numeric value. Now, we also need to create the application, so we conveniently define a struct as follows:

```
Base.@kwdef struct App
    amount_field::TextField
    interest_rate_field::TextField
    interest_amount_field::TextField
end
```

For this example, we will implement a `notify` function to simulate an event that is sent to the text field widget after the user enters a value. In reality, the GUI platform typically performs that function. Let's call it `on_change_event`, as follows:

```
function on_change_event(widget::Widget)
    notify(app, widget)
end
```

The `on_change_event` function does nothing else but communicate to the mediator (the app) that something has just happened to this widget. As for the app itself, here's how it handles the notification:

```
# Mediator logic - handling changes to the widget in this app
function notify(app::App, widget::Widget)
    if widget in (app.amount_field, app.interest_rate_field)
        new_interest = get_number(app.amount_field) *
get_number(app.interest_rate_field)/100
        set_number(app.interest_amount_field, new_interest)
    end
end
```

As you can see, it simply checks whether the widget that is being updated is either the Amount or Interest Rate field. If so, it calculates a new interest amount and populates the Interest Amount field with the new value. Let's do a quick test:

```
function test()
    # Show current state before testing
    print_current_state()

    # double principal amount from 100 to 200
    set_number(app.amount_field, 200)
    on_change_event(app.amount_field)
    print_current_state()
end
```

The `test` function displays the initial state of the application, updates the amount field, and displays the new state. For the sake of brevity, the source code for the `print_current_state` function is not shown here, but is available on the book's GitHub site. The output of the test program is shown as follows:

```
julia> using .MediatorExample

julia> MediatorExample.test()
current amount = 100.0
current interest rate = 5.0
current interest amount = 5.0

* amount is being updated to 200
* interest_amount is being updated to 10.0
current amount = 200.0
current interest rate = 5.0
current interest amount = 10.0
```

The benefit of using the 2 mediator pattern is that every object can focus on its own responsibility and not worry about the downstream impact. A central mediator takes on the responsibility of organizing activities and handling events and communications.

Next, we shall look at the memento pattern.

The memento pattern

The **memento** pattern is a state management technique that you can use to restore your work to a previous state when needed. A common example is the Undo function of a word processor application. After making 10 changes, we can always undo the prior operations and return to the original state before those 10 changes were made. Similarly, an application may remember the most recently opened files and provide a menu of choices so that the user can quickly reopen a previously opened file.

Implementing the memento pattern in Julia is quite simple. We can just store previous states in an array and when making a change, we can push the new state to the array. When we want to undo our actions, we restore the previous state by popping from the array. To illustrate this idea, let's consider the case of a blog post-editing application. We can define the data types as follows:

```
struct Post
    title::String
    content::String
end

struct Blog
    author::String
    posts::Vector{Post}
    date_created::DateTime
end
```

As you can see, a `Blog` object contains an array of `Post` objects. By convention, the last element in the array is the current version of the blog post. If there were five posts in the array, then it means that four changes have been made so far. Creating a new blog is as easy, as shown in the following code:

```
function Blog(author::String, post::Post)
    return Blog(author, [post], now())
end
```

By default, a new blog object contains just one version. As the user makes changes, the array will grow. For convenience, we can provide a `version_count` function that returns the number of revisions that the user has made so far.

```
version_count(blog::Blog) = length(blog.posts)
```

To obtain the current post, we can simply take the last element of the array:

```
current_post(blog::Blog) = blog.posts[end]
```

Now, when we have to update the blog, we must push the new version to the array. Here is the function that we use to update the blog with a new title or content:

```
function update!(blog::Blog;
                    title = nothing,
                    content = nothing)
    post = current_post(blog)
    new_post = Post(
        something(title, post.title),
        something(content, post.content)
    )
    push!(blog.posts, new_post)
    return new_post
end
```

The `update!` function takes a `Blog` object, and optionally it can take either an updated `title`, `content`, or both. Basically, it creates a new `Post` object and pushes it into the `posts` array. Undoing is done as follows:

```
function undo!(blog::Blog)
    if version_count(blog) > 1
        pop!(blog.posts)
        return current_post(blog)
    else
        error("Cannot undo... no more previous history.")
    end
end
```

We can test it with the following `test` function:

```
function test()
    blog = Blog("Tom", Post("Why is Julia so great?", "Blah blah."))
    update!(blog, content = "The reasons are...")

    println("Number of versions: ", version_count(blog))
    println("Current post")
    println(current_post(blog))
    println("Undo #1")
    undo!(blog)
    println(current_post(blog))

    println("Undo #2") # expect failure
    undo!(blog)
    println(current_post(blog))
end
```

The output is shown as follows:

```
julia> MementoExample.test()
Number of versions: 2
Current post
Post: Why is Julia so great? => The reasons are...
Undo #1
Post: Why is Julia so great? => Blah blah.
Undo #2
ERROR: Cannot undo... no more previous history.
```

As you can see, it is quite easy to implement the memento pattern. We will cover the observer pattern next.

The observer pattern

The **observer** pattern is useful for registering observers to an object so that all state changes in that object trigger the sending of notifications to the observers. In a language that supports first-class functions—for example, Julia—such functionality can be implemented easily by maintaining a list of functions that can be called before or after the state changes of an object. Sometimes, these functions are called **hooks**.

The implementation of the observer pattern in Julia may consist of two parts:

1. Extend the `setproperty!` function of an object to monitor state changes and notify observers.
2. Maintain a dictionary that can be used to look up the functions to call.

For this demonstration, we will bring up the bank account example again:

```
mutable struct Account
    id::Int
    customer::String
    balance::Float64
end
```

Here is the data structure for maintaining observers:

```
const OBSERVERS = IdDict{Account,Vector{Function}}();
```

Here, we have chosen to use `IdDict` instead of the regular `Dict` object. `IdDict` is a special type that uses Julia's internal object ID as the key of the dictionary. To register observers, we provide the following function:

```
function register(a::Account, f::Function)
    fs = get!(OBSERVERS, a, Function[])
    println("Account $(a.id): registered observer function $(Symbol(f))")
    push!(fs, f)
end
```

Now, let's extend the `setproperty!` function:

```
function Base.setproperty!(a::Account, field::Symbol, value)
    previous_value = getfield(a, field)
    setfield!(a, field, value)
    fs = get!(OBSERVERS, a, Function[])
    foreach(f -> f(a, field, previous_value, value), fs)
end
```

This new `setproperty!` function not only updates the field for the object, but also calls the observer functions with both the previous state and the current state after the field has been updated. For testing purposes, we will create an observer function as follows:

```
function test_observer_func(a::Account, field::Symbol, previous_value,
current_value)
    println("Account $(a.id): $field was changed from $previous_value to
$current_value")
end
```

Our `test` function is written as follows:

```
function test()
    a1 = Account(1, "John Doe", 100.00)
    register(a1, test_observer_func)
    a1.balance += 10.00
    a1.customer = "John Doe Jr."
    return nothing
end
```

When running the test program, we get the following output:

```
julia> ObserverExample.test()
Account 1: registered observer function test_observer_func
Account 1: balance was changed from 100.0 to 110.0
Account 1: customer was changed from John Doe to John Doe Jr.
```

From the output, we can see that the `test_observer_func` function was called every time a property is updated. The observer pattern is an easy thing to develop. Next, we will look at the state pattern.

The state pattern

The **state** pattern is used in situations where an object behaves differently depending on its internal state. A networking service is a great example. A typical implementation for a network-based service is to listen to a specific port number. When a remote process connects to the service, it establishes a connection, and they use it to communicate with each other until the end of the session. When a network service is currently in a listening state, it should allow a new connection to be opened; however, no data transmission should be allowed until after the connection is opened. Then, after the connection is opened, we should be able to send data. By contrast, we should not allow any data to be sent through the network connection if the connection is already closed.

In Julia, we can possibly implement the state pattern using multiple dispatch. Let's first define the following types that are meaningful for network connections:

```
abstract type AbstractState end

struct ListeningState <: AbstractState end
struct EstablishedState <: AbstractState end
struct ClosedState <: AbstractState end

const LISTENING = ListeningState()
```

```
const ESTABLISHED = EstablishedState()
const CLOSED = ClosedState()
```

Here, we have leveraged the singleton type pattern. As for the network connection itself, we can define the type as follows:

```
struct Connection{T <: AbstractState,S}
    state::T
    conn::S
end
```

Now, let's develop a send function, which is used to send a message via a connection. In our implementation, the send function does not do anything else except gather the current state of the connection and forward the call to a state-specific send function:

```
# Use multiple dispatch
send(c::Connection, msg) = send(c.state, c.conn, msg)

# Implement `send` method for each state
send(::ListeningState, conn, msg) = error("No connection yet")
send(::EstablishedState, conn, msg) = write(conn, msg * "\n")
send(::ClosedState, conn, msg) = error("Connection already closed")
```

You may recognize this as the Holy Trait pattern. For unit testing, we can develop a test function for creating a new Connection with the specified message and sending a message to the Connection object:

```
function test(state, msg)
    c = Connection(state, stdout)
    try
        send(c, msg)
    catch ex
        println("$(ex) for message '$msg'")
    end
    return nothing
end
```

Then, the testing code simply runs the test function three times, once for each possible state:

```
function test()
    test(LISTENING, "hello world 1")
    test(CLOSED, "hello world 2")
    test(ESTABLISHED, "hello world 3")
end
```

When running the `test` function, we get the following output:

```
julia> StateExample.test()
ErrorException("No connection yet") for message 'hello world 1'
ErrorException("Connection already closed") for message 'hello world 2'
hello world 3
```

Only the third message was sent successfully, because the connection was in the `ESTABLISHED` state. Now, let's take a look at the strategy pattern.

The strategy pattern

The **strategy** pattern enables clients to select the best algorithm to use at runtime. Instead of coupling the client with predefined algorithms, the client can be configured with a specific algorithm (strategy) when necessary. In addition, sometimes the choice of algorithm cannot be determined ahead of time because the decision may depend on the input data, the environment, or something else.

In Julia, we can solve the problem using multiple dispatch. Let's consider the case of a Fibonacci sequence generator. As we learned from Chapter 6, *Performance Patterns*, the calculation of the nth Fibonacci number can be tricky when we implement it recursively, so our first algorithm (strategy) may be memoization. In addition, we can also solve the same problem using an iterative algorithm without using any recursion.

In order to support both memoization and iterative algorithms, let's create some new types as follows:

```
abstract type Algo end
struct Memoized <: Algo end
struct Iterative <: Algo end
```

The `Algo` abstract type is the supertype for all Fibonacci algorithms. At the moment, we only have two algorithms to choose from: `Memoized` or `Iterative`. Now, we can define the memoized version of the `fib` function as follows:

```
using Memoize
@memoize function _fib(n)
    n <= 2 ? 1 : _fib(n-1) + _fib(n-2)
end

function fib(::Memoized, n)
    println("Using memoization algorithm")
    _fib(n)
end
```

A memoized function `_fib` is first defined. Then a wrapper function `fib` is defined, taking a `Memoized` object as the first argument. The corresponding iterative algorithm can be implemented as follows:

```
function fib(algo::Iterative, n)
    n <= 2 && return 1
    prev1, prev2 = 1, 1
    local curr
    for i in 3:n
        curr = prev1 + prev2
        prev1, prev2 = curr, prev1
    end
    return curr
end
```

How the algorithm actually works is unimportant in this discussion. As the first argument is an `Iterative` object, we know that this function will be dispatched accordingly.

From the client's perspective, it can choose either the memoized version or the iterative function, depending on what it needs. As the memoized version runs at O(1) speed, it should be faster when n is large; however, for a small value of n, the iterative version would work better. We can call the `fib` function in one of the following ways:

```
fib(Memoized(), 10)
fib(Iterative(), 10)
```

Should the client choose to implement an algorithm-selection process, it can be done easily, as follows:

```
function fib(n)
    algo = n > 50 ? Memoized() : Iterative()
    return fib(algo, n)
end
```

The successful test result is shown here:

```
julia> StrategyExample.fib(30)
Using iterative algorithm
832040

julia> StrategyExample.fib(60)
Using memoization algorithm
1548008755920
```

As you can see, implementing the strategy pattern is quite easy. *The unreasonable effectiveness of multiple dispatch has come to rescue again!* Next, we will go over another behavioral pattern called the template method.

The template method pattern

The **template method** pattern is used to create a well-defined process that can use different kinds of algorithms or operations. As a template, it can be customized with whatever algorithm or functions the client requires.

Here, we will explore how the template method pattern can be utilized in a **machine learning (ML)** pipeline use case. For those who are unfamiliar with ML pipelines, here is a simplified version of what a data scientist might do:

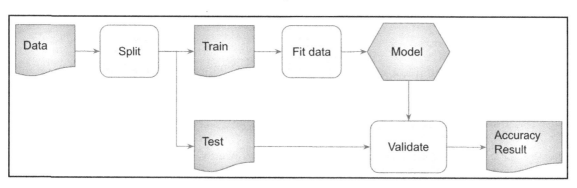

A dataset is first split into two separate datasets for training and testing purposes. The training dataset is fed into a process that fits the data into a statistical model. Then, the `validate` function uses the model to predict the response (also called the target) variable in the test set. Finally, it compares the predicted values against the actual values and determines how accurate the model is.

Let's say we have the pipeline already set up as follows:

```
function run(data::DataFrame, response::Symbol, predictors::Vector{Symbol})
    train, test = split_data(data, 0.7)
    model = fit(train, response, predictors)
    validate(test, model, response)
end
```

For the sake of brevity, the specific functions, `split_data`, `fit`, and `validate`, are not shown here; you can look them up on this book's GitHub site if you wish. However, the pipeline concept is demonstrated in the preceding logic. Let's take a quick spin at predicting Boston house prices:

```julia
julia> using RDatasets, GLM

julia> using .MLPipeline

julia> boston = dataset("MASS", "boston");

julia> result, rmse = MLPipeline.run(boston, :MedV, [:Rm, :Tax, :Crim]);

julia> println(rmse)
6.816627880129819
```

In this example, the response variable is `:MedV`, and we will build a statistic model based on `:Rm`, `:Tax`, and `:Crim`.

The Boston housing dataset contains data collected by the U.S. Census Service concerning housing in the area of Boston, Massachusetts. It is used extensively by much statistical analysis educational literature. The variables that we used in this example are:

MedV: Median value of owner-occupied homes in $1,000's
Rm: Average number of rooms per dwelling
Tax: Full-value property tax rate per $10,000
Crim: Per capita crime rate by town

The accuracy of the model is captured in the `rmse` variable (meaning the root mean squared error). The default implementation uses linear regression as the fitting function.

To implement the template method pattern, we should allow the client to plug in any part of the process. For that reason, we can modify the function with keyword arguments:

```
function run2(data::DataFrame, response::Symbol,
predictors::Vector{Symbol};
            fit = fit, split_data = split_data, validate = validate)
    train, test = split_data(data, 0.7)
    model = fit(train, response, predictors)
    validate(test, model, response)
end
```

Here, we have added three keyword arguments: `fit`, `split_data`, and `validate`. The function is named as `run2` to avoid confusion here, so the client should be able to customize any one of them by passing in a custom function. To illustrate how it works, let's create a new `fit` function that uses the **generalized linear model (GLM)**:

```
using GLM

function fit_glm(df::DataFrame, response::Symbol,
predictors::Vector{Symbol})
    formula = Term(response) ~ +(Term.(predictors)...)
    return glm(formula, df, Normal(), IdentityLink())
end
```

Now that we have customized the fitting function, we can rerun the program by passing it via the `fit` keyword argument:

```
julia> result, rmse = MLPipeline.run2(
           boston, :MedV, [:Rm, :Tax, :Crim],
           fit = fit_glm);

julia> println(rmse)
7.804300451636022
```

As you can see, the client can customize the pipeline easily by just passing in functions. This is possible because Julia supports first-class functions.

In the next section, we will review a few other traditional behavioral patterns.

Command, interpreter, iterator, and visitor patterns

The **command**, **interpreter**, and **visitor** patterns are grouped in this section only because we have already covered their use cases earlier in this book.

The **command** pattern is used to parameterize actions that are to be performed. In Chapter 9, *Miscellaneous Patterns*, in the *Singleton type dispatch pattern* section, we explored a use case where the GUI invokes different commands and reacts to specific actions that the user has requested. By defining singleton types, we can leverage Julia's multiple dispatch mechanism to execute the proper function. We can extend this to new commands by simply adding new functions that take new singleton types.

The **interpreter** pattern is used to model an abstract syntax tree for a particular domain model. As it turns out, we have already done this in Chapter 7, *Maintainability Patterns*, in the *Domain-specific language* section. Every Julia expression can be modeled as an abstract syntax tree without any additional work, and so we can develop a DSL using regular metaprogramming facilities, such as macros and generated functions.

The **iterator** pattern is used to iterate over a collection of objects using a standard protocol. In Julia, there is already an officially established iteration interface that can be implemented by any collection framework. As long as an iterate function is defined for a custom object, the elements in the object can be iterated as part of any looping construct. More information can be found from the official Julia reference manual.

Finally, the **visitor** pattern is used to extend functionalities of an existing class in the OOP paradigm. In Julia, adding new functions to an existing system can be done easily via an extension of generic functions. For example, there are many array-like data structure packages in the Julia ecosystem, such as OffsetArrays, StridedArrays, and NamedArrays. All of these are extensions to the existing AbstractArray framework.

We are now finished with behavioral patterns. Let's move on and take a look at the last group—structural patterns.

Structural patterns

Structural design patterns are used to compose objects together to make bigger things. As you continue developing a system and adding functionalities, its size and complexity grows. Not only do we want to integrate components with each other, but at the same time, we also want to reuse components as much as possible. By learning the structural patterns described in this section, we have a template to follow when we encounter similar situations in our projects.

In this section, we will review the traditional object-oriented patterns, including the adapter, bridge, composite, decorator, facade, flyweight, and proxy patterns. Let's start with the adapter pattern.

The adapter pattern

The **adapter** pattern is used to make one object work with another. Say that we need to integrate two subsystems, but they cannot talk to each other because the interface requirements are not met. In real life, you may have encountered a situation where traveling to a different country is troublesome because the power plugs are not the same. To solve this problem, you would probably bring a universal power adapter, which acts as an intermediary to make your device work with foreign electrical outlets. Similarly, different software can be made to fit with each other by the use of adapters.

As long as the interface for working with a subsystem is clear, then creating an adapter can be a straightforward task. In Julia, we can use the Delegation pattern to wrap an object and provide additional functionalities that conform to the required interface.

Let's imagine that we are using a library that performs a computation and returns a linked list. A linked list is a convenient data structure that supports very fast inserts at O(1) speed. Now, say that we want to pass the data to another subsystem that requires us to conform to an `AbstractArray` interface. In this case, we cannot just pass the linked list as it does not fit!

How do we solve this problem? First, let me introduce the `LinkedList` implementation:

```julia
module LinkedList

export Node, list, prev, next, value

mutable struct Node{T}
    prev::Union{Node,Nothing}
    next::Union{Node,Nothing}
    value::T
end
```

This is a fairly standard design for a doubly-linked list. Each node contains a data value, but also maintains a reference to the node before and after. The typical usage of such a linked list is shown as follows:

```
julia> using .LinkedList

julia> LL = list(1);

julia> insert!(LL, 2);

julia> insert!(next(LL), 3);

julia> LL
Node: 1
Node: 2
Node: 3
```

In general, we can traverse the linked list by using the `prev` and `next` functions. The reason why we need to call `next(LL)` when inserting the value of 3 is because we want to insert it after the second node.

Because using a linked list does not implement the `AbstractArray` interface, we cannot really reference any element by index, nor can we figure out the number of elements:

```
julia> length(LL)
ERROR: MethodError: no method matching length(::Node{Int64})
Closest candidates are:
  length(::Core.SimpleVector) at essentials.jl:593
  length(::Base.MethodList) at reflection.jl:849
  length(::Core.MethodTable) at reflection.jl:923
  ...
Stacktrace:
 [1] top-level scope at REPL[10]:1

julia> LL[1]
ERROR: MethodError: no method matching getindex(::Node{Int64}, ::Int64)
Stacktrace:
 [1] top-level scope at REPL[11]:1
```

In this case, we can build a wrapper (or so-called adapter) that conforms to the `AbstractArray` interface. First, let's create a new type and make it a subtype of `AbstractArray`:

```
struct MyArray{T} <: AbstractArray{T,1}
    data::Node{T}
end
```

As we only need to support a single-dimension array, we have defined the supertype to be `AbstractArray{T,1}`. The underlying data is just a reference to the linked list `Node` object. In order to conform to the `AbstractArray` interface, we should implement the `Base.size` and `Base.getindex` functions. Here's what the `size` function looks like:

```
function Base.size(ar::MyArray)
    n = ar.data
    count = 0
    while next(n) !== nothing
        n = next(n)
        count += 1
    end
    return (1 + count, 1)
end
```

The function simply determines the length of the array by traversing the linked list using the `next` function. To support indexing elements, we can define the `getindex` function as follows:

```
function Base.getindex(ar::MyArray, idx::Int)
    n = ar.data
    for i in 1:(idx-1)
        next_node = next(n)
        next_node === nothing && throw(BoundsError(n.data, idx))
        n = next_node
    end
    return value(n)
end
```

That is all we need to do for the wrapper. Let's give it a spin now:

```
julia> ar = MyArray(LL)
3×1 MyArray{Int64}:
 1
 2
 3

julia> length(ar)
3

julia> ar[1]
1

julia> ar[end]
3
```

Now that we have an indexable array on top of the linked list, we can pass it to any library that expects arrays as input.

In the situation where mutation is required for the array, we can just implement the `Base.setindex!` function as well. Alternatively, we can physically convert the linked list into an array. An array has the performance characteristic of fast indexing at O(1), while being relatively slow for inserts.

Using an adapter allows us to make components talk to each other more easily. Next, we will discuss the composite pattern.

The composite pattern

The **composite** pattern is used to model objects that can be grouped together and yet be treated the same as individual objects. This is not an uncommon case—for example, in a drawing application, we might be able to draw different kinds of shapes, such as circles, rectangles, and triangles. Every shape has a position and size so we can determine where they are located on screen as well as how large they are. When we group several shapes together, we can still determine the position and size of the large, grouped object. Additionally, resize, rotate, and other transformation functions can be applied to individual shape objects as well as grouped objects.

A similar situation happens with portfolio management. I have a retirement investment account that is composed of multiple mutual funds. Each mutual fund may either invest in stocks, bonds, or both. Then, some funds may also invest in other mutual funds. From an accounting perspective, we can always determine the market value of a stock, a bond, a fund of stocks, a fund of bonds, and a fund of funds. In Julia, we can tackle this problem by just implementing a `market_value` function for different types of instruments, whether it is a stock, a bond, or a fund. Let's take a look at some code now.

Let's say we have the following type defined for stock/bond holdings:

```
struct Holding
    symbol::String
    qty::Int
    price::Float64
end
```

The `Holding` type contains a trading symbol, quantity, and current price. We can define a portfolio as follows:

```
struct Portfolio
    symbol::String
    name::String
    stocks::Vector{Holding}
```

```
        subportfolios::Vector{Portfolio}
    end
```

A portfolio is identified by a symbol, a name, an array of holdings, and an array of subportfolios. For testing, we can create a sample portfolio:

```
function sample_portfolio()
    large_cap = Portfolio("TOMKA", "Large Cap Portfolio", [
        Holding("AAPL", 100, 275.15),
        Holding("IBM", 200, 134.21),
        Holding("GOOG", 300, 1348.83)])

    small_cap = Portfolio("TOMKB", "Small Cap Portfolio", [
        Holding("ATO", 100, 107.05),
        Holding("BURL", 200, 225.09),
        Holding("ZBRA", 300, 257.80)])
    p1 = Portfolio("TOMKF", "Fund of Funds Sleeve", [large_cap, small_cap])
    p2 = Portfolio("TOMKG", "Special Fund Sleeve", [Holding("C", 200,
76.39)])
    return Portfolio("TOMZ", "Master Fund", [p1, p2])
end
```

The structure is visualized more clearly from an indented output:

```
Master Fund (TOMZ)
    Fund of Funds Sleeve (TOMKF)
        Large Cap Portfolio (TOMKA)
            Holdings:
                AAPL 100 shares @ $275.15
                IBM 200 shares @ $134.21
                GOOG 300 shares @ $1348.83
        Small Cap Portfolio (TOMKB)
            Holdings:
                ATO 100 shares @ $107.05
                BURL 200 shares @ $225.09
                ZBRA 300 shares @ $257.8
    Special Fund Sleeve (TOMKG)
        Holdings:
            C 200 shares @ $76.39
```

As we want to support the ability to calculate the market value at any level, we just need to define the market_value function for each type. The simplest one is for holdings:

```
market_value(s::Holding) = s.qty * s.price
```

The market value is nothing but quantity multiplied by price. The calculation of market value for a portfolio is just a little more involved:

```
market_value(p::Portfolio) =
    mapreduce(market_value, +, p.stocks, init = 0.0) +
    mapreduce(market_value, +, p.subportfolios, init = 0.0)
```

Here, we use the `mapreduce` function to calculate the market values of individual stocks (or `subportfolios`) and sum them up. As a portfolio may include multiple holdings and multiple `subportfolios`, we need to perform the calculation for both and add them together. As each subportfolio is also a `portfolio` object, this code naturally recurses deeper into sub-`subportfolios`, and so forth.

There is nothing fancy about composites. Because Julia supports generic functions, we can just provide an implementation for individual objects as well as grouped objects.

We will discuss the flyweight pattern next.

The flyweight pattern

The **flyweight** pattern is used to handle a large number of fine-grained objects efficiently by sharing memory for similar/same objects.

A good example of this involves handling strings. In the field of data science, we frequently need to read and analyze a large amount of data that is represented in a tabular format. In many cases, certain columns may contain a large number of strings that are just repeated values. For example, a population survey might have a column stating gender, and so it will contain either `Male` or `Female`.

Unlike some other programming languages, strings are not interned in Julia. This means that 10 copies of the word `Male` are going to be stored repeatedly, occupying 10 times the memory space that is used by a single string of `Male`. We can see this effect easily from the REPL, as follows:

```
julia> s = ["Male" for _ in 1:1_000];

julia> Base.summarysize(s)
8052

julia> s = ["Male" for _ in 1:100_000];

julia> Base.summarysize(s)
800052
```

So, storing 100,000 copies of a `Male` string occupies roughly 800 KB of memory. That is quite a waste of memory. A common way to solve this problem is to maintain a pooled array. Rather than storing 100,000 strings, we can just encode the data and store 100,000 bytes instead so that `0x01` corresponds to male and `0x00` corresponds to female. We can reduce the memory footprint eightfold by using `s` as follows:

```
julia> s = [0x01 for _ in 1:100_000];

julia> Base.summarysize(s)
100040
```

You may wonder why there are 40 extra bytes being reported. Those 40 bytes are actually used by the array container. Now, given that the gender column is binary in this case, we can actually squeeze it further by storing bits instead of bytes, as follows:

```
julia> s = BitArray(rand(Bool) for _ in 1:100_000);

julia> Base.summarysize(s)
12568
```

Again, we reduce the memory usage approximately eightfold (by going from 1 byte to 1 bit) by using `BitArray` to store the gender values. This is an aggressive optimization of memory usage. But we still need to store the `Male` and `Female` strings somewhere, right? This is an easy task because we know they can be tracked in any data structure, such as a dictionary:

```
julia> const gender_map = Dict(true => "Male", false => "Female")
Dict{Bool,String} with 2 entries:
  false => "Female"
  true  => "Male"

julia> Base.summarysize(gender_map)
370
```

To summarize, we are now capable of storing 100,000 gender values in 12,568 + 370 = 12,938 bytes of memory. Compared to the original dumb way of storing strings directly, we have saved more than 98% of memory consumption! How did we achieve such a huge saving? Because all records share the same two strings. The only data that we have to maintain is an array of references to those strings.

So, that is the concept of the flyweight pattern. The same trick is used over and over again in many places. For example, the `CSV.jl` package uses a package called `CategoricalArrays`, which provides essentially the same kind of memory optimization.

Next, we will go over the last few traditional patterns—bridge, decorator, and facade.

Bridge, decorator, and facade patterns

Let me explain how the bridge, decorator, and facade patterns work. At this point, we will not provide any more code samples for these patterns, only because they are relatively easy to implement, as you are already equipped with many ideas from prior design pattern sections. Perhaps not too surprisingly, the same tricks that you have learned so far—delegation, singleton type, multiple dispatch, first-class functions, abstract types, and interfaces—are the same ones that you can use to tackle any type of problem.

The **bridge** pattern is used to decouple an abstraction from its implementation so that it can evolve independently. In Julia, we can build a hierarchy of abstract types for which implementers can develop software that conforms to those interfaces.

Julia's numeric types are good examples of how such a system can be designed. There are many abstract types available, such as `Integer`, `AbstractFloat`, and `Real`. Then, there are concrete implementations, such as `Int` and `Float64`, provided by the `Base` package. The abstraction is designed in such a way that people can provide an alternative implementation of numbers. For example, the `SaferInteger` packages provide a safer implementation for integers that avoids numerical overflow.

The **decorator** pattern is also simple to implement. It can be used to enhance an existing object with new functionalities, hence the term *decorator*. Suppose that we have bought a third-party library, but we are not totally satisfied with the functionalities. Using the decorator pattern, we can add value by wrapping the existing library with new functions.

This can be done naturally using the Delegation pattern. By wrapping an existing type with a new type, we can reuse existing functionalities by delegating to the underlying object. Then, we can add new functions to the new type to gain new capabilities. We see this pattern used over and over again.

The **facade** pattern is used to encapsulate complex subsystems and provide a simplified interface for clients. How do we do that in Julia? By now, we should have seen this pattern over and over again; all we need to do is create a new type and provide a simple API that operates on the new type. We can use the Delegation pattern to forward requests to other enclosed types.

We have now looked at all traditional object-oriented patterns. You might have noticed that many of the use cases can be solved with the standard Julia features and patterns described in this book. This is not a coincidence—it is just that easy to deal with complex problems in Julia.

Summary

In this chapter, we have gone over the traditional object-oriented design patterns extensively. We started with the humble belief that the same patterns in object-oriented programming often need to be applied in Julia programming.

We started reviewing creational design patterns, which include the factory method, abstract factory, singleton, builder, and prototype patterns. These patterns involve various techniques for creating objects. When it comes to Julia, we can mostly solve these problems using abstract types, interfaces, and multiple dispatch.

We also spent a considerable amount of effort looking at behavioral design patterns. These patterns are made to handle collaboration and communication between components in an application. We looked at 11 patterns: chain of responsibility, mediator, memento, observer, state, strategy, template method, command, interpreter, iterator, and visitor. These patterns can be implemented in Julia using traits, interfaces, multiple dispatch, and first-class functions.

Finally, we reviewed several structural design patterns. These patterns are used to construct bigger components by reusing existing ones. This includes the adapter, composite, flyweight, bridge, decorator, and facade patterns. In Julia, they can be handled with abstract types, interfaces, and the delegation design pattern.

I hope you are convinced that building software does not need to be difficult. Just because OOP made us believe that we need all of this complexity to design software, it does not mean that we have to do the same in Julia. The solutions to the problems that are presented in this chapter mostly require the basic software design skills and patterns that you found in this book.

In the next chapter, we will get into a more advanced topic regarding data types and dispatch. *Get ready to rock!*

Questions

1. What technique can we use to implement the abstract factory pattern?
2. How do we prevent a singleton from being initialized multiple times in a multithreaded application?
3. What Julia feature is essential to implementing the observer pattern?
4. How can we customize an operation using the template method pattern?
5. How do we make an adapter to implement a target interface?
6. What is the benefit of the flyweight pattern and what strategy can we use to achieve it?
7. What Julia feature can we use to implement the strategy pattern?

Section 4: Advanced Topics

4

The aim of this section is to provide you with a more in-depth analysis of the Julia language. Understanding such advanced concepts will help you come up with better designs.

This section contains the following chapter:

- Chapter 12, *Inheritance and Variance*

12
Inheritance and Variance

If we had to choose the most important thing to learn in Julia, or in any programming language, then it has to be the concept of the data type. Abstract types and concrete types work together, providing the programmer with a powerful tool to model solutions to solve real-world problems. Multiple dispatch rely on well-defined data types to invoke the right functions. Parametric types are used so that we can reuse the basic structure of an object with a specific physical representation of the underlying data. As you can see, having a well-thought-out design for data types is of the utmost importance in software engineering practice.

In Chapter 2, *Modules, Packages, and Data Type Concepts*, we learned about the basics of abstract and concrete types and how to build a type hierarchy based upon an inheritance relationship between the types. In Chapter 3, *Designing Functions and Interfaces*, and Chapter 5, *Reusability Patterns*, we also touched on the subject of parametric types and parametric methods. In order to utilize these concepts and language features effectively, we need a good understanding of how *subtyping* works. It may sound similar to inheritance, but it is fundamentally different.

In this chapter, we will go deeper and explore the meaning of subtyping and related topics, which includes the following topics:

- Implementation inheritance and behavior subtyping
- Covariance, contravariance, and invariance
- Parametric methods and diagonal rule

By the end of this chapter, you will have a good understanding of subtyping in Julia. You will be more equipped to design your own data type hierarchy and utilize multiple dispatch more effectively.

Technical requirements

The sample source code is located at `https://github.com/PacktPublishing/Hands-on-Design-Patterns-and-Best-Practices-with-Julia/tree/master/Chapter12`.

The code is tested in a Julia 1.3.0 environment.

Implementing inheritance and behavior subtyping

When we learned about inheritance, we realized that abstract types can be used to describe real-world concepts. We can say quite confidently that we already know how to classify concepts with parent–child relationships. With this knowledge, we can build a type hierarchy around those concepts. For example, the personal asset type hierarchy from `Chapter 2`, *Modules, Packages, and Data Type Concepts*, looks like the following:

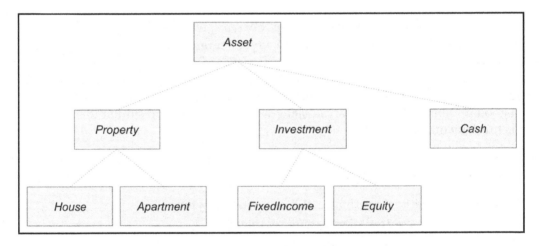

All data types shown in the preceding diagram are abstract types. Going from the bottom up, we know that both **House** and **Apartment** are subtypes of **Property**, and we know that both **Property** and **Investment** are a subtype of **Asset**. These are all reasonable interpretations based on how we speak about these concepts in our daily life.

We also talked about concrete types that are the physical realization of abstract concepts. For this same example, we ended up having `Stock` as a subtype of `Equity` and `Bond` as a subtype of `FixedIncome`. As you may recall, the `Stock` type can be defined as follows:

```
struct Stock <: Equity
    symbol::String
    name::String
end
```

Back then, we did not emphasize the fact that we cannot declare any field inside abstract types, which is something that is given in some **object-oriented programming** (OOP) languages, such as Java. If you come from an OOP background, then you may mistakenly feel that this is a huge constraint in Julia's inheritance system. Why is Julia designed the way it is? In this section, we will try to analyze inheritance in greater depth and answer this very question.

There are two important concepts related to inheritance that are very similar, but fundamentally different—implementation inheritance and behavior subtyping. We will discuss both in the next few sections. Let's start with implementation inheritance.

Understanding implementation inheritance

Implementation inheritance allows a subclass to inherit *both* fields and methods from its superclass. As Julia does not support implementation inheritance, we will switch language for a moment and present the following example in Java. Here is a class that provides a container for holding any number of objects:

```java
import java.util.ArrayList;

public class Bag
{
    ArrayList<Object> items = new ArrayList<Object>();

    public void add(final Object object) {
        this.items.add(object);
    }

    public void addMany(final Object[] objects) {
        for (Object obj : objects) {
            this.add(obj);
        }
    }
}
```

The Bag class basically maintains a list of objects in the items field and provides two convenient functions, add and addMany, for adding a single object or an array of objects to the bag.

To demonstrate code reuse, we can develop a new CountingBag class that inherits from Bag and provides additional functionality for keep tracking of how many items are stored in the bag:

```
public class CountingBag extends Bag
{
    int count = 0;

    public void add(Object object) {
        super.add(object);
        this.count += 1;
    }

    public int size() {
        return count;
    }
}
```

In this CountingBag class, we have a new field called count to keep track of the bag size. Whenever a new item is added to the bag, the count variable is incremented. The size function is used to report the size of the bag. So what is the situation with CountingBag? Let's quickly summarize:

- The count field is available as defined here.
- The items field is available as inherited from Bag.
- The add method overrides the parent's implementation, but it also reuses the parent's method via super.add.
- The addMany method is available as inherited from Bag.
- The size method is available as defined here.

As both fields and methods are inherited, this is called implementation inheritance. The effect is almost the same as if the code from the superclass was copied into the subclass.

Next, let's talk about behavior subtyping.

Understanding behavior subtyping

Behavior subtyping is sometimes called interface inheritance. In order to avoid confusion with the overloaded word *inheritance*, we will avoid using the term interface inheritance here. Behavior subtyping says that a subtype only inherits behaviors from the supertype.

> As we switch the language back to Julia, we will refer to *types* rather than *classes*.

Julia supports behavior subtyping. Every data type inherits functions that are defined for its supertype. Let's try a quick and fun exercise in the Julia REPL:

```
julia> abstract type Vehicle end

julia> struct Car <: Vehicle end

julia> move(v::Vehicle) = "$v has moved.";

julia> car = Car();

julia> move(car)
"Car() has moved."
```

Here, an abstract type, `Vehicle`, is defined with a subtype of `Car`. We have also defined a `move` function for `Vehicle`. When we pass a `Car` object to the `move` function, it still works properly because `Car` is a subtype of `Vehicle`. This is consistent with the Liskov substitution principle, which says that a program accepting type T can also accept any subtype of T and continue to work properly without any unintended outcome.

Now, the inheritance of a method can travel quite far over multiple levels. Let's create another level of abstraction:

```
julia> abstract type FlyingVehicle <: Vehicle end

julia> liftoff(v::FlyingVehicle) = "$v has lifted off.";

julia> struct Helicopter <: FlyingVehicle end

julia> helicopter = Helicopter();

julia> move(helicopter)
"Helicopter() has moved."

julia> liftoff(helicopter)
"Helicopter() has lifted off."
```

We just defined a new `FlyingVehicle` abstract type and a `Helicopter` struct. The `move` function is available for a helicopter as inherited from `Vehicle`, and the `liftoff` function is also available, as inherited from `FlyingVehicle`.

Additional methods can be defined for more specific types, and the most specific one would be chosen for dispatch. Doing this essentially has the same effect as method overrides in implementation inheritance. Here's an example:

```julia
julia> liftoff(h::Helicopter) = "$h has lifted off vertically.";

julia> liftoff(helicopter)
"Helicopter() has lifted off vertically."
```

So far, we have defined two `liftoff` methods—one accepting `FlyingVehicle` and another for `Helicopter`. When a `Helicopter` object is passed to the function, it is dispatched to the one defined for `Helicopter`, because it is the most specific method that works with helicopters.

The relationship can be summarized in the following diagram:

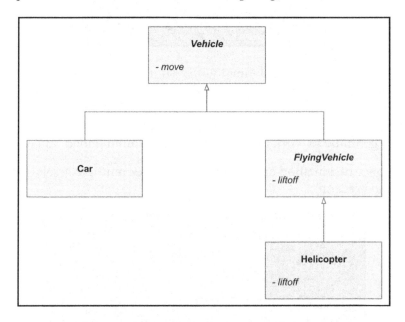

According to behavior subtyping, a car should behave like a vehicle, a flying vehicle should behave like a vehicle, and a helicopter should behave like a flying vehicle and also like a vehicle. Behavior subtyping allows us to reuse the behavior already defined for a supertype.

In Java, behavior subtyping can be achieved using interfaces.

Now that we know about implementation inheritance and behavior subtyping, we can revisit our earlier question: why does Julia not support implementation inheritance? What are the reasons for not following other mainstream OOP languages? In order to understand this, we can review some of the well-known issues with implementation inheritance. Let's start with the square-rectangle problem.

The square-rectangle problem

Julia does not support implementation inheritance. Let's list the reasons:

- All concrete types are final, so there is no way to create new subtypes from another concrete type. Therefore, it is not possible to inherit object fields from anywhere.
- You cannot declare any field in an abstract type because otherwise, it would be concrete rather than abstract.

The core developers of the Julia programming language made a very early design decision to avoid implementation inheritance for a number of reasons. One of them is the so-called *square-rectangle problem*, also sometimes called the circle-ellipse problem.

The square-rectangle problem presents a clear challenge for implementation inheritance. As we know by common sense, every square is a rectangle with an additional constraint that the length of both sides is equal. In order to model these concepts in a class-based, object-oriented language, we may attempt to create a `Rectangle` class and a `Square` subclass:

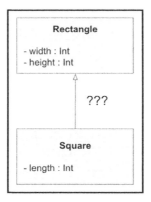

Very quickly, we realize that we have already gotten ourselves into trouble. If a `Square` has to inherit all fields from its parent class, then it would have inherited both `width` and `height`. But we really want to have a single field called `length` instead.

 The exact same issue is sometimes presented as the circle–ellipse problem. In that case, a circle is an ellipse, but there is only one radius rather than major and minor axis lengths.

How do we solve this kind of problem? Well, one way is to ignore the issue and create a `Square` subclass without any field defined. Then, when a `Square` is instantiated with a particular length, both `width` and `height` fields are populated with the same value. Is that good enough? The answer is no. Given that `Square` also inherits the methods of `Rectangle`, we probably need to provide override methods for the mutating methods, such as `setWidth` and `setHeight`, so that we can keep both fields with the same value. In the end, we have a solution that seems to work functionally but is terrible in performance and memory usage.

But how did we get into trouble in the first place? To analyze this further, we should realize that a square, while it can be classified as a rectangle, is a more restrictive version of a rectangle in nature. This is already starting to sound unintuitive—typically, when we create subclasses, we extend the parent class and *add* more fields and functionalities. When do we want to remove fields or functionality in subclasses? It already seems to be logically backward. Maybe we should make `Rectangle` a subclass of `Square`? That does not sound very logical either.

We end up with a conundrum. On one hand, we would like to model real-world concepts properly in code. On the other hand, the code does not really fit without causing maintenance or performance issues. By now, we cannot help but ask ourselves whether we really want to write code to work around problems with implementation inheritance. We don't.

Perhaps you are not yet 100% convinced that implementation inheritance is more evil than good. Let's look at another problem.

The fragile base class problem

Another problem with implementation inheritance is that changes to the base class (parent class) can possibly break functionalities of its subclasses. From the earlier Java example, we have a `CountingBag` class that extends from the `Bag` class. Let's look at the complete source code, including the `main` function:

```
public class CountingBag extends Bag
{
    int count = 0;

    public void add(Object object) {
        super.add(object);
        this.count += 1;
    }

    public int size() {
        return count;
    }

    public String toString() {
        return super.toString();
    }

    public static void main(String[] args) {
        CountingBag cbag = new CountingBag();
        cbag.add("apple");
        cbag.addMany(new Object[] { "banana", "orange"});
        System.out.println(cbag.toString());
        System.out.print("=> has ");
        System.out.print(cbag.size());
        System.out.println(" items.");
    }
}
```

The program simply creates a `CountingBag` object. Then it adds `apple` using the `add` method and adds `banana` and `orange` using the `addMany` method. Finally, it prints out the items in the bag and the size of the bag. The output is shown in the following code:

```
$ java CountingBag
Bag: apple,banana,orange
=> has 3 items.
```

Everything looks fine at the moment. But let's say that the original author of `Bag` realizes that the `addMany` method can be improved by directly adding objects into the `items` array list:

```
public void addMany(final Object[] objects) {          public void addMany(final Object[] objects) {
    for (Object obj : objects) {    An improvement         for (Object obj: objects) {
        this.add(obj);         ──────────────────────▶        this.items.add(obj);
    }                                                      }
}                                                      }
```

[465]

Unfortunately, this seemingly safe change in the parent class ends up in a disaster for
`CountingBag`:

What happened? When `CountingBag` was designed, it was assumed that the `add` method
would always be called when new items are added to the bag. When the `addMany` method
stops calling the `add` method, the assumption no longer applies.

Whose fault is this? Of course, the designer of the `Bag` class cannot foresee who will inherit
the class. The change in the `addMany` method did not violate any contract; the same
functionality is provided, only with a different implementation under the hood. The
designer of the `CountingBag` class thought it was wise to *tag along* and leverage the fact
that `addMany` was already calling the `add` method, and so only the `add` method needed to
be overridden to make `counting` work.

This poses a second issue with implementation inheritance. The subclass developer has too
much knowledge about the implementation of the parent class. The ability to override the
parent class's `add` method has also violated the principle of encapsulation.

How does OOP solve this problem? In Java, there are multiple facilities to prevent the
problem presented in the preceding example:

- A method can be annotated with the `final` keyword to prevent the subclass
  from overriding the method.
- A field can be annotated with the `private` keyword to prevent the subclass from
  accessing the field.

The trouble is that the developer must *anticipate* how classes are going to be inherited *in the
future*. Methods must be carefully examined to determine whether it is safe to allow
subclasses to access or override. Likewise for fields. As you can see, the problem is called
the fragile base class problem for a good reason.

I hope we have shown you that implementation inheritance does more harm than good. For
reference, in the GoF design patterns book, it was also suggested that composition is
preferred over inheritance. Julia took a more radical approach by just disallowing
implementation inheritance altogether.

Next, we will go a little further and look at a specific kind of behavior subtyping called
duck typing.

Revisiting duck typing

There are two ways to implement behavior subtyping: **nominal subtyping** and **structural subtyping**:

- With nominal subtyping, you must explicitly define the relationship between a type and its supertype. Julia uses nominal subtyping, where types are explicitly annotated in function arguments. That is why a type hierarchy needs to be built to express type relationships.
- With structural subtyping, the relationship is implicitly derived as long as the subtype implements the required functions from the supertype. Julia supports structural subtyping when functions are defined with arguments and not annotated with any type.

Julia supports structural subtyping via **duck typing**. We first mentioned duck typing in Chapter 3, *Designing Functions and Interfaces*. The saying is as follows:

> *"If it walks like a duck and quacks like a duck, then it is a duck."*

In a dynamic type language, we sometimes care less about the exact type as long as we get the behavior we want. If we just want to hear a quack sound, who cares if we get a frog? As long as it makes that quack sound, we will be happy.

Sometimes, we want duck typing for good reasons. For example, we do not normally consider horses as vehicles; however, think about the old days when horses were used for transport. In our definition, anything that implements the move function can be considered a vehicle. So, if we have any algorithm that needs something that moves, then there is no reason why we cannot pass a horse object to the algorithm:

```julia
julia> abstract type Animal end

julia> struct Horse <: Animal end

julia> move(h::Horse) = "$h running fast.";

julia> horse = Horse();

julia> move(horse)
"Horse() running fast."
```

For some people, duck typing is a little loose because you cannot easily figure out whether a type supports an interface (such as move). The general remedy is to use the Holy Trait pattern as described in Chapter 5, *Reusability Patterns*.

Next, we will look at an important concept called variance.

Covariance, invariance, and contravariance

As it turns out, the rules for subtyping are not very straightforward. When you look at a simple type hierarchy, you can immediately tell whether one type is a subtype of another by tracing the relationships of the data types in the hierarchy. The situation becomes more complex when parametric types are involved. In this section, we will take a look at how Julia is designed with respect to **variance**, a concept that explains subtyping relationships for parametric types.

Let's first review the different kinds of variance.

Understanding different kinds of variance

There are four different kinds of variance as described in computer science literature. We will first describe them in a formal manner first and then come back to do more hands-on exercises to reinforce our understanding.

Given that `S` is a subtype of `T`, there are four different ways to reason about the relationship between parametric types `P{S}` and `P{T}`:

- Covariant: `P{S}` is a subtype of `P{T}` (`co` here means the same direction)
- Contravariant: `P{T}` is a subtype of `P{S}` (`contra` here means the opposite direction)
- Invariant: neither covariant nor contravariant
- Bivariant: both covariant and contravariant

When do we find variance useful? Perhaps not too surprisingly, variance is a key ingredient whenever multiple dispatch come into action. Based on the Liskov substitution principle, the language runtime must figure out whether the object being passed is a subtype of the method argument before dispatching to the method.

Interestingly, variance is one thing that often diverges between different programming languages. Sometimes, there are historical reasons for this, and sometimes it depends on the target use cases for the language. In the next few sections, we will explore the topic from several angles. We will start with parametric types.

Parametric types are invariant

For the purposes of illustration, we will consider a popular type hierarchy that is used by some of the OOP literature— the animal kingdom! Everyone loves cats and dogs. I have also included crocodiles here to explain related concepts:

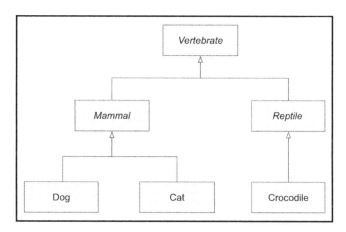

The corresponding code to build such a hierarchy is as follows:

```
abstract type Vertebrate end
abstract type Mammal <: Vertebrate end
abstract type Reptile <: Vertebrate end

struct Cat <: Mammal
    name
end

struct Dog <: Mammal
    name
end

struct Crocodile <: Reptile
    name
end
```

For convenience, we can also define the show function for these new types:

```
Base.show(io::IO, cat::Cat) = print(io, "Cat ", cat.name)
Base.show(io::IO, dog::Dog) = print(io, "Dog ", dog.name)
Base.show(io::IO, croc::Crocodile) = print(io, "Crocodile ", croc.name)
```

Given such a type hierarchy, we can verify how subtypes are handled with the following `adopt` function. As nobody wants to adopt crocodiles (well, not me at least), we are restricting the function argument to subtypes of `Mammal` only:

```julia
function adopt(m::Mammal)
    println(m, " is now adopted.")
    return m
end
```

As expected, we can adopt only cats and dogs, but not crocodiles:

```
julia> adopt(Cat("Felix"));
Cat Felix is now adopted.

julia> adopt(Dog("Clifford"));
Dog Clifford is now adopted.

julia> adopt(Crocodile("Solomon"));
ERROR: MethodError: no method matching adopt(::Crocodile)
Closest candidates are:
  adopt(::Mammal) at REPL[12]:3
```

What if we want to adopt many pets at the same time? Intuitively, we can just define a new function that takes an array of mammals, as follows:

```julia
adopt(ms::Array{Mammal,1}) = "adopted " * string(ms)
```

Unfortunately, it already failed our very first test for adopting Felix and Garfield:

```
julia> adopt([Cat("Felix"), Cat("Garfield")])
ERROR: MethodError: no method matching adopt(::Array{Cat,1})
Closest candidates are:
  adopt(::Array{Mammal,1}) at REPL[18]:1
  adopt(::Mammal) at REPL[13]:3
```

What is going on? We know cats are mammals, so why would an array of cats not be passed to the method that takes an array of mammals? The answer is simple—parametric types are invariant. Here comes the very first surprise for people coming from an OOP background, for which parametric types are often covariant.

By invariance, even though `Cat` is a subtype of `Mammal`, we cannot say that `Array{Cat,1}` is a subtype of `Array{Mammal,1}`. In addition, an `Array{Mammal,1}` actually represents a one-dimensional array of `Mammal` objects, for which each object can be any subtype of `Mammal`. As each concrete type may have different memory layout requirements, this array must store pointers rather than actual values. Another way to say this is that the objects are *boxed*.

In order to dispatch to this method, we must create an `Array{Mammal,1}`. This can be achieved by prefixing the array constructor with `Mammal`, as follows:

```
adopt(Mammal[Cat("Felix"), Cat("Garfield")])
```

In practice, this happens a lot more often when we have to handle an array of objects of the same type. In Julia, we can express such a homogeneous array using the type expression `Array{T,1} where T`. This means that we can define a new `adopt` method that can accept multiple mammals as long as they are the same kind:

```
function adopt(ms::Array{T,1}) where {T <: Mammal}
    return "accepted same kind:" * string(ms)
end
```

Let's test the new `adopt` method now. The results are shown in the following code:

```
julia> adopt([Cat("Felix"), Cat("Garfield")])
"accepted same kind:Cat[Cat Felix, Cat Garfield]"

julia> adopt([Dog("Clifford"), Dog("Astro")])
"accepted same kind:Dog[Dog Clifford, Dog Astro]"

julia> adopt([Cat("Felix"), Dog("Clifford")])
"adopted Mammal[Cat Felix, Dog Clifford]"
```

As expected, the new `adopt` method was dispatched accordingly, depending on whether the array contains `Mammal` pointers or physical values of cats or dogs.

In Julia, the choice of making parametric types invariant is a conscious design decision for practical reasons. When an array contains concrete type objects, the memory can be allocated to store these objects in a very compact manner. On the other hand, when an array contains boxed objects, every reference to an element would involve dereferencing a pointer to find the object, and performance would suffer as a result.

There is indeed one place where Julia uses covariance, that is, method arguments. We will discuss these next.

Method arguments are covariant

It should be quite intuitive that method arguments are covariant because that is how multiple dispatch work today. Consider the following function:

```
friend(m::Mammal, f::Mammal) = "$m and $f become friends."
```

In Julia, method arguments are formally represented as a tuple. In the preceding example, the method argument is just `Tuple{Mammal,Mammal}`.

When we call this function with two arguments that have type `S` and `T` respectively, then it will only be dispatched if `S <: Mammal` and `T <: Mammal`. In this case, we should be able to pass any combination of mammals—dog/dog, dog/cat, cat/dog, and cat/cat. The following screenshot proves this:

```
julia> Tuple{Cat,Cat} <: Tuple{Mammal,Mammal}
true

julia> Tuple{Cat,Dog} <: Tuple{Mammal,Mammal}
true

julia> Tuple{Dog,Cat} <: Tuple{Mammal,Mammal}
true

julia> Tuple{Dog,Dog} <: Tuple{Mammal,Mammal}
true
```

Let's also check whether a crocodile can join the party:

```
julia> Tuple{Cat,Crocodile} <: Tuple{Mammal,Mammal}
false
```

As expected, `Tuple{Cat,Crocodile}` is not a subtype of `Tuple{Mammal,Mammal}` since `Crocodile` is not a `Mammal`.

Next, let's move on to a more complex scenario. As we know, functions are first-class citizens in Julia. How do we determine whether a function is a subtype of another function during dispatch?

Dissecting function types

In Julia, functions are first class. This means that functions can be passed around as variables and can appear in method arguments. Since we have learned about the covariance property of method arguments, how do we handle the situation where functions are passed as arguments?

The best way to understand this is to see how functions are typically passed. Let's pick a simple example from Base:

```
[julia> all(
all(x::Tuple{Bool,Bool,Bool}) in Base at tuple.jl:390
all(x::Tuple{Bool,Bool}) in Base at tuple.jl:389
all(x::Tuple{Bool}) in Base at tuple.jl:388
all(x::Tuple{}) in Base at tuple.jl:387
all(B::BitArray) in Base at bitarray.jl:1627
all(a::AbstractArray; dims) in Base at reducedim.jl:664
all(f::Function, a::AbstractArray; dims) in Base at reducedim.jl:665
all(itr) in Base at reduce.jl:642
all(f, itr) in Base at reduce.jl:724
```

The `all` function can be used to check whether a certain condition is evaluated as `true` for all elements in an array. To make it more flexible, it can accept a custom predicate function. For example, we can check whether all numbers are odd in an array as follows:

```
[julia> all(isodd, [1, 2, 3, 4, 5])
false
```

Although we know it was dispatched correctly, we can also confirm that the type of `isodd` is a subtype of `Function` as follows:

```
[julia> typeof(isodd) <: Function
true
```

It turns out that all Julia functions have their own unique type, displayed as `typeof(isodd)` in the following code, and they all have a supertype of `Function`:

```
[julia> typeof(isodd)
typeof(isodd)

[julia> typeof(isodd) |> supertype
Function

[julia> isabstracttype(Function)
true
```

Because the `all` method was defined to accept any `Function` objects, we can actually pass any function and Julia will gladly dispatch to the method. Unfortunately, this can potentially lead to undesirable results, as shown in the following screenshot:

```
[julia> typeof(println) <: Function
true

[julia> all(println, [1, 2, 3, 4, 5])
1
ERROR: TypeError: non-boolean (Nothing) used in boolean context
```

We are getting an error here because the function being passed to `all` is supposed to take an element and return a Boolean value. Since `println` always returns `nothing`, the `all` function just raised an exception.

In the case that a stronger type is demanded, the specific function type can be enforced as such. Here is how we can create a safer `all` function:

```
const SignFunctions = Union{typeof(isodd),typeof(iseven)};
myall(f::SignFunctions, a::AbstractArray) = all(f, a);
```

The `SignFunctions` constant is a union type that consists of only the types for the `isodd` and `iseven` functions. As such, the `myall` method will only be dispatched when the first argument is `isodd` or `iseven`; otherwise, a method error will be raised, as shown in the following screenshot:

```
julia> myall(isodd, [1, 3, 5])
true

julia> myall(iseven, [2, 4, 6])
true

julia> myall(println, [2, 4, 6])
ERROR: MethodError: no method matching myall(::typeof(println),
::Array{Int64,1})
```

Of course, doing this severely limits the usefulness of the function. We must also enumerate all possible functions that may be passed, and that is not always feasible. So it seems that the means to handle function arguments is somewhat limited.

Coming back to the topic of variance, there is really nothing to talk about when all functions are final and there is only one supertype for all of them.

In practice, when we design software, we do care about the types of functions. As shown in the preceding example, the `all` function can only work with functions that take a single argument and return a Boolean value. That should be the interface contract. How do we enforce that contract, though? At the end of the day, we need to have a better understanding of functions and the contractual agreement between the caller and callee. The contract can be seen as a combination of method arguments and return types. Let's figure out whether there is a better way to handle this issue in the next section.

Determining the variance of the function type

In this section, we will attempt to understand how to reason about function types. While Julia does not provide too much help in formalizing function types, it does not stop us from doing the analysis ourselves. In some strongly typed, static OOP languages, function types are more formally defined as the combination of method arguments and return type.

Suppose that a function takes three arguments and returns a single value. Then we can describe the function with the following notation:

$$Tuple\langle T1, T2, T3 \rangle \rightarrow T4$$

Let's continue the animal kingdom example and define some new variables and functions, as follows:

```
female_dogs = [Dog("Pinky"), Dog("Pinny"), Dog("Moonie")]
female_cats = [Cat("Minnie"), Cat("Queenie"), Cat("Kittie")]

select(::Type{Dog}) = rand(female_dogs)
select(::Type{Cat}) = rand(female_cats)
```

Here, we have defined two arrays—one for female dogs and another for female cats. The `select` function can be used to randomly select a dog or cat. Next, let's consider the following function:

```
match(m::Mammal) = select(typeof(m))
```

The `match` function takes a `Mammal` and returns an object of the same type. Here's how it works:

```
julia> match(Dog("Astro"))
Dog Moonie

julia> match(Cat("Garfield"))
Cat Kittie
```

Given that the `match` function can only return `Dog` or `Cat`, we can reason the function type as follows:

$$Tuple\langle Mammal \rangle \rightarrow Mammal$$

Suppose that we define two more functions, as follows:

```
# It's ok to kiss mammals :-)
kiss(m::Mammal) = "$m kissed!"

# Meet a partner
function meet_partner(finder::Function, self::Mammal)
    partner = finder(self)
    kiss(partner)
end
```

The `meet_partner` function takes a `finder` function as the first argument. Then, it calls the `finder` function to find a partner and finally `kiss` the partner. By design, we are going to pass the `match` function that we defined in the preceding code. Let's see how it works:

```
julia> meet_partner(match, Cat("Felix"))
"Cat Kittie kissed!"
```

So far, so good. From the perspective of the `meet_partner` function, it expects the `finder` function to accept a `Mammal` argument and returns a `Mammal` object. That is exactly how the `match` function was designed. Now, let's see if we can mess it up by defining a function that does not return a mammal:

```
neighbor(m::Mammal) = Crocodile("Solomon")
```

Although the `neighbor` function can take a mammal as an argument, it returns a crocodile, which is a reptile rather than a mammal. If we try to pass it to the `meet_partner` function, we are met with disaster:

```
julia> meet_partner(neighbor, Cat("Felix"))
ERROR: MethodError: no method matching kiss(::Crocodile)
Closest candidates are:
  kiss(::Mammal) at REPL[37]:2
```

What we have just proven is quite intuitive. As the return type of the `finder` function is expected to be a `Mammal`, any other `finder` function that returns any subtype of `Mammal` would also work. So the return type of function types is covariant.

Now, what about the arguments of function types? Again, the `meet_partner` function is expected to pass any mammal to the `finder` function. The `finder` function must be able to accept either a `dog` or `cat` object. It would not work if the `finder` function only takes a cat or dog. Let's see what happens if we have a more restrictive `finder` function:

```
buddy(cat::Cat) = rand([Dog("Astro"), Dog("Goofy"), Cat("Lucifer")])
```

Here, the `buddy` function takes a cat and returns a mammal. If we passed it to the `meet_partner` function, then it would not work when we want to find a partner for our dog `Chef`:

```julia
julia> meet_partner(buddy, Cat("Felix"))
"Cat Lucifer kissed!"

julia> meet_partner(buddy, Dog("Chef"))
ERROR: MethodError: no method matching buddy(::Dog)
Closest candidates are:
  buddy(::Cat) at REPL[67]:14
```

So the arguments of function types are not covariant. Could it be contravariant? Well, to be contravariant, the `finder` function must accept a supertype of `Mammal`. In our animal kingdom, the only supertype is `Vertebrate`; however, `Vertebrate` is an abstract type and it cannot be constructed. If we instantiate any other concrete type that is a subtype of `Vertebrate`, it would not be a mammal (otherwise, it would be considered a mammal already). Therefore, function arguments are invariant.

Stated more formally, this looks as follows:

$$f : Tuple\langle Mammal \rangle \rightarrow Mammal$$

$$g : Tuple\langle T \rangle \rightarrow S \ where \ T = Mammal, \ S <: Mammal$$

Function `g` is a subtype of function `f`, as long as `T` is `Mammal` and `S` is a subtype of `Mammal`. There is a saying about this: *"Be liberal in what you accept and conservative in what you produce."*

While it is fun doing this kind of analysis, do we gain anything, given that the Julia runtime does not support function types as granular as those we have seen? It seems to be possible to simulate a type-checking effect on our own, which is the topic of the next section.

Implementing our own function type dispatch

As we have seen earlier in this section, Julia creates a unique function type for every function, and they are all subtypes of the `Function` abstract type. We seem to be missing an opportunity for multiple dispatch. Taking the `all` function from `Base` as an example, it would be very nice if we could design a type that represents predicate functions rather than letting `all` fail miserably when an incompatible function is passed.

In order to work around this limitation, let's define a parametric type called
`PredicateFunction` as follows:

```
struct PredicateFunction{T,S}
    f::Function
end
```

The `PredicateFunction` parametric type just wraps a function `f`. The type parameters `T`
and `S` are used to represent the types of function arguments and return a type of `f`
respectively. As an example, the `iseven` function can be wrapped as follows, because we
know the function can take a number and return a Boolean value:

```
PredicateFunction{Number,Bool}(iseven)
```

Conveniently, since Julia supports callable structs, we can make it so that
the `PredicateFunction` struct can be invoked as if it was a function itself. To enable this,
we can define the following function:

```
(pred::PredicateFunction{T,S})(x::T; kwargs...) where {T,S} =
    pred.f(x; kwargs...)
```

As you can see, this function merely forwards the call to the `pred.f` wrapped function.
Once it is defined, we can do some small experiments to see how it works:

```
julia> PredicateFunction{Number,Bool}(iseven)(1)
false

julia> PredicateFunction{Number,Bool}(iseven)(2)
true
```

That looks pretty good. Let's define our own *safe* version of the `all` function as follows:

```
function safe_all(pred::PredicateFunction{T,S}, a::AbstractArray) where
    {T <: Any,  S <: Bool}
    all(pred, a)
end
```

The `safe_all` function takes a `PredicteFunction{T,S}` as the first argument, with the
constraint that `T` is a subtype of `Any` and `S` is a subtype of `Bool`. It's exactly the function
type signature we want for predicate functions. Knowing that `Number <: Any` and `Bool
<: Bool`, we can definitely pass the `iseven` function to `safe_all`. Let's test it now:

```
julia> safe_all(PredicateFunction{Number,Bool}(iseven), [2,4,6])
true

julia> safe_all(PredicateFunction{Number,Bool}(iseven), [2,4,6,7])
false
```

Bravo! We have created a safe version of the `all` function. The first argument must be a predicate function that takes anything and returns a Boolean value. Rather than taking a generic `Function` argument, we can now enforce strict type matching and participate in multiple dispatch.

That is enough about variance. Next, we will move on and revisit the rules for the parametric method dispatch.

Parametric methods revisited

The ability to dispatch to various methods based upon subtyping relationships is a key feature of the Julia language. We initially introduced the concept of parametric methods in `Chapter 3`, *Designing Functions and Interfaces*. In this section, we will go a little deeper and examine some subtle situations about how methods are selected for dispatch.

Let's start with the basics: how do we specify type variables for parametric methods?

Specifying type variables

When we define a parametric method, we use the `where` clause to introduce type variables. Let's go over a simple example:

```
triple(x::Array{T,1}) where {T <: Real} = 3x
```

The `triple` function takes an `Array{T}`, where `T` is any subtype of `Real`. This code is very readable, and it is the format that most Julia developers choose to specify type parameters. So what could the value of `T` be? Could it be a concrete type, abstract type, or both?

To answer this question, we can test it out from the REPL:

```
julia> triple([1,2,3])
3-element Array{Int64,1}:
 3
 6
 9

julia> triple(Real[1,2,3.0])
3-element Array{Real,1}:
 3
 6
 9.0
```

So the method does get dispatched on both the abstract type (`Real`) and concrete type (`Int64`). It is worth mentioning that the `where` clause can also be placed right next to the method argument:

```
triple(x::Array{T,1} where {T <: Real}) = 3x
```

From a functional perspective, it is the same as before, whether the `where` clause is placed inside or outside.

There are some subtle differences, however. When the `where` clause is placed outside, you gain two additional benefits:

- The type variable `T` is accessible inside the method body.
- The type variable `T` can be used to enforce the same values if it is used for multiple method arguments.

It turns out that the second point leads to an interesting feature in Julia's dispatch system. We will go over this next.

Matching type variables

Whenever a type variable occurs more than once in a method signature, it is used to enforce the same type as determined across all positions where it occurs. Consider the following function:

```
add(a::Array{T,1}, x::T) where {T <: Real} = (T, a .+ x)
```

The `add` function takes an `Array{T}` and a value of type `T`. It returns a tuple of `T` and the result of adding the value to the array. Intuitively, we want the type `T` to be consistent across both arguments. In other words, we would want the function to be specialized in each of the realizations of `T` when the function is called. Obviously, the function works great when the type agrees:

```
julia> add([1,2,3], 1)
(Int64, [2, 3, 4])

julia> add([1.0,2.0,3.0], 1.0)
(Float64, [2.0, 3.0, 4.0])
```

In the first case, `T` is determined to be `Int64`, and in the second case, `T` is determined to be `Float64`. Perhaps not too surprisingly, we may get a method error when the types do not match:

```
julia> add([1,2,3], 1.0)
ERROR: MethodError: no method matching add(::Array{Int64,1}, ::Float64)
Closest candidates are:
  add(::Array{T,1}, ::T) where T<:Real at REPL[19]:1
```

Since we said that T could be an abstract type, could we dispatch to this method, as T could be considered Real? The answer is no, because parametric types are *invariant*! An array of Real objects is not the same as an array of Int64 values. More formally, Array{Int} is not a subtype of Array{Real}.

It gets a little more interesting when T is an abstract type in the array. Let's try this:

```
julia> add(Signed[1,2,3], Int8(1))
(Signed, [2, 3, 4])
```

Here, T is unambiguously set to Signed, and because Int8 is a subtype of Signed, the method is dispatched properly.

Next, we will look into another unique typing feature called the diagonal rule.

Understanding the diagonal rule

As we learned earlier, it is a nice feature to be able to match type variables and keep them consistent across method arguments. In practice, there are situations where we want to be even more specific when determining the right type for each type variable.

Consider this function:

```
diagonal(x::T, y::T) where {T <: Number} = T
```

The diagonal function takes two arguments with the same type, where the type T must be a subtype of Number. The type variable T is simply returned to the caller.

When T is concrete, it is easy to reason that the types are consistent. For example, we can pass a pair of Int64 values or a pair of Float64 values to the function and expect to see the respective concrete type returned:

```
julia> diagonal(1, 2)
Int64

julia> diagonal(1.0, 2.0)
Float64
```

Intuitively, we also expect this to fail when the types are not consistent:

```julia
julia> diagonal(1, 2.0)
ERROR: MethodError: no method matching diagonal(::Int64, ::Float64)
Closest candidates are:
  diagonal(::T, ::T) where T<:Number at REPL[5]:1
```

While it seems to work intuitively, we could have argued that the type variable T is an abstract type, such as Real. Since the value of 1 is Int64 and Int64 is a subtype of Real, and the value of 2.0 is Float64 and Float64 is a subtype of Real, shouldn't the method still get dispatched anyway? To make this point more clear, we can even annotate the argument as such when calling the function:

```julia
julia> diagonal(1::Real, 2.0::Real)
ERROR: MethodError: no method matching diagonal(::Int64, ::Float64)
Closest candidates are:
  diagonal(::T, ::T) where T<:Number at REPL[5]:1
```

It turns out that Julia is designed to give us more intuitive behavior. It is also the very reason why the **diagonal rule** was introduced. The diagonal rule says that when a type variable occurs more than once in the covariant position (that is, the method arguments), then the type variable will be restricted to match with concrete types only.

In this case, the type variable T is considered a diagonal variable, so T must be a concrete type.

There is an exception to the diagonal rule, though. We will discuss this next.

An exception to the diagonal rule

The diagonal rule says that when a type variable occurs more than once in the covariant position (that is, the method arguments), then the type variable will be restricted to match with concrete types only; however, there is an exception to that rule—when the type variable is unambiguously determined from an invariant position, then it is allowed to be an abstract type rather than a concrete type.

Consider this example:

```
not_diagonal(A::Array{T,1}, x::T, y::T) where {T <: Number} = T
```

Unlike the `diagonal` function from the previous section, this one allows `T` to be abstract. We can prove it as such:

```
julia> not_diagonal([1,2,3], 4, 5)
Int64

julia> not_diagonal(Signed[1,2,3], 4, 5)
Signed
```

The reason is that `T` appears in the first argument in a parametric type. As we know that parametric types are invariant, we have already determined that `T` is `Signed`. Because `Int64` is a subtype of `Signed`, everything matched.

In the next section, we will go over the availability of type variables.

The availability of type variables

An important feature of the parametric method is that the type variable specified in the `where` clause is also accessible from the method body. Contrary to what you might think, this is not always true. Here, we will present a case where the type variable is not available at runtime.

Consider the following functions:

```
mytypes1(a::Array{T,1}, x::S) where {S <: Number, T <: S} = T
mytypes2(a::Array{T,1}, x::S) where {S <: Number, T <: S} = S
```

We can use the `mytypes1` and `mytypes2` functions to experiment with what type variables are derived by the Julia runtime. Let's start with the happy case:

```
julia> mytypes1([1,2,3], 4)
Int64

julia> mytypes2([1,2,3], 4)
Int64
```

However, the picture is not always rosy. In other situations, it may not work 100% of the time. Here's an example:

```
julia> mytypes1(Signed[1,2,3], 4)
Signed

julia> mytypes2(Signed[1,2,3], 4)
ERROR: UndefVarError: S not defined
```

Why is S not defined here? First of all, we already know that T is Signed because the parametric type is invariant. As part of the where clause, we also know that T is a subtype of S. As such, S could be Integer, Real, Number, or even Any. As there are too many possible answers, the Julia runtime decided not to assign any value to S.

The moral of the story is don't assume that a type variable is always defined and accessible from the method, especially for a more complex situation like this.

Summary

In this chapter, we learned about various topics related to subtyping, variance, and dispatch. These concepts are the fundamental building blocks for creating larger, more complex applications.

We first went over the topic of implementation inheritance and behavior subtyping and the differences between them. We reasoned that implementation inheritance is not a great design pattern because of various issues. We came to an understanding that Julia's type system is designed to avoid the flaws that we have seen in other programming languages.

Then, we reviewed different kinds of variance, which are nothing but ways to explain the subtyping relationship between parametric types. We walked through in great details how parametric types are invariant and method arguments are covariant. We then went even further to discuss the variance of function types and how we can build our own data type that wraps a function for dispatch purpose.

Finally, we revisited parametric methods and looked at how type variables are specified and matched during dispatch. We learned about the diagonal rule, which is a key design feature in the Julia language that allows us to enforce type consistency across method arguments in an intuitive manner.

We are now finished with the chapter and the book. Thank you for reading it!

Questions

1. How is implementation inheritance different from behavior subtyping?
2. What are some major issues with implementation inheritance?
3. What is duck typing?
4. What is the variance of method arguments and why?
5. Why are parametric types invariant in Julia?
6. When does the diagonal rule apply?

Assessments

Chapter 1

What are the benefits of using design patterns?

Design patterns help the programmer apply already-proven approaches to common problems. There will be less time wasted in searching for the proper solution or fixing a design issue after a sub-optimal implementation. Anti-patterns provide additional guidance for avoiding common design flaws.

What are some of the key design principles?

The key design principles include SOLID, DRY, KISS, POLA, YAGNI, and POLP. These principles are widely recognized as good guidance for object-oriented programming, but they can be applied equally well in other programming paradigms.

What problem does the open/closed principle solve?

The open/closed principle encourages the programmer to design a system that is easy to extend without having to modify the component that is being extended. It promotes better reusability of software components.

Why is interface segregation important for software reusability?

Interface segregation promotes a minimalistic design for interfaces so that software components can implement the respective interfaces more easily. A large, complex interface is difficult to implement and it makes the component less reusable.

What are the simplest ways to develop maintainable software?

The simplest way to is to adhere to the general design principles such as KISS, DRY, POLA, and SOLID.

What is a good practice for avoiding over-engineering and bloated software?

The best way to avoid over-engineering and bloated software is to only implement functionalities that are absolutely necessary according to the YAGNI principle. Also, keep it simple (KISS) and avoid duplicate code (DRY).

How does memory usage affect system performance?

When the system allocates more memory, it also triggers the **Garbage Collector** (**GC**) more frequently. Garbage collection is a relatively expensive operation and, hence, it can slow down the system. Avoiding over memory allocation is usually one of the best ways to optimize application performance.

Chapter 2

How do we create a new namespace?

A namespace is created using a module block. Typically, a module is defined as part of a Julia package.

How do we expose the functions of a module to the outside world?

Functions and other objects defined within a module can be exposed using an export statement.

How do we reference the proper function when the same function name is exported from different packages?

We can just prefix the function name with the package name. As an alternative, we can use a `using` statement for one package, and an import statement for the other, so that we can use the function name directly for the first package but use the prefix syntax for the other.

When do we separate code into multiple modules?

It is time to consider separating code into modules when the code becomes too big and too difficult to manage. We expect some refactoring to ensure the proper level of coupling between modules.

Why is semantic versioning important in managing package dependencies?

Semantic versioning defines a clear contract about when a breaking change is introduced in a new version. When used properly and consistently, it helps programmers to determine whether the change is compatible with the existing software and whether additional testing is required.

How is defining functional behavior for abstract types useful?

It is useful to define functional behavior for abstract types because the same behavior can be applied for the respective subtypes.

When should we make a type mutable?

It is appropriate to make a type mutable when some parts of the data type are expected to be changed. It is also useful when memory allocation needs to be reduced for performance reasons.

How are parametric types useful?

Parametric types allow a concrete type to be defined without hardcoding the type of its fields, so the same type can be used to generate new variations for different purposes.

Chapter 3

How are positional arguments different from keyword arguments?

Position arguments must be passed in the same order as they are defined in the function signature. They are typically mandatory, but can be made optional when default values are provided. Keyword arguments can be passed in any order that they are written, and they are optional when default value is not provided.

What is the difference between splatting and slurping?

Splatting and slurping have the same syntax but mean different things in different contexts. Splatting refers to the automatic assignment of function arguments from a tuple or array. Slurping refers to the process of passing multiple function arguments, which becomes a single tuple variable accessible from the body of the function.

What is the purpose of do-syntax?

Do-syntax is a convenient way of formatting a block of code that is needed to be wrapped as an anonymous function and passed to another function. It makes the code much more readable.

What tool is available for detecting method ambiguities as related to multiple dispatch?

The `detect_ambiguities` function from the `Test` package can be used to detect method ambiguities within a single module or across multiple modules.

How do we ensure that the same concrete type is passed to a function in a parametric method?

A convenient way to ensure that the same concrete type is passed for the arguments of a function is to designate these arguments as a type parameter (for example, T). Note that this works as long as the type parameter is used as a standalone type rather than part of a parametric type, for example, AbstractVector{T}.

How are interfaces implemented without any formal language syntax?

Interfaces can be implemented according to the contract specified by the designer of the interface even though there is no formal syntax in Julia for specifying interfaces.

How do we implement traits, and how are traits useful?

A trait can be implemented by a function that takes the specific data type(s) and returns a flag. Normally, a trait is defined to return a Boolean value, that is, whether the trait exists or not. However, it can also be designed to return multiple values to indicate various kinds of trait. Traits are useful if the developer needs to programmatically figure out whether a data type (or combination of data types) exhibits a specific behavior.

Chapter 4

What are the two ways to quote expressions so the code can be manipulated later?

One way is to enclose an expression with : (and). Another way is to put the code between quote and end keywords. In general, a quote block is used for multiline expressions.

In which scope does the eval function execute the code on?

The eval function evaluates the code in the global scope. So, if it is used from a function inside a module, then the code that is evaluated will be within the scope of the module.

How do we interpolate physical symbols into quoted expressions rather than being misinterpreted as source code?

To interpolate symbols into quoted expressions, create a QuoteNode object and interpolate that object normally.

What is the naming convention for a macro where it defines non-standard string literals?

Non-standard string literals are defined as macros having names ending with _str. For example, when an ip_str macro is defined for an IP address, it can be written: ip"192.168.1.1".

When do we use the esc function?

The esc function is needed to ensure that the quoted expression is evaluated at the call site, which could be in the local scope of a function.

How are generated functions different from macros?

Generated functions have access to the types of the arguments. They are functions by definition so, unlike macros, they do not have access to the source code. Macros operate at the syntax level and do not have any runtime information. Both generated functions and macros are expected to return expressions.

How do we debug metaprogramming code?

Debugging macros can be challenging. It comes down to making sure that the expression being returned is correct. We can use the @macroexpand macro (or the corresponding macroexpand function) to verify results. Also, because a macro or generated function is defined using regular Julia code, the same debugging technique, such as println, can be used.

Chapter 5

How does delegation pattern work?

Delegation pattern can be implemented by wrapping a parent object in a new object. The function for the new objects can be forwarded (or delegated) to the parent object.

What is the purpose of traits?

The purpose of traits is to formally define the behavior of certain objects. Once a trait is defined, we can programmatically examine whether an object exhibits the trait.

Are traits always binary?

Traits are typically binary, but there is no mandatory requirement. It would be fine as long as the traits are mutually exclusive. Julia's Base.IteratorSize trait is a good example of a multi-valued trait.

Can traits be used for objects from a different type hierarchy?

Yes, traits are not restricted by how the abstract type hierarchy is defined. The same trait can be assigned to objects coming from different type hierarchies.

What are the benefits of parametric types?

Parametric types allow us to define a template for data types. New data types can be created programmatically by filling in parameters. The primary benefit of parametric type is that the code becomes shorter because we do not need to spell out every possible concrete type.

How do we store information with a parametric type?

Additional information can be *stored* in the type itself as a parameter. It is quite convenient to access such data because it is first-class and is available in the function that takes parametric type arguments.

Chapter 6

Why does the use of global variables impact performance?

Global variables are not typed. Whenever it is used, the compiler must generate code that handles any possible data types that it may encounter. Hence, the compiler cannot generate highly-optimized code.

What would be a good alternative to using a global variable when it cannot be replaced by a constant?

We can define a typed global constant as a placeholder. The Ref type may also be used to hold a single value for the variable. Because Ref contains the type of data, the compiler can generate more optimized code.

Why does a struct of arrays perform better than an array of structs?

Modern CPUs can perform many numerical calculations in parallel. When the memory is aligned and packed together as in an array, the hardware cache can quickly look them up. An array of structs may have the objects scattered around in memory, which hurts performance.

What are the limitations of `SharedArray`**?**

`SharedArray` only supports bit types. If we need to process non-bits type data in parallel, then we cannot use SharedArrays.

What is an alternative to multi-core computation instead of using parallel processes?

An alternative is to use the multithreading facility. The Julia 1.3 release implemented a state-of-the-art multi-threading scheduler that supports multiple levels of parallelism.

What kind of care must be taken when using the memoization pattern?

Memoization trades space with time. The use of a cache demands more memory space. Depending on the function result, it may or may not impact the memory footprint of the application. If memory is already constrained in the system, it may not be the best option.

What is the magic behind the barrier function in improving performance?

When using the `barrier` function, the compiler can specialize the function based upon the types of arguments being passed to the function. Even though the type of argument is unstable, when a new type is encountered, a new specialized function is compiled automatically.

Chapter 7

What are afferent and efferent couplings?

Afferent coupling represents how many external components are depending on the current component. By contrast, efferent coupling represents how many external components the current one depends on. These measurements are useful in determining how tightly the current component is coupled with other ones.

Why are bi-directional dependencies bad from a maintainability perspective?

Bi-directional dependencies tend to introduce messy, spaghetti code. To comprehend a single component, the developer must work through and understand the other components that it both uses and depends on.

What is an easy way to generate code on the fly?

The @eval macro can be used to generate code. For example, it can be used inside a for loop so that variables can be interpolated into the definition of a function. The result is that multiple functions are defined, and they are all similar in terms of code structure and logic.

What would be an alternative to code generation?

Sometimes, code generation is not needed. Instead, the developer can choose to use a functional programming technique, such as closure, to reuse existing logic. Code generation may increase the program footprint and makes the program more difficult to debug. So, it would be prudent for a developer to consider other options before plunging into code generation technique.

When and why should we consider building a domain-specific language?

A **Domain-Specific Language** (DSL) is often used for writing code that is clean and easy to understand for people in that particular domain. For example, the DifferentialEquations package allows the developer to write code in a syntax that is very similar to the corresponding mathematical equations. Because the syntax is user friendly, it allows the developer to focus on mathematic modeling rather than the coding aspect.

What are the tools available for developing a domain-specific language?

The MacroTools package provides several convenient macros that are very helpful in writing macros and, in particular, domain-specific languages. The @capture macro allows users to perform pattern matching and parse source code. The prewalk and postwalk functions allow us to surgically replace expressions in an abstract syntax tree. The combination of @capture and prewalk/postwalk makes it a very powerful tool for developing domain-specific languages.

Chapter 8

What are the benefits of developing assessor functions?

Assessor functions are a great way to provide an official API to users of the particular object. The underlying implementation is therefore decoupled from the interface. Should there be any changes to the implementation, there will be zero impact on users of the object as long as the contract of the assessor functions is unchanged.

What would be an easy way to discourage the use of internal fields of an object?

The easiest way to discourage the use of internal fields of an object is to have a special naming convention. A commonly used convention is to have an underscore as the prefix of the field name. If the programmer tries to use the field, then they are reminded that the field is supposed to be private.

Which functions may be extended as part of the property interface?

There are three functions from the `Base` package that can be extended to provide specific functionalities to the dot notation for field access. The functions are `getproperty`, `setproperty!`, and `propertynames`. An important point to remember is that once these functions are defined, all direct field access has to be changed to `getfield` and `setfield!` to avoid the recursion problem.

How can we capture the stack trace from a catch-block after an exception has been caught?

Once an exception is caught, we can use the `catch_backtrace` function to capture the stack frames right before the exception was caught. We can then pass the result to the `stacktrace` function to retrieve an array of `StackFrame` objects.

What is the best way to avoid the performance impact of a try-catch block for a system that requires optimal performance?

The best way to avoid the performance impact of a try-catch block is to not use it at all. We should find other ways to handle exceptions. For example, we can check for any condition that might cause a subsequent function to fail. In that case, we can proactively handle such a scenario. Another option is to catch the exception outside of a loop; hence, we would handle the exception at a higher level.

What are the benefits of using the `retry` function?

The `retry` function is a great way to automatically repeat an operation that may fail. Doing this ensures that important tasks are guaranteed to be completed, barring other types of unrecoverable exceptions.

How do we hide away global variables and functions that are used internally in a module?

We can use a let-block so that global variables are bound as part of the let-block and not exposed to the global scope of the module. Functions that are defined inside the let-block can be declared as global when we need to expose them to the module.

Chapter 9

What predefined data type can be used to conveniently create new singleton types?

The built-in `Val` type can be used to create new singleton types easily. The `Val` constructor function can accept any bits-type value and return a singleton of type `Val{X}`, where `X` is the value being passed to the constructor function.

What are the benefits of using singleton type dispatch?

Using singleton type dispatch, we can eliminate conditional statements that depend on the data type. It also allows us to add new functionalities by just defining new functions, without having to modify an existing function. Because Julia does the dispatch natively, there is no need to create any custom function just for dispatch.

Why do we want to create stubs?

Stubs are very useful indeed in automated testing. First, if a function requires connecting to a remote web service, then it can be inconvenient or even costly to connect to the live service all of the time. In that case, a stub can be used to replace the service. Second, a stub can be designed to exercise all positive and negative scenarios so that desired tests can be included in the automated testing process.

What is the difference between mocking and stubbing?

Stubbing focuses on state verification, that is, what comes out of the **Function Under Test (FUT)** after the stub is used. Mocking, on the other hand, focuses on behavior verification, that is, how the mocked function was used by the FUT. In general, mocking also includes state verification just like stubs.

What does composability mean?

Composability means how easy functions can be combined to create something greater. Composable functions allow applications to be built by reusing existing code. Because functions are first-class in Julia, they can be combined easily, as long as the functions accept only a single argument.

What is the primary constraint for using functional pipes?

The primary constraint of functional pipes is that functions participating in the pipe can only accept a single argument. Functions that need more than one argument can be transformed to a `curried` function such that the higher-order function can participate in the pipe.

How are functional pipes useful?

Functional pipes can be useful for data processing pipelines, especially if the process is linear in nature. The syntax is easy to read for some people.

Chapter 10

What are the risks and potential benefits of Type I piracy?

Type I piracy refers to a situation where a third-party function is redefined with a custom implementation. The risk is that custom implementation may not conform to the contract as expected by the third-party module. Coded incorrectly, the system may become unstable and crash.

What kind of problems can arise due to Type II piracy?

Type II piracy refers to a situation where a third-party function is extended without using your own types in the function arguments. It can be problematic because there is no guarantee that another dependent package also implements Type II piracy, conflicting with your pirate function. The result can be an unstable system.

How does Type III piracy cause trouble?

Type III piracy refers to a situation where a third-party function is extended with your own types but for a different purpose. While the function is defined using a custom type in the argument, there is no guarantee that the third-party module does not end up using your own function due to duck typing. Hence, your pirate function leaks into the third-party module and causes unexpected results.

What should we watch out for when specifying function arguments?

When specifying function arguments, we should avoid making the argument types too narrow. Arguments that are too narrow limit the reusability of the function.

How is system performance affected by using abstract function arguments?

System performance is not affected when function arguments are specified with abstract types. Julia always specifies the function depending on the type that is passed into the function. Hence, there is no runtime overhead.

How is system performance affected by using abstract field types for composite types?

System performance is affected negatively when abstract types are used for fields in a composite type. The Julia compiler must store pointers in memory for these objects because it has to support any data types relevant to those fields. Because pointers must be dereferenced to get to the data, system performance can be degraded greatly.

Chapter 11

What technique can we use to implement the abstract factory pattern?

To implement the abstract factory pattern, we can create a hierarchy of abstract types. Then, we can implement concrete functions that take a singleton type in the argument. By way of multiple dispatches, we should be able to call the right function for the right platform or environment.

How do we avoid a singleton from being initialized multiple times in a multithreaded application?

To avoid multiple initializations of a singleton, we can use a reentrant lock to synchronize the threads. The first thread would be able to obtain the lock and initialize the singleton, while the other threads should wait until the initialization is finished. The lock must be released at the end of the initialization.

What Julia feature is essential for implementing the observer pattern?

We can implement the `setproperty!` function so that all updates to an object's field can be monitored and additional actions can be triggered.

How can we customize an operation using the template method pattern?

We can design the template function to take in customized functions via keyword arguments. A keyword argument may be defaulted to a standard implementation, and at the same time a custom function can be passed by the caller. The expected interface of the function should be clearly documented.

How do we make an adapter to implement a target interface?

We can make an adapter by creating a new type that wraps the original type. Then, we can implement the expected interface on the new type. Using a delegation pattern, the new type can reuse existing functionality by forwarding specific functions to the original type.

What are the benefits of the flyweight pattern and what strategy can we use to achieve that?

We can potentially save a lot of memory space when using the flyweight pattern because objects are shared. The general technique is to maintain a reference table that uses a more compact data element as a lookup key. The key is used to look up the more memory-intensive objects.

What Julia feature can we use to implement the strategy pattern?

We can implement the strategy pattern using singleton types as functional arguments. The function with the proper algorithm (strategy) is automatically selected at runtime by multiple dispatch.

Chapter 12

How does implementation inheritance differ from behavior subtyping?

Implementation inheritance allows a subclass to inherit both fields and methods from a super-class. Behavior subtyping allows a subtype to inherit methods defined for a super-type.

What are some major issues associated with implementation inheritance?

Implementation inheritance is problematic because sometimes, the subclass may not want to inherit the fields from a super-class even when it makes logical sense to define the parent-child relationship. As demonstrated from the square-rectangle problem, a subclass may be more restrictive and take away features rather than adding new functionality on top of the super-class. Second, implementation inheritance suffers from the fragile base class issue, for which changes to the super-class may unintentionally modify the behavior of the subclass.

What is duck typing?

Duck typing is a dynamic feature that allows a method to be dispatched without strong type checking. A function may be dispatched as long as it adheres to the expected interface contract.

What is the variance of method arguments and why?

Method arguments are covariant as they are consistent with the Liskov Substitution Principle, which states that a function that is defined to accept type S should be able to work with any subtype of S.

Why are parametric types invariant in Julia?

Parametric types are invariant in Julia for a very practical reason. The type parameter unambiguously determines the memory layout of the underlying container. When it is invariant, there is an opportunity to achieve high performance by compacting storage data consecutively without having to dereference pointers.

When does the diagonal rule apply?

The diagonal rule is applied whenever a type variable occurs more than once in a covariance position. There is an exception to the rule when the same type variable is unambiguously determined from an invariant position such as in a parametric type.

Other Books You May Enjoy

If you enjoyed this book, you may be interested in these other books by Packt:

Julia 1.0 High Performance
Avik Sengupta, Alan Edelman

ISBN: 978-1-78829-811-7

- Understand how Julia code is transformed into machine code
- Measure the time and memory taken by Julia programs
- Create fast machine code using Julia's type information
- Define and call functions without compromising Julia's performance
- Accelerate your code via the GPU
- Use tasks and asynchronous IO for responsive programs
- Run Julia programs on large distributed clusters

Julia Programming Projects
Adrian Salceanu

ISBN: 978-1-78829-274-0

- Leverage Julia's strengths, its top packages, and main IDE options
- Analyze and manipulate datasets using Julia and DataFrames
- Write complex code while building real-life Julia applications
- Develop and run a web app using Julia and the HTTP package
- Build a recommender system using supervised machine learning
- Perform exploratory data analysis
- Apply unsupervised machine learning algorithms
- Perform time series data analysis, visualization, and forecasting

Leave a review - let other readers know what you think

Please share your thoughts on this book with others by leaving a review on the site that you bought it from. If you purchased the book from Amazon, please leave us an honest review on this book's Amazon page. This is vital so that other potential readers can see and use your unbiased opinion to make purchasing decisions, we can understand what our customers think about our products, and our authors can see your feedback on the title that they have worked with Packt to create. It will only take a few minutes of your time, but is valuable to other potential customers, our authors, and Packt. Thank you!

Index

Made in the USA
Monee, IL
15 October 2020